D0623130

For F*ck's Sake

Sake

Why Swearing Is Shocking, Rude, and Fun

REBECCA ROACHE

OXFORD
UNIVERSITY PRESS

Oxford University Press is a department of the University of Oxford. It furthers the University's objective of excellence in research, scholarship, and education by publishing worldwide. Oxford is a registered trade mark of Oxford University Press in the UK and certain other countries.

Published in the United States of America by Oxford University Press
198 Madison Avenue, New York, NY 10016, United States of America.

Library of Congress Cataloging-in-Publication Data
Names: Roache, Rebecca, author.
Title: For f*ck's sake : why swearing is shocking, rude, and fun / Rebecca Roache.
Other titles: For fuck's sake
Description: New York, NY : Oxford University Press, [2024] |
Includes bibliographical references and index.
Identifiers: LCCN 2023023399 (print) | LCCN 2023023400 (ebook) |
ISBN 9780190665067 (hardback) | ISBN 9780190665081 (epub) |
ISBN 9780197693896 | ISBN 9780190665074
Subjects: LCSH: Swearing.
Classification: LCC GT3080 .R65 2024 (print) | LCC GT3080 (ebook) |
DDC 394—dc23/eng/20230620
LC record available at https://lccn.loc.gov/2023023399
LC ebook record available at https://lccn.loc.gov/2023023400

DOI: 10.1093/oso/9780190665067.001.0001

Printed by Sheridan Books, Inc., United States of America

For my beloved M and O, the noisy centre of my world, who charmingly believed the c-word to be crap *until they found a draft of this book lying around.*

Contents

Why give a shit about swearing?

The late Queen Elizabeth II famously described 1992 as an *annus horribilis* in her televised Christmas Message that year. (It means 'horrible *year*'—be sensible you lot, this is Oxford University Press.) At the time, her words rippled through media reports around the world, as journalists speculated about what particular events (and there were a few candidates) could have pushed her to use her address to the nation to bitch about stuff rather than to reflect on her forty years—it was her anniversary!—on the throne. The speech is still discussed more than thirty years later, and thanks to the Netflix series *The Crown*, a new generation is finding out about it. Part of what raised eyebrows at the time was the fact that Her Majesty's mask of propriety had slipped a bit, and revealed her to be . . . well, pissed off. We can all relate to that, can't we? Even if the way in which she vented her annoyance—in Latin, while standing in front of a gold and red velvet throne—is rather distant from our own frustrated behaviour. But what if it hadn't been? What if the way in which she had expressed herself had been much more akin to how old Geraint down the local pub moans about the roadworks on the lane leading down to his farm?

Let's picture how this might have unfolded. Christmas day, 1992, and you're in the UK. Perhaps it's where you live, or maybe you're just visiting. Bloated and snoozy after your Christmas lunch, you give thanks for the elasticated waistband on your shell suit and settle down in front of the TV to eat as much unhealthy food as possible while watching the Queen's speech. There she is on the screen: coiffed and pearl-necklaced in front of her Guildhall throne, with her husband Prince Philip, Duke of Edinburgh on her left, and Prime Minister John Major on her right, just the other side of the ermine-clad Lord Mayor of London. In the hush that follows, she begins to speak.

'This is not a year on which I shall look back with undiluted pleasure', she says. 'In the words of one of my more sympathetic correspondents, it has turned out to be a fucking shit year. I suspect that I am not alone in finding that it has absolutely sucked arseholes. I'm not going to lie to you cunts. One can't wait to see the fucking back of it'.

What might your reaction have been to witnessing this, do you think? You might respond, at least initially, with shock and disbelief. Perhaps you glance around at your family, a mince pie hovering between your gaping mouth and the crumb-dusted plate on your lap, momentarily speechless. The lot of you might wordlessly seek reassurance from each other that yes, you really did hear what you all thought you heard. After that, in some families, the experience might sour the rest of the day, and you might all gravely ruminate on what the world is coming to. But if your family is anything like mine, your initial shock would instead give way to glee and hilarity. The Queen said *what*? You open another bottle of wine. Argue about who's going to use the phone first to call friends. (It's 1992, remember: only estate agents have mobile phones, and WhatsApp hasn't been invented.) Tell your kids to stop scaring the cats by running around yelling *SUCKED ARSEHOLES!!!!!* Or perhaps, instead, you would just continue watching the TV in rapt silence, not wanting to miss any further sweary outbursts from Her Majesty. Whatever your response, the chances of any of this not making headlines around the world are approximately zero.

But why should any of this be a big deal? People swear all the time. Had you decided to wander to the local pub after lunch instead of watching to see what the Monarch had to say, you would not have batted an eyelid if, during the course of an increasingly alcohol-fuelled afternoon, you heard Geraint embark on *yet another* one of his sweary rants about the roadworks. On the other hand, in other contexts, your reaction to this sort of language would be different still. If somebody had delivered anything resembling the Sovereign's potty-mouthed remarks during the funeral of one of your closest relatives while standing at the graveside watching the coffin being lowered into the ground, it's likely that you would have been horrified, upset, decidedly unamused, and perhaps even angry, even if you're normally the sort of person who doesn't mind swearing at all. And if one of the staff at your toddler's nursery used this language in the presence of the children, you might be alarmed, and you might worry about this person's competence to look after your child. What is it about swearing that leads us to react so differently to it depending on who is swearing and where and how they're doing it? What—if anything—is wrong with swearing? And what sort of *wrong* are we dealing with here?

There are many puzzling things about swearing and its effect on us, but no less puzzling are some of the things we do to try to avoid causing offence through swearing. Let's return to our imaginary Queen's speech, which we left having observed that we could expect to find Her Majesty's tirade reported prominently and internationally in the news. Despite the inevitable interest from the media in reporting an event like this, it's unlikely that we would have found many news outlets reporting an unedited account of what was said. Instead, we'd have seen asterisks sprinkled across the headlines like festive snowflakes. Our Head of State would have been quoted as having described the foregoing twelve months as a *f***ing sh*t year*. In other words, we could have expected to find the newspapers censoring what the Queen said *even as they aimed to report exactly what she said.* Similarly, televised news footage of the speech would have used bleeps to replace the swear words, and perhaps also pixelated the Defender of the Faith's mouth in order to thwart attempts at lip-reading. And yet we'd all know exactly what it was she'd said, even if we hadn't seen the original broadcast. This way of 'sanitising' swear words to communicate them inoffensively is widespread and effective—but how does it work? How does *f**** manage to be less offensive than *fuck*, given that anyone who understands *f**** knows exactly what word is being communicated to them, and given that anyone who writes *f**** intends to communicate *fuck* to their readers? We're going to dive into all this.

It would be difficult to characterise swearing without mentioning its offensiveness, but swearing is much more than merely offensive language. For one thing, it's not always offensive. It can express trust and intimacy, as when friends get together for a chat knowing that they will not be judged or rejected for expressing themselves using swear words that they would refrain from using in different company. It can sometimes be very entertaining, and it plays a large role in comedy. It can even be funny at the same time as being offensive; indeed, in the Queen's speech example, part of why some people are likely to respond with such glee to hearing Her Majesty swearing is precisely *because* they recognise that it is offensive and inappropriate. Of course, reacting with glee to something like this can feel a bit naughty, and when we witness it in the company of people who *are* offended, we often keep a lid on our amusement until later, when we can relax and relate the incident to our friends without offending anyone.

Even so, although it's usually a good and considerate thing to avoid causing offence, there are limits to how much we do and should care about other people being offended. In some cases, people take offence at the wrong things—things much more significant than a word used in poor taste in the wrong context. Some people claim to be offended by interracial marriage, homosexuality, women becoming priests, and breastfeeding in public places. It's far from clear that we should avoid exposing those people to those topics in order to avoid causing offence; on the contrary, more exposure to gains in equality and the changing nature of society is precisely what they need. If Amia is offended by Brandy's homosexuality, then it is Amia who is morally flawed, not those who cause her to feel offended by discussing Brandy's marriage in her company. In that case, how should we respond to someone's taking offence inappropriately? Should we avoid doing what causes them offence? Or, alternatively, does avoiding doing what causes them to feel inappropriately offended make us somehow complicit in their flawed moral judgement? By shining a spotlight on our reactions to swearing, we're going to get at some meatier issues that have to do with offence.

Taking care not to offend others is considerate, but here's something that nobody talks about: having the capacity to offend people by uttering swear words is a privilege. Most of us take for granted that if we utter swear words in a polite context, those around us will be offended. But some people struggle to produce this sort of response in other people no matter what they say. They include some people with disabilities, children, and people who have an unusual appearance or manner. Since they are less able to cause offence, these people lack the capacity for an important and useful way of communicating with others and are worse off as a result. We'll explore this issue too, and we'll see that in an important sense, being offended by people is a way of respecting them.

Back to the idea of avoiding causing offence. Although we generally have no problem working out when (i.e. in which social contexts) swearing would be especially inappropriate, the normative dimension of swearing—the details about how we ought and ought not to swear, and why—is mysterious to us. For some of us, the very idea that there can be norms about how we should and shouldn't swear might seem senseless. Or, rather, it might seem that there is just one norm: we shouldn't do it, ever. (This is what many of us were taught as children.) For others, swearing is an important and valuable form of expression which shouldn't be reined in because some people are too up tight to deal with it—it's just words, after all. We'll see that neither of these approaches gets things quite right. Understanding the oughts of swearing requires digging down below the surface and exploring what gives swearing its power to affect us in the way that it does, what makes some instances of swearing more offensive than others, what we do to mitigate its offensiveness when we really want to communicate a swear word but really don't want to upset anyone, and why we find the whole topic so mysterious in the first place. We'll see that the norms of swearing are built upon a network of attitudes that we hold towards each other, which we typically signal indirectly and often without even realising what we're doing.

You might not agree with some of my conclusions; indeed, I'd be astonished if you were to find my entire argument—which is, in a nutshell, that the offensiveness of swearing isn't about the words at all—uncontroversial. My hope is that I might inspire you to reflect on these issues, discuss them with others, draw your own conclusions, and gain some insight into how and why you and others use and respond to swearing in the way that you do. But disentangling these issues is about more than merely satisfying intellectual curiosity. It has important practical implications too. Our attitudes and responses to swearing shape society and culture in ways that run deep—and this happens despite the difficulties in articulating exactly why we have these attitudes and responses in the first place. In fact, despite it being somewhat mysterious why swearing bothers us so much, inappropriate swearing tends to be dealt with confidently and firmly. And sometimes, this results in injustice.

Let's get technical for a moment (I promise I'm not going to make a habit of it): individuals and organisations have a range of formal and informal ways of discouraging, censoring, and punishing swearing, to which I'm going to refer collectively as *anti-swearing measures*. These range from the informal social norms that reveal themselves in our intuitive sense of when swearing is really *not on*, to formal, explicit rules and even laws prohibiting swearing. The most informal anti-swearing measure, and also the most widely implemented, is simple disapproval. When we find ourselves in situations where swearing is inappropriate—a job interview, for example, or when meeting a romantic partner's parents for the first time—our awareness that those around us will frown upon our swearing is effective as a discouragement. If we forget ourselves and swear in a situation like this, we're likely to feel embarrassed and apologise. In other words, our anticipation of disapproval from the people around us leads us to self-censor: to keep our language clean when we're in polite contexts. In turn, other people's anticipation of our own disapproving attitudes contributes to those people self-censoring. In contexts where swearing is inappropriate, even if nobody actually swears and as a result nobody expresses disapproval, everyone's awareness that if they did, someone might, ensures that they don't, and that if they do, they feel embarrassed and apologise. As a result, without even realising, we are all signed up to an informal, voluntary scheme to regulate swearing. We recognise that there are contexts in which we should not swear, we participate in shaming others who swear in inappropriate contexts, and we respond contritely in cases where we ourselves swear in those contexts and suffer the disapproval of our peers.

So: it's worse to swear in some social contexts than in others. But our intuitions about when swearing is and isn't inappropriate aren't just about what context we're in. Who is doing the swearing also matters. The way we respond to inappropriate swearing, and the pressure on the swearer to apologise, are magnified in cases where the swearer is a public figure; especially if the swearer is (like the Monarch) the sort of public figure that we expect to be a model of decorum. This illustrates that our intuitions about swearing are actually pretty complex: there's a range of factors we take into account (usually unconsciously, of course) when assessing just *how bad* a particular instance of swearing is. But our example involving the Queen raises another point about our responses to swearing too. Inappropriate swearing by a public figure, along with any subsequent apology (or lack of one), is often deemed newsworthy. This places swearing in the spotlight, in a way that doesn't happen when it's Geraint down the pub who's doing the swearing. When swearing makes the news, a contrite response from the swearer provides a public affirmation and reinforcement of the view that swearing is unacceptable; by contrast, shrugging off the incident sends the message that swearing is no big deal. Inappropriate swearing by public figures, then, often provides an opportunity to test wider attitudes to swearing. Such incidents can act as a barometer of swearing's offensiveness, and when the public's response changes over time, this is sometimes taken to indicate that the offensiveness of swearing has changed too.

As an example here, let's compare two related incidents of swearing, twenty-eight years apart. In 1976, British punk band the Sex Pistols famously swore while being interviewed by Bill Grundy on the British teatime TV show, *Today*. The incident cost Grundy his career; a result of the fact that not only did Grundy fail to condemn the first incident of swearing during the interview—in which guitarist Steve Jones said, of the band's earnings, 'We've fucking spent it, ain't we?'—but Grundy then encouraged the band to swear more, which gave rise to *shit*, *bastard*, *fucker*, and *fucking*. There followed outraged headlines, cancelled gigs, and footage of the incident in music documentaries for decades to come.

By contrast, the public responded more apathetically in 2004 when former Sex Pistol John Lydon called a live TV audience of over ten million viewers *fucking cunts* while participating in the British TV reality show, *I'm a Celebrity . . . Get Me Out of Here!* This was despite his sweary outburst being, in an important sense that we'll explore in later chapters, *worse* than what was said in the Bill Grundy incident. One way in which it was worse was that Lydon's *fucking cunts* directly insulted the viewing audience whereas the Pistols' 1976 sweary utterances were either undirected (i.e. used as a kind of punctuation rather than addressed as insults to anyone in particular) or directed at Grundy himself following his encouragement of the behaviour. Another way in which it was worse is that it involved a more offensive word: *cunt* is widely regarded as the most offensive English swear word. Despite this, fewer than a hundred official viewer complaints about this remark were received by the UK's communications regulator Ofcom following Lydon's 2004 outburst. The nation wasn't scandalised, as it had been in 1976. Nobody lost their job, as Grundy did back then. The difference in the public's responses to the 1976 and 2004 incidents of swearing were widely seen as indicative of a shift in attitudes to the acceptability of swearing.[1] Here, then, was a case of the public's attitudes towards swearing being tested and examined via the media, and conclusions drawn.

While we're on the topic of swearing on TV, let's take a look at another aspect of anti-swearing measures. Swearing during a TV show is about more than informal attitudes towards swearing. TV broadcasts are subject to formal rules about whether, when, and how much swearing is permitted, and what happens if these rules are breached. There are regulations like this in place around the world. In the UK, Ofcom's Broadcasting Code restricts swearing to certain contexts and can impose fines on broadcasters when these rules are broken. In the United States, the Federal Communications Commission (FCC) sets rules about swearing in US TV shows, although it is not allowed to fine broadcasters who break these rules. There has been an attempt in the US to tighten rules about swearing: in 2003, the US government considered (but subsequently decided against) implementing the Clean Airwaves Act, which forbade broadcast of

> the words 'shit', 'piss', 'fuck', 'cunt', 'asshole', and the phrases 'cock sucker', 'mother fucker' and 'ass hole', compound use (including hyphenated compounds) of such words and phrases with each other or with other words or phrases, and other grammatical forms of such words and phrases (including verb, adjective,

[1] Despite these claims by journalists, the diminished public outrage in response to the second incident compared to the first does not really show that swearing has become more acceptable over the years. More likely is that the 1976 incident was shocking largely because it was unexpected, given that the Sex Pistols had not yet reached the height of their fame. By contrast, in 2004, the audience knew what to expect from John Lydon, who therefore failed to cause widespread outrage with his on-brand remark.

gerund, participle, and infinitive forms). (Introduction of the Clean Airwaves Act, U.S. Cong., 149 Cong. Rec. E2486 [2003])

The *general* message sent by formal anti-swearing measures is that swearing is unacceptable, at least in certain contexts. However, if we want more specific guidance about exactly how much swearing, and of what sort, is acceptable in a given context, we quickly encounter rules that are so arbitrary as to be bizarre and almost senseless. The UK comedy writer Richard O. Smith related (in conversation) that in writing a half-hour show for BBC Radio 4, he was restricted to 'two shits and a wank'. Leon Wilson, producer of ITV's *Celebrity Juice*, one of the UK's sweariest TV shows, is allowed four *motherfuckers* but unlimited *fucks* per thirty-three-minute show (Zaltzman 2015). Film director Ken Loach, responding to what he viewed as overzealous censorship by the British Board of Film Classification (BBFC) of his 2012 film *The Angel's Share*, complained about the 'world of surrealism' into which discussions descended. He commented that in order for the film to be granted a 15 certificate, 'We were allowed seven cunts . . . but only two of them could be aggressive cunts' (Higgins 2012). The 'surrealism' of rules like these arises from the attempt to capture and quantify all the nuance, vagueness, and messiness of public attitudes towards swearing. In the absence of a rigorous rationale, these rules seem disconnected from our everyday intuitions about swearing. (Most of us would be hard pressed to explain why, if four motherfuckers per thirty-three minutes is basically fine, five crosses the line into unacceptable offensiveness.)[2] There are regular efforts to provide such a rationale—Ofcom, BBFC, and the UK's Advertising

[2] It's worth noting that this point isn't unique to swearing. Any attempt to formalise explicitly the sorts of rules that we tend to think about only in general terms is similarly doomed to 'surrealism'. Imagine trying to specify how close, to the nearest millimetre, it's appropriate to stand to an acquaintance you ran into in the supermarket without risking their thinking you're either uncomfortably close or weirdly distant. Or how loud (in decibels) and how long (in seconds) a murmured conversation in the cinema can be without annoying your fellow filmgoers.

Standards Authority conduct surveys into public attitudes to swearing and use the results to inform regulations—but these generally take public opinion as their authority; as a result, they provide inadequate guidance in difficult or unusual cases, and they are silent on the issue of how to recognise when the public gets it wrong, and how to proceed in those circumstances.

Formal anti-swearing measures are not confined to broadcasting, of course. A schoolteacher who swears at one of their pupils, or a doctor who swears at one of their patients, risks breaching professional guidelines about conduct. Athletes who swear while competing may find themselves punished for unsporting behaviour. This is not to say that swearing is always *explicitly* prohibited in formal rules about conduct; very often, it is not. Instead, that one shouldn't swear in certain contexts is taken to be implied by more general rules about professional conduct and treating others with politeness and respect. That implication itself contains a tangle of unquestioned views about swearing, including judgements about when swearing constitutes disrespect—which, of course, it sometimes does, but not always.

The pinnacle of formal anti-swearing measures is the law. Swearing can get you arrested in many places across the globe. In the US, public swearing in the town of Middleborough, Massachusetts, is punishable by a $20 fine. Swearing in public counts as a class 4 misdemeanor in Virginia, and can attract a $250 fine. Swearing can count as disorderly conduct in several states including Utah, Texas, Arizona, New Jersey, and the District of Columbia.[3] In the UK,

[3] See Nunberg (2012); Theoharis (n.d.); Tex. Penal Code, Disorderly conduct and related offences, tit. 9, ch. 42 (2007) (available at https://statutes.capitol.texas.gov/Docs/PE/htm/PE.42.htm); Ga. Code Ann. Disorderly conduct, tit. 16, ch. 11, art. 2, §16-11-39 (2010) (available at https://law.justia.com/codes/georgia/2010/title-16/chapter-11/article-2/16-11-39); Ariz. State Legislature, §13-2904, Disorderly conduct; classification (n.d.) (available at https://www.azleg.gov/ars/13/02904.htm); New Jersey disorderly conduct. n.d. (available at https://www.sliwinskilawoffice.com/disorderly-persons-offenses/new-jersey-disorderly-conduct/); Council of the District of Columbia, D.C. Code, Disorderly conduct, §22-1321 (2013) (available at https://code.dccouncil.gov/us/dc/council/code/sections/22-1321).

arrests for swearing tend to happen under Section 5 of the Public Order Act, which makes it an offence to use 'threatening or abusive words . . . within the hearing or sight of a person likely to be caused harassment, alarm or distress thereby' (UK Pub. Gen. Acts 1986). In Canada, those who cause a disturbance by swearing in public are guilty of an offence, and in February 2015 the town of Taber, Alberta, introduced fines for swearing (CBC News 2015). You can also get fined for swearing in several Australian states, and in 2014 New South Wales increased on-the-spot fines for offensive language from $150 (£80) to $500 (£270) (Dearden 2014). In 2013, the Australian government introduced a code of conduct for asylum seekers, which reportedly threatened deportation for a range of activities, including swearing (Gander 2014). In Russia, in 2014, the government passed a bill that bans swear words from films, music, and other works of art (Omidi 2014). In Iraqi Kurdistan, the Family Violence Law takes domestic violence to include swearing at children by parents (Parliament of Kurdistan-Iraq 2011). Singapore's 'outrage of modesty' laws have been invoked against swearing and led to the arrest in 2012 of an Australian man for swearing on a flight from Perth to Singapore (Lowe 2013). Convictions under these laws are punishable by two years in prison, twenty-four lashes with a cane, a fine, or a combination of these. In the United Arab Emirates (UAE), 'disgrac[ing] the honour or the modesty of another person', including by swearing, is punishable by imprisonment and/or a fine, with the severity of the punishment depending on whether the person sworn at is a public official, whether the insult is public, whether witnesses are present, and various other factors (Dhal 2013). Swearing is not illegal in China, but public opinion is divided on whether it should be. In 2013, Alpais Lam Wai-sze, a Hong Kong primary schoolteacher, swore at police officers during a confrontation between two political groups. A video of the incident went viral, triggering a demonstration of three thousand people at which there was some violence between Lam's critics and her supporters, who viewed her respectively as a potty-mouthed upstart and a defender of free speech (Tatlow 2013). In the wake of this, a survey of Chinese teachers found that two-thirds believe that swearing in their profession should be regulated by a code of conduct (Wei 2013).

The issue of whether and how swearing should be dealt with by the law is controversial. There is some confusion, it seems, about whether (and under what circumstances) swearing should count as disorderly conduct, or fighting words, or a breach of the peace, or threatening behaviour, or any other category of behaviour for which one can get arrested. A landmark case here is *Cohen v. California*, which we'll return to later. This case saw the court decide that wearing a jacket emblazoned with the words *Fuck the Draft* warranted arrest and imprisonment, only to change its mind on appeal. This 1971 decision marked only the beginning of US law's confusion over *fuck*. The late Christopher M. Fairman, professor at Ohio State University Moritz College of Law, noted in his 2006 article 'Fuck' that since *Cohen* there have been judgements permitting *Fuck Hitler*, *Fucking orders*, and *Fucking genius*; and judgements prohibiting *Fuck the ump* and *Fucking brilliant* (Fairman 2006, 49).

Other English-speaking countries have not done much better. In the UK, Denzel Cassius Harvey's conviction and £50 fine for saying *fuck* while police officers searched him for drugs was overturned in 2011; a controversial decision which prompted Boris Johnson, who was London Mayor at the time, to pledge a zero-tolerance approach to swearing at the police. Four years after these zero-tolerance comments, Johnson was filmed yelling at a London taxi driver, 'Why don't you fuck off and die?', an outburst that suggests that Johnson views taxi drivers as less worthy of respect than police officers, or perhaps that members of the public should be held to higher standards of behaviour than politicians, or perhaps that he simply doesn't know his arse from his elbow when it comes to politics. Confusion about *fuck* and the law is perhaps most comically illustrated by a 2017 Australian case, in which Filip Black replied 'none of your fucking business' to a police officer who asked him what he was doing in the area. Black was arrested, only to be released a minute later when the arresting officer evened out the swear tally by telling Black that he was 'fucking worked up'. Black was then re-arrested when he told the arresting officer to 'fuck it right in your mum's pussy' (McGowan 2017).

Around the world, there is debate between those who oppose harsh penalties for swearing on the ground that they are an unacceptable infringement on free speech and those who support such penalties in the interest of eliminating antisocial behaviour, which some view as likely to lead to more serious transgressions if left unaddressed. It is possible, as we'll see, to take a more nuanced position than either a completely permissive approach or a zero-tolerance attitude to swearing. We can all agree that Filip Black's *none of your fucking business* was in some sense milder than his *fuck it right in your mum's pussy*. That this difference, and other relevant factors, should be reflected in our anti-swearing measures is appropriate. We do, after all, generally view it as appropriate that minor wrongdoings are punished less severely than more serious ones. It remains to map out the sweary landscape by considering what sort of instances of swearing are more serious than others, what makes them so, how to identify them, and how to compare them with wrongs that do not involve swearing.

We've looked at anti-swearing measures that *discourage* swearing, and those that *punish* swearing. But discouragement and punishment are not the only goals of these measures. Swearing is also *censored* in various ways. We're all familiar with seeing *sh*t* instead of *shit* in newspapers, and of hearing bleeped-out swearing on TV and radio, but censorship can take other forms too. Swearing during a live broadcast can get you removed from the airwaves, as happened to Sir Bob Geldof in November 2014 when he said *bollocks* twice during a Sky News interview (Perraudin 2014). Some communication systems make it impossible to swear: the well-to-do British department store Marks and Spencer hit the headlines in March 2015 for banning the word *Christ*, along with the usual swear words, from gift messages when buying flowers online (Willgress 2015). (It later removed *Christ* from the banned list.) You can even opt in to censorship: the Clean Reader app prevents swear words from being displayed in e-books, and has been heavily criticised by writers including Joanne Harris, Margaret Atwood, and Lionel Shriver (Furness 2015; Perry 2015; Shriver 2015). Censorship plays an important role in mitigating the offensiveness of swearing, but it's not always clear exactly how it works (if we communicate *fuck* by writing *f****, how does the latter manage to be less offensive than the former?) and if it's not done right, it can actually cause more offence than would have been caused were it not used at all. We'll look at how censorship works and how it can fail in more detail later.

By considering the various ways in which swearing is formally prohibited, censored, and punished, it is easy to end up with a sense that regulators are bizarrely obsessed with swearing. After all, the planet is burning, and as I'm writing this, people around the world are sheltering indoors while a deadly pandemic rages outside. But it's possible that swearing is more complicated than that. Detective Chief Superintendent Colin Paine, Head of Professional Standards at Thames Valley Police, has (in conversation) suggested that there may be a more nuanced interpretation of arrests for swearing. In some situations in which a member of the public is behaving in a *generally* disruptive and unacceptable way that includes swearing, their swearing is a behaviour that is easy to point to as a justification for viewing their behaviour as unacceptable, and therefore (in some cases) worthy of arrest. After all, often, when we judge someone's behaviour to be disruptive or unacceptable, it is difficult to articulate exactly why. These judgements are often heavily dependent on context, and we take into account factors of which we may not be fully conscious, including subtle changes in body language such as how close they stand to us and how long they hold our gaze. This can make it difficult to explain to a third party why we judged the person's behaviour to be unacceptable; a difficulty that is reflected in some of the vague ways we formulate such explanations: 'She was a bit off with me', 'He was a bit jumpy', 'She didn't say so, but I could tell she didn't want me around', 'He didn't respond but he looked like he wanted to punch someone'. We can sometimes feel foolish if pressed about accounts like this—we might say, in such a case, 'I guess you had to be there'. On the other hand, if the person whose behaviour we judge inappropriate swears, then our job is easier. 'He swore' is more convincing as a justification for such a judgement than 'He didn't respond but he looked like he wanted to punch someone'. Swearing, then, can be a focus for otherwise vague and context-dependent judgements that a person's behaviour or general manner is inappropriate; and a person's swearing can help legitimise our negative evaluation of them. This might help explain why it is mentioned in some regulations about unacceptable behaviour and in explanations for why certain regulations were applied. Such regulations and explanations cannot take into account all the relevant context; swearing helps make this context less relevant.

It is to be expected that it can be hard to explain why we form certain judgements about a person's behaviour, whether we judge them to be rude, threatening, excited, amused, elated, or something else. We take our cues not only from what they explicitly say but also from subtle aspects of body language and from context-dependent factors like the social setting, our history with them, and their interactions with other people present. We shouldn't expect to be able to convey the nuances of these judgements to someone who wasn't there. Sometimes you really did have to be there. But, when these judgements lead to a formal response like arrest, censorship in the media, or a professional reprimand, there are reasons to be concerned. Our inability to articulate why we make certain judgements about other people's behaviour can conceal a variety of biases, many of which we do not even realise we hold. In the US, African Americans are incarcerated at more than five times the rate of whites; in the UK, Black people are more than three times more likely to be arrested as white people (National Association for the Advancement of Colored People 2023; UK Government 2022).[4] Black men tend to be viewed as larger and more threatening than similar-sized white men (Wilson et al. 2017). A 2009 study commissioned by the UK government found that job applicants with a 'white-sounding' name are 74 per cent more likely to receive a positive response than similarly qualified applicants whose name is associated with an ethnic minority. A 2019 Spanish study found that female job applicants are 30 per cent less likely to be called for a job interview than similarly qualified male applicants, and that the penalty for having children is higher for women than for men. These data reveal that—without our even realising, and even if we're well intentioned—our evaluations of people are influenced not only by things like body language and social context but also by factors that ought not to feature at all, such as ethnicity and gender. This gives us a powerful reason to respond to swearing appropriately, in order to avoid the injustice that inevitably results from our decisions being influenced by these biases. If a person's swearing helps legitimise a negative evaluation of them that we have already made but are not sure why, then people from oppressed groups are likely to pay a higher penalty for swearing than those from other groups. We should not expect anti-swearing measures to be able to correct for this bias, but by providing a clear and sensible rationale

[4] Throughout this book, 'Black'—when used to refer to Black people—is capitalised but 'white' is not. This is increasingly conventional in many places, but not yet universal. Luke Visconti, founder and chairman of Diversity.Inc, makes the case for this approach: 'Black' is also accepted by many Black people as an inoffensive description. It is a generalised description and can be supplemented by another description such as Black Canadian, Black African American, Nigerian American or Black Latino. However, many Black people describe themselves simply as being 'Black', and this reality is reflected in a body of literature, music, and academic study.

'I do not believe "white" needs to be capitalised because people in the white majority don't think of themselves in that way. I don't think there's anything wrong with this—it's just how it is. The exception is white supremacists who have a definite vision for what "White" means—and they capitalise the "W"' (Visconti 2020).

Mike Laws of the *Columbia Journalism Review* succinctly echoes this approach: 'For many people, Black reflects a shared sense of identity and community. White carries a different set of meanings; capitalising the word in this context risks following the lead of white supremacists' (Laws 2020).

for rules about when swearing is unacceptable, we can hope that anti-swearing measures that reflect this rationale will promote conscious and reflective decisions rather than supporting the sort of unconscious, difficult-to-explain, 'gut feeling' judgements that can conceal a range of inappropriate biases.

This little skate through some of the ways we, as a society, deal with swearing reveals that any confusion we feel about exactly whether, why, and when swearing is inappropriate does not stand in the way of responding either informally or formally to swearing. That can be useful, for actions-speak-louder-than-words-type reasons: if we feel like we're not sure what we think about swearing, looking at how we actually respond to it can reveal attitudes that we might not have been aware that we have, in roughly the same way that a person can suddenly discover that they don't actually like their job as much as they thought they did when they get fired and then realise that they feel relieved rather than upset. Even so, things are more complicated than this. Our practices do not merely reveal underlying attitudes; they also create them. Punishing, censoring, or officially prohibiting a given behaviour reinforces the view of that behaviour as wrong; punishing it on the grounds that it is a form of abuse reinforces the idea that it is a form of abuse. Our practices can also mask our uncertainty about how a given behaviour should be dealt with. Societies, organisations, clubs, businesses and so on often need to make a decision about how best to deal with a behaviour in the face of disagreement and uncertainty about how to deal with it. They need to respond to the practical demands of keeping everything running smoothly, and sometimes it is more important that *some* decision is made than *what* decision is made. It is easy to overlook this and to forget that the fact that a certain behaviour is regulated in a certain way does not settle the question of how it is most appropriately dealt with, or dispense with the need for further reflection. Once anti-swearing measures are in place, then, it is important to continue to consider whether they are appropriate, or whether instead they are too harsh, inconsistent with the ways we deal with other objectionable behaviours, based on misconceptions about what swearing is, and so on. For these reasons, too, looking at some of our ways of dealing with swearing is a good place to start.

We're going to begin, in Chapter 1, by looking at what swearing is. Yes, I know you already know, but it's going to be useful to make explicit what we all already know about swearing, and to reflect briefly on how it differs from other, similar uses of language. In Chapter 2 we're going to turn to the mysterious issue of where swearing gets its power to shock and offend. We'll look at some common and plausible-seeming explanations that have to do with swear words themselves, but it turns out that none of these is quite satisfactory. Instead, as we'll see in Chapter 3, the secret of swearing's offensiveness does not lie in the words themselves; we find it, instead, in the unspoken messages that we communicate to those around us when we swear. By the time Chapter 4 rolls around, you're probably going to be wondering exactly what we mean when we talk about swearing being offensive, inappropriate, and wrong, so I'll clear this up there. Then, in Chapter 5, I'll address a question that is raised by my argument that swearing's offensiveness doesn't arise from the words themselves: if it's not about the words, then why do swear words all tend to be similar in certain ways? In particular, why do swear words around the world tend to be words for taboo things, and why do they all tend to have a certain sort of sound? Chapters 6 and 7 cover some of the factors that make some instances of swearing significantly more objectionable than others. In Chapter 8 we return to the problem that, as we saw above, regulations about swearing are often confused and incoherent, and I'll explain why this is a problem. In Chapter 9 I'll draw on some influential work in philosophy of language to sketch out a framework that can be used to make sensible decisions about how to regulate swearing. In Chapter 10 I'll explain why relying too heavily on our intuitive sense of how offensive swearing is can lead to bias and injustice—and how we can reflect on and revise our intuitions so that they point us in the right direction. The next two chapters focus on how the offensiveness of certain terms intersects with prejudice: in Chapter 11, we compare swearing to slurs, and look at how and why the norms around swearing differ from those around slurs; and in Chapter 12, we'll see that prejudicial attitudes are to blame for the offensiveness of *cunt* and *cocksucker*. Chapters 13 and 14 deal with some ways, including the use of asterisks, that we can utter swear words (and other offensive terms) in a way that reduces their offensiveness—and with some of the pitfalls and limitations of these strategies. After all that tortuous thought about offensiveness, things become more upbeat in Chapter 15, when we look at the positive side of swearing. And finally, in Chapter 16, I argue that those of us who find ourselves in the position of having to worry about whether we might cause offence with the language we use should count ourselves lucky: there are those who are simply unable to cause offence when they use swear words, and those people suffer a moral wrong as a result.

Get the kettle on and the swear jar at the ready, and let's get started.

1
What is swearing?

Philosophers: always making a song and dance about answering questions to which everyone already knows the answers. But bear with me. I know that, in an obvious sense, we all already know exactly what swear words are, and that we can all rattle off a list of them if we have to. Even so, while we have no trouble listing swear words or identifying them when we encounter them, it's more difficult to articulate exactly what makes a swear word a swear word and what sets swear words apart from other words and expressions. It is no simple matter to answer the question *What, exactly, is swearing?* in a way that does not involve simply giving a list of swear words, but let's give it a try.

Swearing = offensiveness

The Oxford English Dictionary defines swearing as 'The uttering of a profane oath; the use of profane language', while Oxford Learner's Dictionaries offer the somewhat more user-friendly definition of, simply, 'rude or offensive language'. This is a good start, but it is too rough for our purposes. For one thing, 'rude or offensive language' need not involve swearing at all. I am rude or offensive when I tell you that your new baby is ugly, when I respond to receiving your thoughtful gift by complaining that it is not expensive enough, or when I crack a tasteless joke about death after you reveal that you have a terminal illness. Some definitions of swearing get around this issue by specifying that swearing should involve *taboo* (i.e. forbidden) language—but, even combined with the 'rude or offensive' requirement, this is not specific enough. Not all rude or offensive taboo language is swearing. A category of non-sweary offensive taboo language is slurs: words that deride entire groups of people, and that are often associated with hate speech. The best-known slurs are those that deride a person on account of their race, sexual orientation, disability, gender, or religion. Slurs are distinct from swear words, but there is more to say about their relationship to swear words, and we'll focus on them in Chapter 11. Another example is language that is taboo for religious reasons, including curses, blasphemy, and words that are otherwise unspeakable for certain religious groups. For example, the word *pig* is an offensive taboo to many Muslims, but it is not offensive outside this group, and it is certainly not a swear word. Even so, the divisions between swear words and these other categories is not always sharp: consider the word *damn*, which often functions as a swear word (albeit a mild one these days) but which is also a religious taboo word. Slurs, as we'll see, can also be used as swear words. But these overlaps do not matter. It will be useful to make the distinction between swearing, slurs, and religious taboos even if some expressions fall into more than one category.

Offensiveness is not an all-or-nothing phenomenon. There is a spectrum of offensiveness, with some offensive words being more offensive than others. Within the category of swear words, *shit* is less offensive than *fuck*, which in turn is less offensive than *cunt*. This spectrum allows for borderline cases; words that we're not sure whether or not to count as swear words. These might include *crap*, *screw*, and *minge*. (Readers who are unconvinced by these borderline cases are invited to think of their own.) We'll investigate the link between swearing and offensiveness in later chapters, when we address questions like: What makes a word offensive enough to count as a swear word? What quality is possessed by, say, *shit*, in virtue of which it is a swear word, and lacked by the otherwise similar *poo*? Could *poo* grow to equal *shit* in offensiveness? And, what is the link between swearing's offensiveness and taboo language—could a non-taboo word like *book* ever attain the level of offensiveness of a swear word, and if not, why not?

As well as varying in degree, offensiveness varies in kind too. We'll zoom in on what offensiveness is, and what makes swearing offensive, in the chapters that follow—but for now let's simply acknowledge that different offensive things are offensive in different ways and for different reasons. Slurs offend by unjustly deriding members of certain groups. Telling a new parent that their baby is ugly offends by upsetting the new parent. Masturbating on a busy train offends by forcing other passengers to witness something they find alarming and disgusting. And so on. Swearing, too, has its own particular flavour of offensiveness. At a deeper level, though, these behaviours all offend in virtue of those who witness the behaviours taking them to indicate the speaker's (or actor's) lack of respect for certain other people. But we're jumping ahead here. Your takeaway at this stage can be that swearing is about way more than offensive language. It's a very particular type of offensive language.

Swearing = offensiveness + emotion

Aside from being offensive, what else is distinctive about swearing? Well, swearing has a special role in expressing and communicating emotion. The expressions *My car has been stolen* and *For fuck's sake, my fucking car's been stolen!* both assert the same thing, but the second also conveys a sense of anger and annoyance, thanks to the inclusion of swearing. Swearing effectively (though not uniquely) enables the speaker to communicate her emotions without having to describe explicitly what her emotions are. Indeed, it often happens that swearing does a better job of communicating emotion than describing does: other things being equal, we would judge someone who responds to the discovery that her car has been stolen with the outburst, 'For fuck's sake, my fucking car's been stolen!' to be *more* angry and annoyed than someone who is sufficiently composed to articulate the sentence, 'I'm angry and annoyed that my car has been stolen'.

Various writers have picked up on this link between swearing and emotion. Linguist Geoffrey Nunberg remarked, '[s]wear words don't describe your feelings; they manifest them' (Nunberg 2012). Philosopher J. L. Austin wrote, '[w]e might say that we use swearing *for* relieving our feelings' (Austin 1962, 105). And Timothy Jay and Kristen Janschewitz—two psychology professors who have written so extensively on swearing that Jay's institutional website proclaims him to be 'a world-renowned expert in cursing'—have defined swearing as 'the use of taboo language with the purpose of expressing the speaker's emotional state and communicating that information to listeners' (Jay and Janschewitz 2008, 268).

Swearing's characteristic role in expressing emotions is linked to a unique linguistic role, too. What does this mean? Well, suppose we overhear somebody exclaim 'Fuck it!' when he accidentally spills tea in his lap. We don't arrive at an understanding of this exclamation by reflecting on the literal meanings of the words used, as we'd do if the speaker had said 'Eat it!' or 'Wash it!' or 'Wear it!'. In fact, trying to interpret *Fuck it!* along these lines would result in our getting hold of the wrong end of the stick. *Eat it!*, *Wash it!*, and *Wear it!* are imperatives (i.e. commands), but in most cases *Fuck it!* is not. Someone who says 'Fuck it!' in response to slopping tea in his lap is not commanding anyone to fuck anything. In fact, *Fuck it!* in this instance has nothing to do with fucking at all. To understand what a speaker means by it, there is little point in our reflecting on what he is referring to or talking about, because someone who says 'Fuck it!' is not referring to or talking about *anything*. Instead, we need to consider what the expression might indicate about the speaker's emotions. This makes *Fuck it!* more like a scream than an utterance: just like a scream, it expresses emotion without being *about* anything.

To be sure, swear words are not always used to communicate emotion, and the literal meanings of swear words are not always irrelevant to understanding what people say when they swear. *They fucked three times*, *There's bird shit on my car*, *He got kicked in the bollocks*, and *It's bad manners to wank in an open-plan office* are all examples of sentences in which swear words behave like ordinary words and are used to describe what is going on in the world. The late linguist James D. McCawley, writing under the sweary (and racially insensitive) pseudonym Quang Phuc Dong, distinguished between the *fuck* of *Fuck you!* and the linguistically better-behaved *fuck* that appears in sentences like *They fucked three times*, calling them $fuck_2$ and $fuck_1$ respectively (Dong 1971).

We'll return to $fuck_2$ in a moment. First, you might wonder whether $fuck_1$ and other non-cathartic uses of swear words really count as swearing at all. Sentences like *They fucked three times* are ordinary, business-as-usual sentences in which the swear word functions like any other verb or noun. We're doing something very different when we use $fuck_1$ than we are when we use $fuck_2$. If we are keen to flag this distinction, we might distinguish between *swearing* and *using swear words*. We could then stipulate that when someone utters any of the example sentences just considered, they use swear words but they do not swear. Conversely, we might also observe that it's possible to swear without using swear words. To see this, consider the emotion-venting role of swearing described above—the role that is typical of $fuck_2$ utterances. Despite this role being characteristic of swearing, it's possible to use non-swear words to perform this role. If someone frustrates us we might respond with a sweary outburst like, 'You wanker!' But we might be able to realise the emotion-venting function if we dropped the swear word and instead used the right sort of non-sweary insult, like, *You absolute, indescribable, inexpressible fool!*. We could, alternatively, replace *fool* with a slur word; indeed, some people use slurs for this purpose, though not if they are concerned to avoid the additional layer of offensiveness that using a slur conveys. It's also possible to exploit the loophole of swearing without using swear words in order to vent emotion without offending anyone, as when people exclaim

'Shoot!' instead of 'Shit!'—although, of course, the self-restraint required to choose an inoffensive word over a swear word risks diminishing the cathartic potential of the expression. And it's possible to swear without using any words at all: we'll see in Chapter 9 that using offensive gestures like the middle finger can constitute swearing. Since slur words, non-sweary insults, inoffensive substitute swear words, and offensive gestures are not swear words, we could view venting emotion in this characteristically sweary way to constitute swearing without using swear words. This distinction between swearing and using swear words leaves us with a mind-boggling choice of different ways in which swearing can feature in our communication. We can swear using a swear word, we can swear without using a swear word, and we can use a swear word without swearing. But to keep things simple, I'm going to gloss over these distinctions and use the terms *swearing* and *using swear words* interchangeably, relying on the context to make clear what I mean and referring to these distinctions only when the discussion demands it.

Swearing = offensiveness + emotion + linguistic anarchy

The fact that understanding swearing does not always involve considering the literal meanings of swear words helps explain why many swear words are impressively versatile. In his book on the English language, *A Mouthful of Air*, Anthony Burgess reports hearing an army mechanic say of a broken-down truck, 'Fuck it. The fucking fucker's fucking fucked'. Burgess remarks that, here, a single swear word is used as (respectively) an imperative, adjective, noun, adverb, and verb (Burgess 1992, 263). The unusual flexibility of the word *fuck* explains the astonishing fact that we're able to make any sense of the mechanic's pronouncement at all.

Is *fuck* a special case? *Fuck* can, after all, do things that not even other swear words can do. It is, as the philosopher Steve Gimbel has blogged, 'the Swiss army knife of language. There's nothing it can't express' (Gimbel 2006). One powerful illustration of this is provided by a scene from the American crime drama series *The Wire*, in which two detectives spend almost five minutes assessing a crime scene, all the while communicating only through variations of the word *fuck*. So legendary is the word that there is even a Hollywood documentary film about it: *Fuck*, by director Steve Anderson.

So, perhaps *fuck* is not representative of swear words in general. It lends itself easily to the task to which Burgess's army mechanic applies it in a way that other swear words would not. It would have been rather more avant-garde for the mechanic to have said, instead, 'Shit it. The shitting shitter's shitting shitted'. Or even, 'Cunt it. The cunting cunt's cunting cunted'. (This latter formulation is admittedly less bizarre now than it would have been even a few decades ago, when Burgess was writing—*cunting* and *cunted* were added to the Oxford English Dictionary in 2014.)

What is it that prevents other swear words from being put to all the uses to which we can put *fuck*? Several linguists have reflected on the rules governing swear words. They consider what you can and can't do with swear words in an effort to work out what sorts of words they are. Steven Pinker argues that *fucking* is not an adjective because, if it were, *Drown the fucking cat* would be interchangeable with *Drown the cat which is fucking*, just as *Drown the lazy cat* is interchangeable with *Drown the cat which is lazy*. But, clearly, they are not interchangeable—at least, not in cases where *fucking* is used in McCawley's $fuck_2$ sense (i.e. when it is not used to tell us that the cat in question is having sex). McCawley argues at length that *Fuck you* is not an imperative (i.e. a command) like *Wash the dishes*. One reason is that, unlike other imperatives, *Fuck you* cannot be conjoined with other imperatives in a single sentence. We can say, *Wash the dishes and sweep the floor* but not *Wash the dishes and fuck you*. Nunberg suggests that *fucking* is not an adverb like *very* or *extraordinarily*, because while you can say, 'How brilliant was it? Very', and, 'How brilliant was it? Extraordinarily', you can't say, 'How brilliant was it? Fucking'.

There is reason to doubt some of these claims. Anecdotally, when discussing this with others, a couple of friends have claimed that in their part of the world, people *do* say things like, 'How brilliant was it? Fucking'. Ignoring this, what does it mean to say that you *can* or *can't* say things like this? The *can* and *can't* here resemble those of, *You can't say 'Me am hungry', but you can say 'I am hungry'*. Claims like this appear to identify rules about language use that speakers can either follow or break. What sort of rules these are, and what breaking them involves, are tricky issues on which there is no firm agreement in linguistics or philosophy of language. We don't need to get into that debate here, but we can note that the rules about using swear words differ from the rules about using other sorts of words in an important way. We receive much less feedback and guidance about how to use swear words than we receive about how to use other sorts of words. A child who says to a parent or a teacher, 'Me am hungry', is likely to be corrected and told to say, instead, '*I* am hungry'. By contrast, a child who says to a parent or a teacher, 'How brilliant was it? Fucking', is likely to be scolded for swearing, but very unlikely to be scolded for doing it incorrectly. When children start to swear, the first and only rule of swearing that they learn is that they shouldn't swear. And if an otherwise articulate and fluent adult says, 'How brilliant was it? Fucking', we are more likely to think they are being creative with their swearing than that they are an incompetent speaker. It's rare that we receive guidance on how to swear correctly.[1] Indeed, we often celebrate

[1] There is a recent exception to this. In June 2019, the Académie Française published guidance on the correct use of certain French sweary insults. The guidance—entitled *Salop ou Salaud?* ('Male Slut or Bastard?')—explained that, etymologically, a slut (*une salope*) is not simply a female bastard (*un salaud*); and that although a male equivalent of 'slut' (*un salop*) and a female version of 'bastard' (*une salaude*) do exist, these terms are rarely used today. On balance, then, it behooves the conscientious swearer to insult

creative, hitherto unexplored uses of swear words. Consider the hundreds of Buzzfeed articles, blog posts, and YouTube clips devoted to the unusual sweary outbursts of Malcolm Tucker, the notoriously acerbic character from the British political satire show, *The Thick of It*—insults that ranged from the concise 'Shit off' to the more complicated 'You are a real boring fuck. Sorry, I know you disapprove of swearing, so I'll sort that: you are a boring F-star-star *cunt!*' Or the similar online celebration following then-US president Donald Trump's mistaken insinuation on Twitter that Scotland voted to leave the European Union in the UK's 2016 referendum. Scottish citizens accompanied their tweeted corrections with imaginative sweary terms that included *knuckle-brained fart lozenge*, *cock juggling thundercunt*, and *witless fucking cocksplat*. To my knowledge, no concerns were publicly expressed about the sweary competence of Malcolm Tucker or Scottish users of Twitter. On the contrary, *Strong Language*—a long-running, successful blog about swearing by linguists James Harbeck and Stan Carey along with various contributors—celebrates creative swearing each year in a blog post entitled 'The Annual Tucker Awards for Excellence in Swearing'. Among the recent recipients was Wendy Molyneux, for her *McSweeney's* article entitled 'Oh my fucking God, get the fucking vaccine already, you fucking fucks', which included lines like, 'You think vaccines don't fucking work? Oh, fuck off into the trash, you attention-seeking fuckworm-faced shitbutt. This isn't even a point worth discussing, you fuck-o-rama fuck-stival of ignorance' (Molyneux 2021).

My hunch is that our judgements about whether a person is a competent swearer piggy-back on our judgements about whether they are competent users of the language in general. When someone whom we judge to be generally fluent and articulate swears in an unusual way, we are much more likely to view them as swearing

women using *salope* and men using *salaud*. Such explicit, authoritative guidance about how to swear is rare, however (Académie Française (2019)).

creatively than as incompetent at swearing. On the other hand, if someone who is not fluent swears in an unusual way, we are quicker to view them as not knowing how to swear.

Philosopher Joel Feinberg has said, of swearing, 'The words acquire their strong expressive power in virtue of an almost paradoxical tension between powerful taboo and universal readiness to disobey' (Feinberg 1983, 140). We might add to this that swearing also derives its power from the fact that swearing is a realm of language where, once we've flouted the rule not to swear, *anything goes.* We often think that we shouldn't swear, but if we do, it bothers us little if we swear wrong. It is little wonder that swearing can be so cathartic and satisfying.

Swearing and the brain

Don't get excited, this won't be a long and detailed section on the neuroscience of swearing. But before moving on, let's note that as well as its being characterised by taboo language, by its role in expressing emotion, and by the fact that it is less rule governed than other forms of language, swearing seems to be processed in a special way by the brain. For one thing, it is a part of so-called automatic speech. Automatic speech activities are those that we carry out without conscious reflection. Besides swearing, they include counting, naming the days of the week, and conversational fillers like *um* and *ah*. People suffering from aphasia—problems using language correctly due to brain damage resulting from stroke, head injury, tumors, or certain diseases—often find that their automatic speech functions are unaffected. In other words, some people are able to swear even after they have lost the ability to hold a conversation or to read a book. In addition, excessive swearing can result from brain or spinal cord injury and from various neurological and psychiatric conditions, including—famously—Tourette syndrome. This has led researchers to conclude that swearing and regular speech are produced by different systems in the brain (Van Lancker and Cummings 1999).

Swearing's unique role in expressing emotion, and the unique way in which our brains process swearing, make it unsurprising that sometimes only a swear word will do. A common objection to swearing is that it is *unnecessary*: that we always have the alternative of finding a more decorous way of expressing ourselves. Aside from being an odd reason to object to swearing—how much of *anything* we say is necessary, really?—it is also mistaken. When we swear, we are not choosing one of many available, equally satisfactory expressions, as we do when we choose to say, 'Lovely weather, isn't it'? rather than 'Nice day, isn't it'? Swearing enables us to express what cannot be expressed using inoffensive words. As such, far from being unnecessary in such cases, swearing is *absolutely* necessary. As Mark Twain reportedly commented, 'The difference between the right word and the almost right word is the difference between lightning and a lightning bug'.

2
Swearing's secret offensive ingredient

People often wonder what it is that gives swear words their power to shock and offend. The capacity of swear words to affect us in the way they do can seem almost occult. This issue has cropped up in almost every one of the many media interviews I've done about swearing. What, people want to know, does *fuck* have that *funk* doesn't have? Why are people horrified at *cunt* but not at *country*? How can making certain noises, or writing certain symbols, reliably and predictably produce such dramatic emotional reactions in others? I'm going to turn to these questions now.

We already have one answer to the puzzle of where swear words get their power. We considered it briefly in the previous chapter, where I remarked that when, as children, we first start to experiment with swearing, we are met with disapproval from adults. This quickly teaches us that swearing is something to be avoided in polite society; at the same time, marking swearing as taboo in this way opens the door to the excitement of taboo-breaking. We each get the idea that swearing is offensive, then, because we are taught that it is offensive from an early age. And we learn that it has the power to shock because we see that people are shocked when we swear, and because we are taught that we should avoid it.

But this is not a full and satisfying answer to the question of how we came to view swearing as offensive. We also want to know how this all started. Why is swearing's offensiveness a thing? And why is it words like *cunt*, *cock*, *fuck*, *shit*, and *piss* that society has decided to find offensive? Why not—as is sometimes suggested—decide to be offended instead by words that denote truly horrible things, like *torture*, *rape*, and *genocide*? The answer, as we will see in this chapter, is elusive. None of the most obvious candidates for swearing's being offensive is quite satisfactory.

What we say . . .

An obvious first step in considering swearing's offensiveness is to look at what swear words denote; that is, what they refer to, or what they mean—literally, as it were. At least in English, many swear words denote sexual or lavatorial things. Talk of sexual and lavatorial things is frowned upon in many social contexts, so perhaps this helps explain why swear words are offensive. But a moment's reflection is enough to tell us that it is not swear words' denotations that make them offensive—or at least, their denotations will give us only part of the answer. *Cunt*, *cock*, *fuck*, *shit*, and *piss* are offensive, yet other words and expressions denoting exactly the same things—*vagina*, *penis*, *sexual congress*, *faeces*, *urine*—are inoffensive in many contexts where the sweary equivalents are offensive. We even have euphemistic words that enable us to refer to exactly the same things in polite contexts while giving minimal offence: *foo-foo*, *pee-pee*, *sleep together*, *bowel movement*, and *water*. We can distinguish between taboo *things or topics* and taboo *words or expressions*: often the words or expressions that denote taboo things or topics are themselves taboo—as in the case with fucking and the word *fucking*—but some (like *sleep together*) are not; and some taboo things or topics don't have any taboo word or expression that denotes them (cannibalism is taboo, but at least in English, there is no taboo word for it) (Andersson and Trudgill 1992). That swear words tend to focus on taboo topics like sex and defecation is something that demands explanation—we'll return to this in the next chapter—but the fact that *shit* and *bowel movement* denote the same thing yet differ in offensiveness shows that the offensiveness of swear words cannot be fully explained by what they denote. Swearing's offensiveness is not just a matter of what swear words refer to, then, but also of how they refer to it.

It's not just with swear words that the offensiveness of what we refer to can come apart from the offensiveness of how we refer to something. Even without swearing, some things are offensive regardless of how we say them; for example, there is no inoffensive way to assert that some people are inferior to others on account of their belonging to a certain race or gender. In such cases, the offensiveness can be explained by denotation; that is, by the *content* of what is asserted, the claim that is being made regardless of what words are used to make it. Other things can be offensive when expressed in one way but not when expressed in another. It would be offensive for a surgeon, while chuckling, to inform anxious relatives that their seriously ill loved one *croaked* on the operating table but not offensive to use an expression like *I'm afraid we lost him*, or *I'm so sorry but he didn't make it*, delivered with appropriate gravity.[1] When something that we say is offensive, then, this is either because of *what* we said or *how* we said it, or both. We can keep this distinction in mind as we reflect on swearing throughout this book. The fact that swear words denote things that can be less offensively denoted with other words—*fucking* versus *making love*—tells us that their capacity to offend is not exhausted by their denotation. We must look elsewhere to explain their offensiveness. We might, then, look to their *connotation*. If denotation is the literal meaning of a word or expression, its connotation is the 'feel' of it (i.e. the emotions and associations it evokes). A word or expression's connotations can be pleasant or unpleasant, positive or negative. Two words or expressions can have identical denotations but differ in their connotations. This is why, in the example above, *He croaked* is likely to offend, but *I'm afraid we lost him* is not. And as one internet meme puts it, *Have a nice day* is a pleasant thing to

[1] Example adapted from Allen and Burridge (2006, 39–40).

say, but *Enjoy the next 24 hours* sounds rather threatening. When we learn a new language, we master the denotations of its words much more easily than we master their connotations. This helps explain why swearing in a foreign language can be tricky. It is pretty easy for an English learner to grasp that *shit* and *poo* denote the same thing, but it takes longer to grasp their connotations, which involves being able to predict the sort of response that each is likely to elicit in the listener in a given context.

. . . and how we say it

Steven Pinker believes that the connotations of swear words result in their causing an involuntary emotional response in the listener, and that this explains the offensiveness of swear words. By swearing, he tells us, we 'kidnap' the listener's attention and force them to consider something unpleasant (Pinker 2007b). It is undoubtedly true that swearing can be an effective way of getting people's attention. But there are several reasons to be dissatisfied with Pinker's explanation. To begin, there is nothing unique about swearing's ability to 'kidnap' the listener's attention. Pinker himself notes this, with reference to the Stroop effect: a phenomenon famously illustrated by presenting people with a multicoloured list of words naming various colors and asking them to say aloud the colour of the ink in which each word is written, which does not match the colour it names. This task is difficult for literate adults, Pinker explains, because it is so hard to turn off our ability to read the word and instead attend only to its colour. We also have an automatic response to hearing our own name: hearing it 'kidnaps' our attention. So, given that it's possible to 'kidnap' a listener's attention inoffensively, how can it explain swearing's capacity to offend?

Pinker argues that, unlike these other attention-kidnapping phenomena, swearing makes us think of something unpleasant. He sees this combination of attention-kidnapping and unpleasantness as the key to swearing's offensiveness. But this is not convincing. It's true that swear words often denote unpleasant things such as defecation, but the fact that we very often process (and are offended by) swear words without considering their denotation makes it implausible that in general they offend us by virtue of making us think of unpleasant things. If we're dining in an upmarket restaurant and we hear a waiter exclaim 'Shit!' after dropping a fork, we might frown on his impoliteness and lack of professionalism, but his outburst is unlikely to make us think of defecation. The word's denotation wouldn't even occur to most of us in this context. On the other hand, were the waiter to approach our table while we're eating and say 'How is your meal? I'm just going for a shit!', then we might well find our appetites dampened. In this second example, the waiter uses *shit* in such a way as to make us consider its denotation. But he can make us think of that without swearing at all. The non-sweary 'How is your meal? I'm just going to defecate!' is more likely to spoil our appetites—because it is more likely to make us think of defecation—than his sweary exclamation of 'Shit!'

Further, many of the most offensive swear words do not denote anything unpleasant at all. Some focus on sex, the genitals, or religion. And some sweary expressions offend us even though it is unclear what their denotation is. *Fuck you!* can be shocking, but it is not shocking because it makes us think of something unpleasant (unless what is unpleasant is the expression itself, which would leave us without an explanation of *why* it is unpleasant). Making someone think of something unpleasant, then, is not necessary for causing offence. Neither is it sufficient. I can inoffensively make you think of something unpleasant by saying, 'Your daughter should learn to swim in case she ever falls into a river'. Psychotherapists routinely but inoffensively make their clients think of unpleasant things when they encourage them to confront long-buried and traumatic memories. News broadcasts frequently contain unpleasant content without thereby being offensive. Even using attention-kidnapping means to evoke these unpleasant thoughts is not enough to render unpleasant the communication described in these examples: the listener's attention is kidnapped if the speaker uses her name, if the news broadcast is preceded by a catchy jingle, or simply if the communication uses language that the listener understands and therefore cannot help but automatically process.

Finally, while Pinker refers interchangeably to swearing's offensiveness and to its power to evoke certain emotional responses, the offensiveness of swearing—or, indeed, of anything—cannot be explained wholly by the emotional response it arouses in the listener. People respond emotionally to different things in different ways, often in ways that the speaker cannot predict. Even innocently chatting to a friend about your new garden shed could traumatise your friend if it turns out that, unbeknown to you, he once had a distressing experience in a shed that he cannot bear to relive. Despite upsetting your friend, you have not done anything offensive by mentioning your shed.

If swearing's capacity to elicit certain emotions in the listener does not explain its offensiveness, what about its capacity to express the speaker's emotions? As we saw in the previous chapter, when we hear somebody exclaim 'Fuck you!', we do not understand them via a literal interpretation of what they have said. Instead, we take them to be using the expression to communicate their anger, hurt, or annoyance. Swearing is particularly good at enabling us to communicate certain emotions. Can this explain swearing's offensiveness? We do, after all, find certain expressions of emotion offensive, as when someone laughs at a funeral or expresses annoyance when we announce that we have recovered from a deadly illness. However, in cases where people swear to express emotion, it cannot be the mere expression of emotion that causes offence. Saying 'Fuck you!' might well be an effective way to express anger, hurt, or annoyance, but there are plenty of ways to communicate the same emotions inoffensively: we can stamp our feet, say 'I'm angry/hurt/annoyed!', or (especially if we're British) make an understatement like 'I'm not best pleased about this'. While some expressions of emotion are offensive, and while many instances of swearing are offensive, swearing's offensiveness cannot be adequately explained with reference to the emotion that it expresses. Even so, the fact that swearing is a particularly satisfying way to express strong emotions—as is evidenced from the fact that it is more satisfying to yell 'Fuck!' than 'Fiddlesticks!' when we miss our train—demands explanation. We'll return to this later.

The taboo of taboo-breaking

An important aspect of swearing is its relationship to taboos. All swear words, when used to denote, denote something taboo. In addition to denoting what is taboo, swearing itself is taboo: we are not supposed to swear. Let's consider whether the taboo aspect of swearing explains its offensiveness.

A taboo is a behaviour (including speech) or object that is forbidden in society or in a particular social circle or context. Behaviour that is illegal or otherwise officially proscribed counts as taboo according to this definition; but when we talk about taboos, we typically mean behaviour that is *informally* disallowed or frowned upon. In other words, we mean behaviour that may shock, offend, or outrage one's community, and which may get the offender ostracised, but which does not normally result in a formal retaliation from the law. Taboos commonly centre on concerns about contamination, sex, death, and physical or spiritual harm (the latter includes things like bad luck or suffering in the afterlife). Some taboos, such as swearing, blasphemy, and slurs, are linguistic. Being naked in public, having sex with close relatives, defecating in public, and having a punch-up at the graveside at a funeral are all examples of non-linguistic taboos. What is taboo varies across societies, cultures, and contexts: it is taboo for a Sikh man to go without a turban in public but not for women or non-Sikhs to do so; for Muslims, but not for non-Muslims, it is taboo to depict people, and especially to depict God or the prophet Muhammed; in

Japan but not in other cultures, it is taboo to wear outdoor shoes in some buildings; in India but not elsewhere it is taboo to use the left hand for certain purposes, including eating and accepting a gift; in churches it is taboo to wear a hat, but in mosques and synagogues it is taboo to leave the head uncovered. There are even fictional taboos: in the *Harry Potter* series it is taboo to mention Voldemort by name; and in the film *Fight Club*, 'The first rule of Fight Club is: You do not talk about Fight Club'.

How does a type of behaviour become taboo? Typically, this arises from a wish to avoid contamination, death, or physical or spiritual harm. It will perhaps be clear how some of the behaviours just mentioned became taboo. Defecating in public poses a risk of contamination. Interbreeding with close relatives risks physical harm like offspring with genetic disorders. The religious-themed taboos all introduce the threat of spiritual harm via a failure to respect what is sacred. Behaviours can become taboo even in the absence of a satisfactory explanation for their harmfulness; for example, the taboo against incest predates any understanding of the genetic factors that explain its potential effects, and so must have arisen for other reasons, perhaps due to the so-called Westermarck effect (the hypothesis that raising young children together inhibits their being sexually attracted to each other later in life). And behaviours can remain taboo even after the explanation for their harmfulness has been forgotten. Consider the taboo against spilling salt. Salt was once an expensive and precious commodity that also had spiritual significance. As a result, in times gone by, spilling salt was a far more serious matter than it is today, and the ritual of throwing a pinch of the spilt salt over the left shoulder with the right hand had a clear explanation as an attempt to ward off evil forces. Many people continue this ritual today, but usually without any understanding of why spilling salt is something that requires such a response.[2] This reveals how taboos and the rituals around

[2] I've taken this example from Allen and Burridge (2006, 9).

them can easily take on an aura of magic—and some writers have commented on swearing's relationship to magic. Feinberg wrote that the 'shock value of profane words in the past has essentially depended on implicit beliefs in word magic' (1985, 204); and Nunberg (2008) remarked that 'dirty words are magic spells that conjure up their references'.

Understanding swearing's relationship to taboo can help us understand how it developed, and how it assumed the form it has today. Sociologist Edward Sagarin saw swearing as historically rooted in religious language (Sagarin 1962). Using religious language to swear is a form of blasphemy, and blasphemy is taboo. Religious terminology and references play a role in swearing in almost all cultures. In English, religious-themed swearing—using terms like 'Christ', 'damn', and 'hell', often in the form of cursing—is a milder form of swearing than it once was. However, in some other languages, the religious theme features far more centrally and dramatically. Perhaps the most vivid example is Quebecois French, in which the strongest swear words are terms relating to Catholicism. These include *tabernak* (tabernacle), *crisse* (Christ), *baptême* (baptism), *calisse* (chalice), *ciboire* (ciborium), and *osti* (host). *Je m'en calisse* is equivalent to the English 'I don't give a fuck'. These words are considered stronger than the standard French swear words like *merde* (shit), and they can be amplified by combining them with each other and with standard swear words and other expressions. This gives rise to powerful and difficult-to-translate expressions like *Crisse de marde*, *Mon crisse de tabernak*, *J'm va te décalliser la yuele*, and *Crisse de calisse de tabernak d'osti de sacrament*.[3] Religion is a dominant theme in other languages including Italian, Romanian, Hungarian, and Spanish. There are regional differences between

[3] Some of these examples are taken from http://en.wikipedia.org/wiki/Quebec_French_profanity, developed and enhanced with help from Philippe Jacquet. Extra friend-points to Philippe for doing a last-minute WhatsApp survey of his Montreal friends while I was correcting the proofs for this book and needed to know whether *criss* or *crisse* is the correct spelling of this rude word.

practices, but examples include the Italian *Porco Dio* and *Porco Madonna* (respectively, 'God/Madonna is a pig'), the Romanian *Dumnezu să te futǎ* and the Hungarian *Bassza meg az Isten* (both of which mean 'May God fuck you'), and the Spanish *Me cago en Dios* (I shit on God). These examples are from largely religious cultures, but some highly secular cultures also find religious swearing offensive. *Godverdomme* (Goddamn) remains one of the strongest expressions in Dutch. *Perkele* (the name of a pagan deity, now equivalent in meaning to 'devil'), *saatana* (Satan), *jumalauta* (literally 'God help', but used in a similar way to the English 'Goddamn'), and *helvetti* (hell) are all common and powerful ways of swearing in Finnish. There are pagan influences, too, in Estonian: *Pagan võtaks* means, approximately, 'Let the devil take it'. *For fanden*, *For helvede*, and *For Satan* (For the devil's/hell's/Satan's sake) are widely used Danish expressions; similarly, *fan* (Satan), *helvete* (hell), and *jävla* (derived from *djävul*, meaning 'devil') are common Swedish expressions.

For Sagarin, the religious roots of swearing are key to understanding the particular form that many (but not all) of our familiar swears take, and their power to offend. We have already seen that we do not come to understand swears like *Fuck you!* by understanding their literal meanings. This is fortunate given that, in many cases, it can be difficult to make any sense of their literal meanings. There seems no obvious answer to the question of what *Fuck you!*, *For fuck's sake!*, and *I don't give a shit!* mean, leaving aside their capacity to communicate anger, frustration, contempt, or disengagement with one's interlocutor. Sagarin suggests that expressions like these probably developed from religious curses—respectively, *Damn you!*, *For God's sake!*, and *I don't give a damn!*—whose meanings are more straightforwardly comprehensible. As the influence of religion has waned, religious references in these expressions have been replaced by more powerful sexual and scatological words. It does not matter much that the modified expressions make little sense, since what is lost in denotation is amply repaid in connotation.

Pinker takes the capacity of religious curses to evoke strong emotional responses, thanks to their violation of the taboo against blasphemy, to explain why the expletives into which they evolved remain powerful despite the religious terms having been replaced by sexual and scatological ones. Just as many people today worry about breaking the taboo against spilling salt even though the historical reasons for this taboo have long ceased to be relevant, people continue to be offended by swearing even though the religious sentiments that underpin it are much less influential today than they once were. However, this leaves unexplained the fact that not just *any* expression that evolves out of a religious curse is offensive. If that were the case, then *Darn you!* and *Fuck you!*, both of which have evolved out of *Damn you!*, would be equally offensive; as would *For goodness' sake!* and *For fuck's sake!*, having both evolved from *For God's sake!* Clearly this is not the case: *Darn you!* and *For goodness' sake!* arose as replacements to the religious curses precisely to *reduce* their offensiveness. Given that replacing words like *God* and *damn* in religious curses with words like *fuck* and *shit* did not diminish the emotional force of the original expressions, this must be due to the replacement expressions somehow being sufficiently forceful.

What, then, makes *fuck* and *shit* sufficiently forceful? Well, like religious curses, they relate to taboos. Specifically, they relate to taboos about sex and contamination. Along with religious expressions, sexual and lavatorial ones play a starring role in swearing. This is true not only of British swearing but of swearing in almost all cultures. Wherever you go in the world, the chances are that you'll come up against the equivalent of *fucks*, *cocks*, and *shits* at some point. Swearing in some cultures also makes use of taboos in ways that diverge from the sex/toilet theme. French swearing contains insults relating to menstruation, such as *Viens boire mes règles* (Come drink my menstrual blood). And references to sodomy and homosexuality feature in swearing in many languages, including French.

Sex and defecation are not the only common non-religious themes in swearing, however. Many swears make reference to physical harm; specifically, to disease. In English, insults that accuse the listener of being diseased have a childish, playground feel, but they are more widely used elsewhere. Dutch swearing has many expressions relating to disease: *kankerlijer*, *teringlijer*, *tyfuslijer*, and *aidslijer* (cancer/tuberculosis/typhus/AIDS sufferer) are common insults, and the disease terms can be combined with other insults to amplify them, as in the strong but somewhat out-of-fashion *kankerhoer* (cancer-whore). Mental disability features in swearing, too. Korean swearing includes the insults 바보 (*babo)* and 병신 (*byeongsin*), both of which mean 'idiot'; 미친놈 (*michinom*), meaning 'crazy'; and the less common 염병할 (*yeombyeonghal*), an insult that refers to typhoid fever, or to infectious disease in general. Calling someone 'idiot' in English is a way of insulting them without actually swearing—but strictly speaking, insulting someone by suggesting they are mentally or physically disabled is a way of slurring people with disabilities, which is not only rude but also morally problematic. We'll return to this issue in Chapter 11 when we take a closer look at slurs. There are some insults that relate to physical harm but not to disease or disability, and which do not have the character of slurs; although they're pretty rare. Examples include the Korean 육시랄 (*yuksiral*) and 오사랄 (*osaral*), which refer to methods of execution in which one is torn into six and five pieces, respectively, along with 오라질 (*orajil*), a term that translates to 'fit to be tied up like a criminal', 주리를 틀 (*jurireul teul*), meaning 'fit to have one's legs twisted with sticks inserted between them', and 난장맞을 (*nanjangmajeul*), meaning 'fit to be flogged'—but the first two expressions are not commonly used and the rest are now rather old-fashioned.[4]

In addition to swears born of religious, sexual, and contamination-related taboos, there are swears characterized by taboos relating to hierarchy. These involve expressing

[4] I'm grateful to Brian Jongseong Park for these insights about Korean swearing.

inappropriate disrespect—often through sexual references—for certain individuals, commonly the mother of the person insulted.[5] Examples in English are limited to 'motherfucker' and 'son of a bitch', but they are more common in other languages. There are the Croatian expressions *Pička ti materina* (Your mother's cunt) and *Jebo ti pas mater* (May a dog fuck your mother); the Filipino *Putang-ina* (Whore-mother); the Romanian *Futu-ţi dumnezeii mă-tii* (Fuck your mother's gods) and *Morţii mă-tii* (Fuck your mother's dead relatives);[6] the Spanish *Me cago en la leche de tu madre* (I shit in your mother's milk), *Me cago en tu tia* (I shit on your aunt), and *Putamadre* (Whore-mother); the Turkish *Ananı sikeyim* (I fuck your mother); the Korean 네미 붙을 (*nemi buteul*), 제미 붙을 (*jemi buteul*), 네미랄 (*nemiral*), and 제미랄 (*jemiral*), all of which are contractions of expressions that correspond to 'motherfucking'; and the Mandarin 肏你祖宗十八代 (Fuck your ancestors to the eighteenth generation). 'Son of a bitch' has equivalents in many languages including French (*Fils de pute*), German (*Hurensohn*), Italian (*Figlio di troia*), Turkish (*Orospu çocuğu*), and Korean (개새끼 (*gaesaekki*)); and German has absorbed and translated the term 'motherfucker' (*Mutterficker*).

Insulting the listener's mother has a lofty historical pedigree. The following 'ur mum' joke appears in William Shakespeare's *Titus Andronicus*:

Demetrius	Villain, what hast thou done?
Aaron	That which thou canst not undo.
Chiron	Thou hast undone our mother.
Aaron	Villain, I have done thy mother.

[5] Should we view religious taboo as a special case of taboos relating to hierarchy? I think there is a case for keeping the two separate, since breaking religious taboos is associated with a fear of spiritual harm (such as going to hell), which is not associated with breaking other hierarchy-related taboos.

[6] For an enlightening discussion about Romanian swearing, I'm grateful to Emilian Mihailov, who shared various insults in a pub in Oxford the first time I met him, in what remains one of the funniest scholarly discussions of my career.

Japanese offers a striking example of a hierarchy-themed insult. There are fewer swear words in Japanese than in many other languages, and Japanese swearing is generally viewed as *yakuza* (gangster) language, to be avoided by ordinary people. Instead, one of the most effective ways to offend somebody in Japanese is to address them as てめ (*teme*), which is a very derogatory form of 'you'. To understand why this is so insulting, note that Japan is a highly hierarchical society, and this is reflected in the existence of a great many pronouns and word endings that imply a difference in status between speaker and listener. Addressing someone using てめ tells them that you view them as worthless. Korean, too, contains different speech levels to reflect the relationship between speaker and listener, and it is possible to insult one's listener by addressing them in an overfamiliar way.

To a less dramatic extent, it's possible to insult one's listener with overfamiliarity even in languages that don't have such pervasive ways of reflecting the relationship between speaker and listener. Many languages, including Welsh, French, and German, have different forms of *you* to reflect (among other things) the formality of the relationship between speaker and listener, which introduces the possibility of insulting one's listener by addressing them with inappropriate familiarity. While we don't have this pronominal distinction in English, it's nevertheless possible to insult someone by being inappropriately informal. Saying 'Cheers, Chuck!' in the course of being knighted by King Charles III is likely to result in offence, as is using terms like *Bud*, *Darling*, or *Sugar tits* to address the judge who is presiding over one's murder trial. Even addressing one's parent or grandparent using their first name, when precedent requires using words like *Mum* and *Grandma*, can cause offence.

It's also possible, although rarer, to insult someone by addressing them with inappropriate formality. Imagine a group of work colleagues who are in the habit of addressing each other formally while at work—as 'Ms X', 'Mr Y', 'Dr Z', and so on. Imagine that they occasionally socialise outside work and that, in this less formal context, they fall to addressing each other by their first names. If there were one colleague in the group whom the others continued to address formally even in this less formal context, despite his efforts to make friends with his colleagues, he could reasonably conclude that he is being excluded and snubbed by his colleagues.

Does swearing's focus on taboo explain why swearing is offensive? Not quite. Swear words refer to taboo topics when used to denote, but—as we have seen—swear words have many inoffensive synonyms. This means that merely referring to, relating to, or evoking a taboo topic is not enough to make a term offensive. So, what is it about the way in which swearing relates to these topics that makes it offensive? We have already noted that swearing is taboo in two separate senses: swearing is itself a taboo activity, and swear words have taboo denotations. That it's possible—using terms like *number two*—to refer inoffensively to what is taboo shows that a word or expression's being taboo in the second sense does not explain why it is taboo in the first sense. We must, then, look elsewhere to find out why swearing is offensive.

Where shall we look? We could continue to scrutinise swear words in the hope of finding the secret of their offensiveness—but perhaps we should pay heed to the pattern that is beginning to emerge. We've already seen that swearing's offensiveness cannot arise solely from what swears denote or connote, nor from the emotions that the speaker expresses by swearing, nor from the fact that swear words relate to taboo topics. This is because there are inoffensive ways of communicating all these things. Moreover, with the exception of connotation (to which we'll return), these factors do not vary with context, whereas the offensiveness of swearing does vary with context, and so considering these factors can tell us nothing about why swearing is more offensive in some contexts than in others.

We're likely to end up with similar results if we look to other context-insensitive aspects of swear words for the key to their offensiveness. Some writers have pointed to the sound that swear words make. Pinker remarks that 'imprecations tend to use sounds that are perceived as quick and harsh' (Pinker 2007a, 339), and Kate Warwick hypothesises that the peculiar offensiveness of *cunt* results from a combination of its meaning and 'the sound of the word and the physical satisfaction of lobbing this verbal hand grenade' (Warwick 2015). There is, to be sure, something plausible about this. Trying to express anger using a swear word full of gentle, soft sounds—like the words *whiffy* and *slush*—would be decidedly unsatisfactory; the verbal equivalent of angrily trying to slam a door fitted with a compressed air hinge. Even so, the sound of swear words cannot fully account for their offensiveness, for reasons that have become familiar. Many inoffensive words also sound 'quick and harsh', and some swear words have benign alternative meanings (consider *prick* and *cock*), or sound identical to parts of inoffensive words (*cunt* sounds identical to the first syllable of *country*—a fact not lost on John Donne, who 'sucked on country pleasures'; nor on the anonymous author of the rugby song *A Soldier I Will Be*, whose sweary lines include 'Asshole, asshole, a soldier I will be' and 'To fight for the old cunt, fight for the old cunt, fight for the old country').

That swear words tend to centre on taboo topics, and that they tend to sound a certain way, are things that demand explanation, and we'll be considering that explanation in Chapter 5. But to find a satisfactory account of what makes swearing offensive, we need to cast our net wider and look to the relationship between swearer and listener. Let's turn to this now.

3
There is no secret ingredient

We've explored a few features characteristic of swear words: their focus on certain taboo topics like sex and defecation, the way they sound, and the fact that swearing is itself a taboo. *Why* these features are associated with swearing is something that needs explaining, and we'll come to that eventually. But let's not get ahead of ourselves. We started out, at the opening of Chapter 2, wanting to know how swear words get their power to shock and offend. And none of the features that swear words always and everywhere have—their sound, their link to taboo—can explain their power to shock and offend, precisely *because* they are features that swear words always and everywhere have. As we saw in the introduction, swear words' power to shock and offend is not a quality that they always and everywhere have. An f-bomb dropped by the monarch during an official television broadcast is more shocking and offensive than the very same word bandied about between a couple of geezers sitting in the pub venting about the disruption caused by local roadworks. Swearing's power to shock and offend, in other words, is context dependent. That means that, if we want to understand this power, it's a mistake to look to those features of swearing that don't vary with context.

You might be wondering whether, setting aside the way swear words sound, what they refer to, and their being taboo, there is anything left to explain how swearing manages to shock and offend. What else *is* there? In this chapter, we're going to find out.

Context is (almost) everything

Swearing's offensiveness depends on its context. What do I mean by 'context' here? Well, a few different things.

Context can relate to the particular sort of social environment in which we are speaking: swearing on a building site is less likely to offend than swearing during a church service, and there is a long history of swearing being frowned upon in the company of women and children. Context can also relate to what sort of person the speaker is. The middle class tends to be held to greater account for bad language than the working or upper classes; indeed, in their work on taboos, Keith Allan and Kate Burridge coin the term *middle-class politeness criterion* to describe the standard by which certain expressions are typically judged polite or the reverse. The criterion, they explain, is meant to apply to people who fall between 'those so rich and/or so powerful that they can disregard social conventions observed by the mass of the community' and 'those so uneducated, poor and deprived that they are unaware of, or cannot afford to observe, the niceties of such social conventions' (Allen and Burridge 2006, 35).

Context can also relate to the wider cultural environment, which can vary with time and place. Similar swear words have different connotations at different times and in different cultures and places. In the UK, religious swearing has come to be seen as less offensive over the past few decades. By contrast, as we saw in the previous chapter, religious terms remain highly offensive in some countries and in some languages. *Cunt*, while highly offensive throughout much of the English-speaking world, can be used inoffensively and affectionately in many communities in Scotland—a point stressed by film director Ken Loach in his wrangling with the British Board of Film Classification over the classification of his 2012 film, *The Angel's Share*, which focuses on the Glasgow working class—and its Welsh equivalent, *cont*, can also be used inoffensively in many contexts where the English equivalent would be highly offensive.

Wanker is a moderately offensive English insult, but the Greek equivalent—*μαλάκας* (*malakas*)—while also an insult, is commonly used affectionately.

Context can relate to what the speaker is responding to: we are more tolerant of the sort of involuntary swearing that occurs as a response to the speaker's trapping her hand in a door than we are to swearing in calmer situations. And context can relate to the expectations that the audience has of the speaker; for example, we sometimes forgive offensive language in polite company in cases where the speaker is a young child or a non-native speaker, because we recognise that children and non-native speakers may not fully grasp informal rules about when certain expressions are inappropriate. (Other times, of course, these sorts of speakers are judged extra harshly for swearing.) These rules, along with other contextual factors, can interact in complex ways that affect the extent to which a given instance of swearing is offensive. For example, while we would not normally reprimand someone who swears involuntarily in response to suffering a painful injury, there are contexts in which we would view this as unacceptable. Loudly exclaiming 'Fucking hell!' after stubbing one's toe during a wedding service is likely to raise eyebrows, even if it would be overlooked in less austere contexts.

To understand swearing's offensiveness, then, we have to take context into account. But how can we begin to do this, given the diverse and complex ways in which context can influence the offensiveness of swearing?

Offence escalation

It would be a mistake to expect some deep and profound insight about swearing's offensiveness to emerge from reflecting on precisely how this offensiveness can be determined by uttering those particular words in those particular contexts. After all, there is often no good reason for why we find offensive the particular things we find offensive. To see this, let's go back to one of the examples of taboo behaviour described in the previous chapter. We saw that taboo behaviour can vary across cultures, and that while it is taboo for men to wear a hat in a church, in a mosque it is taboo to leave the head uncovered. Despite the contrast between the behaviours proscribed by these taboos, they arise from the same source: the desire to express respect for what is sacred. There is undoubtedly a (causal, religious, cultural) story to be told in each case about how the particular way of respecting what is sacred was settled upon—but if we want to understand why it is offensive to keep one's hat on in church, it would be misguided of us to look for the key to the offensiveness in the particular phenomenon of hat-wearing in church. When people are offended by men who wear hats in church, this offence is caused by those men's failure to respect what is sacred via the established cultural norms. When people are offended by men who enter mosques with uncovered heads, this offence is caused by the failure to respect what is sacred according to a different set of established cultural norms. Setting aside these norms and the culture in which they operate, there is nothing that is either respectful or disrespectful about the act of (not) removing one's headwear in a religious building. The ability of that act to convey respect or disrespect derives from the cultural context in which it occurs—as is illustrated by the fact that Christians associate removing one's hat in church with conveying respect while Muslims associate uncovering one's head in a mosque with disrespect.

How do these reflections apply to our exploration of why swearing is offensive? Well, we might view them as a caution against focusing too narrowly on context-insensitive features of swear words. To discover what makes swearing offensive, we must instead look more widely at the sort of speech behaviour that involves and surrounds swearing, and the way in which it arises in social situations. Swearing's offensiveness arises from the interaction between two features of the language we use. The first is that, as we have seen, when we use language, we communicate much more than is conveyed by the denotations of the words we use. The second is that we have preferences about which words and expressions people use. Many of these preferences are taboo related in that we generally prefer that people avoid referring to taboo topics especially in certain formal or sacred settings. Once preferences for certain forms of speech are established, it is easy to see how forms that are merely dispreferred should grow to be offensive while preferred forms become expected. This will happen as our choice of which form of words to use comes to be influenced by our knowledge about what preferences our listeners have for certain expressions over others.

We can illustrate this by means of an analogy with an expression that nobody would be tempted to deem offensive. Imagine the following scenario, which is based on an actual and recurring series of events. Suppose that you make a new friend named Rebecca, and you fall into the habit of addressing her as 'Rachel'. After you have done this a couple of times, she politely points out that her name is Rebecca, not Rachel. If, after she has drawn your attention to this, you persist in calling her 'Rachel', she is likely to begin to feel annoyed, and she might repeat the request to call her Rebecca. If you ignore her request a second time, and perhaps also a third time, then—provided that she has no reason to believe you have failed to understand her requests, nor that you are incapable of easily complying with them—she will come to view your behaviour as offensive. What started out as merely a dispreferred (by Rebecca) way of speaking, then, becomes offensive.

How does this happen? Well, the first time you call Rebecca 'Rachel', Rebecca takes you to have made an innocent and regrettably common mistake, and she assumes you meant no harm. When you continue to address her by the wrong name even after she has corrected you, she concludes with mild annoyance that you are being unacceptably inattentive to her wishes. But when you persist in using 'Rachel' even after Rebecca has pointed out several times that this is not her name, it is difficult for her to avoid the conclusion that either you are deliberately calling her by the wrong name in order to upset her or you respect her so little that you regard getting her name right as pretty unimportant. Having started out assuming that you meant no harm, she comes to view your attitude towards her as hostile. And, indeed, leaving aside outlandish possibilities like your being blackmailed into calling her 'Rachel', it is hard to see how she could be mistaken.

In this example, the offensiveness of your calling Rebecca 'Rachel' is not due to 'Rachel' being an offensive word. 'Rachel' is about as inoffensive a word as it is possible to get. Rather, your behaviour of calling Rebecca 'Rachel' grows to be offensive after it has filtered through a series of inferences that the speaker and the listener make about each other and about each other's inferences. In essence, you know that Rebecca's name is not 'Rachel', and you know that she prefers not to be called 'Rachel', yet you nevertheless continue to call her 'Rachel'; Rebecca knows that you know all this and concludes from your behaviour in light of this knowledge that you are hostile towards her; you, in turn, know all *this* yet persist in calling her 'Rachel'; Rebecca notices that you do this and so takes offence.

Let's call the way in which your calling Rebecca 'Rachel' becomes offensive in this situation *offence escalation*. Offence escalation is the process by which a behaviour that is merely dispreferred grows to be offensive as a result of the audience's (1) taking the person exhibiting the behaviour to realise that the behaviour is dispreferred, and (2) taking this person's decision to behave in this way in spite of this realisation as indicative of this person's lack of consideration of, or even hostility towards, her audience.

It's helpful, having considered this example, to reflect on what Joel Feinberg has to say about the experience of getting offended. Feinberg was an American political and legal philosopher who, in the mid-1980s, became well known for arguing for an *offence principle* to supplement the *harm principle* associated with the nineteenth-century English philosopher, John Stuart Mill. Mill's harm principle stated that the only legitimate reason for the state to exercise power over citizens against their will is to prevent harm to others. Feinberg's view was that the harm principle was not enough, and that under certain circumstances a state may legitimately exercise power over citizens to prevent offence. At this point, though, we're not interested in whether or how the state should respond to what's offensive; our focus is simply on what offensiveness *is*. Feinberg noted that there are two different senses of *offence*. In one sense, something is offensive simply if someone *feels* offended by it. In the other sense—which Feinberg calls *wrongful offence*—something is offensive when (among other things) it is a consequence of someone doing something that they ought not to do. He explained:

> I am offended (or 'take offence') when (a) I suffer a disliked state, and (b) I attribute that state to the wrongful conduct of another, and (c) I resent the other for his role in causing me to be in the state. The sense of grievance against the other or resentment of him for wronging me in this way is a phenomenological component of the unpleasant experience itself, an element that actually reenforces and magnifies its unpleasantness. (1985, 2)

In what follows I'm going to use the term *offence* to mean *wrongful offence*, rather than to refer to the feeling of offence, and when I want to discuss feeling offended, I'll say so. We're going to consider how we should interpret Feinberg's 'wrongful' in the next chapter. For now, note that Feinberg's focus here is on one person's act of wronging another, and on that other's response. He does not, at least at this stage in his account, focus on what specific sort of behaviour the first person engages in. It's all about people responding to each other.

Back to your calling Rebecca 'Rachel'. What Feinberg says here neatly describes the stages of the process by which your use of

'Rachel' comes to offend Rebecca. Being called by the wrong name starts out merely as a disliked state for her, but it grows into something that offends her when your behaviour produces in her a 'sense of grievance'.

Armed with this understanding of offence escalation, we can say something more about the example from the previous chapter, in which you unknowingly upset your friend by chatting about your new garden shed. I mentioned there that despite upsetting your friend, you do nothing offensive. You do nothing offensive because *shed* is not generally viewed as an offensive (or even dispreferred) term, and because you could not be expected to know that your friend finds the term upsetting. In Feinberg's terms, you're responsible for (a) (causing your friend to suffer a disliked mental state) but you haven't done anything wrong, so you haven't pushed your friend into (b) or (c). However, you *would* end up doing something offensive if you were to continue to talk about sheds even after learning that your friend prefers you not to talk to him about sheds, and if your friend ends up resenting you as a result. The lesson from these examples is that we don't need to use offensive words to cause offence with the language we use. We can, instead, use language in a way that indicates our disrespect for the person we're talking to. In other words, it's not about the words, it's about what we convey by the way we use the words.

These two examples differ in an important way from swearing. Swear words are recognised by all users of the language as offensive words, which we can—given the right context—use to cause offence. By contrast, in the Rebecca/Rachel example, the name 'Rachel' becomes offensive only when it is used by *you* to address Rebecca. If, later on, Rebecca meets a new person who also addresses her as 'Rachel', then this new person's behaviour will not be offensive to her unless it, too, goes through an offence escalation process involving Rebecca and this new person. Analogous remarks apply to the shed example. It is difficult to think of a story about how the word *Rachel* (or talk about sheds) might become *universally* offensive; that is, offensive not just when used by you to address Rebecca (or when talking to your shed-phobic friend) but when used by anyone when addressing anyone else.

On the other hand, unlike in the examples just discussed, swear words' capacity to offend does not require the audience first to explain to the speaker that she prefers him not to use swear words. Even so, the same process of offence escalation explains why swearing is offensive.

The recipe for offensiveness

We have seen that, to work out why swearing is offensive, we must look beyond the words themselves. Swearing is offensive not because of some magic ingredient possessed by swear words and lacked by other words but because when we swear, our audience knows that we do so in the knowledge that they will find it offensive. You are offended by my saying *fuck* in a polite context because *fuck* is a dispreferred word, you know that I know that it is a dispreferred word, and you take my choosing to utter it anyway as indicative of my lack of consideration, or even hostility, towards you. *This* is why context is important: there are some contexts in which we judge that swear words are not strongly dispreferred and can be used without causing offence—or even used to produce positive effects like amusement or intimacy; something we'll explore in Chapter 15. When we swear in contexts like this, our listeners' knowledge that we did so in the belief that we will not cause offence helps ensure that we do not cause offence. This also explains why we are (sometimes) more forgiving of swearing by children, by people with certain disabilities, and non-native speakers of our language: we realise that people in these groups may lack insight into what their listeners will make of their swearing, and so we are less likely to suspect them of being inconsiderate of their listeners when they swear inappropriately. Offence escalation also explains how the offensiveness of swear words can change over time. In the UK, religious terms have declined in offensiveness over the past few decades, and the offensiveness of sexual swear words surged during the Victorian period. These fluctuations in offensiveness reflect changing attitudes towards various terms—specifically, changes in the extent to which certain words are dispreferred—resulting from various cultural forces. In turn, this affects how serious a matter it is to use these terms, which determines their offensiveness.

While offence escalation forms the core explanation of swearing's offensiveness, it is not the whole story. We will see in Chapter 5 that there are some features of swear words that have helped them along their path to offensiveness. A word's being linked to a taboo topic helps ensure that it can undergo offence escalation on the culture-wide scale necessary to become a swear word, rather than simply a word that causes offence when used by a particular speaker, as was the case with the examples we considered in this chapter. And a word's sounding a certain way makes it more satisfying to use as a swear word, which makes taboo-related words that sound 'quick and harsh' more likely than other words to develop into swear words.

Before we get to that, though, let's take a closer look about what's offensive about swearing, and what—if anything—we do wrong when we swear.

4
Different kinds of wrong

Context, I've claimed, is (almost) everything when it comes to swearing's power to shock and offend. Most of us can recognise inappropriate swearing when we encounter it. Often, it's a matter of *feeling* it: inappropriate swearing is surprising, often even shocking, and it gets our attention. As we saw in the introduction, witnessing the monarch swear during a formal, televised address to the nation is arresting in a way that witnessing Geraint swearing down the local pub is not. Most of us, too, are able to recognise at least some cases when inappropriate swearing is *so* inappropriate as to be morally wrong. If you arrive home from a night out to find your babysitter yelling at your toddler to 'Shut the fuck up and go back to sleep!', you're likely to feel—even without taking the time to reflect on it—that you've caught them doing something immoral.

These everyday intuitions about when swearing is inappropriate or immoral versus unremarkable or a-bit-naughty-but-basically-okay form the starting point from which to dig into normative issues—that is, the *oughts* and *ought nots*—around swearing. But, given the scrutiny to which we're going to subject swearing, we need something more substantial than these intuitions. We need an understanding of what underlies them: of what makes swearing inappropriate in cases when it's inappropriate, and of the link between causing offence with swearing and doing something wrong. This will be our focus in the current chapter.

When is swearing inappropriate?

Let's start off by looking at what we're saying when we call an instance of swearing inappropriate. The category of inappropriate swearing is pretty large: swearing is inappropriate in cases where it is rude or bad mannered, and also in cases where it's morally wrong. We're going to start off by focusing on instances of swearing that are rude or bad mannered—that is, contrary to etiquette. This will lead us naturally to the topic of moral wrongness, since etiquette and morality are closely linked.

Deeming an instance of swearing to be inappropriate is usually a matter of etiquette. We can approach the question *What is the difference between appropriate and inappropriate swearing?* in a similar way to other questions relating to etiquette, like *What is the difference between appropriate and inappropriate use of a person's first name to address them?* Swearing inappropriately—like addressing someone in an overfamiliar way—is contrary to etiquette. Often, though, swearing is not inappropriate. Situations in which swearing is not inappropriate tend to be informal settings—socialising in a pub in the evening, chatting with close friends, and so on—where it's understood that it's okay to be relaxed with the language one is using. It's not all about formality, though: if you're spending the evening in a pub with your new boss, you might want to watch your language despite the informal setting. Conversely, the seminars, talks, and interviews I've given on swearing have not exactly been informal, but they have been contexts in which swearing is not inappropriate—although generally some caution is required to ensure that any swearing falls clearly into the category of *necessary in order to make points relevant to the topic under discussion* and outside the category of *exploiting the opportunity of a discussion about swearing to say rude words for fun.*

I'll tighten up exactly what I mean by *inappropriate* and *not-inappropriate* swearing in a moment. First, though, note that so far I've been contrasting *inappropriate* swearing with swearing that is *not inappropriate*. What about *appropriate* swearing? Can we usefully distinguish between swearing that is appropriate and swearing that is merely not inappropriate? Yes, I think we can. We can call swearing *appropriate* in cases where it is somehow required; I'll call it *not inappropriate* when it's permitted without being required. By *required*, I mainly mean demanded by the norms of etiquette, or perhaps by other relevant norms, such as professional norms or the norms that develop around a particular friendship or other relationship. *Not* swearing in a case where swearing is appropriate would itself be inappropriate; whereas not swearing in a case where swearing is merely not inappropriate would not be inappropriate. (Of course, simply as a matter of logic, the category of *not-inappropriate swearing* includes all cases of *appropriate swearing* in addition to the permitted-but-not-required cases I've just described. But I'll reserve the term *not inappropriate swearing* for swearing that is neither inappropriate nor appropriate, which I think is how most people would intuitively understand it.)

Is swearing ever appropriate in the sense I've described? There are indeed cases in which, as a matter of etiquette or other norms, swearing is appropriate. An undercover police officer who is trying to infiltrate a gang of sweary criminals in order to gather evidence against them for a prosecution needs to adopt the criminals' behaviours (the legal ones, at least) in order to be accepted by them. Swearing in the way that the criminals do is, in such a case, not merely *not inappropriate* but *appropriate*. It is, after all, necessary if the police officer is serious about getting the job done. We could expect such an officer who, on receiving details of their mission from their superior officer, responds by saying, 'I'm happy to do this, but I'm not going to swear, because that would be rude', to be met with exasperation and perhaps even a stern reprimand. In this case, refusing to swear would be contrary to the officer's professional obligations.

Less dramatically, and as a matter of etiquette, we might think of swearing as being appropriate in cases where abstaining from swearing would make the people around us uncomfortable. Perhaps you've had the experience of hanging out with a group of friends with whom it's normal to swear in the course of chatting, and a member of the group brings along a person whom none of the others have met before, and who stiffly avoids swearing. We understand that, in cases like this, it takes a while for a new group member to feel their way into the culture of the group, and so some reservation about relaxing into the group's sweary ways is to be expected. But if this new group member continues to hang out with the group, and conspicuously continues to avoid swearing—perhaps substituting words like *heck* and *darn* in place of the terms that the other group members freely use—even after becoming familiar with how the group behaves, then it's likely that other group members will feel that they are not able to be their usual relaxed selves when this person is around. In a case like this, the new group member behaves inappropriately by not swearing. After all, while it's true that swearing is often contrary to etiquette, so too is behaving in a way that sours the camaraderie and enjoyment of a group of friends who have welcomed you into their midst.[1] As philosopher Karen Stohr puts it in her book, *On Manners*, '[t]he politeness of a given action is tied to the underlying moral aim, not to the behaviour itself' (Stohr 2012, 35).

Note that, in thinking about the 'underlying moral aim' of polite behaviour, we encounter a bridge between etiquette and morality. As Stohr also tells us, 'the principles of manners are moral principles, and specific rules of etiquette get their authority from their relationship to those moral principles' (Stohr 2021, 23). The moral aim underlying the norms of etiquette is to respect others; complying

[1] This example—like many thought experiments in philosophy—is somewhat artificial. It's likely that, in reality, someone who joins a group of friends and fails to take on their patterns of swearing will also be failing to fit in with the group in other ways too. Some of these ways may not be obvious: the original group members may simply experience the newcomer's manner as a bit 'off'. Swearing, in the wild, does not happen in isolation from other social interactions.

with etiquette—the demands of which vary between cultures, and between different social contexts even within a culture—is how we express our commitment to the underlying moral aim. Generally in cases where we think we should avoid swearing, we avoid it in order to convey respect to others. But in the case we've just considered, the new group member can most effectively convey respect to the other group members by adopting the established culture of the group, which includes swearing. *Respecting others*, in this context, means treating people as beings who have value in themselves (as opposed to their merely being useful as a means to someone else's end), and as beings to whom we have moral obligations. This echoes the view of the eighteenth-century German philosopher Immanuel Kant, who argued that humans should be treated as ends in themselves and not merely as means.

Let's link this back to swearing and its inappropriateness or otherwise. Weighing the question of whether swearing is appropriate, inappropriate, or not inappropriate involves reflecting on the underlying principles of etiquette. Often, especially in formal settings, swearing is inappropriate because it would express disrespect to others. This is a point that emerged in the previous chapter: when we swear in a context where we know that the person to whom we're talking will dislike it, and where that person knows that we know this, that person can justifiably conclude that we don't care very much about their comfort, and that by swearing we're *expressing* that we don't care very much about them, which is a way of disrespecting them. The importance of respecting others is why we have expressions like *please* and *thank you*; it is why we dress in a smart, sober manner for formal occasions like job interviews; and it is what guides emerging etiquette norms surrounding recent technologies, such as the view that it is impolite to stare at one's phone while engaged in conversation with someone who is right next to us. Acting in accordance with norms like these generally enables us to express respect. But that's not always the case, because sometimes the best way of communicating respect involves doing something that runs contrary to the usual expectations of etiquette. For example, sometimes, prior to a funeral, attendees are informed that the deceased explicitly requested that those attending their funeral should dress in a vibrant and cheerful manner. In a case like this, turning up in a severe black suit would fail to communicate respect for the deceased, despite being in accordance with the usual rules of etiquette. And in our earlier example, although the new member of the sweary group of friends, by avoiding swearing, is following etiquette norms that usually enable one to express respect to others, their refusing to swear in this particular case results in their failing to express respect for the group members who have welcomed them.

The link between swearing and expressing respect provides a useful framework to help us think about what makes swearing appropriate, inappropriate, or not inappropriate. Swearing is inappropriate in cases where it is likely to be taken by others to express disrespect to them. This is a pretty rough guide: *likely* is doing some heavy lifting here, and there are questions around how much the speaker can know (or be expected to know) about how other people will react to what they say. But it's supposed to be rough. The rules of etiquette need to be simple enough to be grasped by busy people and implemented with confidence most of the time, and that wouldn't happen if mastering etiquette required memorising and becoming proficient in the application of the rules along with a precise and meticulous explanation of how and when they apply. In any case, the rules of etiquette aren't mastered in a vacuum, as a theoretical exercise. We learn them as part of our upbringing. By the time we reach adulthood, we've developed a feel for when the rules apply. It's often our gut, rather than our head, that tells us not to swear in a certain situation. (There are exceptions, of course: some of us are better than others at reading the room; and some people, like many on the autism spectrum, find it especially tricky.) Very often, the explicit guidance we receive about matters of etiquette doesn't amount to much more than *Don't call your olders and betters by their first names* and *Say thank you to someone who does you a favour*. If we want more specific guidance, or information about when exceptions apply, we can ask those who are doling out the advice, discuss it with others, or—in relatively rare cases for most of us—consult etiquette books and etiquette columnists. The etiquette around swearing is especially difficult to master, because the guidance children receive in this area often amounts to nothing more than *Don't swear*. Children who press for information about exceptions typically receive a less cooperative response than those who press for information about exceptions to other rules of etiquette.

So, *Swearing is inappropriate in cases where it is likely to be taken by others to express disrespect to them* is about as much as you're going to get by way of explicit guidance about what inappropriate swearing involves, although we're certainly going to be taking a closer look at some of the factors that exacerbate or contribute to swearing's inappropriateness (and, in some cases, to its immorality). By contrast, swearing is *not* inappropriate in cases where it is unlikely to be taken by others to express disrespect to them. Chatting with friends who are secure in their knowledge that you respect them, shooting the breeze in the pub, reacting to a tense sports match that you're watching alongside fellow spectators, sounding off in response to driving over yourself after eating too many jacket potatoes—these are all cases in which you are probably able to swear without those around you taking you to express disrespect to them. Which is not to say that it's impossible to swear inappropriately in these contexts, and the same process of enculturation that equips us with a feel for whether swearing is innocuous in a given context also helps us detect when someone's benign swearing crosses the line into inappropriateness.

Finally, swearing is appropriate in cases where *not* swearing is likely to be taken by others to express disrespect to them. We've seen an example of this with the person who joins a sweary group of friends and refuses to swear. But our other example—that of the undercover police officer who jeopardises their infiltration into a group of sweary criminals by refusing to swear—highlights that the appropriateness (or otherwise) of swearing can be due to norms other than etiquette. The police officer in our example is bound by professional norms, as well as by the usual norms of etiquette. By refusing to swear in the course of their undercover investigation, the officer jeopardises the investigation that they are being paid to undertake. If you're inclined to think that the officer *ought* to swear in the course of their investigation, then you've probably reasoned as follows: you've noted that the officer faces a conflict between different sets of norms and has made the wrong call. Specifically, the officer deems that etiquette demands that they refrain from swearing while on the job, but they also cannot help but recognise that their obligation to catch the criminals they have been assigned to catch requires them to swear. Faced with conflicting sets of norms, the officer must make a decision about which set of norms is more important. If we conclude that swearing is appropriate in this case, we do so not because refraining from swearing is likely to convey disrespect to others but because we think that etiquette is not the most important consideration in this case. For an undercover police officer charged with an important investigation, their professional obligations are more important than being polite.

There's another sense, too, in which we sometimes talk of swearing being appropriate. This sense has to do with a recognition that swearing is sometimes the best way to express something. Someone who, with dawning horror, exclaims 'Oh, fuck!' on arriving home to find their house ablaze might be thought to be swearing appropriately—because isn't this speaker likely to be experiencing exactly the sort of intense emotion that swearing is uniquely placed to express? Judging this sort of swearing to be appropriate has nothing to do with etiquette or other norms; rather, the thought is that the swearing is psychologically or linguistically appropriate.[2]

There are, then, various ways in which swearing can be appropriate, not all of which involve its being demanded by etiquette. This is a pretty intuitive, commonsensical point, and doesn't need much explanation. Things are more complex (and interesting) when we try to account for what makes the difference between inappropriate and not inappropriate swearing.

Speaker intentions

The intentions of the speaker are another factor to consider in trying to understand swearing's inappropriateness or otherwise. I've defined inappropriate swearing as swearing in cases where it is likely to be taken by others to express disrespect to them. Does it matter whether or not the swearer *intends* to express disrespect to others? It depends. Certainly, the disrespect we read into another person's inappropriate swearing is likely to be felt more acutely in cases where we recognise that the speaker is intentionally expressing disrespect to us. It's never pleasant, after all, to realise that another person has deliberately set out to let us know how little they think of us. Even so, it's often appropriate to read disrespect into someone's swearing in cases where they don't intend to express disrespect. As Stohr notes, 'many forms of rude behaviour are really forms of inattentiveness: texting while walking down a busy sidewalk, letting a door slam in someone's face, failing to notice that someone in need of a seat has entered the waiting room or gotten on the subway' (2012, 64–65) Similarly, a speaker can express disrespect to others by swearing inappropriately even if they

[2] I've argued that swearing can be appropriate according to norms other than etiquette. Is something similarly true of inappropriate and not inappropriate swearing? Undoubtedly. But probably those cases are rarer.

don't intend to convey any such thing. They manage this by failing to attend to how their words might affect others around them. Sometimes this is easily forgivable, as when the swearer is not fluent in the language they are speaking and did not realise that what they said is rude. And sometimes it's a more serious matter, as when the swearer seems not to care very much about how their words impact other people.

Conversely, it's possible for a speaker to swear with the intention of expressing disrespect yet fail to swear inappropriately. One example of how this might happen is if a speaker tries to offend people by swearing in a context in which swearing is not inappropriate, and those around them fail to pick up on the disrespect that the speaker was trying to convey. This example brings out a subtle distinction between *expressing* and *communicating*. When we express disrespect (or some other psychological state), we often also communicate it, but not always. Typically, when we tell someone to fuck off, we express our disrespect for them, and we also communicate it; that is, by telling someone to fuck off we let them know that we disrespect them. By contrast, I can express disrespect for my neighbour by poking out my tongue when their back is turned, but I don't communicate disrespect by doing this if my neighbour never finds out about it. We've seen that complying with etiquette is an important way in which we express respect for others, but this expression of respect is almost always communicative too; in other words, by following etiquette we express *and also communicate* our respect to others. Etiquette governs our *interactions* with others, after all; and there's little scope for interaction in private expressions of (dis)respect that communicate nothing to other people.[3]

[3] Are there any examples of cases in which we follow etiquette in order to express, without communicating, respect to others? We find some in our customs around death. Complying with funeral etiquette and carrying out the wishes expressed by people who have since died are ways that we express respect to the dead but without also communicating that respect to the dead. (By complying with etiquette in this area we also, of course, communicate to others—such as our fellow mourners at a funeral—our respect for the dead person.)

Having said that, there's a sense in which trying but failing to communicate our disrespect to other people isn't exactly innocuous in relation to etiquette, even if it falls short of rudeness. There's something icky, etiquette-wise, about trying to communicate our disrespect to others, even if the communication fails. This intuition has to do with a link between etiquette and moral character. As Stohr puts it, '[m]anners . . . are the outward expression of moral character' (2012, 13) It is important to us that other people, through their good manners, express respect because it is important to us that the people we interact with have good moral character (roughly: are good people), and we take their good manners to constitute evidence of their good moral character. We'd rather not be interacting with nasty people. Because of this, trying but failing to communicate disrespect to others strikes us as icky because it's the sort of thing that only a nasty person (i.e. a person of poor moral character) would do, even if their nastiness never shows up in their manners.

Inappropriate swearing, wrongness, and offence

What's the link between swearing inappropriately and causing offence? Let's remind ourselves of what Feinberg has to say about offence:

> I am offended (or 'take offence') when (a) I suffer a disliked state, and (b) I attribute that state to the wrongful conduct of another, and (c) I resent the other for his role in causing me to be in the state. The sense of grievance against the other or resentment of him for wronging me in this way is a phenomenological component of the unpleasant experience itself, an element that actually reenforces and magnifies its unpleasantness. (1985, 2)

Taking offence, if we think about it like Feinberg, involves judging that the person causing offence has done something wrong. Being offended by someone's swearing, then, involves judging that the speaker has done something wrong. Let's unpack this a bit. What sense of *wrong* are we dealing with here?

We're apt to cause offence by swearing if we swear inappropriately; in other words, if we swear in a context where it is likely to be taken by others to express disrespect to them. Swearing inappropriately is contrary to etiquette—meaning that, in this case, *wrong* equates to *rude*—but disrespecting others is contrary to the moral aim that underlies etiquette, making *wrong* equivalent to *morally wrong.*

Wow. That escalated quickly. So, whenever we swear inappropriately, not only do we act rudely but we also do something morally wrong? Well, not quite. There's quite a gap between swearing inappropriately and failing to respect people, which means that there is plenty of scope to swear inappropriately without failing to respect people. Let's take a look at how this might happen.

Failing to respect people is morally wrong. In general, we disrespect others when, for no good reason, we behave in a way that we know they dislike. Let's add that, sometimes, even if we *don't* know for sure that others will dislike our behaviour choices, we disrespect them when we make those choices. This is because ignorance is not always an excuse: we expect each other to make some effort to find out how to behave in unfamiliar situations. If you attend a wedding or a swingers' club or a football match for the first time, you'll probably be forgiven for the odd *faux pas*. But if you clearly have no idea what's expected of you, it's likely that others will read disrespect into your behaviour. They're likely to think that you ought to have made some effort to find out beforehand how you should behave. By contrast, when you distress your friend from the previous chapter by talking about garden sheds, not realising how upsetting they find this topic, your ignorance is understandable. The difference is that weddings, swingers' clubs, and football matches are all contexts in which people interact with each other in ways that they do not usually do in their everyday lives, which means that there are norms governing interactions in these contexts that do not apply outside those contexts. Anyone entering one of these contexts for the first time having not made an effort to familiarise themselves with the norms in question risks annoying other people, partly because their repeated slip-ups are likely to be disruptive, and partly because their inattentiveness to what's expected of them itself conveys a lack of respect to those around them. On the other hand, your friend's dislike of the topic of garden sheds is completely unexpected. There were no signs, prior to your broaching the topic, that you were entering conversational territory where unusual rules might apply. Your broaching this topic does not betray a lack of respect for your friend.

Back to swearing. One way in which a person can swear inappropriately without failing to respect others involves the speaker not realising that they are swearing in an inappropriate context, and their failure to realise that their swearing is inappropriate is understandable. By *understandable* I mean that, applying commonsense standards of how attentive we expect people to be to what's required of them in a particular situation, we would excuse the speaker's failure to realise what norms apply in the situation they're in. Here's an example to illustrate this sort of situation. Imagine that a comedian, famous both for swearing and for playing pranks on audience members, is booked to perform at a particular venue at a particular time, but due to an advertising mix-up, the published event for that venue and that time is a talk by a local gardener entitled 'Japanese knotweed: tips from the trade'. The comedian, unaware of the mix-up, delivers their routine, understandably assuming that the members of the audience have knowingly chosen to attend a sweary performance. Meanwhile, the horticultural audience, assuming that the comedian deliberately misadvertised the performance as part of a prank, take the comedian's swearing to express disrespect to them. In this case, we have an example of inappropriate swearing in which the speaker does not fail to respect others. Despite swearing inappropriately, then, the speaker has not done anything morally wrong. More specifically—to use Stohr's framework—by (unwittingly) swearing inappropriately, the comedian has (unwittingly) acted contrary to the norms of etiquette governing the situation in question but has not acted contrary to the underlying moral aim of respecting others.

There are also some cases in which a speaker can *knowingly* swear inappropriately without doing anything wrong. An obvious way in which this can happen involves recognising that while it is important to express respect for others via adhering to etiquette norms, this is not our only obligation, and in some circumstances a speaker may be justified in prioritising some other concern over refraining from swearing inappropriately, such that it would be inappropriate to conclude from the fact that the speaker knowingly swore inappropriately that they do not respect others. This claim is pretty difficult to grasp in the abstract, so here's an example: the building is on fire, and you need to interrupt a meeting in order to alert the participants so they can escape to safety. But the participants are immersed in heated discussion and it's likely to be difficult for you to get their attention, even if you raise your voice. Since the meeting is a context in which swearing is inappropriate, you decide that the best course of action is to enter the meeting room and start yelling obscenities in order to shock the participants into silence. The discussion stops, and you are able to convey your urgent message and ensure everyone hurries out of the burning building. In this example, it's likely that, initially, the participants of the meeting will take your yelling swear words at them as an expression of disrespect. You've intentionally shocked them into silence, after all. But as soon as they realise that you swore inappropriately in order to save their lives, their sense of being disrespected by you is going to vanish. Instead—if they're sensible people, at least—their realisation that you are working hard to help them will result in their feeling valued and respected by you. (And, frankly, if they grumble about your language during the time in which—if you hadn't rescued them—they would otherwise be burning to death, fuck them!)

Another way of knowingly swearing inappropriately without doing anything wrong involves what has been termed *conscientious offence*: causing offence as a way to invite people to reflect on and revise their feeling of offence. Non-linguistic examples of this include mass breastfeeding protests in response to controversial restrictions on where mothers can nurse their babies, and mass gay kissing protests in response to homophobia. The thought here is that despite knowingly acting in a way that others find offensive, it's not the protesters—the nursing mothers or the kissing gays—who are doing wrong; the wrong is committed by the people who feel offended, since being offended by breastfeeding or homosexuality helps perpetuate harmful attitudes. We're going to consider conscientious offence in relation to swearing in Chapter 12.

As a final example of how it might be possible that someone can knowingly swear inappropriately without failing to respect others, sometimes we can find ourselves confronted with conflicting norms, so that we end up doing something wrong whatever action we take. Suppose that you've recently been introduced to the group of sweary friends whom we met earlier in the chapter, and that you're trying to fit in and adopt their culture. You're all in a pub, enjoying a typically sweary conversation. You are a kindergarten teacher, and you notice the parent of one of the young children you care for taking a seat at a nearby table. The two of you nod your acknowledgement to one another. The pub is not a context where swearing is inappropriate, but your relationship with this parent certainly is, and you feel uncomfortable about these two worlds colliding. You fear that joining in with the swearing would risk offending the parent, who will certainly overhear; but you also fear that failing to participate in the group's swearing will lead the other members to think that you are aloof and unfriendly. You very much want to act respectfully towards everyone present, but you don't see how that's possible. Whatever you do, someone is going to read disrespect into your behaviour. Yet, you do not actually fail to respect anyone.

There is, then, plenty of scope for situations to arise in which people are offended by someone's swearing—that is, in Feinberg's terms, people suffer a disliked state which they resentfully attribute to the wrongdoing of the swearer—without the swearer doing something morally wrong, as they would if they were to fail to respect others. This scope exists because of the gap that exists between what people view as expressions of disrespect and what actually constitute expressions of disrespect.

Swearing and moral character

Before moving on, there's something else worth saying about swearing and its capacity to cause offence, and this goes back to what Stohr had to say about moral character. We dislike people being rude partly because we take their rudeness to reflect their moral character, and we don't like to find that we're dealing with someone with poor moral character. This applies to inappropriate swearing: we take someone's inappropriate swearing to be evidence for their having a poor moral character. But inappropriate swearing, like other etiquette breaches, doesn't happen in isolation. When someone offends us by swearing inappropriately (or, for that matter, committing some other breach of etiquette), our taking offence often isn't the end of the matter. We're also waiting to see what this person will do next. Will they continue to behave in a way that betrays their lack of respect for others, or will they apologise or redeem themselves in some other way that prompts us to write off their earlier inappropriate behaviour as a momentary lapse by a generally respectful person? In other words, we're getting a sense of their moral character. A single instance of inappropriate swearing provides us with *some* evidence about what sort of moral character the speaker has, but it's not alone enough to form firm, reliable conclusions. Sometimes good people slip up and their behaviour fails to meet their usual standards; in particular, people who are generally respectful of others can occasionally behave in way that does not express that respect. This is why our codes of etiquette include ways to apologise.

This observation reveals another gap between inappropriate swearing and acting in a way that is morally wrong. We've looked at why failing to respect people is morally wrong. Let's be a bit more specific here: a person whose lack of respect for others is a stable character trait is morally flawed. When such a person swears inappropriately, what they express is a fundamental and enduring lack of respect for others; a mark of their flawed moral character. When a generally respectful person has a lapse and swears inappropriately, they don't express a fundamental and enduring lack of respect. They don't have any such thing to express. Their behaviour is rude, but not morally wrong. Even so, it might be difficult for onlookers to tell the difference here: taken in isolation, the inappropriate swearing of a respectful person having a momentary lapse might look just as disrespectful as that of the generally disrespectful person. It's not always easy to spot moral wrongs.

I suspect that the thought that inappropriate swearing is a window into the speaker's moral character lies behind some of the vehemently anti-swearing views we sometimes encounter. The beliefs that swearing is always morally wrong, that people who swear are not nice people, that increased tolerance of swearing heralds the downfall of civilisation, and so on, can seem puzzling and overdramatic. But if inappropriate swearing—and there are some who view *all* swearing as inappropriate—betrays a flawed moral character, then perhaps we should take it more seriously. By tolerating swearing, we communicate to swearers that their flawed moral characters are acceptable, and we perhaps encourage them to relax and indulge in other ways of expressing their nasty natures. Who knows what horrors might follow next? Better that we take a zero-tolerance approach to swearing. That way, we send a clear message that nasty people are not welcome in society, and that they should go away and work on some self-improvement before interacting with the rest of us.

Thankfully, this view is muddled. Inappropriate swearing does not always betray a flawed moral character. It's not always morally wrong, since it doesn't always express a fundamental and enduring lack of respect on the part of the speaker. Sometimes, it's just rude: upsetting to others, since it looks to them like an expression of disrespect, but ultimately a false alarm. Tolerating swearing—even welcoming it—in certain contexts is compatible with acknowledging the importance of respect for others.

Is swearing wrong?

What's the takeaway from this chapter? Is there anything wrong with swearing, and if so, what? The answer I've argued for is this: we don't necessarily do anything wrong when we swear, even when we swear inappropriately. That's because inappropriate swearing is swearing that those around us are likely to view as expressing disrespect to them, and sometimes those around us are wrong. Sometimes, when we swear, those around us take us to be expressing disrespect to them even when we're not. But when the people around us *aren't* wrong, and our swearing *does* express our disrespect for them, then we do something wrong. What sort of wrong depends on the circumstances. Sometimes—as when we're generally respectful of others but, owing to a momentary lapse, we swear because we're not being as attentive as we should be towards what's expected of us in the situation we're in—we do something wrong in the sense of doing something contrary to etiquette. We're rude, in this situation, but we don't do anything morally wrong. At other times, our swearing is a more serious matter. When our inappropriate swearing expresses our fundamental lack of respect for others, we do something morally wrong, because failing to respect others is a moral flaw. It's this lack of respect for others that lies at the heart of swearing's moral wrongness, in cases where it is morally wrong—although we'll see in Chapters 6 and 7 that there are other factors that can push swearing into the realm of moral wrongness. An upshot of this focus on respect is that while *not* swearing is usually the most reliable way to behave respectfully towards others, in certain circumstances—as when we're invited to spend an evening in the pub with the sweary friends we met earlier—being respectful involves being willing to swear.

5

Taboo, aggression, and harsh sweary sounds

The offence escalation process, which I described in Chapter 3, explains how a word can acquire a power to shock and offend. It's at the heart of why *cunt* and *fuck* are, despite some superficial similarities, worlds apart from *country* and *fork*. Even so, offence escalation doesn't give us the whole story about what sets swear words apart from other words. It doesn't tell us, for example, why it is that swear words tend to have sexual, lavatorial, religious, or other taboo themes. Nor does it tell us why swear words tend to sound—to use Steven Pinker's expression—'quick and harsh'. And we might want to know, too, how the shockingness and inappropriateness of swearing fits in with shocking and inappropriate behaviour more generally. We're going to zoom out from offence escalation in this chapter and take a look at these other aspects of swearing.

Swearing and taboo, again

How are swear words born? The process begins with certain words being widely dispreferred within a given community. This sets the scene for the offence escalation process to occur on a community-wide level, resulting in words that offend the entire community. The process cannot, as in the Rebecca/Rachel and shed examples we looked at in the previous two chapters, be restricted to the response of a particular listener or the use of the word by a particular speaker.

We all have different preferences about the words we use, but words that are *widely* dispreferred within a community are linked to recognised taboo topics like sex, defecation, religion, and so on. As we've seen, it's not impossible to use taboo-related words inoffensively in polite company: a new parent might manage inoffensively to refer to defecation by remarking that their baby has 'soiled herself', or someone might politely refer to sex by sharing that a mutual friend has ended their relationship after catching their partner 'in bed with' someone else. Remarks like these can pass off without so much as raising an eyebrow even in cases where the listener is someone who would be horrified by other ways of introducing the same topics—but this takes some skill on the part of the speaker. Part of that skill involves knowing which euphemisms to use: *soiled herself* and *in bed with* instead of *defecated* and *having sex with*—or, worse, words like *shit* and *fucking*. Choosing one's words carefully in this way helps to signal to our audience that we recognise that the topic is not a pleasant one and that we do not wish to cause offence by discussing it. But it's not all about the words we use. Even euphemistic references to defecation and sex can end up causing offence if the speaker keeps returning to the topic, discusses it too gleefully, introduces it at the wrong moment, or in other ways fails to convey that she finds the topic as uncomfortable as her audience does. One wrong move—an indelicate word here, a second too long spent on the topic there—and the speaker risks embarrassing, disturbing, or offending their audience.

An important lesson that arises from the fact that it's possible (albeit risky) for a skilled speaker to introduce a taboo topic into a polite conversation without causing offence is this: when we cause offence by talking about taboo topics in polite company, it's not the taboo topic itself that offends our listeners, it's what we signal to our listeners about our attitudes to them. Specifically, by talking about taboo topics we risk signalling to our listeners that we don't care about their feelings. After all, we're choosing to talk about a topic that we know people in our community—including those we're addressing—dislike. The strategies speakers employ to avoid causing offence in these circumstances—strategies like using euphemisms and moving on from the taboo topic as soon as possible—work by conveying to their listeners that they (the speakers) are being solicitous of the feelings of their listeners. Dealing sensitively with a taboo topic in a polite conversation is possible when the speaker manages to strike the right balance between signalling *I care about having a conversation with you* and *I care about ensuring that you are comfortable during this conversation.*

The ease with which one can cause offence by discussing taboo topics makes taboo words ripe for offence escalation. When we talk about recognised taboo topics with a fellow member of our community—or with multiple members of our community, including ones we've never met or spoken to before—our listener knows that we know that the topic is dispreferred. Offence escalation of taboo words can, as a result, occur on a much larger scale than in the Rebecca/Rachel and shed examples described above. Further, offence escalation of taboo words can skip the stage—required in the Rebecca/Rachel and shed cases—where the audience points out to the speaker that the expression used is disliked, since everyone will take the speaker to understand this already. This means that offence escalation can get started even when the speaker knows nothing about the personal likes, dislikes, and sensitivities of their listeners.

All this means that words referring to taboo topics are much better suited than neutral words like *book* to develop via offence escalation into swear words. We saw, when we discussed the Rebecca/Rachel and shed cases, that in some cases it may be possible to offend someone with a neutral expression when offence escalation occurs on a one-to-one basis and one comes to learn that one's listener has an unusual dislike for a neutral expression. But offence escalation of a neutral expression cannot get started when addressing a larger audience, precisely because the expression is neutral (i.e. not widely dispreferred).[1]

There is an additional reason why taboo-related expressions have a head start over neutral ones when it comes to developing into swear words: breaking widely recognised taboos can be thrilling. This idea is already familiar, since it is one of the reasons why swearing—itself a taboo behaviour, of course—can be thrilling. The thrill of taboo-breaking helps explain why children delight in toilet jokes, why it can sometimes feel liberating to let rip and be rude, and why we are often entertained (even if also horrified) to witness somebody put their foot in it by unwittingly doing something inappropriate, like complaining about a colleague's ineptitude to the colleague's spouse. That breaking taboos can be fun gives us a

[1] Here's a question for the philosophers, which I'm relegating to a footnote because it is likely too pedantic to engage the general reader. Could a neutral word—like *book*—become a swear word in a scenario where, despite not being widely dispreferred by the community, the community nevertheless knows that the speaker falsely *believes* that it is widely dispreferred? In this situation, the listeners could reasonably take the speaker's utterance of what they take to be a dispreferred word to indicate the speaker's lack of consideration of (or even hostility towards) the listeners, which could result in the listeners being offended by the speaker's utterance of the word despite the fact that the speaker is mistaken about the word being dispreferred. If, as I am arguing, what matters for offensiveness is the attitude that the speaker conveys by their use of the word, and what the listener takes the speaker to convey by their use of the word, rather than any context-insensitive property of the word such as its sound or its denotation, then perhaps it does not matter whether the word really *is* dispreferred. Perhaps all that matters is that the listeners know that the speaker *believes* it to be dispreferred. There is some plausibility in this; however, if the speaker's utterance of *book* in these circumstances were an isolated incident, I doubt that the speaker could succeed in causing much offence. This is because, although the listeners are able dispassionately to conclude that they have reason to object to the speaker's utterance of *book* in these circumstances, they would lack the sort of negative emotional response to the word that would develop through the offence escalation process of a word that is genuinely dispreferred. A neutral word can acquire negative associations, but only after repeated use. Were the speaker in our example to persist in uttering *book*, and also to persist in the belief that the listeners dislike it, we could expect the word to develop negative associations for the listeners when uttered by this particular speaker. Since this effect is unique to a particular speaker and a particular set of listeners, it is comparable to the Rebecca/Rachel and shed examples rather than to the offence escalation of swear words. It is probably worth conceding, too, that a scenario in which a speaker repeatedly utters *book* in these circumstances, without anyone ever disabusing them of the mistaken belief that it is disliked, is the sort of unlikely thought experiment that gives philosophers a bad name.

motivation to do it; an observation made no less accurate by the fact that our motivation to break taboos is generally outweighed by our motivation not to break them. By contrast, there is no comparable, community-wide motivation to use neutral words like *book* for thrills, which makes those words less likely to be used in a way that would give rise to offence escalation.

But there's more. Not only is breaking taboos fun, it is also widely recognised that breaking taboos is fun. This observation adds an extra layer to the offence escalation of taboo words. To see this, let's begin by considering that sometimes, when we have a good enough reason, it's acceptable to break taboos. Yelling at work colleagues is generally unacceptable, but if the purpose is to warn them that the building is on fire, then it is acceptable. Asking a stranger when they last defecated is usually frowned upon, but not if one is a doctor trying to diagnose a digestive disorder. Curtly telling another person to shut up is usually bad mannered, but not if spoken to someone who is verbally abusing another person. And so on. In cases like these, no sensible person who recognises that the speaker has a good reason for breaking the taboo is likely to disapprove of the taboo-breaking. Even so, breaking taboos is risky. Given that we all recognise that breaking taboos can be fun, when we break them we run the risk that those around us will suspect that we are doing it merely (or mainly) because it's fun, and we do not generally regard having fun as a good enough reason to cause distress to others. Etiquette, as well as morality, demands that we take into account other people's feelings when deciding how to act. This is part of what's involved in respecting others. If we anticipate that a certain course of action will be fun for us but unpleasant for others, we are expected to avoid it, unless we have a good reason *not* to avoid it. What might such a good reason look like? Well, it could involve having permission from the affected others, as when we go ahead and throw a noisy party after getting the go-ahead from our neighbours. Alternatively, it could involve an action being *very* fun for us but only *mildly* unpleasant for others, as when we take a relaxing vacation that will make our colleagues feel even more downhearted about their dreary lifestyle. Or, the affected others might deserve the unpleasantness that our action will cause them, as when I humiliate you (and enjoy doing so) after suffering months of harassment from you. And so on.

In cases where we break a taboo without good reason, we not only give our own fun greater weight than other people's distress, we also *demonstrate* that we have done so. There's an element of performance to breaking taboos in this way; a flavour of *Look at me being all naughty—I know you don't like this but I'm having fun!* Our audience can reasonably conclude from this that we do not respect them very much. When we break taboos, then, we had better hope that it is clear to our audience that we are doing so with good reason if we want to avoid causing offence.

Here's the upshot of this for swearing. Taboo-breaking in general can be fun, but it's more common—and satisfying—to break some taboos rather than others for fun. Few of us get our kicks by asking strangers about their defecation habits, which loses much of its sparkle once we're over the age of eight. While bad manners are rather more common, being bad mannered is not something we think of as fun or thrilling. By contrast, we all recognise that uttering taboo words can be fun, and even funny—even those who don't enjoy this form of taboo-breaking themselves typically acknowledge (while shaking their head regretfully) that there are others who do. This enjoyment is reflected by the large role that swearing plays in comedy.[2] It means that when we swear, there's a risk that those around us will suspect that we're doing so for fun, a risk that doesn't really arise when we break other sorts of taboos. Since taboo-breaking for fun sends our audience a strong and clear message that we place little value on their feelings—their feelings are, after all, less

[2] Taboo-breaking in general plays an important role in comedy, but few other taboo breaches are capable of delivering the effortless and immediate laughs often provoked by the utterance of swear words. A good (and entertaining) illustration of this is George Carlin's famous 'seven words' routine, which can easily be found and watched online.

important than our own fun—swearing can be more shocking than the breaking of many other sorts of taboo. And our recognition that swearing's capacity to shock is greater than that of some other taboo-breaches makes taboo-breaking by swearing even *more* fun, which in turn emphasises to the audience the disregard in which they are held by the inappropriate swearer—and so on.

I have explained swearing's focus on taboo topics by arguing that taboo-referring words get a head start over other words in the community-wide offence escalation process that is required in order for a word to become a swear word. As such, I have provided a causal explanation for the role that taboo-referring words play in swearing; in other words, I've explained how swearing grew out of words relating to taboo. But it also seems likely that, over time, the association between taboo topics and swearing has grown stronger, to the extent that now we might not recognise as a swear word a word that doesn't have a taboo denotation. If that's the case, then there's another kind of explanation of why swear words tend to focus on taboo topics. According to this explanation, swear words *by definition*, or *necessarily*, have a taboo denotation. This amounts to claiming that the link between taboo topics and swearing is not merely causal but also conceptual, which would make the idea of swear words that do not denote taboo topics incoherent, in much the same way that there is something incoherent about the idea of a square circle or an invisible colour. This is a much stronger claim than I'm going to argue for here. I will, instead, content myself with the causal claim, along with the observation that the conceptual claim *might* be true.

The sound that swear words make

Besides their focus on taboo topics, other features of swear words demand explanation. One is the way they sound. Pinker, as we have seen, notes that 'imprecations tend to use sounds that are perceived as quick and harsh' (Pinker 2007, 339). We saw that the sound of swear words cannot alone explain their offensiveness, since many inoffensive words also sound quick and harsh, and some swear words have benign alternative meanings (consider *prick* and *cock*), or—like *cunt*—sound identical to parts of inoffensive words. Even so, the fact that swear words sound a particular way is something that demands explanation, and this explanation is not provided by offence escalation.

While the quick and harsh sound of swear words doesn't alone explain their offensiveness, it is certainly a factor in determining which words catch on and go through the offence escalation process to end up as swear words. This has to do with the way swear words are used. We've already noted that, often but not always, we use swear words to vent emotion, and that some sounds are more suited to this purpose than others. This point is not unique to the language we use: just as some *sounds* are more suited than others to enabling us to vent our anger, some general *behaviours* are more suited than others to this purpose. It is easier to vent anger, frustration, and other strong emotions if we can shout, frown, stand up, throw our arms about, and point an accusing finger than if we must whisper, smile, lie down, and gently cradle a sleeping kitten. We tend towards making quick, harsh sounds when expressing our anger for the same reasons that we tend to shout and point. Our swear words need to sound like little explosions—a point to which Kate Warwick alludes when she compares uttering *cunt* to 'lobbing [a] verbal hand grenade' (Warwick 2015). As a result, a word whose sounds are not well-suited to venting emotion would make a second-rate swear word. Words that sound quick and harsh are, then, better placed to make it through the offence escalation process and attain the status of swear words, simply because they are satisfying for people to use to vent emotion. This helps explain why *cunt*, *cock*, and *arse* are more sweary than their less quick and harsh but also taboo synonyms, *muff*, *willy*, and *bum*.

What explains the fact that some swear words are more offensive than others even when they refer to the same taboo topic and sound similarly quick and harsh? For example, *cunt* is more offensive than the synonymous and equally quick and harsh *twat*, *shit* is more offensive than *crap*, and *cock* is more offensive than *dick*. To some extent, we can explain this in terms of offence escalation, which has bestowed *cunt* with greater power to offend than *twat*. But if we want to know *why* offence escalation has worked more powerfully on *cunt* than it has on *twat*, there may be no really satisfying explanation. The best explanation may be that there is no explanation. Our conventions about swearing, like our other conventions, contain an element of arbitrariness. Recall the example of covering one's head in religious buildings: in mosques and synagogues it is customary for men to cover their heads to express respect, whereas in churches it is customary for men to remove their hats for the same reason. There is no 'deep' reason to explain this difference. The convention in each case has developed out of the preference of the community in question for one type of behaviour over another; a preference which, in the early days before the convention evolved, may be arbitrary. Similarly, there is no deep reason to explain why in the Caribbean, India, Japan, Australia, the UK, and Ireland, it is conventional (and legally required) to drive on the left, whereas in the US and most other countries people drive on the right. In the early days of driving, it didn't matter which side people chose to use, as long as they all agreed on the same side. This sort of arbitrariness tends to be a feature of *all* conventions: we have settled on one form of behaviour where another would have done just as well. We eat with our fork in our left hand, but our right would have done just as well. We use certain expressions and gestures when greeting each other, but others would have done just as well. And so on. So, it should not be surprising to find that although offence escalation has ensured that *shit* is the most offensive way to refer to shit, *crap* would have done just as well.

Offence and expressing emotion

Swearing's important role in expressing strong emotion adds another layer to understanding why hearing it can be shocking. Expressing strong emotion in the wrong context can be alarming even when it doesn't involve swearing. A person who is clearly incandescent with rage while travelling in an otherwise peaceful train carriage, or weeping with despair in a restaurant, or doubled over with laughter at the cinema during a gruelling film about the Holocaust is likely to attract the attention and anxiety of people nearby, who will be uncertain about how to respond or what to expect next. How free one should feel to express emotion obviously varies with context, and we are more sympathetic to the public expression of some emotions than others. In particular, we are more disapproving of public displays of anger than we are of public displays of grief or pain, perhaps because we feel threatened by the former and sympathetic towards the latter, and perhaps also because—reasonably or otherwise—we feel that people ought to control their anger but not that they ought to control their grief or pain.[3] It should not, then, be surprising that we are less tolerant of angry swearing than we are of swearing linked to grief or pain. This observation is borne out both by a tendency to associate offensive swearing with displays of anger—recall that the dictionary definition that we considered in Chapter 2 linked swearing to the expression of anger—and by the fact that the public is more tolerant of swearing on TV when it results from the swearer having hurt herself than when it arises from other considerations (Millwood-Hargrave 2000). In the case of swearing that expresses anger, then, it is not merely the inappropriate use of swear words that explains

[3] It could be that anger is more valuable than we typically realise, and that it can be a force for good in the world. Myisha Cherry argues that not only is anger an appropriate response to racism, it is also essential to countering it (Cherry 2021).

our feeling offended by it but also the expression of the underlying emotion of anger.

One reason why we are particularly uncomfortable with angry swearing—and perhaps also why the law sometimes gets involved in swearing—is that we fear that it might escalate into violence. This could happen if the swearer himself turns violent; alternatively (or additionally), it could provoke others to become violent. People have different views about this. Some doubt that swearing, even aggressively, makes violence more likely: Kristen Jay (previously known as Kristen Janschewitz) and Timothy Jay, two psychologists who have written extensively about swearing, claim never to have witnessed swearing escalate into physical violence. Others—including me and my fellow patrons of certain remote, rural Welsh nightclubs in the 1990s—have had different experiences. What lies behind this fear?

One important factor is that inappropriate swearing and inappropriate displays of anger are both contrary to etiquette and other social norms, and so someone who engages in either of these things—and especially those who engage in both—reveals themself to be at least temporarily unconstrained by some important norms that apply in the current context. Being confronted with someone who disregards social norms in this way can make us feel uneasy. Perhaps the offender is consciously and deliberately disregarding important norms of politeness, which introduces the possibility that they might also take themself to be excused from other norms, including the norm that forbids us from physically attacking other people. Or perhaps the offender has deviated from normal standards of politeness because they have lost control, which might lead us to fear that they lack the self-restraint necessary to abstain from violence. Whatever the explanation, we are left anxiously wondering, in the words of Feinberg, 'Who knows . . . what this gross vulgarian will do next?' (1985, 280). The worry here is not that inappropriate angry swearing *causes* the angry swearer to become violent; rather, it is that inappropriate angry swearing can be a warning sign that the angry swearer is the sort of person who might become violent.

Inappropriate swearing along with an inappropriate expression of anger can, then, lead us to fear that the offender themself might turn violent. But, equally, we might fear that their behaviour might cause others to turn violent. One reason is that their disregard of the relevant norms of politeness might encourage those around them to disregard those norms, too: we often take ourselves to be justified in being rude (or worse) to people who were rude (or worse) to us first. As above, we might also worry that disregarding some relevant norms will lead others to being disregarded, including those who keep our conflicts with others non-violent. Another reason—and here I'm touching on issues that will be explored in more detail in later chapters—is that while disregarding etiquette in general can be viewed as a sign of disrespect, swearing inappropriately is a particularly overt and direct way of signalling disrespect. This is especially true of swearing that is directed at an individual: *Fuck you!*, addressed to another person, is more offensive than an undirected *Fuck it!*. The more overt and direct a show of disrespect towards another person, the more likely it is to provoke a violent response from that person—especially if it is also aggressive, as angry swearing generally is when directed at others. Let's take a moment to explore this idea.

Thankfully, people are not generally inclined to respond violently to expressions of disrespect towards them. Often we don't respond to our abuser at all, even if we feel annoyed—as when we (or perhaps just we British) sarcastically but inaudibly mutter 'You're welcome' when we hold the door for a stranger who fails to thank us. Other shows of disrespect are harder to ignore. A key factor here is the concept of *face*, which is familiar from our everyday ideas of *saving face* and *losing face*, and which has been explored and expanded upon by the sociologist Erving Goffman and discussed at length by theorists of politeness. Face, in this context, is the image of ourselves that we present to the world. We lose face when we are humiliated, when another person demands something of us, and when we apologise; we gain face when we are publicly praised, when someone concedes to us, and when others express gratitude to us. When other people show disrespect to us, they threaten our face, and an appropriate response can make the difference between losing and saving (or even gaining) face. We can afford to ignore covert expressions of disrespect not witnessed by others—as in the case of the stranger who fails to thank us for holding the door—because while such insults can smart, they don't affect other people's opinions of us. Other expressions of disrespect do demand a response in order to avoid loss of face. If a senior work colleague marches over to us and loudly accuses us of incompetence while everyone else in the workplace looks on, even the most placid among us would feel compelled to respond in order to save face. Some ways of responding will be ineffective; for example, 'Actually, I'm the best person in the entire building at turning on the lights, it's just the rest of my job I struggle with' is unlikely to save face. Other responses—such as challenging the accuser to a pistol duel or smashing up their car—are overreactions, and risk loss of face by making us appear ridiculous or deranged. The success of some responses depends on the context and one's relationship with the abuser and any onlookers. 'I only accept accusations of incompetence in writing' is unlikely to save face if onlookers view it as an endorsement of the accusation, but it may well save face if taken to be a comedic attempt to brush off the accusation, because—depending on the social dynamics of the workplace—it may successfully emphasise that the target of the attack is strong enough to withstand the accuser's harsh words.

In some contexts, for some shows of disrespect, and for some people, any non-violent response may be viewed as inadequate as a way of saving face. Responding to an insult by challenging the insulter to a duel was not, after all, always and everywhere regarded as an overreaction, and it is not unheard of today for verbal disagreements in bars to escalate into violence following the invitation of one of the participants to step outside to resolve the issue. Indeed, the capacity of certain expressions of disrespect to lead predictably to face-saving violent reactions has, in extreme cases, led to legal sanctions against those expressions of disrespect. An example is the category of speech known in US law as *fighting words*. Fighting words are words intended to provoke violence, and they are not protected under the First Amendment; that part of the US Constitution that, among other things, protects freedom of speech. While not all swearing constitutes fighting words, the law states that 'argument is unnecessary' to demonstrate that certain sweary insults 'are likely to provoke the average person to retaliation, and thereby cause a breach of the peace'.[4] Further, the manner of delivery matters: the 1940 judgement in *Cantwell v. Connecticut* included the remark, 'The English language has a number of words and expressions which, by general consent, are "fighting words" when said without a disarming smile'. Just as a smile can neutralise an insult, an aggressive manner can emphasise it and increase the chance of violent retaliation. There will be more to say in Chapters 6 and 7 about how the offensiveness of inappropriate swearing can be aggravated by various factors, including whether and to whom it is directed, and the manner in which it is delivered.

Before moving on, let's pause to note that there is a positive side of angry swearing, even when it is inappropriate. Even if aggressive swearing can be a precursor to physical violence, a precursor to violence is not itself violence, and we have already seen that swearing is an effective way of expressing emotion. There is reason to welcome behaviour that enables us to express emotion—especially venting anger—yet stops short of violence. We recognise this when we advise angry friends to vent their anger by punching a cushion, going

[4] From the judgement in *Chaplinsky v. New Hampshire* (315 U.S. 568 [1942]), which claims this of the epithets *damned racketeer* and *damned fascist*. Note that in 1942, when the judgement was made, *damned* was far more offensive in the US than it is today.

for a run, hitting a squash ball, and so on. That we advise our angry friends to do things like this reveals a few important things about our attitude to anger. First, given that we offer this advice in the hope that it will make our friend feel better, we must believe that expressing anger is a way to feel calmer and less angry. Second, we encourage our friends to vent their anger by punching cushions but not by punching people or smashing up cars because we believe that activities like punching cushions are *healthy* ways to express anger, in that they don't involve causing harm. Third, we encourage people to vent their anger because we think it preferable to do that (in healthy ways) than not to vent it at all; indeed, not expressing emotion—'bottling it up'—is widely recognised as a bad idea, and Sigmund Freud himself viewed anger as itself the consequence of suppressing other emotions. We can, then, plausibly view angry swearing as a way to *avert* violence rather than as something that makes violence more likely. This could happen in two ways. First, given the cathartic function of swearing, it may enable us to release some of the emotional pressure that might otherwise escalate into violence. Second, while swearing can be aggressive and intimidating, it is a low-cost form of aggression and intimidation compared to physical violence. Fighting words don't always result in fighting, and sometimes both parties feel better afterwards. Doing battle with strong words may be something that we would prefer to avoid, but it is preferable to fighting with fists and weapons. Mere swearing, even when aggressive and inappropriate, never put anyone in hospital.

Offensiveness beyond words

As well as helping us understand the offensiveness of inappropriate swearing, offence escalation helps us understand the offensiveness of breaching etiquette more generally. Comparing and contrasting inappropriate swearing with etiquette breaches in general will be helpful in understanding our attitudes to swearing and its power to affect us in the way it does.

Let's begin by observing that offence escalation can explain the offensiveness of things other than swear words. While I have characterised offence escalation as a process by which some varieties of *verbal* communication (i.e. the utterance of certain expressions) become offensive, we can generalise it to explain how certain sorts of *non-verbal* communication become offensive. In Chapter 1, I introduced the idea that gestures like the middle finger should be viewed as varieties of swearing. Like the utterance of swear words, these non-verbal gestures can be offensive and cathartic, and some even argue that—like swear words—they are based on taboo topics.[5] We can explain their capacity to offend in the same way that we can explain the capacity of swear words to offend: these gestures, dispreferred on account of taboo associations, grew to be offensive when people used them despite knowing that their use was disliked by their community, and when community members became aware that those using the gestures knew that their use was disliked.

Offence escalation can explain the offensiveness of behaviours that are even further removed from language, and from communication in general. Some conventions of etiquette (like the customs around *please* and *thank you*) are linguistic, but others (like the rules about which cutlery to use and how to hold it) are not. Breaching these conventions can be rude, impolite, or bad mannered, but it is not normally harmful or otherwise morally wrong. In an article co-authored with Gunther S. Stent, Judith Martin—who, under the name Miss Manners, pens a regular etiquette advice column that is published in hundreds of newspapers worldwide—characterises etiquette as a set of rules with which we comply

[5] Anthropologist Desmond Morris explains that the middle-finger gesture represents a penis, although the taboo origin of some offensive hand gestures (including the V-sign and the *bras d'honneur*) is not always clear, and very often produced without conscious thought (Morris 2005; Nasaw 2012).

voluntarily (i.e. without the threat of 'fierce sanctions' for non-compliance). The rules of etiquette regulate our social behaviour to ensure harmony, make our relations with others predictable, and to facilitate rituals, such as the behaviour characteristic of weddings and funerals. Martin and Stent see a large overlap between etiquette and morality:

> If a distinction is to be made between them, then it could be said that the moral point of view tends to be concerned with aspects of the human condition that involve matters of potentially grave consequence for life, limb, and property, whereas aspects of concern to manners tend to involve matters of potentially less grave consequences, such as offences against personal dignity, sacred and profane ritual, and the aesthetic sense. (1990, 253)

This view of etiquette as related to morality, concerned with everyday matters of less grave consequences, and having an important role in conveying respect for the dignity of others, is echoed by various philosophers. Sarah Buss argues that, in many cases, to be bad mannered is to be immoral, and that an important function of manners is to express respect and to acknowledge the moral status of others. Indeed, she argues that saying 'please' is equivalent to saying 'you are worthy of respect' (Buss 1999, 802). Karen Stohr, whose work we encountered in the previous chapter and who discusses Martin throughout her 2012 book, *On Manners*. Stohr remarks that 'polite behaviour is an extension of morality into small corners of our lives' (Stohr 2012, 4). This echoes ancient views about manners: philosophers such as Aristotle and Confucius wrote about manners alongside morality as they considered the more general question of how to live well.

The conventions of etiquette are many and diverse, and they vary by culture. They include removing a hat on entering a church, covering the head when entering a mosque, saying 'please' when we make a request, addressing people with a level of formality fitting to the occasion, standing an appropriate distance from someone with whom one is conversing, and refraining from 'liking' all the Facebook photos that one's ex has posted with their new partner. The ways in which these conventions developed, too, are many and diverse: some are set out in explicit rules, including those in religious texts, while others—like many of those governing appropriate behaviour on social media—arise organically, in the wild, as we navigate the rewards and awkwardness of our everyday interactions. In some cases, it is difficult to say exactly what the convention is, even when we have no trouble complying with it and recognising when it is breached. (Are you confident, for example, that you could specify exactly how close you could stand to a professional colleague without them feeling that you are uncomfortably close, without trying out various distances to see how they feel? I don't think I am.) However they arise, established conventions of etiquette become expected in the contexts in which they apply, and failure to abide by them risks causing offence. And while we are all more committed to some of these conventions than to others, we are all capable of being offended by those who refuse to comply: as Martin and Stent observe, even the most lawless drivers can become violently enraged by their fellow motorists' failure to abide by the simple conventions of traffic etiquette, as one victim of a roadside assault demonstrated by 'pulling in front of the assailant's car so that he was forced to slow down' (Martin and Stent 1990, 246). In short, once a convention of etiquette has become established, failure to abide by it becomes dispreferred by the community, and anyone who fails to abide by a convention we care about is likely to offend us, especially in cases where we know that they know that we dislike their failure to abide by it.

We can use offence escalation to explain how breaches of etiquette manage to be offensive. Conventions of etiquette develop when certain behaviours become expected in certain situations. This leads the community to disprefer failure to abide by these conventions. When people in a community fall into the habit of, say, bringing a small gift—a bottle of wine, chocolates, flowers—for the host of a dinner party to which they have been invited, a community member risks causing offence by failing to offer a gift in these circumstances. Often, community members will view a failure to follow convention on a single occasion as an excusable oversight, but repeated failures are unlikely to be viewed as benign. In such a scenario, if the host is confident that the guest knows that it is customary to bring a gift, that doing so would not unduly burden the guest, and that circumstances did not make it difficult for the guest to comply on this occasion, then the host can reasonably assume that the guest who arrives at the dinner party without a gift is insufficiently respectful of the host. The host can justifiably feel offended as a result. Breaches of etiquette, then, are liable to offend in much the same way that swearing inappropriately is liable to offend.

We saw, in the previous chapter, that in cases where swearing inappropriately is objectionable, it is objectionable because it is rude (i.e. because it is contrary to etiquette). As a result, inappropriate swearing lies at the 'less grave' end of Martin and Stent's spectrum. But sometimes, as we've seen, swearing can be a more serious matter. This can happen when it expresses the speaker's fundamental disrespect of others. There are other things to consider here too. Sometimes, the way we swear can turn it from something that is merely rude into something that is morally wrong. We're going to look at how this can happen in the next two chapters.

6

How to be a really offensive swearer

The extent to which swearing is objectionable depends on context, which words we use, and whether or not we express disrespect to others. It also depends on *how* we swear, who we are, who we're swearing at or in the presence of, who else is around, and—in a sense that will become clear in Chapter 9—what we're doing when we swear. How all these factors combine can affect whether swearing is innocuous, inappropriate but easily overlooked, objectionable, or even harmful. Between this chapter and Chapter 10, we're going to work out how we can make sensible, proportionate, and fair judgements about how objectionable particular instances of swearing are; how we can spot judgments that *aren't* sensible, proportionate, and fair; and how these insights can be used to improve formal regulations that target swearing.

Some background: nuisances

We can start with some general points about what can make offensive behaviour more or less of a problem. Feinberg drew on nuisance law to gauge how concerned we should be about offensive behaviour. In US law, he wrote, 'We demand protection from nuisances when we think of ourselves as *trapped* by them, and we think it unfair that we should pay the cost in inconvenience that is required to escape them' (Feinberg 1985, 5). He argued that the seriousness of offensiveness depends on three things: how intense and long-lasting is the offended person's offence (assuming that they're not abnormally sensitive to offence), how easy it is to avoid the offensive behaviour, and whether or not the witnesses willingly took the risk of being offended. On the other side of the scales, we should pay attention to the importance of the behaviour to the person behaving offensively and the wider social value of freedom of expression, whether the behaviour could be moved to a place and time where it would cause less offence, and whether the behaviour is motivated by spite (Feinberg 1985, 26).

If we apply all this to swearing, we end up with various sensible-sounding results: it's worse to swear at a captive audience than at people who can simply walk away, it's worse to swear in a primary school than a pub, people who attend a show by a famously sweary comedian aren't justified in complaining about hearing swearing during the show, and so on. These points aren't specific to swearing, though—they apply to other sorts of offensive behaviour too, like making loud noise and bad smells. These general considerations don't tell us everything we need to know about the offensiveness of swearing, though—there are some swearing-specific factors too. Here are some important examples.

Tone and body language

One thing that affects the offensiveness of our swearing is the tone we use when we swear. Suppose that, while commuting on a busy but quiet train, the stranger in the seat next to you opens a can of drink, accidentally spills it in their lap, and responds with a loud 'Fuck it!'. Even if you're pretty tolerant of swearing, how comfortable you feel about this will depend on what tone the speaker has used. If your seatmate is clearly in good humour, then you might be amused and sympathetic. But if the tone is clearly very angry, you are more likely to be alarmed. Loudly swearing on a busy but quiet train breaks social norms regardless of how it is done, but doing so angrily also breaks the norm against expressing strong negative emotion in public. If your seatmate is willing to express anger in this way, you might worry, then perhaps they might express it in more destructive ways too. This is why swearing angrily is more offensive than swearing good-humouredly. Other negative tones have a similar effect: a survey commissioned by the UK's communications regulator Ofcom found that, in broadcasting, an aggressive, malicious, or mocking tone makes swearing more offensive to the audience (Ipsos MORI 2016).

Body language, too, makes a difference to the offensiveness of swearing. Pairing swearing with aggressive body language—jabbing a finger at the person we're speaking to, standing very close to them, shaking a fist, and so on—makes swearing a more serious matter. Our body language can reduce the offensiveness of what we say, too. This is something that's explicitly recognised in US law: the judgement in *Chaplinsky v. New Hampshire* includes the remark that, to count as 'fighting words', our provocative speech needs to be delivered 'without a disarming smile'.

Of course, tone and body language are important in communication generally; they don't suddenly become important when people start swearing. Which tone we use can convey whether we're asking a question, making a suggestion, asserting something, and so on. Tone is even more important in certain languages: the Chinese languages, Hausa, and Mohawk (among others) are tonal languages, meaning that the tone one uses can make a difference to which word one is uttering. Body language, too, can convey our mood and our intentions towards the person we're speaking to—are we friendly, aggressive, joking, flirtatious?—and which body language is appropriate varies with culture and context.

With swearing, though, the stakes are higher: the tone and body language we use when we swear can determine whether or not we're doing something wrong, as the reference to the disarming smile in the *Chaplinsky* judgment illustrates. Swearing—and doing wrong with swearing—is a whole-body, surround-sound experience. It's difficult to make an accurate judgement about how offensive an incident of swearing is without taking into account the speaker's tone and body language.

Direct and indirect swearing

Next, we've seen that inappropriate swearing risks causing offence by conveying disrespect. But not all ways of conveying disrespect are equal. We're more likely to offend by expressing these attitudes *directly* than if we express them *indirectly*. Here's an example. If you and I are having a polite conversation, I might offend you if I casually use a swear word—by saying something like, 'Lovely fucking weather we're having'. But you will be much more offended if, instead, I say 'Fuck you!'. Offence escalation takes us part of the way to understanding why you are offended here: people dislike *fuck* in this sort of context, we both know this, we both know that the other knows it, which means that you take my *fuck* to express disrespect. This doesn't tell us the whole story, though. If my saying 'Lovely fucking weather we're having' and 'Fuck you!' both offend you because they express my disrespect towards you, why is the latter *more* offensive than the former? We need to look beyond offence escalation for the answer, which I think is this: both expressions express disrespect, but one does so more directly than the other. *Fuck you!* shows another person, in a way that leaves no room for doubt, that the speaker disrespects them or even holds them in contempt; in fact, *I hold you in contempt* is a reasonable (if clumsy and less expressive) non-sweary translation of *Fuck you!*. By contrast, saying 'Lovely fucking weather we're having' does not directly express any negative attitude to the listener. If you end up being offended, it's because you take my choice of words to be inconsiderate of you, and you infer from this that I disrespect you.[1]

All of this fits with a general point about politeness. Typically, it's more offensive and less polite to express negative attitudes explicitly and directly rather than indirectly and ambiguously. That's why it's more polite to end a conversation by saying, 'Well, I'd better let you go now' than by saying, 'I don't want to talk to you any more'. Both expressions convey that the speaker wants the conversation to end, but only the former does so indirectly. How direct and explicit a speaker can be while still being polite is, again, something that varies with culture and context. Germans, for example, communicate with a directness that would border on rudeness in Britain. We can return, here, to the concept of *face*. According to Penelope Brown and Stephen C. Levinson—the socio-linguists who set out politeness theory in the late 1970s—expressing our negative attitudes indirectly prevents the listener's loss of face. Saying 'I don't think that dress does anything for you' is more polite than 'You look awful in that dress' because while both convey to the listener our negative opinion of how they look, the directness of the latter makes a public show of the negativity, which diminishes the listener in the eyes of any bystanders—and even if there are no bystanders, we might care about what they would think if there were. For similar reasons, saying 'Lovely fucking weather we're having' is less face-threatening to the listener (because less direct) than saying 'Fuck you!', even though both are ways of conveying disrespect or contempt.

[1] This view that direct swearing is worse than indirect swearing is reflected in the 1971 judgment of *Cohen v. California*, in which Paul Robert Cohen's conviction for disturbing the peace by wearing a jacket emblazoned with the words *Fuck the Draft* inside a public courthouse was overturned. The judgement mentioned, as a factor that reduced the offensiveness of Cohen's behaviour, that '[n]o individual actually or likely to be present could reasonably have regarded the words on appellant's jacket as a direct personal insult' (403 US 15 (1971)).

How about witnessing swearing directed at someone else? Saying 'Fuck you!' is direct, but if it's not addressed to me, *I* don't lose face. Even so, we are more likely be offended by witnessing someone say 'Fuck you!' to a third person than we are by witnessing 'Lovely fucking weather we're having' addressed to a third person. Empathy is part of the explanation for this. We're not purely selfish, so it's not just our own face that we care about—we don't like to see others insulted or humiliated either. But how offended we're likely to be by witnessing someone say 'Fuck you!' to a third person depends on a few other factors too, including who the addressee is and the relationship between the swearer and the swearee. We're going to return to this in the next chapter.

Accidental or deliberate

Another factor relevant to the offensiveness of swearing is whether or not it is accidental. We tend to be more tolerant of the sort of swearing that slips out accidentally than of the more deliberate sort. This view is reflected in the findings of an Ofcom survey on public attitudes towards swearing in broadcasting, which found that participants 'found offensive language much less acceptable when they felt that professional broadcasters . . . had intentionally used strong language' (Ipsos MORI 2016, 4), and recommended that broadcasters 'should, in general, be held to higher standards for pre-recorded programmes than for live broadcasts' (8). This reflects a more general attitude: we tend to be more forgiving of objectionable things that people say in the heat of the moment, without adequate forethought, than we are of objectionable things said after careful consideration. Everyone makes mistakes sometimes, after all, and we take what people say after careful consideration to be more likely to represent their true thoughts and feelings. Swearing aggressively at another person following careful consideration, we think, is likely to reflect the swearer's true attitude towards the swearee; by contrast, swearing aggressively in haste may merely reflect the speaker's momentary annoyance, tiredness, grief, or some other negative but temporary state.

Repetition

Finally—at least, the final aggravating factor that we will consider in this incomplete list—repetition can increase the offensiveness of swearing. Perhaps this is because repeated swearing strikes us as more likely to be deliberate, and more likely to indicate that the swearer is working really hard to offend. This is borne out by the participants of Ofcom's survey, who view repeated swearing to indicate the swearer's desire to draw attention to the swear word. Where repeated swearing does *not* reflect the speaker's intention to offend, it doesn't lead us to view swearing as more offensive. This happens in coprolalia, the tendency to utter swear words and other inappropriate language frequently and involuntarily. Coprolalia is associated with Tourette syndrome, although relatively few Tourette patients have it, and it can arise in other conditions too. Nobody who understands coprolalia is likely to be offended by it—although they may prefer not to hear the language that the speaker utters. This shows us it's not due to the repetition itself that swearing is more offensive when it's repetitive; it's because of the inferences that repetition usually leads us to make about the speaker's intentions.

The factors we've just considered interact, of course. Swearing is a more serious matter when it is done both angrily and repeatedly; repetitive swearing at nothing in particular is less objectionable than repetitive swearing at a person, and so on. In the next chapter, we're going to add something else to the mix, when we see how the relationship between the speaker and their listener can affect how objectionable swearing is.

7
You talkin' to me?

How objectionable is it to say 'Fuck you!' to another person? The previous chapter enables us, I hope, to give a somewhat sensible answer to this question. But it's not the whole story, because it says nothing about the relationship between the person swearing and the person being sworn at—and this makes a huge difference. If you're a liberal sort who likes to think of themself as open-minded about swearing, you might happily tolerate a good-humoured *Fuck you!* between friends in a relaxed and informal setting. But you might wince if you heard the same thing said by a teenager to one of their schoolteachers, or—even worse—vice versa. And if you were to hear an adult say the same thing to a toddler or to a very elderly person, you'd probably judge them to be acting not merely rudely but immorally.

Now, there's a long tradition of viewing swearing as worse when it's directed at (or in the presence of) certain people. The ears of women and children have historically been considered especially delicate in this regard. Let's take a look at how swearing's offensiveness intersects with who is swearing and who is around to witness it.

Swear power

Generally speaking, witnessing an adult saying 'Fuck you!' to another adult whom we do not know, and who is roughly equivalent to the speaker in size, age, and social and professional status is less likely to offend us than being sworn at ourselves. In other cases, though, we are *more* offended by swearing addressed to another person than by swearing addressed to ourselves. This can happen if the addressee is someone we care about, or someone who is powerless or vulnerable compared to the swearer, or someone to whom the swearer has particular duties. It is worse for an adult to swear at a child than at another adult, it is worse for an employer to swear at one of their employees than at a professional equal, it is worse for a physically fit and strong person to swear at someone smaller and weaker than at someone of their own size, it is worse for a doctor to swear at one of their patients than at someone they're not treating, and so on. In all these cases, the swearer is in some sense more powerful than the swearee. Our sense that swearing is worse in these circumstances reflects our more general disapproval of people who attack those who are smaller and weaker than themselves; a disapproval that is expressed in expressions like *Pick on someone your own size!* and in the norm against 'punching down' in comedy. Things are even worse when the swearer is not only stronger than the swearee but also has a duty to protect, nurture, or care for them. Doctors who swear at their patients and teachers who swear at their pupils behave especially badly by attacking those whom they ought to be protecting, nurturing, and supporting.

What about when the swearer is *less* powerful than the swearee? Things are trickier here. On the one hand, we are less likely to be intimidated by someone less powerful swearing at us than by someone more powerful. But on the other hand, such cases can strike us as especially outrageous. People are particularly shocked when a member of the public swears at a police officer, a priest, or a member of medical staff, or when a student swears at their teacher. I think that it is not the power relations that explain our shock in cases like these. Instead, they're shocking because of the widespread belief that people like the swearee are especially deserving of respect from people like the swearer. Widespread views about what sort of people are especially deserving of respect are not always well founded and can reflect prejudice, but since these views are entrenched in our norms and our moral intuitions, they help explain our reactions to what we find offensive nevertheless. In Chapter 10, we will consider how to respond to offence that is based on prejudice.

In some cases of swearing-at, there is room for disagreement about whether or not it is especially objectionable. In the past, and even in some contemporary circles, it was thought especially objectionable for men to swear in the company of women (and, for that matter, for women to fucking swear at all). For those who hold such a view, it is more objectionable for a man to swear at a woman than it is for him to swear at another man. This view has its roots in the sexist view that women are delicate creatures who can be corrupted by swearing and who need to be protected from it. Sensible people reject this sexist view—but it is not obvious what attitude we should take towards the view that swearing at women (by men) is especially objectionable. On the one hand, we might think that since it is not the case that women are delicate creatures who must be protected from swearing, it is no worse for a man to swear at a woman than it is for him to swear at another man. On the other hand, continuing sexism, misogyny, and violence against women mean that there is still work to do to reduce disrespectful treatment of women, which might lead us to object more strongly to swearing at women by men than to swearing at men by men. Analogous problems arise when we consider swearing at members of other oppressed groups—people with disabilities, LGBTQ + people, members of ethnic and religious minorities, and so on—especially by people who are not members of those groups. Should we view such swearing as especially objectionable given that it adds to the burden of mistreatment that these people bear, or is it in some way disrespectful to treat oppressed people differently to others when it comes to swearing?

There will be more to say in Chapter 10 about how concerns about oppression interact with offensiveness, but let me come down on one side of this fence. Swearing at a member of an oppressed group by someone who is not a member of an oppressed group is more objectionable than swearing at someone who is not a member of an oppressed group. Taking this view need not be based on patronising, paternalistic, or otherwise disrespectful attitudes towards members of oppressed groups, such as the view that the latter are delicate creatures who need protection from strong language. It can instead be motivated by a recognition that members of disadvantaged groups experience more than their fair share of disrespect and abuse compared to people who are not members of disadvantaged groups, and that the offensiveness of swearing at them is likely to be magnified by its fitting into an oppressive pattern of disrespect and abuse.[1] By contrast, although swearing at a person who is not a member of an oppressed group can be offensive, and is typically more offensive than swearing at nobody in particular, it is less offensive than swearing at a member of an oppressed group, since it does not fit into an oppressive pattern of disrespect and abuse.

Setting an example

Who is doing the swearing can make a difference to its offensiveness. If you're the sort of person who is (expected to be) a model of politeness and decorum, you have greater capacity to shock and offend by swearing. This is an instance of a more general, familiar phenomenon: the concept of *noblesse oblige* embodies the thought that the privileged should be held to a higher standard of behaviour than everyone else. We saw an illustration of this in the opening example of this book: it would have been especially shocking to hear the Queen swearing during her Christmas address, in part because the Queen was *not the sort of person* one expected to hear swearing. We expected her to be a model of decorum. The same

[1] That swearing at is more objectionable when it is directed at a member of a disadvantaged group because of its place in an oppressive pattern of disrespect and abuse makes it comparable to microaggression, as characterised by Regina Rini (2021).

applies to other people to whom we look for guidance on behaving well: priests, police officers, teachers, judges. It often happens that those people we uphold as models of decorum are also people of high social or professional status, which often means that they hold positions of privilege and power; as a result, the offensiveness of their swearing, if it is directed at an individual, can be aggravated by the fact that they hold a position of power relative to the swearee. Sometimes a person's swearing is made especially objectionable by the fact that we view them as models of decorum *and* by the fact that they are swearing at a relatively powerless person. These combined aggravating factors apply when a teacher swears at a pupil, or when a police officer swears at a member of the public.

Simply being middle class can also make one's swearing more objectionable. As we saw in Chapter 3, due to the middle-class politeness criterion, we are often less shocked by swearing from very underprivileged people and by swearing from very highly privileged people. This develops the sorts of double standards that have resulted in Conservative politicians escaping unpunished for swearing (even aggressively) at the public, while ordinary people have been arrested and fined for the same thing.

Won't somebody think of the children?

Swearing by adults in the company of children is frowned upon, although not simply because children tend to be more vulnerable compared to adults (even though they are) or because children are an oppressed group (even though, perhaps, they are). Let's take care to separate swearing *in the company* of children from the idea of treating children aggressively. Swearing *at* children—by shouting things like *Fuck you!* at them or by swearily calling them names—or allowing them to witness one behaving in this way towards others is certainly objectionable, for reasons we discussed above. But what about simply allowing children to witness the sort of swearing that doesn't come with any aggravating factors? Many people believe there's something wrong with even this. The presence of children has been used in law and broadcasting to justify punishing swearing: the presence of children can turn relatively innocuous swearing into swearing that warrants punishment (see Fairman 2006, 60ff). Swearing in the presence of children is generally thought to be far more objectionable than swearing in solely adult company. This view has its roots in the idea that it is possible somehow to corrupt children by exposing them to swearing; something that Supreme Court Justice Stevens, who in 1978 condemned Pacifica for broadcasting George Carlin's 'filthy words' skit on a New York radio station, apparently took to be self-evident when he gravely remarked that 'Pacifica's broadcast could have enlarged a child's vocabulary in an instant' (FCC v. Pacifica Found. 1978).

This idea that a child can be corrupted by a mere word is incoherent, as Feinberg observes: either children who overhear a swear word do not recognise it as such, in which case they are not corrupted by it; or they do recognise the word to be a swear word, in which case they are already 'corrupt'. But perhaps enlarging their vocabulary by teaching them swear words that they did not previously know could be viewed as corrupting, as Justice Stevens believed? This, too, is implausible. Learning swear words (and how to use them) is a normal part of language development; something that everyone reading this book has gone through at some point. If it's corrupting, then it's a form of corruption that happens to us all. Would it be better if we could avoid being corrupted in this particular way? Unlikely. To avoid being corrupted by learning swear words, we'd need to be protected from sources of sweary vocabulary enlargement. Those sources include not only edgy radio broadcasts but also wholesome things like books and normal social interactions with peers. It is difficult to imagine how it might be possible to meet children's needs while also shielding them from swearing. Much as many people dislike the idea of children being exposed to swearing, then, taking decisive steps to ensure that they aren't exposed to swearing looks to be at odds with healthy ways of raising children. And what's more, children who are thoroughly protected from swearing would grow into adults who have not mastered a particular part of their language—a part that those who would protect them from it get to enjoy themselves. Such adults would, in some small (or perhaps not-so-small) way, be less equipped for life and social interaction than other people. With all this in mind, the claim that it is harmful to expose children to swearing looks hopelessly implausible.

Even so, many of us who would not want to claim that swearing harms children nevertheless avoid swearing in their presence. Why? Does our distaste for swearing in front of children make sense? I think so. We can make sense of the thought that it's better to avoid swearing in front of children with reference to etiquette. Let's consider, first, the case of swearing in front of one's own children. Is it objectionable to allow one's own children to overhear one swearing in a non-aggressive way that is not directed at anyone? If this is objectionable at all, it is objectionable in a 'setting a bad example' sort of way. Part of good parenting is instilling in one's children a knowledge of etiquette and (more generally) the standards of behaviour that will be expected of them throughout their lives, and an ability to conform to those standards. To neglect this part of a child's education places them at a significant disadvantage when it comes to interacting with others, since it will impede their ability to cooperate with others. We naturally teach our children how to act in accordance with etiquette by acting that way ourselves, and by correcting them when they fail to follow our example. By failing to act in accordance with etiquette while we are parenting, we fail to set a good example for our children to follow, and as a result we risk failing to socialise them effectively. Even so, this is only a risk if we *consistently* set a bad example. Allowing children to witness the occasional, infrequent lapse in etiquette—by swearing, by treating someone rudely, by being inappropriately informal, and so on—hardly risks undermining their general command of etiquette, and may even enhance it by exposing them to the sorts of reactions that one is likely to provoke by breaching etiquette. Swearing in front of one's own children is, then, objectionable only when it happens regularly enough to threaten their grasp of etiquette. If we are the sorts of people to disapprove when we witness a parent swearing in the presence of their child, it seems plausible that the reason we disapprove is not that we believe this particular instance of swearing to be harmful to their child but because we suspect that the parent in question *routinely* swears in front of their child, in which case they are not taking steps to socialise their child properly. We disapprove of this behaviour because it disadvantages the child, and because it contributes to a wider problem: it is bad for everyone if people reach adulthood without learning to treat people with respect. We view parents as responsible for ensuring that their children reach adulthood knowing how to treat people with respect via their grasp of etiquette.

What about swearing in front of other people's children? This, too, is viewed as objectionable, yet we are not responsible for parenting other people's children. Even so, what is objectionable about swearing in front of other people's children is, in part, roughly similar to what is objectionable about swearing in front of one's own children. Parents bear the main responsibility for setting a good example to their children, but the wider community bears a responsibility to do the same. This is apparent from the fact that we generally expect adults to modify their behaviour in front of children—to behave politely and to refrain from doing things that it would be undesirable for the children to emulate. So, we disapprove of people who set a bad example to other people's children by swearing in front of them. In addition, we view swearing in front of someone else's children as disrespectful to those children's parents.

The considerations that lead us to avoid swearing in the presence of other people's children guide our behaviour in other ways too. There are many things that we can do to someone else's children that are not remotely harmful, and which may even be beneficial, but which we refrain from because we would view it as encroaching on the remit of the parents. The sorts of activities in question vary with culture but might include giving a child a radical new haircut, buying them an expensive toy, or enrolling them in an after-school music class. Without gaining the permission of the child's parents, these things could all be viewed as rude and disrespectful, even if done in response to a request by the child themself. The reason is that we view decisions about cutting a child's hair, whether they are allowed to have an expensive toy, and what they will be doing after school to be up to the child's parents. It is customary to defer to parents' judgments about how to raise their children, and—except in extreme cases where the child is placed in danger—this involves not interfering in decisions parents make about their children even when we think those decisions are not justified. These reflections highlight another reason why we think there is something wrong with swearing in front of other people's children. Given that we view setting standards of behaviour for a child as largely the responsibility of the child's parents, and that it is normal for parents to raise their children to think that it is wrong to swear, swearing in front of other people's children is disrespectful of those children's parents' efforts to teach them that swearing is unacceptable. This holds regardless of one's own views about how it is best to raise children: a parent who deems it acceptable to swear in the company of her own children is expected to refrain from swearing in the company of other children out of deference to the efforts of those other children's parents to raise them according to different standards. It also holds regardless of whether the reasons that the child's parents wish to avoid exposing the child to swearing are coherent or not. If a child's parents want to avoid their child encountering swearing because they believe, say, that swearing is capable of causing brain damage to the child and we know them to be mistaken, this does not justify our swearing in front of the child. To do so would be insufficiently respectful of the child's parents' freedom to raise their child as they see fit—a freedom that, except when it involves actually harming the child, we take to be part of parenting.

When deciding how objectionable an instance of swearing is, then, it matters who is doing the swearing, who (if anyone) is being sworn at, who else is around, and what the relationship is between these people. This broad focus on the act of uttering swear words in our interactions with others, rather than on the much narrower topic of the words themselves and what they refer to and sound like, is perhaps unsurprising given the offence escalation account, which explains swearing's capacity to shock and offend in terms of the unspoken sentiments that the speaker conveys to the listener and to those around them when they swear. Next, we're going to look at some of the rules that are used to deal with swearing in the wild, and how they could be improved.

8

A regulatory fucking mess

Around the world, rules designed to prohibit, censor, or punish swearing are enshrined in broadcasting codes, professional and sporting practices, and even the law. How can we work out whether our rules about swearing are fair and consistent? How can we spot and correct overreactions and wrong calls before people are silenced and punished inappropriately? We've made some progress towards understanding our responses to swearing by identifying some of the factors that make swearing more or less offensive. Let's continue in that vein now, by zooming in on the problem of how to make and apply sensible rules about swearing. In doing so, we're going to be led by a need to find a sensible answer to the question: what are we *doing* when we swear?

Who cares what we do with swearing?

The answer to this question matters. Usually, when we object to something that someone says, we're objecting not to the words they use but to what they are doing with those words. former US president Bill Clinton's notorious pronouncement, 'I did not have sexual relations with that woman, Miss Lewinsky', is notorious not because of the particular words he uttered but because by uttering those words in the context he uttered them, he *lied* about a politically important matter (and also, of course, because the lie was about the salacious topic of the president's inappropriate sexual relationship with his intern). His words would not have been at all objectionable if they had been true. And if he'd lied by using a different arrangement of words—like, 'It's false that Monica Lewinsky and I had any sexual interaction'—his utterance would have been just as objectionable as the one he in fact made.

Judgements about exactly what someone is doing with their words can have life-or-death consequences. The tragic case of Derek Bentley is a vivid illustration of this. Bentley was a mentally disabled British man who was hanged for the murder of a police officer in 1953, when he was nineteen years old. Bentley and his sixteen-year-old friend, Christopher Craig, were caught by police attempting to burgle a warehouse. When a police officer asked Craig to hand over his gun, Bentley reportedly shouted, 'Let him have it, Chris!'. Craig began to fire, injuring one police officer and killing another. In court, Bentley's fate hinged on the question of whether by shouting 'Let him have it, Chris!', he had been *ordering Craig to fire at the police*—in which case, given what happened afterwards, it makes sense to view Bentley as a murderer—or whether he had simply been *urging Craig to hand over the gun*, in which case he didn't murder anyone. It was under the former interpretation that Bentley's exclamation was introduced in court by the prosecution. Both Bentley and Craig were convicted of murder, but since Craig was a minor, only Bentley faced the death penalty. The case was controversial from the outset. It was the focus of the 1991 film, *Let Him Have It*, in which Christopher Ecclestone played Bentley. Bentley was granted a posthumous royal pardon in 1993, and his conviction was overturned in 1998.

Even in less dramatic situations, it can be difficult to work out what people are doing with their words. Was your colleague who suggested continuing your discussion over dinner asking you on a date or simply letting you know that he was hungry? Was that neighbour who described your outfit as 'bold' insulting you or complimenting you? Was that stern stranger who just advised you not to park your car outside her house threatening you or merely cautioning you?

Grappling with ambiguities like these is a common feature of our communication with others. Things can be even more confusing when swearing is involved. Our strong emotional reactions to swearing can get in the way of thinking clearly about what the speaker was doing. We might get the impression that someone was threatening us simply because they swore, but perhaps we were wrong. We might feel that the swearer was being aggressive, but perhaps it's just our shock at their unexpected swearing that led us to think that. To make sensible judgements about when swearing is objectionable, we need a way to cut through our emotional responses to swearing—but we also need a way to judge when our emotional responses to swearing *are* relevant.

A lack of clear fucking guidelines

Analysing the offensiveness of swearing by looking at what the speaker is doing when they swear does sometimes happen in the wild. We've seen, from the US concept of fighting words, that in certain circumstances a person who swears is viewed as provoking violence. Over the years, various court cases have explored the difference between swearing that constitutes fighting words and swearing that does not. Swearing looks ideally suited to fighting words: it's a good way of expressing disrespect, and expressing disrespect can be highly provocative. But not all ways of swearing are provocative in the right way: we've seen that some ways of swearing are more powerful and dramatic expressions of disrespect than others, and some aren't expressions of disrespect at all. Not all ways of swearing can plausibly be viewed as acts likely to breach the peace. This is something that the courts have learned the hard way, as when Paul Robert Cohen was arrested in 1968 for 'maliciously and willfully disturb[ing] the peace . . . by . . . offensive conduct' and imprisoned for thirty days after wearing a jacket emblazoned with the words *Fuck the Draft* (a reference to the draft of US men into the army to fight in the Vietnam War) inside the Los Angeles County courthouse, but successfully appealed his conviction in 1971. The resulting decision—*Cohen v. California*—remains a landmark in the debate about what sort of swearing can get you arrested. In reaching the decision, the court considered what Cohen had been *doing* by wearing the jacket. After noting that he didn't act violently, threaten violence, or even speak before his arrest, the Court reflected: 'The conviction quite clearly rests upon the asserted offensiveness of the words Cohen used to convey his message to the public. The only "conduct" which the State sought to punish is the fact of communication'. In other words, apart from using a swear word to communicate his opinion about—as the Court put it—'the inutility or immorality of the draft', Cohen didn't *do* anything that could have got him arrested. The Court ruled out the possibility that Cohen's wearing of the jacket could constitute fighting words, and in doing so, it made reference to one of the factors we considered in the previous chapter: it noted that Cohen's swearing was not *direct*. 'No individual actually or likely to be present could reasonably have regarded the words on appellant's jacket as a direct personal insult', said the Court.

The *Cohen v. California* judgement was a satisfyingly clear analysis of what Cohen was doing by wearing his sweary jacket in the context where he wore it—but anyone hoping that this was the first step on a path to clear and systematic thinking about swearing in US law is going to be disappointed. A confusing series of decisions followed. In 1973, a US radio station played George Carlin's 'filthy words' comedy skit about the seven words you can't say on the airwaves. The broadcast included the seven words in question, which are *shit*, *piss*, *fuck*, *cunt*, *cocksucker*, *motherfucker*, and *tits*. A father who claimed to have been listening with his fifteen-year-old son complained to the Federal Communications Commission (FCC). The broadcaster, Pacifica, responded by noting that it had aired a warning about the 'sensitive language' in the monologue, and defended its value as a commentary on attitudes towards language.

The FCC upheld the complaint and the Supreme Court agreed, taking the view that listeners should be able to expect not to have 'indecent' material broadcast into their homes and the ears of their children (FCC v. Pacifica Found. 1978).

From this point, things get really confusing. When the Irish singer Bono accepted an award at the Golden Globes in 2003 with the words 'This is really, really *fucking* brilliant', the FCC initially took no action in response to the 234 complaints it received. The rationale for this inaction was that, in saying what he did, Bono did not describe sex or excretion, which he would have needed to do in order to bring his utterance under the remit of indecency regulation—and anyway, he only swore once. Less than a year later, however, following lobbying by pro-censorship groups, the FCC changed its mind. This time, it reasoned that 'given the core meaning of the "F-Word", any use of that word or a variation, in any context, inherently has a sexual connotation' (Federal Communications Commission 2004). According to this line of thinking, every time you say 'fucking', you're talking about sex. This means that Bono's remark translates as something like—and I'm just guessing here—*My erect penis is especially honoured by this recognition of my work*. The view of *fucking* taken by the FCC here contradicted previous legal rulings (including *Cohen*) as well as the opinion of linguists writing about *fuck* and made it difficult for broadcasters to guess what sort of language might attract unwanted attention from the FCC. Caution was the result. The chilling effect on free speech was dramatically illustrated eight months later in November 2004, when the American ABC Television Network decided to air the *fuck*-filled World War II movie *Saving Private Ryan* in honour of Veterans Day. Sixty-six ABC affiliates decided against broadcasting the movie and mentioned confusing FCC decision-making as the reason for their caution (Fairman 2006). But its broadcast by the remaining affiliates led to yet another confusing result. The broadcast attracted *fuck*-based complaints to the FCC, yet despite the FCC's every-*fuck*-is-indecent ruling in response to complaints about Bono a decade earlier, it decided that the use of *fuck* in *Saving Private Ryan* was acceptable. Anyone studying these rulings in the hope of drawing conclusions about what makes swearing acceptable in some cases and unacceptable in others is going to be left scratching their head.

A large part of the problem here is the way that the FCC operates: rather than proactively creating polices around what words it is acceptable to broadcast and under what circumstances, it relies upon complaints from the public to bring problematic cases to its attention. This system is open to influence by pro-censorship lobbying groups, like the Parents Television Council and the American Family Association, whose campaigns have led the FCC to rule as unacceptable instances of swearing that most people do not regard as problematic.[1] Other groups, like the UK's BBFC and Ofcom, do periodically undertake and publish audience research to develop specific guidelines around acceptable language. But even so, the helpfulness of such guidelines is limited, since they reflect audience views but do not analyse, question, or challenge those views. As a result, although those guidelines are a useful reference point for most cases of everyday, common-or-garden swearing, they are less useful—even harmful—in unusual cases. Unusual cases include those where a film realistically depicts a community in which certain words that are widely viewed as offensive are used inoffensively or even affectionately—as *cunt* can be in certain Scottish communities; a point made by the team behind the Glasgow-based 2012 film, *The Angel's Share*, in response to the BBFC's decision to rate it 18 rather than 15 due to the film's copious *cunts*. While organizations like the BBFC aim to reflect public opinions rather than create them, the effect of their enforcing their guidelines is to reinforce the prevailing view—in the case of *The*

[1] Fairman reports: 'Of the 234 total complaints received [by the FCC with regard to Bono's appearance in the Golden Globe Awards show], 217 were part of an organized campaign launched by the Parents Television Council' (2006, 38).

Angel's Share, the view that *cunt* is always a highly offensive word. This makes it more difficult to challenge public opinions about the offensiveness of certain words.

A way forward: the nudity analogy

We need to avoid confusion and promote fairness in regulations around swearing. Were rule makers to provide specific guidance about what sorts of factors make an instance of swearing particularly objectionable, this could clear up confusion and promote free expression, since people could more confidently anticipate the likely reaction to their swearing and avoid swearing in a way that is likely to attract more retaliation than they are prepared to deal with. To see approximately what such guidance might look like, we can look to the legal guidance around public nudity. Exposing one's body in public is, like swearing, an activity that can be benign or morally concerning, depending on the circumstances. Laws around public nudity vary by state in the US, with some states simply prohibiting nudity. In the case of other states, however, the intent of the person who goes nude matters. For example, in Colorado, nudity 'done with intent to arouse or to satisfy the sexual desire of any person' is an offence. In many cases, it also matters whether the person could be expected to anticipate the reaction of any onlookers: in Arkansas, indecent exposure must happen either in a public place or '[u]nder circumstances in which [the person who exposes themself] knows [their] conduct is likely to cause affront or alarm' (HG.org 2022). In the UK, the guidance is relatively clear. The CPS explains what naturism is and states that, in regulating it, 'a balance needs to be struck between the naturist's right to freedom of expression and the right of the wider public to be protected from harassment, alarm and distress' (CPS 2022). Like swearing, public nudity can, in the UK, amount to an offence under section 5 of the Public Order Act provided that certain conditions are met: to qualify, the nudity must be accompanied by threatening, abusive, or disorderly behaviour, and it must take place within hearing or sight of someone likely to be caused harassment, alarm, or distress. Where the nudity has a sexual content—such as where the nude person intends to cause alarm or distress as a result of someone seeing the genitals specifically—it may amount to a sexual offence. Other countries, of course, have stricter laws about public nudity, and even liberal France takes a dim view of it: in July 2015, Swiss performance artist Milo Moiré was arrested and spent a night in jail after posing naked for selfies with tourists in Paris. She had previously done something similar in Switzerland and Germany without getting arrested (Hall 2015).

How do we get clear about the ways in which the offensiveness of swearing interacts with the intentions of the swearer and the effects (or likely effects) on other people? We'll zoom in on this in the next chapter.

9

How to do things with swearing

We've arrived at quite a mind-boggling list of factors that can affect how offensive swearing is. Confronted with another person's *Fuck you!* our calculations about how offensive they're being need to take into account who they are, who they're speaking to, the relationship between who they are and who they're speaking to, who is listening, what tone they're using, how polite the social context is, whether the context makes it likely that they're threatening or harassing or bullying the other person . . . with so much to think about, it's little wonder that our reactions to (and regulations about) swearing are all over the place. How on earth are we supposed to react sensibly to swearing, in practice? This is what we're going to turn to next. Armed with our theoretical insights about things that make swearing more or less objectionable, we're going to come up with a framework upon which regulators can build sensible and coherent rules about swearing.

Acts, effects, intentions, predictions

If you can bear just a little more theory, traditional philosophy of language can help us out here. In 1955, Oxford philosopher John Langshaw Austin delivered a series of lectures at Harvard University entitled *How to Do Things with Words*. Austin began from the observation that language is not simply a tool to describe or refer to things in the world. We also use language to perform various speech acts. For example, we can use words to promise, assert, apologise, challenge, ask, resign, accept an offer, issue a warning, and so on.

In some cases, there is nothing more to doing a certain act than uttering certain words. If you want to apologise to Marley, you can simply say 'I apologise' to Marley. Once you've done that, you've apologised. And if you want to promise Owly that you'll pay him £100 tomorrow, you can do that simply by saying to him 'I promise to pay you £100 tomorrow'. When we say things like 'I apologise', 'I promise', 'I resign', 'I accept', we're not simply describing or referring to things in the world. Just by saying those things, we're performing certain acts (apologising, promising, resigning, accepting). Austin calls acts like these, which we can perform simply by uttering certain words, *illocutionary acts.*

It's pretty easy to work out that someone who says 'I apologise' is apologising, and that someone who says 'I promise' is promising, but usually we can perform illocutionary acts without actually saying that we're doing it. We can apologise by saying 'I'm sorry', and promise by saying 'I give you my word that . . .', or simply 'I will . . .' in the right context. With some illocutionary acts, we almost never say explicitly which one we're performing, even though we could. For example, we don't usually begin our assertions with 'I assert that . . .' and our threats with 'I threaten that . . .'.

Another category of speech act has to do with the effects of our words on the person we're speaking to. I can *threaten* you by saying 'If you don't make me a cup of tea right now, I'll strangle you', but if I want to *intimidate* you, something else is needed. For me to intimidate you, you need to end up feeling intimidated. Something similar is true for convincing, amusing, offending, annoying, alarming, and impressing. A speaker can *try* to do these things, but they only succeed if their listener is convinced, amused, offended, annoyed, alarmed, or impressed as a result. Austin calls these sorts of acts *perlocutionary acts*, and the effects that they have on the listener *perlocutionary effects.*

Austin, as it happens, very briefly discusses swearing in *How to Do Things with Words*. He notes that swearing expresses our feelings, and he remarks that swearing doesn't neatly fit the framework he's sketched. Swearing, he tells us, is neither an illocutionary nor a perlocutionary act.[1] So, why the little crash course on Austin? Well, because when we swear, we perform other acts too, and these acts make a difference to how objectionable our swearing is. In fact, understanding what *else* we're doing when we swear is absolutely key to unpacking our judgements about it. Austin's account provides us with a framework we can use to do this. Let's take a closer look.

One thing that Austin makes vivid is that some of the things we do when we speak relate to the effects of our words on our listeners, while we can do other things regardless of what effect we have on listeners. Rules that regulate swearing—and other sorts of objectionable behaviour, for that matter—are concerned with behaviour that affects other people in certain ways. Nobody is interested in making rules to prohibit or censor swearing by people who are alone and out of earshot of anyone else, or in TV shows that will never be broadcast to the public. This focus on the effects of swearing is reflected in the language used in rules that are commonly used to regulate swearing: laws that prohibit behaviour likely to breach the peace, distress onlookers, provoke violence, and so on. People who swear in certain ways and in certain contexts can be arrested under these laws. We saw above that some organisations that regulate swearing take things a step further by proactively researching how swearing will affect people, and using this research to inform their

[1] Why not an illocutionary act? His explanation here is limited and involves an appeal to (his own) intuition. Even so, he remarks that 'the illocutionary act is a conventional act: an act done as conforming to a convention' (Austin 1962, 105). So, in order for saying 'I apologise' to count as apologising or saying 'I promise' to count as promising, speakers of the language must take saying those words to be performing those acts. For Austin, the test of whether something is an illocutionary act is whether we could, if we wanted to, perform it simply by saying we're performing it. This means that while apologising, promising, threatening, and asserting are illocutionary acts, swearing is not: we can't swear simply by saying, 'I swear'. (We can, of course, use this form of words to swear in another sense of 'swear'—the sense that has to do with promising or sincerely asserting something.) Something similar is true, as Austin notes, of insinuating and implying, which are not illocutionary acts. We can't successfully insinuate or imply something by saying 'I insinuate' and 'I imply'.

rules; this approach is taken in the UK by Ofcom and the BBFC. The FCC relies on complaints from the public before enforcing rules against broadcasters for the language they use. This focus on the *effects* of swearing suggests that, when we're trying to work out whether someone who swears is doing something wrong (and if so, how wrong), we should focus on their perlocutionary acts. That means that perlocutionary acts like offending, upsetting, alarming, intimidating, and distressing people are relevant to judging what's objectionable about swearing. Illocutionary acts like asserting, threatening, promising, reprimanding, and warning look to be less relevant.

Except . . . not so fast. Things are more complicated. We all know that certain illocutionary acts tend to go hand in hand with certain perlocutionary acts. By *threatening* someone (an illocutionary act), we often *intimidate* them (a perlocutionary act); by *reprimanding* someone (illocutionary), we often *humiliate* them (perlocutionary); by *forgiving* someone (illocutionary), we often *soothe* them (perlocutionary); and so on. Whether or not a speaker performed a certain illocutionary act can make a difference to whether or not it's appropriate to hold the speaker morally responsible—that is, praiseworthy or blameworthy—for the perlocutionary effects on the listener. If your neighbour feels intimidated because you threatened them, it's appropriate to blame you for their feeling intimidated. But if your neighbour feels intimidated merely because you offered to mow their lawn, it's inappropriate to blame you.

Not only do certain perlocutionary effects predictably follow from certain things that we say, but sometimes we say what we say *because* we want to bring about certain perlocutionary effects. I might threaten you *because* I want to intimidate you. I might reprimand you in public *because* I want to humiliate you. Or I might forgive you *because* I want to soothe you. If we're inclined to blame or praise someone for the perlocutionary effects of what they say, we're going to blame or praise them even more in cases where they *intended* those perlocutionary effects than in cases where they merely *foresaw* those effects.

In fact, acting with the intention to bring about certain effects, and whether a person could be expected to predict that their behaviour will have certain effects, is often more important than whether those effects actually occur. The law in many countries prohibits and penalises attempted murder, conspiracy to commit a crime, and dangerous driving even in cases where nobody is harmed. And laws that are used to regulate swearing focus on the *likely* effects of swearing, rather than its actual effects. In the US, fighting words—which, as we've seen, have been taken to encompass certain instances of swearing—are words that 'are *likely* cause a fight'. In the UK, Section 5 of the Public Order Act prohibits 'threatening or abusive words . . . within the hearing or sight of a person *likely* to be caused harassment, alarm or distress thereby'. Breach-of-the-peace legislation, which in several countries has been used to arrest people for swearing, applies in cases not only where someone has actually breached the peace but also in cases of behaviour *likely* to do so.[2] What we intend, and what is likely to follow from our actions, is important regardless of the effects we actually produce.[3]

[2] A few examples: in England and Wales, the leading authority is the 1982 case of *R v. Howell* (QB 416; [1981] 3 All ER 383 (Ct. App.). Australian law has also adopted the conception set out in *Howell.* In Scotland, the relevant legislation is Criminal Justice and Licensing (Scotland) Act §38(1) (2010). In the US—where attempts to prosecute breaches of the peace have occasionally been challenged on the basis that they are unconstitutional—the 1936 Texas case *Head v. State* (96 S.W.2d 981 (Ct. Crim. App.) defines breach of the peace as an act 'which disturbs, or threatens to disturb, the tranquility enjoyed by citizens'.

[3] Why have I focused on the law here, rather than on other sorts of rules around swearing? Simply because the law is a particularly rich source of explicit information about how it's possible to behave objectionably merely by attempting to do something that one fails to do, and by doing something likely to lead to certain effects which don't occur. The reason for the law's detail here is probably practical: criminalising even failed attempts at wrongdoing and behaviour that is likely to lead to certain effects even if it doesn't means that prosecutors are not burdened with having to prove that any negative effects actually occurred, and that people can be intercepted and arrested before they actually do any harm.

Sweary acts

Let's bring this back to swearing. Offending people by swearing is a perlocutionary act, and therefore not entirely within the control of the speaker. But causing offence is an easily predictable effect of swearing—at least for those of us who are fluent in the language we're using, able to understand applicable social norms and adjust our behaviour accordingly, and familiar enough with the culture we're in to grasp whether it's inappropriate to swear in the current social context. (That's not to say that we never misjudge things. Many of us have experienced the awkwardness that can follow an ill-advised *Bollocks!* in the company of people who turn out to be disapproving. Reading the room isn't an exact science.) In general, then, it's appropriate to hold people responsible for causing offence when they swear. And indeed, this is what we do.

However, our informal attitudes towards swearing are one thing; formal rules are another. When it comes to formulating and enforcing rules about swearing, offence is only a very small part of the story. A person who causes offence by swearing, but who doesn't use the strongest swear words, who doesn't swear in the sorts of aggravating ways described in the previous chapter, and who doesn't, in the course of their swearing, also do anything that would be objectionable even without swearing (such as threatening or slandering another person), does something only very mildly objectionable. An example is someone who unthinkingly exclaims 'Shit!' after accidentally dropping food on their lap. Such a person might raise eyebrows if they're in polite company, but punishing them would be inappropriate. It would be comparable to punishing them for other potentially offensive minor infractions of etiquette, like addressing another person in an overfamiliar way or not following a strict dress code. Rules about swearing need to focus on behaviour that's rather more heavyweight than this, which is to say that they need to focus on behaviour that does more than merely cause people to feel offended. That means we need a way to evaluate aspects of sweary behaviour other than what was said and whether anyone was offended.

Here is where Austin's framework is useful. To work out how objectionably a person behaves when they swear, we can ask: what else was the speaker doing, besides swearing? Did they merely mutter 'Oh, bollocks!' to nobody in particular when they used the wrong spoon to add sugar to their tea at the church fundraiser? Or did they swear in a way that expressed disrespect, by doing something like screaming 'Fuck you, Father!' while the vicar was announcing the results of the embroidery contest? If the speaker's swearing expressed disrespect, we can then focus on the perlocutionary effects of the speaker's behaviour to work out how serious a matter it is. What did the speaker do that involved an effect on other people? Perhaps the vicar dropped her tea; perhaps the organist choked on his custard cream; perhaps those around the swearer feared for their safety. Were any of these effects morally concerning—that is, were they negative, undeserved by whoever experienced them, and the sorts of effects that we'd view as significant enough to warrant considering taking action against the speaker even if they hadn't involved swearing? If so, can the speaker reasonably have been expected to foresee that those effects were likely?[4] If so, did the speaker intend to produce those effects?

[4] To keep things relatively simple, I'm glossing over an important issue here. Often, it's appropriate to blame a person who foresees that certain effects of their actions are merely possible, even if not likely. For example, people who drive while drunk are widely viewed as blameworthy even when it's not *likely* (i.e. highly probable) that they will cause any harm by doing so. It matters only that it is *somewhat* probable that they might cause harm. How much risk of negative consequences we're willing to tolerate before blaming someone varies depending on the possible consequences: if those consequences are very bad, we'll want to avoid even a small risk that they might occur.

Were any morally concerning negative effects likely or intended even if they didn't actually arise? These questions—and, admittedly, it's quite a mind-boggling list—help us work out whether the speaker did anything wrong, and if so, how wrong. Importantly, they are questions that we can ask of non-sweary behaviour, too, in trying to work out how objectionable it is. Comparing sweary behaviour with similar non-sweary behaviour can help ensure that we respond proportionately to swearing—in other words, it can help ensure that a person's swearing doesn't lead us to view their behaviour as more objectionable than it actually is.

Now, as I said, this is quite a perplexing range of factors to consider when making judgements about swearing. Thankfully, though, there's a way to simplify it a little. One way involves using our intuitions about non-sweary behaviour to calibrate our judgements about swearing, in order to help ensure that our judgements about swearing do not get knocked off course by the visceral responses we sometimes have to rude words. In addition, we can specify what, at a minimum, must be true of a speaker in order for them to be justifiably judged blameworthy for swearing, in particular. This minimum standard is as follows: it must be the case that it was reasonable to expect the speaker to have foreseen that significant, morally concerning, negative effects on others were likely to follow from their behaviour—regardless of whether any such effects actually materialised. Any speaker who does not meet this condition is not blameworthy for swearing. All this is summarised in the diagram below.

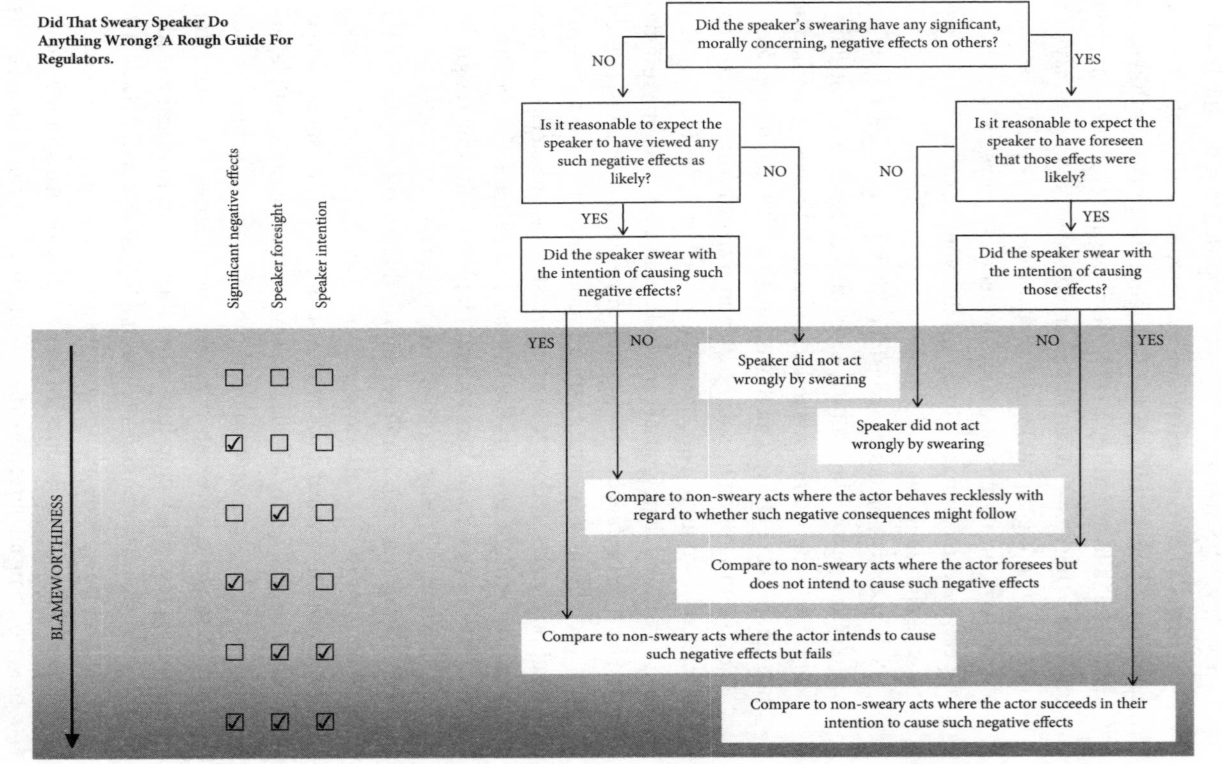
Did That Sweary Speaker Do Anything Wrong? A Rough Guide For Regulators.
Did the speaker's swearing have any significant, morally concerning, negative effects on others?
NO
YES
Is it reasonable to expect the speaker to have viewed any such negative effects as likely?
Is it reasonable to expect the speaker to have foreseen that those effects were likely?
NO
NO
YES
YES
Did the speaker swear with the intention of causing such negative effects?
Did the speaker swear with the intention of causing those effects?
Significant negative effects
Speaker foresight
Speaker intention
YES
NO
NO
YES
Speaker did not act wrongly by swearing
Speaker did not act wrongly by swearing
Compare to non-sweary acts where the actor behaves recklessly with regard to whether such negative consequences might follow
Compare to non-sweary acts where the actor foresees but does not intend to cause such negative effects
Compare to non-sweary acts where the actor intends to cause such negative effects but fails
Compare to non-sweary acts where the actor succeeds in their intention to cause such negative effects
BLAMEWORTHINESS

You might be wondering: if we're supposed to judge the blameworthiness of sweary behaviour by comparing it to non-sweary behaviour, how is this a way of judging the blameworthiness of *swearing* at all? According to this view, swearing looks like merely an aggravating factor: it can make already-objectionable behaviour (like, say, making threats) worse, but without any other objectionable behaviour, it's not objectionable enough to regulate. In this respect, we can compare it to things like volume of speech and aggressive body language.

Let's take a moment to consider this idea of swearing as an aggravating factor. The reality is more nuanced than it might at first seem. Swearing cannot make the difference between whether or not the speaker performs an illocutionary act. Chucking a *fuck* or a *bollocks* into an utterance can't turn it into an order or a question or a threat if it would not otherwise have been an order or a question or a threat, and removing swear words from a warning or a resignation or an acceptance can't stop it being a warning or a resignation or an acceptance. Swearing can, however, alter the mood of our illocutionary acts. It does this by expressing the speaker's emotions and their attitude towards the listener and perhaps also the social context. A person who says to their employer 'I fucking resign', instead of simply 'I resign', not only resigns but also expresses a certain attitude towards their employer and/or their job. By expressing the speaker's attitude in this way, it can intensify the act that the speaker is performing: swearing in the course of threatening someone typically emphasises the threat, making it seem more credible, authentic, and—well, *threatening*. If the illocutionary act in question is objectionable, as threats often are, the addition of swearing can be an aggravating factor. It can, in other words, make an already-objectionable act yet more objectionable. But this is not always the case, and it depends on the context and the relationship between the speaker and the listener. In some cases, swearing in the course of performing an objectionable illocutionary act can indicate to the listener that one is not serious, and so mitigates or cancels rather than aggravates the act. In cases where the illocutionary act in question is not objectionable, mitigating or cancelling it can turn it into something objectionable. The sweary insult in 'I apologise, you shithead' might indicate to the listener that the speaker's apology is insincere, which undermines the reconciliatory effect that apologising typically has, and might make a future reconciliation more difficult. But context is key: in some cases, the same utterance might be *more* reconciliatory than a swear-free apology, because the swearing might inject a welcome bit of levity into an otherwise solemn business. And while swearing may in general lend a sense of urgency to an order, in World War I the familiar, everyday order to 'get your fucking rifles' was recognised as much less grave and urgent than the order to 'get your rifles' (Brophy and Partridge 1930).

The ways in which swearing can affect the mood of illocutionary acts, emphasising some and undermining others, might seem hopelessly complicated. An awareness of the factors that produce these effects helps lend some order to the chaos. We looked at some of those factors in the previous chapter. Considering questions, like *Would this utterance been more or less objectionable if it had been made in a different tone of voice/by a different sort of speaker/to a different sort of listener/accompanied by different body language?* can help us compare and evaluate different cases and isolate whether it was the swearing itself or some other aspect of the behaviour that made the act objectionable.

Things are different with perlocutionary acts. In some cases, swearing might be merely an aggravating factor: a speaker who intimidates another person might intimidate them even more if they swear, and if intimidation is objectionable, it is more so if it is emphasised. But, unlike with illocutionary acts, swearing can make the difference between whether or not certain perlocutionary acts are performed at all. A speaker who intimidates a listener by swearing might not have intimidated them at all had they not sworn. A speaker might, by swearing, fail to persuade a listener who would have been persuaded had the speaker not sworn. And so on. When we're trying to assess how objectionable a speaker's behaviour is when the speaker has sworn in the course of performing a certain perlocutionary act, then, we can make progress by considering questions like *If the speaker had not sworn, would the listener still have been intimidated/distressed/shocked/traumatised by the speaker's behaviour?* and *Had the speaker not sworn, what other behaviours could they have engaged in that would have likely produced similar effects on the listener?* The former sorts of questions will help us work out how much of a contribution the speaker's swearing made to the objectionable nature of the behaviour: if the behaviour would have been about as objectionable even without the swearing, then the swearing is a red herring; if the behaviour would have been much less objectionable without the swearing, then we need to explore why. The latter sort of question is helpful in keeping swearing in perspective: if, for example, aggressive body language would probably have produced similar effects in the listener, then the speaker's swearing looks to be about as objectionable as using certain body language.[5]

What about cases in which swearing is *explicitly* forbidden by the rules—as it is, for example, in many rules governing broadcasting—and in which those who break the rules face punishment? Is swearing more objectionable in cases like this? Well, yes and no. We saw, from the offence escalation story, that there is something objectionable about behaving in a way that one knows to

[5] Though we also need to consider questions about whether the speaker could have been expected to foresee the effects of their behaviour, and whether they intended such effects. It's perhaps plausible to hold that speakers have a greater awareness of the likely effects of their swearing than they do of the likely effects of their body language, and that they have greater control over the former than the latter. For example, the speaker's swearing and being tall are both things that could potentially contribute to a listener's being intimidated by the speaker. However, while we can reasonably expect the speaker to foresee that their swearing is likely to intimidate the listener and to exercise the choice to abstain from swearing in order to avoid intimidating the listener, it might not be reasonable to expect the speaker to foresee that their being tall is likely to intimidate the listener (we're often unaware of exactly how we're perceived by others), and it is certainly not reasonable to expect the speaker to choose not to be so tall.

be disliked—at least, without good reason. The more salient to the listener is the fact that the speaker knows it to be disliked, the more objectionable is the swearing to the listener. If there is an explicit rule against swearing, which it's reasonable to expect the speaker to know about, there's a sense in which this makes the speaker's swearing more objectionable than it would have otherwise been. On the other hand, though, it tends to happen that explicit rules about swearing just formalise what everyone is expected to know anyway. While breaking explicit rules is a new way for a sweary speaker to express their disrespect for those around them, swearing in such a context expresses disrespect even without explicit rules.

Something different applies in cases where there are explicit rules against swearing in contexts where it is otherwise not clear that swearing is inappropriate. Pubs are generally contexts where swearing is tolerated, although some pubs, at some times of day, are more family-oriented, in which case swearing is more likely to be inappropriate. Often, it is difficult for newcomers to distinguish between pubs where swearing is tolerated and those where swearing is not tolerated. Because of that, the management of the latter sorts of pubs sometimes have signs, prominently displayed near the bar, asking customers not to swear. A new customer who walks into a pub where swearing is not tolerated and proceeds to have a sweary conversation behaves objectionably if the pub is one of those that prominently displays signs asking customers not to swear but does not behave objectionably if there is no such sign.

Of course, people break rules for all sorts of reasons, and doing so is not always wrong or bad. Some rules are bad rules. Rosa Parks broke the rules when, in 1955, she refused to give up her seat on an Alabama bus to a white person, but she did nothing wrong. Rules that regulate swearing, like other sorts of rules, should on balance make the world a better place than it would be if there were no such rules. Creating rules that meet this standard is often difficult—and one purpose of the arguments we're looking at here is to try to make that task a little easier.

Beyond speech acts

In comparing sweary and non-sweary objectionable acts, we don't have to stick too closely to Austin's framework. Our lesson from Austin can be: speaking is a way of doing things, some of which relate to the effects of the speaker on others and some of which are predictable ways of bringing about effects on others, and the things we do when we speak can often also be done in other ways. For our purposes, *doing things* can incorporate more than illocutionary and perlocutionary acts. Acts like lying, slandering, insinuating, and insulting are neither illocutionary nor perlocutionary acts, but they are ways in which speakers can produce morally concerning effects, sometimes with foresight or intention.

There's another interesting thing that emerges from reflecting on speech acts: some speech acts can be performed without using words at all. Usually, we use language to make promises (*I promise to . . .*) but sometimes children make promises to each other by 'pinky promising': entwining their pinky fingers. We can issue a warning using words (*Look out!*), with images (think of those warning signs depicting falling rocks), or with a gesture, like holding up a hand. We can intimidate using words, gestures, or—as in *The Godfather*—a horse's head in a bed. It should not come as a surprise, then, that it's possible to swear without using words. In many cultures, holding one's middle finger aloft is regarded as an offensive gesture. Known as 'the bird', 'flipping off', or simply 'the finger', it originated in ancient Rome and Greece, where the cynic philosopher Diogenes is said to have used it (Diogenes Laërtius c. 300, VI.2.34). It means approximately the same thing as *Fuck you!*: the finger is used in roughly the same way as this expression, it is offensive in roughly the same contexts, and it offends for the same reasons (i.e. it expresses disrespect). Like swear words, it has taboo connotations: the gesture has long been taken to represent the penis and to be associated with sexual penetration (Rosewarne 2013, 51ff). Also like swear words, its offensiveness can be explained by offence escalation: it is a gesture that is disliked and known to be disliked, and in light of this, we are offended when people whom we know to understand all this make the gesture at us. At the same time, just like its verbal equivalents, there are contexts where the middle finger can be used in a humourous or even in an affectionate way.

The finger is not the only gesture that can be understood as a non-verbal form of swearing. Others include the V-sign (which resembles a backward 'victory' or 'peace' gesture), used in the UK, Ireland, Australia, and New Zealand, which is a slightly less offensive version of the middle finger; the fist-raising, bicep-slapping gesture known by various names including the *bras d'honneur* and Italian salute; the Greek *moutza* (arm extended, fingers spread, palm facing the person one is addressing, sometimes emphasised by slapping the back of the extended hand with the other hand); the thumbs-up gesture (offensive in Islamic cultures); the 'fig' gesture, used in Turkey and elsewhere (which resembles the hand gesture that, in places including the UK and the US, adults use when pretending to steal children's noses); the gesture used in the US and other cultures to mean *okay* (thumb and index finger making a circle, other fingers extended), which is offensive in Brazil; and the palm-up, index-finger-curling gesture that in some countries is used to beckon, but which is offensive in many Asian countries. These gestures typically have taboo origins, although these origins are often unknown by the people who use the gestures, and sometimes—as in the case of the V-sign—it is unclear what its origins are.[6] They can all be thought of as non-verbal forms of swearing, although the variety of ways in which one can swear with these gestures is more limited than the ways in which one can swear with words. The middle finger is an effective way to express *Fuck you!* but cannot adequately express, say, *Whichever Tory fucklump*

[6] For more on offensive hand gestures, see LeFevre (2011).

decided that British schools must promote 'British values' is an embarrassing fantasist bell-end.

Right then. We have a framework for making sensible decisions about swearing. Where does this leave our gut-feeling judgements about when it's appropriate to feel offended by swearing? Am I trying to convince you that those judgements are wrong? Well, no. But our gut-feeling judgements do leave room for bias, which—if our judgements are allowed to shape formal regulations without any sort of sense-check—could lead to injustice. In the next chapter we'll explore how this might happen, and how we can be on guard against it.

10

Fairer swearers

You might be forgiven for thinking that all this theory about speech acts is a bit much. After all, thinking about what speakers are doing when they swear, as a way to gauge the offensiveness of their swearing, is not a novel idea. Unconsciously, we do this all the time when we form intuitive, gut-feeling judgements about how serious an instance of swearing is. Swearing's power to shock and offend very often means that, when someone swears, we *hear* (rather than infer) the threat they are making, or the anger they are expressing, or the contempt they are conveying. It's not something we need to stop and think about; it's something we perceive directly and unmediated. In this respect, the way in which we pick up on what people are doing when they swear resembles the way in which the philosopher Ludwig Wittgenstein claimed we pick up on how they are feeling. In *Zettel*, he wrote:

> 'We *see* emotion'.—As opposed to what?—We do not see facial contortions and make inferences from them (like a doctor framing a diagnosis) to joy, grief, boredom. We describe a face immediately as sad, radiant, bored, even when we are unable to give any other description of the features.—Grief, one would like to say, is personified in the face. (1970, 225)

Because of this, it might seem that we don't need Austin and his speech acts in order to work out what someone is doing when they swear—whether, for example, one person's *Get the fuck away from me* constitutes a threat, or whether another person's *He's a bit of a cunt* is a warning. What does the framework sketched in the previous chapter add to our existing understanding?

Putting the brakes on bias

Being reflective and explicit about how we translate our gut-feeling judgements about the offensiveness of swearing into explicit claims about what a person was doing when they swore and how that affected the offensiveness of their swearing has great benefits for understanding swearing and responding to it fairly and appropriately. For one thing, it's useful in enabling us to assess and compare the offensiveness of separate instances of swearing. Thinking about what acts the swearer was performing in each case, and how we know, helps us catalogue and compare what (if anything) the swearer did wrong in each case; which in turn gives us a way to work out whether our gut-feeling responses were correct in each case. And sometimes our gut-feeling judgements do get it wrong. They can conceal prejudice and bias, which—if we care about treating people fairly—are important to identify and set aside. For example, there's empirical evidence that Black men tend to be viewed as larger and more threatening than similar-sized white men, especially by white people (Wilson et al. 2017). This means that, if we rely solely on gut-feeling judgements about how offensive swearing is, people are more likely to view swearing as threatening when the swearer is a Black man compared to when the swearer is not a man or not Black. This in turn will lead to Black men being judged (and in some cases punished) more harshly for swearing than other people.

There is evidence of this happening. In the UK, Denzel Cassius Harvey's 2010 conviction (later overturned) for swearing at the police during a drugs search was based on a pretty mild case of swearing. He said, 'Fuck this, man. I ain't been smoking nothing', 'Told you, you wouldn't find fuck all', and (when asked if he had a middle name), 'No, I've already fucking told you'. Apart from swearing repetitively at a police officer, he wasn't *doing* anything objectionable that could have justified his arrest. He wasn't making a threat, defaming anyone, or even uttering an insult. While it's reasonable to view his choice of words as disrespectful—some might say justifiably so, given that he was not carrying any drugs, and given that Black men are disproportionately targeted by the police for on-the-spot drugs searches—any disrespect was expressed indirectly. By contrast, the Conservative MP Andrew Mitchell's act of calling police officers *fucking plebs*—for which he was not arrested, let alone convicted—was a more serious instance of swearing. His use of the word *plebs*—a British slur for the lower classes—expressed his sense of social superiority to the people he addressed, which made this an instance of a more powerful person swearing contemptuously at a less powerful person; something that, as we saw in the previous chapter, aggravates the offensiveness of swearing.

Of course, we can't cure racism and other prejudices just by trying to respond sensibly to swearing. But we can make progress towards fair judgements. If, instead of relying on our gut feelings to compare the offensiveness of different instances of swearing, we identify individual factors that make swearing more or less offensive and which do not refer to swearers' race, gender, accent, or other irrelevant considerations, we help ensure that our judgements are based on relevant considerations.[1] A person whose gut feeling leads them to view a Black man's swearing as more threatening than similar swearing by a white man is more likely to revise their judgement if

[1] What makes a consideration 'irrelevant' in this context? We can refer to broader conceptions of equality and discrimination to answer this question. If an act is offensive, harmful, or otherwise wrong, it is not made more so by the offender's being a member of a certain group based on their ethnicity, gender, religion, sexual orientation, and so on, except when certain features of the act make these considerations relevant. For example, desecrating a religious building is worse when the offender is a member of a group that has historically oppressed followers of the religion in question, and we will see in Chapter 11 that the use of slurs is generally more offensive when the speaker is not a member of the group targeted by the slur.

they reflect on *why* they found the former more threatening than the latter than if they don't reflect at all.

Consciously reflecting on the basis of our judgements about swearing is a good way for us as individuals to ensure that we respond fairly and appropriately to swearing, but doing so is especially important for organisations that make and enforce regulations about swearing—the police, broadcasters, sports organisations, and so on—since such organisations have greater power than the average person to punish and censor, and they typically face a greater demand to justify their decisions about swearing, especially in novel or unusual cases. There's a spectrum of ways in which we can engage in the right sort of reflection on swearing. At one end, for organisations that punish or censor swearing, making and justifying judgements about the offensiveness of swearing with reference to an explicit checklist of exacerbating factors will help in promoting fairness, consistency, and transparency. Such a checklist could include the sort of things that we've discussed from Chapter 6 onwards. At the other end of the spectrum, people who simply want to understand and question their own attitudes to swearing can systematically interrogate their judgements by considering why they responded to a certain instance of swearing in the way they did, and whether they might have responded differently if the person swearing had been a different gender, social class, race, and so on. Midway along the spectrum we might find parents who want to encourage their children to take a sensible, curious attitude to swearing, and who approach this task by discussing things like context, tone of voice, relationship between the speaker and listener, and what else the speaker was doing besides swearing.

Educating our intuition

Questioning and reflecting on our gut-feeling judgements before we act on them is not always practical or sensible—if we're alarmed by a gunshot unexpectedly and at close range it's best to dive for cover immediately rather than wait until we've reflected on whether the sound indicates a genuine threat—but when there's no great urgency to act on our judgement, and especially when getting it wrong can result in unfairness to others, we can and should reflect before acting. As we reflect on, correct, and discuss our gut-feeling judgements, we train those judgements to be more accurate.

Social psychologist Jonathan Haidt's 'social intuitionist' model of moral judgement provides a framework that can help us understand how this might happen. He believes that the moral judgements we make are not the outputs of a process of reasoning. According to this view, we come to believe things like *murder is wrong* and *equality is good* without the help of our rational faculties. This idea strikes us as strange; after all, we tend to think of beliefs like these as ones that can be defended with reason, and we like to think that we hold them *because* they can be defended with reason. However, Haidt believes that although moral reasoning does have a role in moral judgement, it's not quite the role we think. He has argued that our moral judgements are usually formed on the basis of our intuition; that is, on the basis of 'quick, automatic evaluations' in a process that is 'more akin to perception' than 'rational reflection' (Haidt 2001, 814). Moral intuitions can be emotional: they include the visceral horror we feel when we hear accounts of the Holocaust and the disgust that we feel in response to reports of sexual abuse. Moral reasoning comes into the picture only when we're asked by others to explain or defend our moral judgements, or when we're trying to persuade someone else to change their beliefs about a moral issue. So, our moral judgement about a particular issue—that murder is wrong, say—comes *before* our moral reasoning about this issue. The judgement is not caused by the reasoning. We start to reason about it only when someone asks us, 'Hey, why do you think murder is wrong?', or when we encounter someone who insists that there's nothing wrong with murder, and when as a result we feel the need to convince them otherwise.

While Haidt (2001) believes that 'moral reasoning is rarely the direct cause of moral judgement' (815), it influences our moral judgements indirectly. The moral intuitions that we have are shaped, in part, by our own and other people's reasoning about them. As a result, the moral intuitions that we start out with can change following reflection and discussion with others, which in turn leads our moral judgements to change. We often see this happening at a societal level—take, for example, the increasing recognition of same-sex marriage in societies around the world over the last decade or so. We could tell the following social intuitionist story about this. Same-sex marriage was initially prohibited because of a widespread intuition that homosexuality was wrong. But arguments against discrimination on the basis of sexual orientation have led many people to reflect on, question, and eventually reject their intuitive aversion to homosexuality—and at a societal level this has been reflected in measures like recognising same-sex marriage. Here, we have a change in moral judgement—specifically, a rejection of the judgement that homosexuality is wrong—on the basis of moral reasoning. But according to the social intuitionist story, the change in moral judgement was not a direct result of the moral reasoning. The change was mediated by intuition: moral reasoning about homosexuality led to changes in people's moral intuitions about it, and this in turn led people (and, eventually, societies) to change their moral judgements about homosexuality.

Sweary self-improvement

Let's link this back to swearing. Not everyone agrees with Haidt's social intuitionism about moral judgement, in part because of how general it is. It's a bold move to claim that *all* moral judgement happens in this way; something that Haidt acknowledges by emphasising that he does not present his model as 'an established fact' (Haidt 2001, 815). Even so, it fits the way in which we generally respond to swearing extremely well. Swearing's seemingly magical capacity to shock us makes us especially likely to form moral intuitions about its wrongness. After all, when we find ourselves judging that a fellow motorist acted wrongly when they screamed at us to 'Get the fuck out of my way!', our judgement is not usually the outcome of a dispassionate process of moral deliberation. Rather, we simply perceive, without needing to think about it, that this person wronged us. The immediacy of this sort of judgement, as we have seen, means that bias can creep in unnoticed, with the result that some people may unjustly be judged more harshly than others for comparable acts of swearing. But Haidt's social intuitionism offers hope here. If he's right, then although our moral judgements about swearing may be intuitive and immediate, there is scope to influence them with reason and to make them consistent and fair. This is something we can do by explicitly reflecting on what's wrong with swearing, and by examining and questioning the factors that underlie our moral judgements about it.

The upshot of this is that, contrary to first impressions, we do need to theorise about swearing—not because we're incapable of forming moral judgements about swearing without reflecting on what lies behind those judgements but because it's important that our judgements about swearing should be sensible, consistent, and fair. If you found yourself rolling your eyes while reading about the FCC's response to Bono's *fucking brilliant* in Chapter 8, or siding with Ken Loach when he complained about the view taken by the BBFC of swearing in his films, this is something you can help with right now. Chat with friends about your responses to swearing. Be curious about how you (and they) respond as you do. Be open to questioning and, if necessary, revising your thinking about it. Organisations that regulate swearing tend to take their lead from the public, and the more sensible the public is, the better the rules will have to be.

Ensuring a fair and just approach to dealing with offensive language isn't just about reacting appropriately to it, however. Sometimes the language itself, and the act of using it, propagates prejudice and oppression. We're going to look at this in the next chapter, where we consider how the norms of swearing compare to those of slurs.

11
Swears vs. slurs

Suppose you're one of those people who think of themselves as pretty liberal about swearing. You don't see the fuss about the odd swear dropped into conversation, and you're certainly not going to clutch your pearls and fret about how the world is going to hell in a handcart simply because it's possible to find the odd uncensored *shit* on the internet. People need to calm the fuck down about swearing, right? But you are likely to react differently to other forms of offensive language. Especially if you're one of these liberal sorts, the thought of using a slur is apt to wipe the smile off your face pretty quickly. Swears are a bit of fun; slurs are horrifying. What's the difference?

We've touched on slurs and how they compare and contrast with swears a few times over the previous chapters. There are some similarities between swearing and slurs. Both involve taboo language—in some sense, they're words that we *ought not* to use. Both are also forms of language that often convey the speaker's disrespect. Both are tolerated—or even welcomed—in some contexts, and condemned (sometimes strongly) in others. Despite these similarities, there are important differences too. They attain their power to offend in different ways. The sort of offence they cause is different. And they're different morally, not just in degree but in kind. Slurring is a more serious matter than swearing. Let's take a closer look.

The journey to offensiveness

Swear words, as we've seen, come to be offensive via offence escalation. Offence escalation plays a different, and relatively minor, role in how slurs come to be offensive. Generally speaking, offence escalation isn't at all necessary for slurs to become offensive.

As a case study, let's take what is probably the most notorious English-language slur: the n-word. (I'm going to avoid writing it out in full, for reasons we'll explore in Chapter 13.) This word is derived, via Spanish and French, from the Latin word for *black*. Over the centuries, it has had a variety of uses, not all of them negative. The Oxford English Dictionary lists 1577 as the earliest written use of it, and 1775 as the earliest written use 'as a hostile term of abuse or contempt'. Exactly how and when it became a slur is unclear, but for our purposes it will suffice to make two observations. First, it has long been widely used by white people to talk about Black people in a disrespectful and contemptuous way. Second, much of its use in this way predates widespread recognition by white people that Black people are not deserving of disrespect and contempt on account of their being Black. As a result, while it's a taboo word today, this wasn't always the case. For many years, it could be used in polite conversations among white people without causing anyone to recoil. The view that there is anything wrong with the word follows on the heels of advances in the battle for universal recognition that Black people are equal to non-Black people. This battle is a very long way from being over, and even the most basic advances in this area are still very recent: in the US, slavery legally ended with the Thirteenth Amendment in 1865, and legally enforced racial segregation ended only in 1964 with the Civil Rights Act.

Was the n-word, used by white people 'as a hostile term of abuse or contempt', *offensive* in the years before it became widely recognised that Black people are equal to non-Black people? Was it offensive before it became widely dispreferred? Was it a slur in those years? Is there anything wrong with using it today 'as a hostile term of abuse or contempt' in a context where one can be sure that nobody who hears it is going to feel offended by it—as might happen if, for example, a white supremacist who lives in his parents' soundproofed basement invites some fellow white supremacists to their home for an n-word-riddled discussion about politics? The answer to all of these questions is *yes*, and the same applies to other slurs too.

Before going on to take a look at why the answer to these questions is *yes*, let's pause to note that we've hit upon some important differences between swears and slurs. Swears, unlike slurs, are not hostile terms of abuse or contempt about members of a particular group. We can certainly swear (or, for that matter, use neutral terms) in a way that is hostile, abusive, and contemptuous, but swearing doesn't have to be hostile, abusive, or contemptuous, and indeed much swearing doesn't fall into any of these categories. Swears, to count as swears, must be widely dispreferred; slurs need not be widely dispreferred. Swears, unlike slurs, are not offensive words before they become widely dispreferred. And while there's nothing wrong with swearing in a context where one can be sure that nobody who hears it is going to feel offended by it, slurs are offensive regardless of whether anyone feels offended.

We can make sense of some of these differences between swears and slurs by noting that they are offensive in subtly different ways. Recall, from Chapter 3, Feinberg's two different senses of *offence*. In one sense, something is offensive simply if someone *feels* offended by it. In the other sense—'wrongful offence'—something is offensive when, among other things, it involves wrongdoing. It's possible for something to be offensive in one sense without being offensive in the other. For example, homosexuality is offensive in the sense that there are some people who *feel* offended by it, but it does not itself involve any wrongdoing. And, conversely, a group of Nazis waving the Hakenkreuz (Nazi flag) while marching through what they know to be a predominantly Jewish neighbourhood does something wrong, even if—because nobody happens to see or hear about the march—nobody *feels* offended.[1] We might say that people who are offended in the first case aren't justified or entitled to feel offended; in the second case, we might say that *had* anyone ended up feeling offended, they would have been justified or entitled to feel offended.

How does this relate to swearing and slurs? Well, the *feeling* of offence is an important part of how swear words become offensive. If nobody cares one way or the other whether a particular word is used in their company, then that word can't develop into a swear word. According to offence escalation, to become a swear word, a word needs to start off by being disliked. Once a word has become a swear word, it's important that it retains its power to cause people to feel offended—not in all contexts, but in polite contexts. If it loses that power, it's no longer a swear word. Despite the centrality of the *feeling* of offence to swearing, wrongful offence is relevant too, as we saw in Chapter 4. If a speaker knows that swearing in the company of a particular listener is going to cause that listener to feel offended, then the speaker does something wrong by swearing in that listener's company without good reason, since they fail to treat the listener with respect.

[1] I'm drawing here on National Socialist Party of America v. Village of Skokie, 432 U.S. 43 (1977); a Supreme Court ruling that ultimately resulted in the Illinois Appellate Court deciding that displaying the Hakenkreuz is not protected by the First Amendment. I'm using the term *Hakenkreuz* instead of the more common *swastika* because, despite the negative connotations that the latter term has attained in the West, it is derived from Sanskrit, and the term and the symbol to which it refers have positive connotations throughout much of Asia. For thousands of years the swastika has been, and continues to be, a sacred symbol in several Asian religions including Hinduism, Jainism, and Buddhism. *Hakenkreuz* ('hooked cross') is the term used by Hitler in his description of the design of the flag in *Main Kampf.* It is capitalised here simply because it is a German noun, and in German all nouns are capitalised. I am grateful to Indu Viswanathan for talking through with me how I can best refer to the Nazi flag in a way that does not contribute to promoting an association between Nazism and those Asian religions and cultures for whom the swastika is sacred.

Slurs and the feeling of offence

The offensiveness of slurs does not depend on their producing a feeling of offence. They are offensive because they express contempt and disrespect towards members of a particular group simply for being members of that group. What's more, the most powerfully offensive (in both senses of *offensive*) slurs target groups that are oppressed, or that have been oppressed in fairly recent history: ethnic and religious minorities, women, LGBTQ + people, people with disabilities, poor people, and so on. There are slurs for dominant and non-oppressed groups, but they are milder. You can slur white people with *honky*, but it doesn't have anything like the bite of the n-word. There are more slur terms for women than there are for men—and, notably, the most offensive ways of slurring men don't express contempt and disrespect towards them on account of being men but rather by suggesting that they belong to some oppressed group (gays, women, people with disabilities, etc.) (Saucier et al. 2015). The 'always punch up, never punch down' tradition in comedy is relevant here: the empowered and privileged are fair game; the disempowered and oppressed are not. Slurs are part of the arsenal of oppressors, which makes slurring members of more vulnerable groups especially objectionable.

By expressing an attitude of contempt and disrespect towards members of an oppressed group—and expressing it in a way that others recognise as contemptuous and disrespectful, such as by using a slur—one contributes to the continued oppression of that group. This makes slurs offensive even if nobody *feels* offended by their use. And indeed, it's often the case that slurs develop in contexts where their use does not cause people to feel offended. The n-word began to be used as a term that expressed contempt and disrespect for Black people at a time and in a culture where expressing racist views was much more widely accepted than it is today. And it was widely accepted precisely because of the oppression of Black people, whose views about the word were ignored, if they dared voice them at all. As a result, using the word was less likely to cause people to *feel* offended then compared to now. Linguist John McWhorter, writing in *The New York Times*, reflects on this change with reference to the children's rhyme, 'Eeny, meeny', which today tends to include the word *tiger*—historically pronounced *tigger*—in place of the n-word. McWhorter remarks:

> [T]he original version of the 'Eeny, meeny' doggerel is a window into how brutally casual the usage of '[n-word]' once was, happily trilled even by children at play. For eons, it was ordinary white people's equivalent of today's 'African-American'. (McWhorter 2021. The n-word appears in full in the original.)

These reflections help us to make sense of the idea that (white) racists do something wrong when they use the n-word to talk about Black people, even when they do so in a private gathering where nobody who is likely to feel offended witnesses what's going on. This way of using the n-word might be inoffensive in the sense that it doesn't cause anyone to *feel* offended, but it's offensive in the sense that Black people are wronged by the expression and acceptance of the attitudes that are expressed, accepted, and encouraged in this context.

It's pretty obvious how it's possible for the n-word to be used during a private gathering of white racists without causing anyone to feel offended, but it's common to hear people express a stronger claim than this. It's common to hear people remark that certain slurs *used to* be inoffensive but at some point *became* offensive. Sometimes this observation is expressed as a complaint: 'You can't say anything these days', 'Freedom of speech is under threat', 'People are too quick to get offended nowadays', and so on. The thought here seems to be that it used to be possible to use certain slurs without *anyone* feeling offended, and that those who are offended by slurs are unreasonable.

The thing is, this isn't quite true. What people are noticing when they say things like this is that it's more common to encounter complaints about slurs than it was in the past. An important couple of reasons for this is that more people today recognise that members of oppressed groups are wronged when they are treated with contempt, and that the often slow and incomplete journey out of oppression that the members of those groups are making means that their views and perspectives are expressed and heard in a way that they weren't in the past. The teacher and writer Paul Hartzer identifies this phenomenon in an article criticising *The Simpsons* creator Matt Groening's dismissive response to controversy over Apu Nahasapeemapetilon, the show's sole recurring Indian character, who is portrayed in an unflattering, stereotypical way. Asked in a 2018 interview with *USA Today* if he had any thoughts on criticism of Apu, Groening replied, 'Not really . . . people love to pretend they're offended' (Keveney 2018). Responding to this remark, Hartzer wrote:

> We haven't really reached a point in society where Apu is suddenly offensive. We've reached a point in society where we have a high enough density of celebrities from the Indian subcontinent that their voices can be heard. . . . Some people do love to pretend they're offended, Mr. Groening, but at the same time, people who are powerless and feeling offended have learned to just smile and take it. Being confused and dismissive about that is just more punching down. (Hartzer 2018)

When white people claim that the n-word used to be inoffensive—or that slurs against gays, women, people with disabilities, poor people, and so on used to be inoffensive—what they generally mean is that members of dominant groups used to be able to use these words without anyone complaining, and if anyone else was offended, the hegemony of the dominant group's view of the world ensured that those divergent views remained largely unvoiced, or if voiced, largely unheard.

What's our lesson from these reflections on the offensiveness of slurs? Well, in short, slurs are not offensive in quite the same way that swearing is offensive. It's easier to make sense of the view that slurs can be offensive even when they don't cause anyone to feel offended than it is to make sense of the analogous view about swear words. And while swearing can, like slurring, express disrespect, only slurs tap into and reinforce a subtle network of beliefs about which groups in society are superior to which other groups.[2] This means that slurring oppressed groups contributes to their oppression. Because of this, when it comes to slurs that target oppressed groups and speakers who do not belong to those groups, using slurs is always morally wrong.

Becoming offensive, becoming inoffensive

We've seen that even the worst sorts of slurs could, in the past, be used without causing a widespread feeling of offence. Are there offensive slurs in use today whose offensiveness as slurs we don't even notice because the contemptuous attitudes we use them to express don't cause people to feel offended, or because the views of those who are offended by them are so oppressed that their offence passes unheard in society?[3] Undoubtedly. We are more enlightened today

[2] Robin Jeshion describes how this happens: 'Attitudes of contempt towards others do not *in and of themselves* compel a sense of self-satisfaction or superiority on the part of the contemnor. Yet because of contempt's evaluative qualities, it easily stimulates and encourages such reflexive attitudes. When attitudes of contempt towards particular targets or groups are shared and are common knowledge, they naturally spawn shared identities amongst the contemnors *as superior*' (Jeshion 2018, 94).

[3] Note that what I *don't* have in mind here are cases where a well-intentioned person, who does not hold contemptuous attitudes towards an oppressed group, uses a word that they do not realise is a slur. This sort of case made the news in 2022 when the American singer-songwriter Lizzo released a song, 'GRRRLS', whose lyrics featured a word that is a well-known ableist slur in the UK but is not regarded as a slur in the US. In the controversy that followed, Lizzo changed the lyrics and issued a statement acknowledging the 'harmful word' and emphasising her opposition to 'derogatory language' (Lizzo 2022).

about the offensiveness of certain slurs than previous generations were, but there is still progress to make. There are some slurs that, only a few years ago, could be used without causing a widespread feeling of offence but whose use increasingly is recognised as offensive. An example is *whore*, a word that has long been recognised as a contemptuous way to refer to certain types of sex worker but has only recently started to be viewed as an offensive slur. (More precisely, whereas *whore* has long been a word to avoid in polite company, any offence its use caused was *because* of contemptuous attitudes toward sex workers—a group of people regarded with such contempt that they were deemed unfit for discussion in polite company—rather than because sex workers were thought to be undeserving of contempt.) The term *sex worker*—coined by sex worker and activist Carol Leigh in 1978—has become the acceptable term (Leigh 1978).

It is interesting to note the change in attitudes that underlie this change in views about what counts as appropriate language. *Whore* expresses contempt; *sex worker* does not. It's not that those who hear *whore* without feeling offended don't notice that it expresses contempt; rather, they notice the contempt but do not object to it, because they believe that it's appropriate to express contempt to those to whom the word refers. The move to *sex worker* as the preferred term goes hand in hand with a growing awareness that women who have sex in exchange for money are not deserving of contempt, and that speaking contemptuously of them is offensive. There are other slur terms that can still be used without causing a widespread feeling of offence but which we can expect—like *whore*—to become increasingly recognised as unacceptable as more and more people come to see that they express inappropriate contempt for certain groups. Some examples are *wino*, *hobo*, and *fatso*, which refer respectively to alcoholics, homeless people, and fat people. These are

Despite using a slur, Lizzo did not hold contemptuous attitudes towards people with disabilities.

words whose use causes some people to feel offended, but by no means most people. The process happens in the other direction, too: what were once slurs can become benign and inoffensive. *Tory* and *limey* were once slurs, but have—as Luvell Anderson and Ernie Lepore put it—'lost their offensive intensity' (Anderson and Lepore 2013, 20).

By contrast, while the offensiveness of swear words can change over time, and while there are perhaps words we use inoffensively today which will, in the future, develop into swear words, there's no sense in which the swear words of the future are *already* offensive but we just don't realise that yet.

An important difference between swearing and slurring is that the offensiveness of slurs is not context-dependent in the same way that the offensiveness of swearing is. While there are many contexts in which one can swear inoffensively, slurring oppressed groups is almost always offensive. Almost, but not always. The offensiveness of slur words depends on who is using them. These words can often be used inoffensively, or even positively, by members of the group targeted by the slur. This is called *reappropriation*. Many Black people use the n-word inoffensively—not to slur their fellow Black people, but to address each other in a spirit of camaraderie, or just as a neutral term. By contrast, people who are not Black are mostly unable to use the n-word in this way. Something similar is true for many other slurs: it's possible for members of the target group to use the term inoffensively, but much harder for people outside the target group to do so. Why is this?

Luvell Anderson uses the concept of a *community of practice* to explain this. A community of practice is a group of people with a common set of interests and goals, who end up doing things in a particular way—examples are 'bowling teams, book clubs, crack houses, and friendship groups' (Anderson 2018, 19, paraphrasing Eckert 2006). Around the world, there are various communities of practice defined by, among other things, race. Anderson tells us that 'a characterisation of the African American speech community will include a unifying experience or set of experiences and distinctive patterns of language use' (Anderson 2018, 20). The same is true of Black people living outside the US. Within the community, Anderson tells us, there developed a practice of 'reappropriating a signature verbal tool of abuse as a mechanism for expressing solidarity. And because the use had this function, it was important to tie appropriate use of the expression to the having of a certain insider status' (Anderson 2018, 20). This means that membership of the right community of practice—which tends to require being Black—is necessary for being able to use the n-word in an inoffensive way. Something similar is true for other slurs that are reappropriated and used inoffensively by members of the target group but remain offensive in the mouths of those outside that group.

Some slurs are so successfully reappropriated that it becomes possible for people outside the target group to use them inoffensively, and the original derogatory connotations become so comprehensively replaced by benign or affirming connotations that it can be difficult to use the slur in an insulting way. *Queer* is an example of this. What was once a slur against non-heterosexual people has become so thoroughly reclaimed by the targeted communities that people outside these communities can use it as a neutral term—as demonstrated by the fact that there are academic disciplines (and university departments devoted to studying them) with names like *queer studies* and *queer history*. To use the term *queer* as an insult, a speaker would need to signal that they understand the word in its archaic sense, which they could perhaps do if other attitudes that they expressed were aligned with using the word in that way. But even so, we could expect the word to lack much of the punch that it once had.

Efforts to reappropriate slurs are controversial within the target group. Oprah Winfrey is vocal about her opposition to the n-word: she believes that nobody should use it, regardless of their race and whether or not they are attempting to reappropriate it. In a 2017 interview with *Access Hollywood*, she referred to a photograph of a Black family witnessing a lynching that is being cheered on by a white mob. She said:

> I always think of that family. I actually had this conversation with Jay-Z, when he was saying, 'We can take the power back, we can take the power out of the word. We're changing the power'. I go, 'You will *never* change it for that family. You will never change it for whom it was the last word they heard when they were hung or they were dismembered or they were degraded'. (Quoted in Todd 2017)

Russell Simmons, founder of the hip-hop record label Def Jam, and the British poet Dean Atta are among those Black people who are also opposed to reappropriation of the n-word (Wyatt 2015; Atta 2013). Among members of the group targeted by a slur, the offensiveness of reappropriated uses of the slur more closely resembles a swear word than a slur. Reappropriated uses of a slur by members of the target group are not offensive in the way that the slur is offensive in the mouths of non-members. Those reappropriated uses do not denigrate the target group in the way that regular uses do.[4] Despite this, members of the target group who oppose reappropriated uses of a slur will dislike hearing such uses and may feel offended by them. Such members will be more offended if the reappropriated slur is uttered by a speaker who knows that they (the listener) dislike even reappropriated uses of the slur than if it is uttered by a speaker who does not realise that their listener dislikes reappropriated uses. This is because the listener may take the speaker's decision to go ahead and utter the slur despite knowing that the listener dislikes

[4] Many people who are opposed to reappropriated uses of slurs might disagree with this, depending on their reasons for opposing reappropriation. But I'm going to take it for granted nevertheless. In doing so, I follow the thinking of many oppressed people who have, throughout history, attempted to reappropriate slurs that were used to denigrate them; I also follow the thinking of a great many writers on this topic, including Luvell Anderson (2018), Geneva Smitherman (2006), and Claudia Bianchi (2014).

it to indicate the speaker's disregard of the listener, which the listener resents. This resembles the offence escalation account of what makes swearing offensive. Reappropriated uses of slurs between members of the targeted group can, then, end up being offensive in a manner that more closely resembles offensive swearing than slurring.

Slurs, oppression, and desert

Just as some swear words are more offensive than others, some slurs are more offensive than others. Slurs that target oppressed groups tend to be regarded as more offensive than those that target groups that are not oppressed. *Honky*—a slur term for white people—is less powerful than the n-word. But why? And, should we feel free to use slurs, just as long as we stick to those that target non-oppressed groups? I think that there is a clear sense in which slurs against non-oppressed groups are less offensive than those against oppressed groups. Part of what makes slurring oppressed groups wrong is that by doing so one contributes to the oppression of members of that group; so, if the group is not oppressed then slurring them can't be a way of contributing to its members' oppression. Even so, slurs against non-oppressed groups can be offensive even without an obvious sense in which the members of that group are (or have been) oppressed. There are slur terms for various nationalities, including Germans, Italians, French, Spanish, and British, none of which picks out an obviously oppressed group.[5] These terms are not quite as offensive as the n-word because, unlike

[5] Except, perhaps, *foreigner*: using nationality-focused slurs constitutes xenophobia, and foreigners are often oppressed when living abroad. But this is a fairly abstract and context-relative way of thinking about oppression, and one that applies to all of us: we are all foreigners when we are abroad. Being German (or Italian, or French, or Spanish, or British) is not a way of being a member of an oppressed group in the clear and obvious way that being Black, gay, transgender, or disabled is.

the n-word, there is scope for people outside the target group to use them non-contemptuously, or even affectionately: it's easier to imagine a person who is not German affectionately and inoffensively calling their German friend a *Kraut* than it is to imagine a non-Black person affectionately and inoffensively calling their Black friend the n-word.

Finally, some slurs derogate groups that deserve to be derogated. Robin Jeshion gives *pimp* as an example: 'individuals who exploit women and children by selling their bodies to others for sex are, and are widely seen as, deserving of contempt for that exploitation' (Jeshion 2013, 237). As a result, using *pimp* to refer derisively to a pimp is not likely to offend anyone.[6] Other examples are *paedo* (an adult who has sex with children) and *despot* (a person who uses their power to oppress others). There's an obvious sense in which using these terms contemptuously is inoffensive, or even appropriate; indeed, perhaps we *ought* to be contemptuous of these groups, in which case refusing to express contempt of them is offensive.

But even while some people might be deserving of the contempt that slurring them expresses, we should be wary of condoning the use of slurs in these cases and leaving it up to individuals to make a judgement about whether or not the person they are about to slur is a deserving target. One reason for such caution is that sometimes progress in improving conditions for oppressed groups can lead people from outside those groups to view people in those groups as no longer oppressed, or even as having gained too much power—a phenomenon captured in the oft-seen expression of unknown origins, 'when you're accustomed to privilege, equality feels like oppression' (Quote Investigator 2016). A 2020 survey of young people in the UK found that half of men between the ages of 16 and 24 believe that 'feminism has gone too far' (Carter 2020), despite the fact

[6] Although, of course, using 'pimp' to refer to someone who is not a pimp *is* likely to cause offence.

that women in the country remain underpaid compared to men, that women remain underrepresented in politics, and that gender parity in the UK has been getting worse in recent years (World Economic Forum 2019). And sometimes the world's most powerful and privileged people are not beyond presenting themselves as oppressed: former US president Donald Trump was fond of claiming to be persecuted by the press, and in 2020 he even claimed during a Fox News interview that he was treated worse than Abraham Lincoln, whose presidential term ended in 1865 with his assassination (Fox News 2020). Former First Lady Melania Trump, too, claimed during a 2018 ABC interview to be 'the most bullied person in the world' (Bruggeman 2018). Condoning the use of slurs against non-oppressed groups risks encouraging the slurring of oppressed groups by people who want to claim falsely that those groups are not oppressed, a consequence that would harm members of oppressed groups. Better—because safer and simpler—to avoid slurs completely.

Comparing slurs

Different slurs, then, are differently offensive. This is not just a matter of whether the target group is oppressed or whether the group deserves contempt, but—as Robin Jeshion has argued (Jeshion 2013)—for a range of other reasons too. These reasons include the semantics (roughly, the meaning) of the words themselves, how hearing the slur affects members of the target group, what sort of stereotypes exist about the group, how intense is bigotry about the group, whether the speaker is a member of a group responsible for the oppression of the slurred group, and perhaps also how much public awareness there is of individual members of the target group *as* individuals rather than merely—and fungibly—as members of the group. But facts about the targeted group (and how its members are perceived and treated in society) are not the only things that affect the offensiveness of a slur against that group. After all, there are often multiple ways of slurring a particular group, and some of those ways are more offensive than others. The n-word, for example, is more offensive than other ways of slurring Black people. How can different slurs for the same group vary in how objectionable they are?

I think the answer here has to do with the ways in which speakers and listeners understand each other, and how those ways feed into the meaning of the terms themselves. Consider an analogy. Suppose that Leticia, while speaking to Yoshiaki, derogates his intelligence. There are various ways she can do this, some of which are more contemptuous than others. *You're certainly not the brightest star in the sky, Yoshiaki* is pretty subtle compared to something like *Yoshiaki, you're really not very smart*, which in turn is less intense than *Yoshiaki, you truly are an absolute moron*. Suppose that there is no chance that Leticia is speaking affectionately or bantering with Yoshiaki. What explains the differing intensities of the three expressions we've considered?

One possibility is that each ascribes a different degree of stupidity to Yoshiaki. In the first, Leticia metaphorically tells Yoshiaki that he is not the world's most intelligent person, which is compatible with him nevertheless being extremely intelligent; the second tells Yoshiaki that he is not *very* intelligent, which still leaves scope for him being *pretty* intelligent; and the third categorises Yoshiaki as the most stupid kind of person. But, really, this isn't the way that anyone would use these expressions. People don't use any of these expressions about someone whom they think is pretty intelligent. When we hear someone say, 'You're certainly not the brightest star in the sky', we don't interpret the speaker literally as asserting merely that the person they're addressing is not the world's most intelligent person. Instead, we think something like, 'The fact that Leticia has said this at all shows that she thinks Yoshiaki is really stupid'. We'd think something similar were we to hear Leticia say, 'Yoshiaki, you truly are an absolute moron'—but in that case, we'd also think something like, 'The fact that Leticia has made this point so explicitly and emphatically shows that she's really contemptuous of Yoshiaki because of his low intelligence'. What's more, assuming that Leticia is a competent speaker of the language she's using, she will anticipate that Yoshiaki (and anyone witnessing her words) will have these reactions to her words, and this will be a factor in her choices about how to express herself. So, if she chooses to say, 'Yoshiaki, you truly are an absolute moron' rather than 'You're certainly not the brightest star in the sky, Yoshiaki', she recognises that her listeners will take her to be especially contemptuous of Yoshiaki—and her listeners, also being competent speakers, will recognise that Leticia has chosen her words in the knowledge that she will be taken to be especially contemptuous of Yoshiaki, which in turn makes Leticia's contempt all the more emphatic. In the other direction, if Leticia chooses to say, 'You're certainly not the brightest star in the sky, Yoshiaki', when she *could* have chosen a more forceful way of expressing herself, her listeners will take her to be somewhat measured in her negative evaluation of Yoshiaki.

Something similar explains why different slur terms for a particular target group can vary in their offensiveness. At some point, the n-word became associated with an emphatically contemptuous attitude towards Black people: for competent speakers of the language, the word calls to mind the vicious disregard that slave masters had for the Black people they exploited and oppressed, and anyone using the expression today vividly expresses that attitude. For non-Black speakers, using the word while knowing its connotations, knowing that one's listeners know its connotations, and knowing that one's listeners know that one knows its connotations (and so on) involves emphatically expressing contempt for Black people.

Other slurs for Black people, while also contemptuous, do not have quite the same connotations as the n-word. *Spook*, for example, does not have the same offensive force as the n-word—which is perhaps unsurprising given its history. Its use to refer to Black people can be traced back to World War II, when segregation in the US presented obstacles for Black people wanting to enlist in the military. Black people who joined the US Air Force trained at Tuskegee Institute in Alabama. These Tuskegee airmen referred to themselves as 'Spookwaffe', after *Luftwaffe*, the German term for the air force (Motley 1975; Williams 1992; Donnella 2017). Despite initially being used as a term of solidarity among Black people, *spook* acquired derogatory connotations when used by non-Black speakers to refer to Black people. Its status as a slur term is now widely recognised, and when the US store Target offered a 'Spook Drop Parachuters' toy in the run-up to Halloween in 2010—packs of black figurines attached to orange parachutes—the resulting public outcry led Target to apologise and withdraw the toy from sale (Mendoza-Denton 2010).

Spook and other slur terms for Black people are less well-known and less powerful than the n-word. We can ascribe this to their lacking the powerfully negative connotations that the n-word is widely recognised to have. In addition, when we encounter a racist speaker who derogates Black people using *spook* or some other slur term other than the n-word, it's reasonable to interpret their choice of word to indicate that although they are contemptuous of Black people, they wish to stop short of expressing their contempt as emphatically as they would do were they to use the n-word. It's reasonable, too, to expect speakers to anticipate that their listeners will interpret their word choice in this way, and to expect listeners to realise that speakers anticipate that their listeners will interpret their word choice in this way, and so on. This mutual, unspoken understanding between speakers and listeners serves to underline the distance—in terms of the offensive power with which a speaker expresses contempt—between the n-word and other slur terms: by choosing a slur that is less offensive than the n-word, a speaker tempers the racism that they express, which draws attention to the fact that their chosen slur is less offensive than the n-word, which in turn cements its status as a less offensive term. We can expect this to work in the other direction, too. Just as a racist speaker's using a slur other than the n-word to derogate Black people highlights that they choose not to express their racism as emphatically as they could; so too does their using the n-word highlight that despite the availability of milder slur terms for Black people, the speaker has chosen to express their racism using the most emphatically offensive term possible, thus bolstering the offensive power of using the n-word and cementing its status as the most offensive slur for Black people.

Let's wrap up this discussion about slurs. We've seen that although, like swears, slurs are offensive terms, there are many important differences. One is that, unlike swears, slurs do not attain their offensiveness via causing people to *feel* offended. As words that denigrate members of an entire (typically oppressed) group of people, the words that we recognise as slurs today are ones that always were offensive, even though there was a time when—due to the oppression of the target group—they were not widely recognised as offensive. Because of this, identifying a word as a slur is more like discovering something that was always there rather than creating something anew. The discovery involves recognising that the oppression of the target group is, and always was, wrong. And since, setting aside reappropriative uses, using the slur is a form of oppressing the target group, using slurs is wrong.

The same cannot be said of swearing. It's not the case that, as can happen with slurs, we suddenly discover that a word we have been using without causing anyone to feel offended is in fact a swear word. Swears are not closely linked with oppression the way that slurs are. Even so, issues of oppression sometimes arise in the case of swearing, and those issues are relevant to deciding how and when it is permissible to use certain swear words. We're going to consider some examples of this in the next chapter.

12

Cunt and cocksucker

Slurs are offensive because using them contributes to the ongoing oppression of certain groups of people. Contempt of oppressed groups contributes, albeit in a different way, to the offensiveness of certain swear words too. In English, *cunt* is the most offensive swear word. In the US, it is an abusive, slur-like term for women; in English-speaking cultures other than the US, it is a more general-purpose insult.[1] It has a long history of being offensive. It appears in Francis Grose's 1785 *A Classical Dictionary of the Vulgar Tongue* in the censored form *c**t*, where its meaning is given as 'a nasty name for a nasty thing'. Elsewhere in that dictionary, it is referred to as '****' or simply as 'an indecent monosyllable'. Even so, it has not always been so offensive: between the thirteenth and sixteenth centuries, several English towns and cities, including Oxford, London, and Shrewsbury, boasted streets by the name of Gropecunt Lane, apparently because of the prostitution that went on there (Holt and Baker 2001). The word is also featured in people's names: there are records of a Gunoka Cuntles, a John Fillecunt, and a Robert Clevecunt dating from thirteenth- and fourteenth-century England. It even appeared in the English translation of a

[1] Why do I say that, in the US, *cunt* is a 'slur-like term' rather than that it is a slur? Well, it's *like* a slur in that it is a term that tends to be used to express contempt for women. But it falls short of being a slur in a number of ways. For example, slurs have what Anderson and Lepore call neutral counterparts: slurs are offensive words used to denote a particular group of people, but there is always an equivalent, inoffensive term with exactly the same denotation. The n-word, for example, has the same denotation as the inoffensive term *Black person*. By contrast, the terms *cunt* and *woman* do not have the same denotation. There are other reasons not to regard *cunt* as a slur; for a detailed analysis of what properties slurs have that are lacked by other pejoratives, see Anderson and Lepore (2013).

fifteenth-century Italian textbook on surgery, which taught that '[I]n wymmen, þe necke of the bladdre is schort & is maad fast to the cunte' (c. 1400, 172).

It's not clear precisely how, when, and why *cunt* morphed from its Middle Ages matter-of-factness into the highly offensive term that, as Grose's dictionary entry shows, it clearly was by the eighteenth century, and which it remains today. But these are questions for another day. Here, let's consider the unusual offensiveness of *cunt*, and what we can do to avoid propagating the misogynistic attitudes that underlie its offensiveness.

Offensiveness and misogyny

It's notable that a term for a woman's genitals has attained the number one slot on the sweary offensiveness leaderboard while even the most offensive male equivalents dangle impotently in the midranks. *Cock* is the strongest of the male equivalents, yet it can't hold a candle to *cunt*. This is interesting, because—as the linguist Kate Warwick, quoting David Crystal's *Cambridge Encyclopaedia of the English Language*, remarks—'the phonetics of a word like *cock* ought to make it more offensive than *cunt*. [*Cock*] has the typical phonetic characteristics of a swear word, what Crystal describes as "the really important sounds . . . the velar consonants, especially the voiceless ones, especially when these are in final position"' (Warwick 2015, quoting Crystal 2003, 251). On paper, *cock* should be more offensive than *cunt*. The explanation for the difference in offensiveness of the two words must—how could it not?—involve misogynistic attitudes. As Michael Adams, professor of English at Indiana University Bloomington and past president of the Dictionary Society of North America, remarks, 'nothing insults a man more than being called by words for women's sexual parts—and women don't especially like that' (Adams 2016a, 62). The difference between the offensive powers of *cunt* and *cock* means that during the offence escalation processes that elevated them to the status of swear words, *cunt* must have been more vehemently disliked than *cock*.

It's not only in English that misogyny shapes offensiveness, and the effects of misogyny aren't limited to *cunt* and its equivalents. As we saw in Chapter 2, many languages have swear words and expressions that insult the listener by insulting their mother. There is no father-disparaging equivalent. Nor is sexism the only prejudice that makes its way into swearing. In English, homophobia has elevated *cocksucker*—an insult used exclusively against men—to the status of a swear word.[2] Other languages contain more diverse resources for injecting homophobia into one's swearing.[3] Despite being a product of misogyny and homophobia, words like *cunt* and *cocksucker* are not slurs. They are not insulting words *for*, respectively, women or gay men. Rather, it's through their power to offend that misogynistic or homophobic attitudes are expressed. Calling someone a cunt or a cocksucker is offensive because *cunt* and *cocksucker* are understood to be offensive words, and they are offensive words because, during the offence escalation process that elevated them to the status of swear words, women's genitals and the act of performing fellatio were regarded with distaste. This does not entail that people who use the words *cunt* and *cocksucker* today are consciously expressing distaste for those things—more often than

[2] Why isn't *cocksucker* used against women? Perhaps due to the homophobic thought that it's bad for men, but not women, to perform fellatio. As George Carlin remarked, 'For some reason, now *cocksucker* means *bad man*. It's a good woman' (Carlin 1972).

[3] Not that *cocksucker* is devoid of misogyny. There is apparently no equivalent pejorative term for a person whose cock is sucked rather than the person doing the sucking. We might hypothesiee that this reflects a general view that, in sexual encounters, it is demeaning to receive a cock into one's body, but not to put one's cock into another person's body—a view reflected by common attitudes of approval and even admiration for men who have sex with a lot of women, yet contempt for women who have sex with a lot of men. These attitudes are essentially misogynistic and are found in other sweary expressions too. For example, Catharine MacKinnon discusses the power relations expressed by statements containing *to fuck* (which can be used in a general way to mean 'to dominate') and *to get fucked* (i.e. to be dominated or oppressed) (MacKinnon 1989; see also Cornell 1990).

not, people use those words simply because they are the right swear words for the occasion, and give little or no thought to their literal meaning or how they came to be as offensive as they are. Even so, we might worry that attitudes to these terms reflect and reinforce misogyny and homophobia in our society (more specifically, in the societies where *cunt* and *cocksucker* are offensive words), and that prevailing views about their offensiveness ought to be challenged.

This creates a dilemma for those of us who not only care about equality and justice but also care about interacting politely with others. On the one hand, equality and justice demand that we challenge patterns of offensiveness that embody discriminatory attitudes. Sometimes, people take offence inappropriately, and being offended inappropriately can be harmful; for example, finding homosexuality or interracial relationships offensive has contributed to the denial of proper respect to homosexuals and interracial couples. When faced with someone who finds these things offensive, we have good reason to avoid pandering to and reinforcing their prejudices by declining to challenge their view of homosexuality or interracial relationships. Similarly, the capacity of *cunt* and *cocksucker* to offend embodies discriminatory attitudes, and by continuing to treat them as offensive—by, among other things, avoiding them in polite company—we reinforce those attitudes.

On the other hand, interacting respectfully with others requires that we comply with norms of politeness, which means acknowledging the offensiveness of *cunt* and *cocksucker* by (among other things) avoiding them in polite company, which in turn reinforces the norms governing their use and the discriminatory attitudes that underlie those norms. These underlying discriminatory attitudes involve viewing female genitals and homosexuality with distaste. When it comes to words like *cunt* and *cocksucker*, being polite involves avoiding those words and sucking up the discriminatory attitudes that one thereby propagates, whereas challenging discriminatory attitudes involves using those words and expecting others to suck up their distaste for these terms. What is a well-intentioned person to do?

When etiquette gets it wrong

Karen Stohr is a philosopher who has thought about this issue. Some rules of etiquette, she notes, embody unjust attitudes. For example, during the time of racial segregation in the US, it was customary not to address Black people using the honorific titles—*Miss*, *Mr*, and so on—with which whites were addressed, and which express respect. Instead, Black people were commonly called *boy* or the n-word. This disparity was mentioned by Martin Luther King Jr. among a list of complaints about the unjust and discriminatory treatment of Black people in his 1963 'Letter From a Birmingham Jail'. Waiting for justice—as, he explains, Black people are constantly asked to do—is 'difficult' when, among other things,

> you are humiliated day in and day out by nagging signs reading 'white' and 'coloured'; when your first name becomes 'n*****', your middle name becomes 'boy' (however old you are) . . . and your wife and mother are never given the respected title 'Mrs'. (King 1963)[4]

A key function of etiquette, remember, is to express respect; yet as Stohr remarks, '[p]eople who followed that convention [of withholding honorifics from Black people] were, deliberately or not, communicating disrespect and contributing to the oppressive structures of racism'. By contrast, '[i]t was the people who bucked social convention and used the same titles for people regardless of

[4] King, in his letter, wrote the n-word in full. Why have I sanitised his language here? I'll explain in the next chapter.

race who were behaving in the most morally defensible way' (Stohr 2012, 32).

So, in the case of unjust customs, does etiquette express respect or not? Stohr answers this by distinguishing between the actual conventions of etiquette that are in use in a society and the principles underlying those conventions. She tells us that 'the criterion for whether something is a legitimate rule of etiquette is not simply whether it is the convention actually in use, but whether it is consistent with the underlying principles of manners' (Stohr 2012, 32). This gives us a framework to critique etiquette: rather than blindly following etiquette because not doing so would fail to express the proper respect, we can ask whether the principles underlying a particular rule of etiquette are defensible. If not, they need to be revised and the rules of etiquette based upon them changed to reflect the revised principles. If the principles are defensible, we can ask whether the rule of etiquette in question properly reflects them; if not, we need to change the rule. Stohr tells us that, in the case of the custom of addressing whites more respectfully than Blacks, the problem lies not with the rule of etiquette itself but with the underlying principle, according to which, in the US at the time, white people were deemed more deserving of respect than Black people. It is—as King sets out in his letter—this principle that needed to be revised, and the rules of etiquette based on it updated to reflect more just principles.

On the other hand, some rules of etiquette are problematic not because of the underlying principles, but because the rule itself does not adequately reflect those principles. So, 'deliberately setting a table with an unusual array of forks so as to trip someone up' (Stohr 2012, 35) might involve following the relevant etiquette about which forks go where, but employing the etiquette in question in order to confuse and humiliate someone is inconsistent with the underlying principles of providing an orderly and easy-to-navigate dinner table and, more generally, respect. This distinction allows Stohr to claim that a white person in the segregation-era US who addresses a Black woman as *Mrs* fails to follow etiquette yet is not being rude (because such a person acts in accordance with the principles that *should* be in play), while a person who uses a complicated arrangement of forks in order to humiliate a diner acts rudely despite following etiquette (because such a person acts contrary to the principles underlying the rule).

How does this bear on *cunt*? Stohr's distinction between the actual conventions of etiquette and the principles underlying them can help us make sense of what's going on here. Now, to be sure, there are plenty of ways in which the dehumanieing segregation-era conventions around honorifics are *not* like the ways in which *cunt* is used—but what we're focusing on now is the rather narrow issue of how we can best convey respect in our interactions with others in cases where the conventions that we'd usually follow to enable us to convey respect are themselves, in one way or another, unjust. And despite their differences, both of these sets of conventions embody injustice. Just as the segregation-era convention of using honorific titles for white people but not Black people reflected a society in which white people were valued and respected more than Black people, so the greater offensive power of *cunt* compared to *cock* reflects a society in which women's genitals are viewed with greater distaste than men's genitals—and, by extension, a society in which women are viewed with greater distaste than men. However, while it's pretty clear that, in the face of customs that required white people to be addressed more respectfully than Black people, a well-intentioned person should ignore those customs and address Black people in the respectful way usually reserved for white people, it's less clear what a well-intentioned person should do in the face of treating *cunt* as a highly offensive word—more offensive than *cock*. While a segregation-era white person who addressed Black and white people with equal respect is obviously acting respectfully, someone who takes an analogous approach to *cunt*—by using it as if it is no more offensive than *cock*—is unlikely to be viewed as acting respectfully, even by people who share the view that *cunt* ought not to be more offensive than *cock*. She does, after all, understand that using *cunt* is very likely to offend her listeners, and her listeners know that she understands this, and she knows that they know that she understands this, and so on, just as in any other case where a person offends by swearing. Despite this, she is well intentioned because by using *cunt*, she aims to challenge and reduce misogynistic attitudes—a goal that is important enough to justify causing offence along the way. Or so she thinks.

A dilemma for sweary feminists

There are some obvious ways in which freely using *cunt* might challenge and reduce misogynistic attitudes. First, since taboos around a particular behaviour are reinforced when we avoid that behaviour, breaking the taboo around *cunt* by freely saying *cunt* will weaken the taboo—especially if other people also follow suit and break the *cunt* taboo; something that the speaker might hope to encourage by their behaviour, because their avoiding the word amounts to their respecting and reinforcing the taboo. Second, since the sort of speaker we're considering is not a misogynist, they will use *cunt* in contexts that are not misogynistic, which means that they lead by example in showing how the word can be used without expressing misogyny. And third, they might hope that their listeners, after feeling offended by their behaviour, might reflect on their response, consider why they find the word so much more offensive than other words, and reevaluate their attitudes, with the result that they come to regard *cunt* as no more offensive than *cock*.

The approach that the speaker adopts to challenge people's reactions to *cunt* is comparable to the approach taken by people who organiee mass breastfeeding protests and mass gay kissing protests in response to negative attitudes to, respectively, public breastfeeding and gay people behaving affectionately towards each other in public. In 2016, in Buenos Aires, two police officers approached Constanza Santos, who was nursing her baby in a public square, told her (mistakenly) that it was illegal to breastfeed in public, and forced her to leave when she challenged them. Santos told her story on Facebook; it went viral, and mass nursing protests were organieed in Buenos Aires and across Argentina. Hundreds of women occupied public spaces, where they nursed their children and displayed signs that asserted their rights to nurse unmolested (Iricibar 2016; 'Argentine Mothers Hold Mass Breastfeeding Protest' 2016). The same sort of approach has been used to protest homophobia: in 2013, gay rights activists gathered outside the Russian parliament in Moscow and kissed their same-sex partners to protest a bill banning homosexual 'propaganda' that the parliament was preparing to pass (Grove 2013). Protests like these aim to normaliee a certain behaviour while also challenging people to reflect on why it is viewed as offensive. The message they express is: *Look, what we're doing is completely harmless—you shouldn't be offended, but if you are, that's your problem!*

Freely using *cunt* in an effort to challenge prevailing attitudes to the word, along with mass breastfeeding and mass gay kissing protests, are examples of what Donald Vandeveer has called *conscientious offences*: they are designed to 'provoke and upset' and 'to shock the complacent into a reevaluation of their position' (Vandeveer 1979, 187). Despite the offence they cause, acts of conscientious offence are motivated by a desire to create a better world. Conscientious offence is not the only route to creating a better world, of course—but it can be an effective strategy. Vandeveer observes that this is because furthering one's aims through offensive conduct is more likely to attract media attention than doing so inoffensively, and that makes it more likely that one will 'get a hearing'.

There's another important way in which conscientious offence might be thought to create a better world: it involves causing people to feel offended while simultaneously calling upon them to reflect on why they feel offended and demonstrating that people are being harmed by their offended reaction, in the hope that those who feel offence will realiee that their reaction is inappropriate and become motivated to override it in the future (by noticing when they start to feel offended, reminding themselves that their reaction is inappropriate and even harmful, and over time training themselves not to react with offence). So, for example, a gay kissing protest might aim at causing homophobes to feel offended, while inviting them to reflect on why they feel offended and highlighting the harm that homophobia causes to gay people, in the hope that those who feel offended will accept that they are reacting inappropriately and harmfully, and that they will consequently be motivated to curb their feelings of offence when they encounter homosexuality in the future. Viewed as such, using conscientious offensiveness as a strategy to create a better world is valuable not merely because it grabs media attention but also because there is something valuable about actually causing feelings of offence in order to challenge them. By actually causing the feeling of offence that one wants to challenge, the challenge is more immediately relevant than it would be if one were to talk hypothetically about offence. People are more likely to reflect on their own feelings in response to the message, *How you're feeling right now is a problem* than in response to the more general and less immediate, *Sometimes people react in this way and that's a problem.*

One big problem with conscientious offensiveness, however, is that—as Feinberg observes—in practice it can be difficult to distinguish from offensive conduct that is motivated by 'malice and spite' (Feinberg 1985, 41). The conscientious offender causes offence in an attempt to reform attitudes precisely because they view it as unfortunate that their conduct provokes feelings of offence; the malicious offender causes offence simply for the pleasure of doing so and relishes the fact that their conduct provokes feelings of offence. It's usually pretty clear that mass breastfeeding protests and mass gay kissing protests are not instances of malicious offence, partly because of the cultural context in which they occur (usually in response to controversy around a decision that implies that breastfeeding or homosexuality is offensive), and partly because breastfeeding and kissing are just not the sort of things that people do when they are intent on maliciously offending people. They are, instead, recognieed as activities that are done for reasons other than offending people.

When it comes to saying *cunt*, things are more complicated. While there are people who believe that *cunt* should not be regarded as being as offensive as it is, that view is pretty niche compared to the views that publicly breastfeeding or homosexuality are offensive. In addition, saying *cunt* in polite company is exactly the sort of thing that people do when they are intent on maliciously offending people. As a result, anyone who liberally uses *cunt* as an act of conscientious offence runs a high risk of appearing maliciously offensive. Their behaviour would not come with the sort of clues that, in the cases of breastfeeding and kissing protests, reveal their behaviour to be motivated by a desire to create a better world. As an act of conscientious offence, this could backfire: without drawing attention to the conscientious motivation to reduce misogynistic attitudes, it could legitimiee the use of *cunt* and with it the misogynistic attitudes currently associated with it. The result could be that, especially in the US where *cunt* is used in a slur-like way to insult women, expressing contempt or disrespect of women becomes increasingly viewed as an acceptable thing to do.

None of this means that increasing our use of the word *cunt* as an act of conscientious offence is doomed to misunderstanding—but it does point to the importance of doing so in the context of wider efforts to tackle misogynistic attitudes. If all we do is start using *cunt* in polite company, we're going to achieve little more than upsetting people. *Cunt* alone can't cure misogyny. To challenge the misogyny behind attitudes to the word, there needs to be a wider effort to raise public awareness of the issue. Against a backdrop of that awareness, it's more likely that people who use *cunt* for conscientious reasons will be recognieed as doing so.

Gently increasing cunt love

How might we reduce the offensiveness of *cunt* in non-confrontational, non-aggressive ways? Our options might include memes and fictional characters who model ways of using *cunt* in non-misogynistic ways. It could also involve taking the opportunity, when we encounter someone who expresses offence at *cunt*, to discuss their attitudes in a curious and respectful way—which enables us to challenge the response without uttering the word ourselves.

An excellent reference point here are cultures—including Wales, Ireland, Scotland, and Australia—in which *cunt* is used relatively inoffensively. The benign Scottish use of *cunt* was demonstrated to the public one morning in December 2018, when the British live-broadcast TV show *Saturday Kitchen* held a phone-in to offer viewers the chance to ask culinary advice from a panel of chefs. A caller introduced as 'Dan from Edinburgh' had the following question: 'You ken [know] what it's like this time of year, every cunt's banging on about parsnips and all that, so what's a barry [good] side for Christmas?' Dan's tone was friendly and polite, and the reaction of the host, Matt Tebbutt—who immediately grinned—revealed that he interpreted Dan's choice of words as benign. (Later in the show, Tebbutt apologieed to viewers for Dan's language.) A more dramatic example dates from 2010, in which a Glaswegian supporter of Rangers football club was interviewed by local TV news in Manchester in advance of a match, two years after Rangers' defeat in the Europa League final had resulted in rioting. The supporter commented: 'It was only a minority that spoilt it for us last time. This time is going to be, it's going to be a good game of football and every cunt's going to hopefully get on with each other'. Given the backdrop of tense concern about whether the match would pass off peacefully, this fan's use of *cunt* with reference to the supporters could have been explosive—but his clearly respectful and diplomatic manner ensured that viewers had no difficulty interpreting his comment as benign. Indeed, the speaker's *cunt* apparently passed unnoticed by the show's producers and was broadcast repeatedly to viewers across the North West of England, being removed only when a Glaswegian living in the area alerted the broadcaster.[5]

The way in which *cunt* can be used affectionately by Australians emerges in the following anecdote shared on my Facebook page by Yasmin Haskell, professor of Classics and Ancient History at the University of Western Australia:

> Ten years ago my mate and I were hanging out with some off-duty goldminers on a beach in remote Western Australia—we were down there for birding but they were spending the summer fishing. We were sharing a few beers and stories and one of the old fellas was reminiscing about his beloved wife, who had died of cancer a few years before. As we gazed out to the ocean, he choked up with emotion and exclaimed, with eloquent passion, 'God I miss the cunt'.

The offensiveness of *cunt* is often overstated even outside cultures with established practices of using the word benignly. In his 2016 book, *In Praise of Profanity*, Michael Adams, remarks that while many swear words can be used as terms of endearment, 'it's hard to imagine when *cunt* isn't [face threatening]' (Adams 2016a, 146). Reviewing the book on his *Strong Language* blog, the editor and writer Stan Carey views this 'Americocentric suggestion' as a 'lapse' (Carey 2016). A few weeks later, in a guest post on the same blog, Adams not only accepted Carey's criticism, but went further:

> As if parochialism weren't bad enough, I may have been wrong about the American status of *cunt*, too. I've come across evidence

[5] For a discussion of both of these incidents, along with video footage, see Thoms and Jamieson (2018).

of *cunt*'s reappropriation as a term of endearment—not unalloyed BFF endearment but a grudging, competitive willingness to get along well supported by a word all the riskier because it's used in unfriendly ways against women. (Adams 2016b)

One of the examples given by Adams is a scene from the American TV show *Six Feet Under*, which ran for five seasons between 2001 and 2005. At a high school graduation party, two female friends, Parker and Claire, bond awkwardly while sharing a joint. Claire laughs at a comment made by Parker, and Parker responds, 'It isn't that funny, cunt', while passing Claire the joint. *Cunt*, observes Adams, functions here as 'a troubling endearment'.

Adams (2016b) compares these American attempts at reappropriation of *cunt* to the reappropriation of slurs, but there are important differences between *cunt* and slurs that make the road to reduced offensiveness rockier for *cunt*. Reappropriation of a slur involves members of the target group taking a word that has been used as a weapon against them and putting it to use as a term of camaraderie, or at least neutrality. Reappropriating a slur that targets a group to which we belong can be empowering, an effect described by Simon Tam, bassist and founding member of Asian American rock band The Slants, who in 2009 was refused permission by the US Patent and Trademark Office to trademark the band's name on the ground that it was disparaging to Asian people. Tam took his battle to the US Supreme Court, and following his victory in 2017, he made the following comments: 'There's power in claiming an identity, saying: "You can't use this against me. This belongs to me." When you are very deliberate and intentional about that, it can be very powerful'.[6]

Cunt is not like this, however. We saw above that while misogyny explains the superlative offensiveness of *cunt*, it is not a

[6] Quoted in Hodgkinson (2019). Tam's sense of empowerment is an instance of a general phenomenon: see Galinsky et al. (2013).

term that is used primarily to disparage women (although its use in the US comes close). Outside the US, it is used as often—if not more so—against men. Because of this, it is difficult to imagine women experiencing the sort of identity-claiming empowerment from using *cunt* that Tam experiences from using *slant*. This makes it likely that women will be less motivated to use *cunt* than members of groups targeted by slurs are motivated to reappropriate those slurs.

Another difference between the sort of reappropriation of *cunt* that we're concerned with here and reappropriation of slurs is that the end goals are different. With *cunt*, the goal is a general reduction in the word's capacity to offend, which applies always and everywhere, so that there is no context in which *cunt* is a more powerfully offensive word than *cock*, regardless of who utters it. Reappropriation of a slur, by contrast, aims specifically to counter the harmful effect of the slur term on members of the target group by establishing an empowering use of the term within the target group. Reappropriated slurs remain offensive when used by those who are not members of the target group, and even those members of the target group who are actively promoting a reappropriated, empowering use of the term tend to oppose non-members using the term, even when those non-members attempt to use it in the same non-weaponieed way that members use it. This was highlighted in May 2018, when rapper Kendrick Lamar was performing at Hangout Fest in Gulf Shores, Alabama. Lamar often invites fans on stage to rap with him during his live shows, and it has become a recognieed norm among his fans that those who are not Black should omit the n-word where it appears (reappropriated) in the lyrics. On this occasion, a white fan named Delaney came on stage and sang the n-word as it appeared in the lyrics three times before Lamar stopped the track. He explained to her, patiently and politely, 'you got to bleep one single word', just as another non-Black fan who 'knew the rules' had done earlier in the show. The crowd can be heard jeering and yelling in the background. Lamar's response,

Delaney's immediate apology, and the hostility of the crowd all point to the reappropriated n-word being off limits for people who are not Black, even when it comes to singing lyrics penned by a Black performer.[7] This norm was underlined a year later, when the American actress Gina Rodriguez posted a video on Instagram featuring her rapping along to a Fugees song that featured the n-word. Rodriguez uttered the word, and in the backlash that followed she removed the video and apologieed (Romano 2019).

As we've seen, it would be fantasy to imagine that the goal of realieing a situation where 'there is no context in which *cunt* is a more powerfully offensive word than *cock*' can be achieved by reducing the taboo around *cunt* alone. Misogyny is about more than rude words. But there is reason to hope that by changing attitudes to *cunt*, it can be removed from the misogynist's armory. One promising way to do this would be to lead the way with regulatory decisions. When it comes to creating and enforcing rules around swearing, regulators generally aim to reflect public opinion rather than to influence it. But a little pushing at boundaries can go a long way. We saw in Chapter 8 that use of *cunt* by Glaswegian characters in the 2012 film *The Angel's Share* led to its receiving from the

[7] BlackTree TV (2018); Santiago (2018). For footage of another white fan, Payton Renner, rapping with Lamar three years earlier without uttering the n-word, see Renner (2015). Following the Delaney incident in 2018, media coverage included discussions about whether Lamar was at fault. He had, after all, invited a white person to rap lyrics that were replete with the n-word—what did he expect? However, given that the offensiveness of the n-word in the mouths of non-Black people is well known, the need for non-Black fans to omit the n-word when on stage with Lamar was a well-established norm, and the gentleness with which Lamar raised the issue with Delaney, it would be uncharitable to blame Lamar here. Even without the established norm about how non-Black fans should behave on stage at Lamar's concerts, it would be highly reckless for a non-Black person to take an invitation to sing on stage as a license to utter the n-word, especially to a large crowd, despite the lyrics of the song. It is certainly not *obvious* that it is permissible to utter the n-word under such circumstances; at best it is ambiguous, and faced with such ambiguity the appropriate way forward is to err on the side of *not* causing offence. For a fan, being invited on stage by Lamar to rap with him is comparable to being a guest in his home and invited to 'make yourself at home'. We know not to take such invitations literally: our host may have food in the cupboards and their phone lying on the table, but the polite guest refrains from helping themself to a snack and scrolling through their host's private messages.

BBFC the most restrictive possible classification—a decision that the makers of the film claimed failed to recogniee the nuances of the often inoffensive ways that *cunt* is used in Scotland. By taking a more permissive approach in cases like this, the BBFC could call public attention to the fact that *cunt* is not always and everywhere a truly offensive word, which would have been an important step in dismantling some of the misogyny associated with it. Complaints could be used as an invitation to educate and change attitudes.

Taking this approach, however, would involve acknowledging that decisions about how to regulate swearing should not be solely guided by and reflective of public opinion. It would involve recognieing that such decisions also have a role in shaping public opinion. The question of what public opinion ought to be is more difficult to answer than the question of what public opinion currently is, and the process of attempting to shape public opinion is tricky and potentially open to abuse. Even the expression *shape public opinion* has a somewhat sinister air; after all, whose standards are the 'right' ones here, and who gets to decide? Such shaping is best done with a light touch, perhaps by focusing on the question: What unjust views might decisions about what is offensive embody, and how could regulators best ensure that they do not unwittingly reinforce those views? Such a policy would involve taking seriously the possibility that the offensiveness of certain swear words is influenced by misogyny, homophobia, and other prejudices—even in cases where the people who find those words offensive are committed to justice and equality—and, in order to avoid propagating those prejudices, making less restrictive regulatory decisions about those words than would have been made were the aim solely to reflect public opinion. This approach could be incremental: there's no urgency to jump right in with a Scottish TV show aimed at toddlers entitled *Wee Cunts.* Over time, one well-judged regulatory decision at a time, the benign *cunt* would eclipse the misogynistic. As Raskolnikov observes in Dostoyevsky's *Crime and Punishment*, 'Man grows used to everything, the scoundrel'!

13

Cunt and 'cunt'

Let's not get ahead of ourselves. All that hand-wringing in the previous chapter about reducing the offensiveness of certain swear words and whether it's okay to *cunt* at people in the course of a crusade against misogyny, as if all ways of saying or writing offensive words are equal—yet the truth is that they're not. There are some pretty familiar devices that we routinely use when we want to strike a balance between saying the (rude) words we want to say and avoiding causing offence. We're going to get into this now.

If we want to avoid offending anyone in contexts where swearing is inappropriate, we can simply avoid swearing. But what if, for one reason or another, we don't want to do that? Often, we want to be able to utter (i.e. speak or write) swear words in contexts where swearing is inappropriate. And we often want to be able to do that without shocking anyone, and without attracting disapproval or the sorts of penalties that swearing attracts in certain formal contexts. Suppose, in a polite context, we want to give an accurate report of what another person said, and what that person said contained swearing. Assuming that we value both accuracy and politeness, we face a dilemma. Accurately reporting what the person said requires us to utter a swear word, which is impolite; but politely reporting what was said requires us to omit the swear word, which compromises the accuracy of our report. This dilemma is especially acute for news outlets. Accuracy is central to their business (the respectable ones, at any rate)—but so, too, is avoiding alienating their audience through offensive language.

Thankfully, there are some ways for us to have our cake and eat it too. It's possible to communicate swear words politely—or, at least, it's possible to make them less impolite for the purposes of reporting them.

Sanitisation

One familiar device is what I'm going to call *sanitisation*, in which we partially or wholly censor a swear word by replacing some or all of the letters in a written swear word with asterisks or other symbols, or obscure part or all of a spoken swear word with a bleep. (The latter, of course, is really only available in broadcasting; it's not something we're easily able to do in the conversations we have in the wild.)

News outlets use sanitisation all the time. Swearing, after all, can be very newsworthy, especially when it's done by a public figure who we think should know better. But, while no news outlet wants to miss out on a gripping story, many news outlets—particularly the mainstream ones—have policies restricting the use of swear words in their reports. Those outlets must find ways to balance conveying to their audience what was said with adhering to their own policies around language use. This happened in the UK in July 2015, when His Royal Highness The Prince Philip, Duke of Edinburgh, late husband of the late Queen Elizabeth II, was filmed asking a journalist to 'Just take the fucking picture' during a photoshoot. Given that *toilet*, *perfume*, and *pardon* are among the words that members of the British royal family will not utter, it is unsurprising that Prince Philip's *fucking* was interesting to many.[1] The incident was widely covered in the news, with much of print and internet news media using asterisks to obscure some of the letters in *fucking*. Where video footage was shown by news outlets, His Royal Highness's *fucking* was obscured with a bleep. Asterisks and bleeps are widely

[1] See Fox (2004) for more on words that the British royal family, and the British upper classes in general, will not utter.

recognised methods of sanitising language in such instances. This is despite the fact that these techniques are usually applied sparsely enough to leave the audience in no doubt which particular word is being reported. Swear words are rarely sanitised as much as they could be. *Fucking* becomes *f**king*, *f***ing*, or *f******, but rarely *******; bleeps, too, often begin only after the word's initial consonant has been enunciated, and while in video footage the speaker's mouth is sometimes visually obscured to make it difficult to use lip movements to help identify the bleeped-out word, this is far from always being the case.

The practice of using asterisks (and other techniques) to censor taboo words has a long history. In Judaism, it has long been blasphemous to name the god of the Jews. In Jewish writing it is customary to omit letters from God's name, to refer to God indirectly as *Ha Shem* (The Name) or *Adonai* (Lord), or to write *G—d*. The latter technique was once used by Christians too, although it is now obsolete. The belief that uttering or writing certain words is taboo, but that partially censored versions of those words are acceptable, is not unique to swearing. It might seem that sanitisation shouldn't work—it doesn't prevent the communication of the word to the audience, after all—but it does. We'll consider how it works in the next chapter.

Quoting and mentioning

First, though, we're going to focus on how we can mitigate the offensiveness of even unsanitised swear words. One way involves quoting swear words. Another involves mentioning swear words rather than using them. (I *mention* swear words when I observe that our list of familiar swear words includes *shit*, *piss*, *fuck*, and *cunt*. By contrast, in this fucking sentence I am *using* swear words like that shit is going out of fashion.) The use/mention distinction is central to traditional philosophy of language: the late philosopher Donald

Davidson recalled, as a student, receiving 'a stern sermon on the sin of confusing the use and mention of expressions' (Davidson 1979, 79). There's a murky nook in philosophy full of head-scratching about precisely how to articulate the use/mention distinction, but that needn't worry us here. Our commonsense grasp of the distinction will enable us to look at what happens, offensiveness-wise, when we mention swear words rather than use them. As we'll see in this chapter, mentioning swear words is a way to reduce their offensiveness—but it's not a foolproof mechanism.

The UK newspaper *The Guardian* makes an exception to the widespread practice in mainstream news media of sanitising swear words. *The Guardian*'s style guide on swearing says the following:

> We are more liberal than any other newspapers, using language that our competitors would not. . . .
>
> The editor's guidelines are as follows:
>
> . . . use such words only when absolutely necessary to the facts of a piece, or to portray a character in an article; there is almost never a case in which we need to use a swear word outside direct quotes. (Marsh and Hodsdon 2021)

Isn't *The Guardian* daring? Well, not as daring as it would have us believe. Swear words are much less offensive when they are quoted: consider the difference in offensiveness between saying to somebody, in a polite context, 'Fuck you!' and 'He said, "Fuck you!" '. The conclusions that we draw about a speaker's beliefs, intentions, and attitude to others are different when they quote a swear word compared to when they utter a swear word without quoting it.

This point is not unique to swearing. Consider the following. In 1997, three years before the end of the controversial ban on LGBT people serving in the UK Armed Forces, the satirical news documentary TV program *Brass Eye* featured a fictional British Navy captain, Sir Hugh Maharggs, who made the following argument against permitting gay men to join the Royal Navy:

> Homosexuals can't swim, they attract enemy radar, they attract sharks, they insist on being placed at the captain's table, they get up late, they nudge people whilst they're shooting, they muck about. Imagine the fear of knowing you have a gay man on board a boat. When you retire at night, you think to yourself: God, will I wake up and find everybody dead? You can't run a ship like that. (Morris 1997)

What conclusions did you draw about my own views on LGBT people serving in the Royal Navy after reading that last paragraph? Hopefully, none. The only views on this topic that appeared in the paragraph above were formatted as a block quotation and ascribed to a fictional character, which you understand means that the quoted remarks don't reflect my own views. Had the quoted remarks *not* been formatted as a quotation, nor ascribed to another speaker, however, you could take them to express my own views. But there's more. Although you can't take those quoted remarks to reflect my own views about LGBT people serving in the Royal Navy, there are other conclusions you can draw from the fact that I've quoted them in the context that I've quoted them. You can, for example, conclude that I am trying to make a point about quotation, and—given the point I'm trying to make—that I definitely *don't* hold the views quoted. Something similar happens when offensive remarks are quoted in the news. Not only can quoted remarks not be ascribed to the person who quotes them, but the fact of that person's uttering the quotation can support certain inferences about that person. When *The Guardian* quotes unsanitised swear words, its readers understand that it would be inappropriate to take offence at the newspaper or the author of the article in question, and also that the decision to leave the swear words unsanitised expresses certain things about the newspaper. These things include, perhaps, that it is committed to conveying 'the facts of a piece' and that it trusts its readers' sober love of truth will not be knocked off course by the odd *fuck* or *shit*. Both of these inferences reflect quite well on *The*

Guardian, and because of this, for *The Guardian*, the decision not to sanitise swear words is win-win—but such a decision requires its readers to recognise the significance of the distinction between quoted and unquoted swear words.

When it comes to neutralising the offence of an uttered word, a close cousin of quotation is the use/mention distinction. The distinction between using offensive language and merely mentioning it hit the headlines in June 2015 after then-US president Barack Obama said the n-word during a podcast interview. The majority of news stories that covered this incident were scandalised and reported him as having *used* the word. In fact, he merely mentioned it, as the context makes clear. What he said was, 'It's not just a matter of it not being polite to say [n-word] in public. That's not the measure of whether racism still exists or not. It's not just a matter of overt discrimination'.[2]

Quotation, mention, and slurs

Neither quotation nor mentioning provide the speaker with complete protection against causing offence, however. Generally, when we quote something offensive that somebody else has said, our listeners' offence will be directed at the person whose remarks we are quoting, rather than at us. So, if I say to you: 'Nigel said, "It's not my fault I'm late for work, I'd have been on time if there weren't so many immigrants on the roads"', any offence you feel is going to be directed at Nigel, not at me.[3] But sometimes speakers do not escape unscathed when quoting offensive remarks. This can happen when quoting slurs. In May 2020, Stanford University law

[2] Writing in the *Huffington Post*, Harvey Simon was in a minority of journalists to note that Obama had mentioned rather than used the word, and to draw out the difference this made to how offensive (or not) Obama's remarks were (Simon 2015).

[3] The quoted passage paraphrases remarks made by Nigel Farage in 2014. See Rawlinson (2014).

professor Michael W. McConnell read aloud an eighteenth-century quote by Patrick Henry, which contained the n-word. McConnell is white, and his utterance of the n-word was viewed with outrage by his students and condemned by the dean of the law school, Jenny S. Martinez (Anderson 2020). Not everybody working in education views it as offensive for non-Black people to quote the n-word—anecdotally, among non-Black philosophers working on slurs, I've attended some talks by white philosophers who will utter the word during the course of their talk on slurs, and some who won't—but it remains controversial, largely due to the fact that the emotional response it provokes in Black people does not distinguish between quotation and non-quotation, or between use and mention.[4] (It's for this reason that I, a white person, did not quote Martin Luther King's remarks in full in the previous chapter, nor those of John McWhorter in Chapter 11, nor those of Barack Obama above.) Recall Oprah Winfrey's comments, quoted in Chapter 11, on being unable to hear the n-word without thinking of lynching and degradation. The writer Mahad Olad, whose Somali parents moved the family to the US when he was very young, expands further. The n-word, he writes, 'carries a lot of power and can elicit a visceral reaction', and while he supports Black people's efforts to reappropriate it, he 'will probably never be comfortable with non-Black usages of n—a and especially n—er, even if they're merely referring to it and not using it' (Olad 2019).

[4] Why don't those philosophers who utter the n-word make the news, as McConnell did? Perhaps because the context in which they utter it—during talks dealing with the semantics, pragmatics, and offensiveness of the n-word and other slurs—is recognised as a context in which it is difficult to avoid uttering it. Perhaps because invariably such talks are premised on the recognition that the n-word is offensive, so the speakers are recognised as opposed to its general use, as well as recognised as having spent a lot of time and attention researching the word. Perhaps also because, depressingly, although philosophy undergraduates are fairly racially diverse, the population of PhD students and professional philosophers—who generally make up the audience at these sorts of talks—remains mostly non-Black in countries like the UK, the US, and Australia, which means that utterances of the n-word by non-Black speakers during research talks tend not to be utterances of the word in the presence of Black people, who are those most likely to have a strong reaction to the n-word.

What's going on in these contexts? Did those students who were offended by McConnell's quoting of the n-word simply not understand that he was quoting somebody else rather than expressing the quoted sentiments himself? That seems unlikely. A more promising explanation for their reaction lies elsewhere. We saw above that when a person quotes something, there are conclusions we can draw from the fact that they've quoted the words in question in the context in question. McConnell's students recognised that his utterance of the n-word occurred within a quotation, but perhaps concluded from his quoting it that the word came rather too easily to his lips and therefore that he had failed to grasp its significance. They might also have concluded that clearly he was confident—even without consulting his Black students about the matter before the class—that the word's enclosure within quotation marks would render it inoffensive. It's far from clear that the n-word becomes inoffensive even in the context of a quotation that is relevant to the subject being discussed, as the remarks of Oprah Winfrey and Mahad Olad demonstrate. But even ignoring that, the fact that McConnell did not consult his students prior to uttering the quotation is itself significant.

Even if—as many people apparently believe—it *is* sometimes appropriate to utter the n-word in the course of quoting another person, this does not mean that it's polite or respectful to do so without first consulting or at least warning one's listeners. Especially in the last few years, it's become increasingly familiar in educational spaces to warn students in advance about offensive or upsetting content in classes and reading material. This includes appearances of the n-word: in August 2022, Exeter University in the UK made the news for following various American schools' practice of providing students on its American literature module with a warning about the language in Mark Twain's 1884 novel, *Huckleberry Finn*. The warning stated that the novel 'is problematic in a number of ways, not least because of Huck's use of the n-word' (Brown 2022).

Preceding an utterance of the n-word with a trigger warning, however, is useful only in cases where we've already decided that it's appropriate to utter the word. It's not clear that it would have been appropriate for McConnell to utter the n-word in his class, even if his students had been forewarned. Issuing a warning, after all, would not have involved consulting his students about whether it was acceptable to utter the word in the first place—and perhaps that's what was needed here. Perhaps, at the very least, McConnell ought to have consulted his students in order to enable himself to quote the n-word in a way that was considerate and respectful of his students.

To make this point clear, consider an analogy. When visiting someone's home for the first time as a guest, it's appropriate to sit on their furniture and to use their toilet if needed. Even so, it would be rude to make oneself comfortable on their sofa without being invited to sit down, or to wander off to use their toilet without first asking for permission. We wait for permission in this context not because we think that sitting on the sofa or using the toilet might be inappropriate but in order to signal our acknowledgement that our host is in charge. Awaiting permission says *I recognise that any use I make of your home while I'm here is a favour from you to me.* Similarly, had McConnell discussed with his students—and given particular weight to the views of his Black students—his plans to quote the passage containing the n-word during class, his act of consulting them would have expressed something like *I recognise that my being able to quote this word inoffensively during class is a favour from you to me.* For him to utter the word without prior discussion was the equivalent of entering someone's home as a guest and sprawling on their sofa before one has been shown into the living room and invited to sit down. Both are objectionable, regardless of whether or not *quoting the n-word in relevant educational contexts* and *sitting on one's host's furniture* are generally appropriate.

The limitations of sweary quotation

Quoting swear words isn't likely to get you into the sort of hot water in which McConnell found himself, but you still need to tread somewhat carefully to avoid falling foul of certain conclusions that your audience might draw from the fact that you've quoted the words in question in the context that you've quoted them. A single quoted swear word, in order to communicate accurately what another person has said, can reflect well on both speaker and audience, as we saw from *The Guardian* case. But take it too far—for example, by repeatedly uttering the quotation—and you risk your audience concluding that you're not quoting swear words because of a noble commitment to clear communication but because you simply enjoy saying rude words.

In the case of news outlets, we can draw an analogy between quoted swearing and gore. When news outlets report a murder, it's often appropriate for them to mention some aspects of how the murder occurred, such as what weapon was used, what injuries the victim suffered, where the crime occurred, and so on. But we would find it distasteful and gratuitous were a news report about a murder to include lingering, close-up footage of the victim's wounds and lengthy descriptions of the last moments. With gore in the news, as with swearing, we expect *enough* but not *too much*. What constitutes enough and too much is, of course, a matter of social convention, and varies with context—what constitutes too much gore in a mainstream news report may be appropriate in a documentary about a serial killer—but we expect news outlets to do a decent job of reflecting the prevailing views of its audience about this.

The swearing/gore analogy is not perfect. As we've seen, swearing (at least when certain people do it) can itself be newsworthy; gore generally isn't. In cases where swearing is newsworthy, swearing is not a peripheral detail which can be omitted; it's the main point of the story. Mentioning swear words might seem straightforwardly and obviously appropriate in those cases, while sanitising them (as some news outlets and broadcasters do) might seem bizarre and nonsensical. But, in fact, things are much more complicated. Incidents of swearing—particularly those involving British royalty—are routinely reported in the news in a way that indicates that the very readers who are interested in being kept up to date about when members of the British royal family utter swear words are very much *not* interested in encountering the swear words uttered. A striking example of this is a story from 2019, in which the British tabloid *Express* ran a story about how Prince Philip swore at Queen Elizabeth II using unknown words 'between 1949 and 1951' (Bet 2019). It's also apparently newsworthy—and here we risk getting thoroughly entangled in theoretical distinctions—when members of the British royal family merely *mention* swear words. In 2013, during an episode of the British comedy quiz show *Was It Something I Said?*, the actor Brian Blessed related an encounter with the Queen in which she mentioned *fuck*:

> The Queen said to me, 'You know, Mr Blessed, the other week when you were on [British comedy quiz show] *Have I Got News For You*, you did say "F. U. C. K". thirty times, you know you didn't care to swear—but, of course, it's an Anglo-Saxon word, *fuck*, it means "spreading of seed". (Channel 4 2013)

Much audience laughter followed this anecdote, and the host of the quiz, comedian David Mitchell, responded with an incredulous, 'Have you heard the Queen say *fuck*? That is amazing'. Reporting this exchange seven years later, *Express* included a video clip in which Blessed's spelling-out of *fuck* was left uncensored but his utterance of *fuck*, despite its offensiveness being double-bagged as a mention within a quotation, was obscured with a bleep. In the accompanying text, *fuck* was rendered as *f**k* (Scarsi 2020). Clearly, despite *Express* taking its readers to be sufficiently interested in royal swearing to want to hear about sweary incidents that occurred more than seventy years earlier, it does not take those readers to be so interested as to want to encounter the uncensored words themselves, even when those words are merely quoted, merely mentioned, or both.

Let's pause to take stock of where we are. Words that are offensive when we use them can be inoffensive when they are quoted or mentioned—but not always. Some words uttered by some speakers—including slurs uttered by people outside the target group and swear words uttered by the late Queen—are so shocking to some listeners or readers that it hardly matters whether the words are used, mentioned, or quoted; the effect of the words is felt regardless. Sometimes, we manage to act offensively despite quoting or mentioning a certain word because of the conclusions that our audience draws about our quoting or mentioning the word. If our audience thinks that we are quoting or mentioning the word in question more than is necessary, they might conclude that we're enjoying uttering the word, which leads them to respond to us as if we'd used the word. If the quoted or mentioned word is a slur and the speaker is not a member of the target group, the audience might conclude that the speaker's willingness to utter the word betrays their inadequate grasp of the word's power to oppress and offend, which leads them to react to the speaker as if they had used the word. Sometimes, quoting or mentioning an offensive word—particularly a slur—without prior discussion with one's audience can be disrespectful and rude. To get away with quoting or mentioning an offensive word without causing offence, a speaker needs to ensure that the conclusions that their audience will draw about them will be positive ones. *The Guardian* manages to do this. By aiming to minimise the swear words appearing in its reports, but not shrinking from printing them in full where not including them would be awkward, it manages to convey a serious-minded commitment to news reporting.

In some unusual cases, however, even when all the right boxes are ticked, it's still possible to offend with quoted or mentioned remarks. Here's an example that was described to me by David Edmonds just before he and Nigel Warburton interviewed me about swearing for their hugely successful podcast, *Philosophy Bites*. Imagine that, during a heated but polite discussion with a professional colleague whom you do not know well, your colleague says to you, 'I'm tempted to call you an arrogant prick, but since I want to keep this polite, I won't.' In saying this, your colleague stops short of calling you an arrogant prick—instead, they merely mention the term—but even so, they manage to convey their negative opinion of you just as effectively as if they'd used the term. Your colleague in this example is comparable to Stohr's dinner host, whom we met in the previous chapter, who deliberately sets the table with a complicated collection of cutlery in order to trip someone up. Both act in accordance with relevant rules of etiquette, which, respectively, prohibit one from calling colleagues *arrogant pricks* and set out the way in which cutlery should be arranged on a dinner table; but both act contrary to the underlying principles of manners, which require treating people with respect.

In terms of offensiveness, then, there is a difference between, on the one hand, using swear words, and on the other, quoting or mentioning them. But the whole area is an offensiveness minefield. There are plenty of ways in which we can cause offence with quoted or mentioned swear words. This makes it surprising that so many of us succeed in quoting or mentioning swear words *without* causing offence—something that is perhaps explained by the fact that in polite company most of us, like *The Guardian*, quote or mention swears 'only when absolutely necessary to the facts.' While many people, when reporting verbatim what others have said, will give voice to language that they would never include in their own vocabulary, it's often clear that they utter the words in question only reluctantly and in the service of communicating clearly. This helps to ensure that their audience does not view them as taking pleasure in uttering the words, or failing to understand their offensiveness, or any other conclusion that reflects negatively on the speaker. In general, fluent speakers of a language do understand the significance of uttering swear words in polite company, and where it's necessary to utter them, they do so with discomfort; this discomfort helps ensure that they are not viewed as acting offensively when they quote or mention swear words.

But, what about sanitisation? It may well be true that there is a strong case for the relevance of swear words in certain news reports and some other contexts. But there are also universally recognised methods of sanitising swear words using asterisks and bleeps. How can uttering swear words in full ever be 'absolutely necessary to the facts' when sanitisation is an option? How does sanitisation even work—after all, anyone who knows what *fuck* means also knows what *f**** means? We'll turn to these questions in the next chapter.

14

How the f*** do asterisks work?

In 2014, the *International Journal of Advanced Computer Technology* accepted a paper by David Mazières and Eddie Kohler, who are professors of computer science at Stanford and Harvard universities, respectively. The paper was entitled 'Get Me Off Your Fucking Mailing List'. The entirety of the text, along with two diagrams, consisted of the sentence *Get me off your fucking mailing list*, repeated over ten pages and formatted like a standard scientific paper. The paper's acceptance highlighted the problem of predatory academic publishers: organisations that spam thousands of academics with offers to publish their research—for a fee—in journals that have lofty-sounding titles but which are not particularly selective about what they publish. (Despite being accepted, 'Get Me Off Your Fucking Mailing List' ended up not being published, since the authors did not pay the $150 publication fee.)

Academic publishing practices are not usually of interest to the general public, but this incident made the news around the world. I learned of it in 2014 via a story on a news website—sadly, I don't recall which one—in which all mention of the content of the paper in the headline and accompanying text was sanitised as *Get me off your f***ing mailing list*, yet the story was illustrated with an image of the front page of the article, which contained dozens of uncensored, unsanitised *fuckings*. It was this news story that triggered my philosophical interest in swearing. *What was going on with the asterisks?*, I wondered. The word they were censoring was right there on the screen. And even if it hadn't been, anyone likely to be interested in the story can easily work out what the partially obscured word is.

The practice of sanitising swear words with asterisks or other symbols (and the audio equivalent of using bleeps during broadcasts and recordings, or saying things like *effing* in place of *fucking*), is widely used as a way of communicating swear words without causing offence, and apparently it is pretty effective. *How* it manages to be effective is puzzling, and there are those who believe it shouldn't be effective and that it shouldn't be used. In her 'editor's preface' to the second edition of Emily Brontë's *Wuthering Heights*, Charlotte Brontë condemned the practice of sanitisation even while acknowledging its effectiveness in reducing offence:

> A large class of readers, likewise, will suffer greatly from the introduction into the pages of this work of words printed with all their letters, which it has become the custom to represent by the initial and final letter only—a blank line filling the interval. I may as well say at once that, for this circumstance, it is out of my power to apologise; deeming it, myself, a rational plan to write words at full length. The practice of hinting by single letters those expletives with which profane and violent persons are wont to garnish their discourse, strikes me as a proceeding which, however well meant, is weak and futile. I cannot tell what good it does—what feeling it spares—what horror it conceals. (Brontë 1850)

The Guardian style guide, after permitting the appearance of swear words inside quotation marks, approvingly quotes Brontë as it instructs its writers to 'never use asterisks, or such silliness as b——, which are just a cop-out' (Marsh and Hodsdon 2021).

Both Brontë and *The Guardian* are clearly frustrated by the practice of sanitisation. The thought is: either swear or don't swear, but don't mess about with half measures. Reminding ourselves yet again of Feinberg's distinction between two senses of *offence* helps us understand their attitudes here. Feinberg, remember, distinguished between a general sense of *offence* and a normative sense. Something is offensive in the general sense when it causes people to *feel* offended. Something is offensive in the normative sense when it involves wrongdoing, which for our purposes includes rudeness or impoliteness. For us to view someone's feeling of offence as reasonable or understandable, we expect it to be explainable by what is happening at the normative level: as Feinberg puts it, 'the unpleasant mental state [i.e. feeling offended] must be caused by conduct that really is wrongful' (1985, 2). Sanitisation is frustrating because, although it really does work to stop people from *feeling* offended, it is not clear what sanitisation changes at the normative level that could explain this result. By writing *f****, we still communicate *fuck*, after all. How can *f**** enable us to communicate *fuck* to our audience while also telling them not to feel offended? This seems rather like punching someone in the face while also telling them not to be hurt. It's a mystery how this could possibly work, which leads people like Charlotte Brontë and the editors of *The Guardian* to conclude that sanitisation should not work, and that it should not be used.

So, how does sanitisation work (or not work)? What difference does it make to the sanitised swear words themselves? Well, not much. There's more to say on this, but, in short, sanitisation does not work by stopping short of communicating swear words, or by communicating something inoffensive in place of swear words. It works, rather, by signalling something about the speaker's intentions and attitudes towards her audience: that she cares about her audience's feelings and that she does not wish to offend them. This means that sanitisation works in a similar way to many other widely accepted ways of expressing respect, such as saying *please*.

Sanitisation: it's not about the word

Trying to explain how sanitisation works to mitigate the offensiveness of swear words by looking at what it changes about the words themselves does not lead us anywhere satisfactory. There are a few forms that such an explanation could take.

First, we could try to explain how sanitisation works by claiming that we view the sanitised version of swear words as literally different words to the unsanitised versions. So, *f**** is less offensive than *fuck* because *f**** and *fuck* are different words. We have already seen that swear words tend to have inoffensive synonyms: *fuck* and *copulate* are expressions that (for certain uses of *fuck*, at least) mean the same thing, yet they differ in their offensiveness. So, perhaps we could tell a similar story for *fuck* and *f****: they both mean the same thing, but one is more offensive than the other.

This is not a plausible story, however. *F**** and *fuck* are not different words. They are the same word. Writing *f**** is simply a way of writing *fuck*. We learn what *f**** means by first learning what *fuck* means, and if you wanted to explain to someone what *f**** means, you'd do it by explaining that it's *fuck* with most of the letters replaced by asterisks. When we write *f****, we assume that our readers will understand us to mean *fuck*. When Prince Philip said, 'Just take the fucking picture' to a photographer and was reported in the news as having said 'Just take the f***ing picture', those reports were not inaccurate. They did not report him as having said something other than he did, and we don't interpret them as such. When we read a report that says, 'Prince Philip said "Just take the f***ing picture"', we take it to mean that Prince Philip said 'Just take the fucking picture'. All these reflections point to *f**** and *fuck* being the same word. Which, given that the word *fuck* is offensive, makes it difficult to understand how *f**** manages to be less offensive.

What, then, accounts for the difference in their offensiveness? Perhaps the answer is that, while *fuck* is a swear word, *f**** is not. On the face of it, this view is highly appealing, because it fits with the way in which people use the *f****. Someone who chooses to say *f**** instead of *fuck* believes that, by doing so, they avoid swearing. They use the sanitised version because they do not want to utter a swear word. Even so, if we scratch the surface of this account, it makes little sense. We have already seen that *f**** and *fuck* are the same word. We also know that *fuck* is a swear word. This means that *f**** must also be a swear word. One and the same word cannot both be and not be a swear word.

Second, even if *f**** and *fuck* are not different words, perhaps we don't have to concede that they are the same word. Perhaps *f**** is not a word at all. After all, the asterisks are not letters, but placeholders for missing letters. The asterisks are linguistic IOUs. It might be that, by writing *f****, one stops short of writing a word, even if the context makes it clear to the audience what word one would have written had one gone ahead and written a word. This would explain how *f**** manages not to be an offensive word: something cannot be an offensive word unless it is a word. In this sense, *f**** is rather like the catchphrase that Homer utters before strangling Bart in *The Simpsons*: 'Why you little—!' Homer stops short of saying something offensive, but the inoffensive words that he does say leave us in no doubt about how his sentence would have been completed had he decided to complete it. The catchphrase *suggests* something offensive without needing to say it. Perhaps *f**** communicates the offensive word *fuck* by inoffensively suggesting it. And just as Homer's catchphrase is not a complete sentence, perhaps *f**** is not a complete word.

However, it is implausible to claim that *f**** is not a word. It functions linguistically exactly as *fuck* does. Anything that we can say with *fuck*, we can also say with *f****, which means that since *fuck* qualifies as a word, it is difficult to deny word status to *f****. And if we wrote '*F**** is a four-letter word' and someone were to reply 'No, it's a one-letter-and-three-asterisk not-word', we wouldn't take them seriously—we'd think they were being overliteral and (perhaps deliberately) missing our point.

*F**** might lack the cathartic, expressive power of *fuck*, but that is not enough to disqualify it from wordhood. Almost all words, after all, lack the cathartic, expressive power of *fuck*. Despite its being comprised mostly of asterisks, and the fact that we use it as much for what it enables us to *avoid* saying as for what it enables us to say, the case for claiming that *f**** is not a word is weak.

Third, we might try the following explanation. When we say that *f**** and *fuck* are the same word, we mean that they are both ways of expressing or communicating the same word. But nobody could deny that they are each different ways of expressing or communicating that same word. One way involves writing all the letters of the word; the other involves substituting most of those letters for asterisks. This is the only difference between the unsanitised and the sanitised ways of communicating the word—at least in their written forms. That one of them is more offensive than the other must be because one is a more offensive way of communicating the word *fuck* than the other. One way of viewing this, which accurately reflects our motivation for using *f**** instead of *fuck* in certain contexts, involves claiming that by writing *f****, we spare the reader the word *fuck*. We allow the reader a glimpse of the word—just enough to see what's going on—without making them dwell on it. Reading *f**** is to reading *fuck* as watching a horror movie from behind the sofa is to being forced to view it, our eyes propped open like Alex in *A Clockwork Orange*. This view of things certainly seems to be held by news editors who require their journalists to sanitise swear words. Editorial guidelines that require the news that Prince Philip said *fucking* to be expressed as 'Prince Philip said "f***ing"' aim at communicating to readers precisely what Prince Philip said but in a way that spares them the offensive word that he uttered.

On the surface, this talk of sparing the reader (or listener) sounds plausible—but actually, if sparing the reader is the concern, there are far better strategies than sanitisation. If we really wanted to spare the reader the offensive word, we could avoid including the word at all. It is, after all, possible to report that Prince Philip swore without conveying exactly what word he used. A report could say that Prince Philip uttered a swear word, and perhaps that the word in question was one of our strongest swear words. If news editors really were serious about sparing their readers swear words, this is what we should expect them to do. Or they could use asterisks (or bleeps) to obscure the *entire* word, rather than just part of it, as tends to be the custom. But, in fact, the way in which asterisks and bleeps tend to be used makes clear that we don't want it to be at all obscure which word we are using. We typically leave enough of the original letters or sounds to leave the reader in no doubt about what word is being used. We *want* our audience to know which word we're using. Communication is, after all, the whole point of language.

In any case, if we really do wish to spare readers swear words, using asterisks or bleeps to sanitise swear words is an ineffective way to go about it. Often, this strategy has the opposite effect. By partially obscuring swear words, we force the reader to work harder in order to work out which word we are using. This can result in the reader having to devote *more* attention to the mystery swear word than would be necessary had we left the word unsanitised, as David Marsh, writing in *The Guardian*, illustrates with the following anecdote:

> [A] Twitter user commented that, before he saw the word 'knobhead' in the *Guardian*, he did not know what the word denoted by another newspaper as k******* was supposed to be. I sympathise. How is the poor reader expected to differentiate between b******* and b*******? (The former, of course, is 'bastards'; the latter, 'bollocks'.) (Marsh 2012)

Consider also the following list from the *Daily Mail*, which had appropriated a report from *Slate* about the most commonly used swear words on Facebook. The *Daily Mail* reported the top ten words as follows:

1. F***
2. S***
3. Bloody
4. P***
5. B****
6. Crap
7. C***
8. C***
9. Damn
10. D*** (Bloom 2014)

It takes more time and thought to make sense of this list than it would had the swear words been left unsanitised. What, for example, are we to make of words 7 and 8 in this list? Is 7 *cunt* and 8 *cock*, or vice versa? We know that neither of them can be *crap*, which appears unsanitised at number 6; although its synonym, *shit*, is sanitised at (where else?) number 2. The *Daily Mail* has failed to spare its readers the trauma of encountering swear words. And indeed, in this case and many others, the swear words are the entire point of the story. It's a story *about* swear words. Running a news story about swear words while also attempting to spare readers the swear words is too bizarre to make sense. Sanitisation cannot be about sparing the audience the swear words.

What we communicate besides the words

If sanitising swear words with asterisks does not spare the reader the swear word, perhaps it instead allows the writer to communicate the swear word while also communicating that they recognise its offensiveness and want to mitigate that offensiveness. This would fit nicely with our earlier observations about the relevance of what the reader (or the listener) takes to be the writer's (speaker's) intentions in using swear words. A large part of what makes swearing offensive, we saw, is that when we swear, we know that we are likely to offend our audience, but we go ahead and do it anyway. Our audience, seeing that we are being insufficiently considerate of their sensibilities, resents us for inflicting the word on them, and takes offence. However, when we use asterisks to sanitise swear words, we effectively say, 'I want to communicate to you the word *fuck*, but I know that writing that word will offend you, and I don't want to offend you, so I'm writing *f**** instead'. Asterisks, then, give us a way to swear without setting off the usual chain of inferences between us and our audience that culminates in their taking offence at what we say.

This explanation sounds right. We do recognise and mitigate the offensiveness of *fuck* by instead writing *f****. But this is merely a restatement of our original point that many people prefer reading *f**** to reading *fuck*. It doesn't give us any additional insight into how *f**** manages to communicate *fuck* while also being less offensive than *fuck*. On the contrary, it presupposes that *f**** is less offensive than *fuck*. After all, if *f**** were not less offensive, then using it would not enable us to mitigate the wrongness of writing *fuck*, because by writing *f**** we would be doing something as offensive as writing *fuck*. Doing something offensive while recognising its offensiveness does not mitigate its offensiveness. Quite the opposite in fact: using disliked terms while recognising that they are disliked leads to offence escalation, as we've seen already. If *f**** is less offensive than *fuck* in part because it enables the speaker to communicate that she recognises the offensiveness of *fuck*, we need a plausible story about how this works to mitigate offensiveness.

Thankfully, a plausible story is available. Recall Feinberg's account of what (wrongful) offence is: we are offended when we experience a mental state that we dislike (disgust, shock, horror, etc.), when we attribute that state to the wrongful conduct of another person, and when we resent that other person for causing that state. Applied to swearing, we are offended by swear words when encountering them causes us to feel bad (shocked, unsettled, uncomfortable), when we attribute that bad feeling to another person's having sworn inappropriately, and when we resent that person for causing us to feel bad. That sense of resentment, in the case of swearing, commonly takes the form of a belief that the speaker could easily have avoided swearing but did not, and the fact that they did not prompts us to infer that they hold a disrespectful or contemptuous attitude toward us. We've seen that swearing's power to shock and offend has less to do with the words themselves and more to do with the attitude that the speaker manages to convey by swearing. Another way of putting this point is: encountering swear words is only mildly unpleasant for people who take offence at swearing—the bulk of their displeasure results from encountering (what those people take to be) the disrespectful and contemptuous attitudes of people who swear.

Sanitisation works not by shielding us from offensive words (although there's a sense in which it does do that, as we'll discuss below) but by enabling the writer to signal that she do not hold a disrespectful or contemptuous attitude towards the reader, which in turn prevents the reader from resenting her role in any displeasure caused by encountering the easily recognisable sanitised word. When a writer sanitises a swear word, she does not merely signal her recognition that the word is offensive (which, as we saw above, would not alone explain how sanitisation manages to reduce the offensiveness of swear words). She also makes a sacrifice: she could have written the word in full, but chose not to, due to her solicitude towards her reader. Uttering the word in full would have been more satisfying than uttering a sanitised version. This sacrifice is not lost on her reader. As we saw in Chapter 5, swearing (and taboo-breaking in general) can be fun. Sanitising swear words is a recognised way to avoid the taboo of swearing, which means that by opting to sanitise, one opts to forgo the fun of breaking the taboo. But not only is sanitising swear words a recognised way of avoiding the taboo of swearing—it's a recognised way of doing so in order to avoid offending one's reader. This means that what our reader takes from our use of sanitisation is: *I care about your feelings*. The writer who uses sanitisation conveys that she is trying to do her best to strike a balance between communicating using language and protecting her reader's feelings; a balance that is difficult to strike when swearing is important to what she wants to communicate. What the writer signals, in such an instance, is incompatible with the attitude of disrespect and contempt that we risk conveying when we swear unsanitised. As a result, sanitisation, when used wisely, cancels out that attitude. In doing so, it removes the primary means by which swearing causes offence.

It may seem, at this point, that sanitisation has a 'house of cards' feel about it. By sanitising, we manage to signal our solicitude toward our reader, yet we do so by substituting an offensive word for something that is barely less offensive. How can this possibly work? The answer, I think, is: it doesn't matter. There are plenty of examples in etiquette where we signal solicitude through behaviour that, on close scrutiny, doesn't make sense. We hold the door open for the person behind us, and in doing so signal solicitude towards them even when we have no doubt that they are capable of opening the door themself. We say *Good morning* to our neighbours as we pass them on the street even on mornings when it seems that world events have rendered the morning anything but good. We offer to compensate a colleague who has done us a favour even when it is clear to us that they will decline our offer. When it comes to signalling solicitude, it's the thought that counts. The mechanisms via which we do it—sanitisation, holding doors open, and so on—enable us to do it not through doing something practically useful or helpful but simply through being recognised ways of signalling solicitude. As Sarah Buss has argued, the word *please* (and its equivalents in other languages) means, simply, *You are worthy of respect*. Something similar is true of sanitisation, and of the other ways of signalling solicitude described here.

When asterisks don't cut it

I've claimed that sanitisation cancels out the attitude of disrespect and contempt that we risk conveying to our reader through unsanitised swearing *when used wisely*. This qualification is important. For sanitisation to work in reducing the offensiveness of swearing, we need to use it sparingly. It needs to be plausible to our reader that we are caught in a dilemma: we want to communicate something that makes the use of swearing difficult to avoid, and we want to minimise the damage to our reader's sensibilities. Overusing sanitised swear words, or using them in a way that leads the audience to suspect that the author is deriving glee or cathartic pleasure from using them, undermines sanitisation's capacity to signal solicitude to the reader. The notoriously sweary character, Malcolm Tucker, in the 2009 movie *In the Loop* (a spin-off of the TV show *The Thick of It*), did not signal solicitude to Linton Barwick when he said the following to him: 'I mean, you are a real boring fuck! Sorry, I know you disapprove of swearing, so I'll sort that: You are a boring eff-star-star cunt'! In this case, Tucker's liberal use of unsanitised swearing, along with his aggressive and generally impolite tone, ensures that the small amount of sanitisation he utters does nothing to dilute his contemptuous attitude.

Here's another example. Consider again that heavily sanitised list of swear words published by the *Daily Mail*. Imagine if, instead of printing the sanitised words in a list, it had offered them up in the form of the following sweary puzzle for its readers:

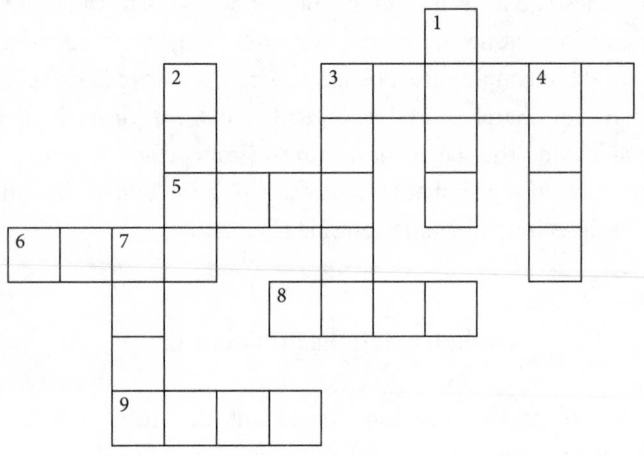

ACROSS	DOWN
3. Of the fluid that is pumped by the heart	1. Male bird
5. Female genitals	2. Abbreviated form of the name 'Richard'
6. Copulate	3. Female dog
8. Solid waste from the body	4. Condemn by God
9. Liquid bodily waste produced by the kidneys	7. Solid waste from the body

In some ways, this puzzle would have done the same job for the *Daily Mail* as the sanitised list that appeared in the published article. It communicates the relevant words to the reader without having to write them in full. It's actually even more sanitised than the sanitised list: the sanitised list displays at least part of each rude word, whereas they are not displayed at all in the puzzle, only hinted at by clues that do not contain swear words. Even so, it's difficult to imagine the *Daily Mail*'s readers being impressed by this puzzle. I'm not aware of any research comparing attitudes to regular sanitisation with attitudes to sweary puzzles, but my hunch is that the *Daily Mail* readership's response to a sweary puzzle would more closely resemble its response to unsanitised swearing than its response to regular sanitisation. Complaints would be rife. But why, given how thoroughly sanitised are the swear words in the puzzle?

The reason is that what the *Daily Mail* signals to its readers via the sanitised list is different to what would be signalled with the puzzle. With the sanitised list, the message is: *We recognise that these swear words will offend you and because we care about not offending you we're not printing them in full.* With the puzzle, the message is different. Puzzles are fun! A sweary puzzle would have signalled to readers: *We think you'll enjoy guessing these swear words and because we care about your enjoyment we're not printing them.* A newspaper that publishes a crossword puzzle omits the answers from the puzzle not because it wants to help its readers avoid the words in question but because it expects that the readers will have fun working out the words from the clues and writing them in the puzzle. This shows that sanitisation does not render swear words less offensive by covering them up but through the unwritten message of solicitude that it enables the writer to convey to the reader.

Sanitisation does not succeed in completely protecting the reader or listener from the shock and offensiveness of swearing. For this reason, it is not regarded as suitable for certain audiences, including those consisting of young children. *Clangers* is a British stop-motion TV series for children. It was initially broadcast during the 1960s and 1970s, although it was reprised with new episodes in 2015. Each episode of *Clangers* has a script, but actors use whistles rather than words to give voice to the characters, and the whistles follow the same cadence of the scripted speech. The show's creator, Oliver Postgate, described in an interview that in one of the original episodes, Major Clanger responds to a stuck door by whistling, 'Oh sod it, the bloody thing's stuck again!'. Despite the fact that the words were whistled rather than spoken, and therefore can be regarded as sanitised, the BBC objected to the line on the ground that 'people will know' (Banks 2005). Communicating even a sanitised form of swearing is, it seems, unacceptable in certain contexts.

This capacity of sanitisation to convey a residue of whatever is objectionable about swear words has been used to comic effect. The 'unnecessary censorship' segment of the American talk show *Jimmy Kimmel Live* features video footage of public figures speaking, censored with bleeps despite the fact that no swearing occurs. The effect, which turns on the association that the audience makes between bleeping and swearing, is to make the speakers appear far more foul-mouthed than they really are. There are written examples of this too: in 2021 the Toronto-based financing software company, Wave, published an advertisement that read, 'Wave Money is changing the whole ***king industry'. The censored word, in this case, is *banking*.[1] Also in 2021, an advertisement for *Clarkson's Farm*, an Amazon Prime documentary show about the efforts of disgraced British journalist Jeremy Clarkson to become a farmer, featured the headline 'Jeremy Clarkson is a f***er'. In both these cases, sanitisation is used to lend shock value to inoffensive words by—to borrow Nancy Friedman's expression—swearifying them.

Sanitisation, then, is sometimes ineffective at reducing offensiveness. But there's more. Sometimes sanitisation makes things worse.

[1] For this and some similar examples, see Friedman (2021).

It does this by encouraging a lazy attitude to reducing offensiveness, which sometimes results in failing to address what is really offensive. An example of this involves the footballer John Terry, who in 2012 stood trial for calling fellow footballer Anton Ferdinand a *fucking Black cunt* during a match. The first and third of these words were sanitised in almost all newspapers that covered the story. In a story about the coverage, *The Guardian* printed a letter from a reader, who wrote:

> Thanks, in any event, to *The Guardian* for reporting without coyness what Mr Terry is alleged to have said to Anton Ferdinand. I never cease to be amazed by newspapers which shyly make him say 'f***ing black c***', leaving intact the one word which aroused Mr Ferdinand's wrath. (Marsh 2012)

This reader raises exactly the worry we are considering here: that sanitising swearing can distract us from other, more serious, sources of offence. Terry, after all, was not standing trial for swearing but for racial abuse. He would not have ended up in court had he omitted the word *Black* and restricted himself to calling Ferdinand a *fucking cunt* (although he may, perhaps, have been punished by sporting or broadcasting authorities). It was the inclusion of *Black* that turned a mere sweary insult into a slur. Conversely, the word *Black* is not offensive, but it became so when weaponised in the way that Terry used it. Should Terry's outburst, then, have been sanitised (if at all) as *f***ing B***k c****? No: I think doing this would have been unsatisfactory for at least two reasons. First, *Black* is not a word that is generally sanitised, and sanitising it would therefore have been puzzling to readers. Second, given that *Black* is generally used in a neutral or positive way to refer to Black people, implying (through sanitisation) that it is offensive would have been insulting. Terry's expression was, in effect, unsanitisable. By mindlessly following a 'sanitise rude words' rule, newspapers that published *f***ing Black c**** failed to grapple with these wider issues, while also sending a shoulder-shrugging *We've done enough* signal.

A more dramatic example—because it contains a slur—comes from the consistently awful *Daily Mail* in January 2022. The tabloid's Twitter account shared a link to a story entitled 'Model is filmed calling Asian club doorman "a little [p-word] f**k"'. The *Daily Mail* printed the p-word in full. While the *Daily Mail* later deleted the tweet and sanitised the slur on their website, the journalist Lorraine King tweeted a screenshot of the original tweet with the words, 'Is it just me that finds the p-word much more offensive than the f-word?' The resounding reply from her followers was: No.

The need to align one's sanitisation practices with more widely implemented values goes beyond decisions about which words to print and which to censor. The British daily tabloid *The Sun* published a photograph of a topless model on page 3 of every issue between November 1970 and January 2015. This was always controversial, and the practice finally ended following a high-profile 'No More Page 3' campaign that had run for several years. At the same time, *The Sun* has long had a policy of not printing the word *tits* in full—it prints a sanitised version, *t*ts*. This sanitisation policy suggests that *The Sun*'s editors take a solicitous attitude towards any readers who might be offended by *tits*, yet almost forty-five years of printing uncensored photographs of tits, despite controversy, betray a different attitude. As in the John Terry case and the *Daily Mail* case, *The Sun*'s approach to mitigating offensive content is brainless: it sanitises the usual words yet fails to engage with wider questions about offensiveness.

These examples illustrate that sanitising swear words can go hand in hand with a complacent and thoughtless attitude towards mitigating offence. If we are serious about taking steps to ensure that we do not cause undue offence, then we should be prepared to invest more care, thought, and effort into this than is required by simply substituting asterisks for letters in certain words. Mitigating offensiveness requires a level of empathy and sensitivity to the feelings of others that is absent from the examples of sanitisation that we just considered; it also requires reflection on when the importance of not causing offence is outweighed by other considerations, such as the importance of reporting the news accurately, or the importance of highlighting an injustice. But this itself is not an argument against sanitisation; it is, rather, a cautionary tale about the importance of not underestimating what is required in order to avoid giving undue offence. And while the examples above provide an interesting contrast between, on the one hand, vigilance against giving offence, and on the other, a thoughtless or even reckless attitude towards offending other people, they do not provide evidence that sanitising swear words leads one to be *more* offensive. There are more important things we can do to avoid causing offence than sanitising swear words, but this does not entail that sanitising swear words is a bad idea.

15

Swearing as a force for good

Our focus, so far, has been on offensive swearing: what makes it offensive, how it compares to other offensive language, and how its offensiveness can be mitigated. But, isn't there an upside to swearing—and even to offensiveness more generally? Consider the following anecdote from journalist Joan Acocella:

> The philosopher Noël Carroll told me once of an international conference in Hanoi in 2006. On the first day, to break the ice, the Vietnamese and the Western scholars, taking turns, had a joke-telling contest. The first two Vietnamese scholars told off-color jokes, but the Westerners, still fearful of committing some social error, stuck to clean jokes. A stiff courtesy reigned. Finally, the third Western contestant (Carroll, and he recounted this proudly) told a filthy joke about a rooster, and everyone relaxed. The conference went on to be a great success. (Acocella 2017)

Three cheers for Noël Carroll, his 'filthy joke about a rooster', and the death of 'stiff courtesy'. Let's take a look at the good that swearing can do, in spite of—or even because of—its capacity to offend.

Respect the power of swearing

Plenty has been written about the advantages of swearing. Perhaps the most well-known recent work in this vein is a series of studies by psychologist Richard Stephens and his colleagues, who showed that swearing can help us withstand pain. Stephens had his experimental subjects submerge a hand in a bucket of very cold water for as long as they could. Doing this is, after a while, painful, not simply cold. Some participants repeatedly swore while their hand was submerged. Others remained silent, or uttered a neutral word, like *solid*. Those who swore during the experiment were able to withstand the pain for longer than those who remained silent, or who uttered a neutral word. Stephens and colleagues then introduced some invented swear words—*fouch* and *twizpipe*—to test whether the analgesic effect of swear words was due to their being funny and distracting. The real swear words came out on top (Stephens and Umland 2011; Stephens and Robertson 2020). And it's not just the pain we feel in our bodies that swearing can help us withstand: a study by psychologists Michael Philipp and Laura Lombardo found that swearing helps us cope with the 'social pain' resulting from being ostracised (Philipp and Lombardo 2017).

Stephens and his co-authors suggest that swearing helps us cope with pain because it increases emotional arousal. Even so, among those participants who swore during the experiment, the analgesic effect was greater for those who tend not to swear a lot during their daily lives than for those who swear a lot. This points to one way in which swearing regularly can rob the words of some of their power for the person who swears—their 'power', in this case (and if Stephens and his collaborators are right about why swearing helps people withstand pain), is the emotional change we undergo when we swear.

The worry that swearing too much robs swear words of their power is a pretty commonly expressed objection to swearing—and it implicitly recognises the value of swearing. After all, why worry about swear words losing their power if their power is not something worth preserving? This concern was brought out by the comparison that we considered in the introduction between the British public's outraged reaction to the Sex Pistols swearing on TV in 1976 and the far milder reaction to former Sex Pistol John Lydon swearing on TV in 2004. The comparison did not pass unremarked at the time of the second incident, with various people—including Mark Lawson in *The Guardian*—asking whether this heralded the demise of swearing (Lawson 2004). This concern has not gone away: I was asked to write an article on exactly this topic for *The Ethics Centre* in 2015 (Roache 2015). The worry is that swearing's power to shock and offend means that it has expressive power that other words lack, and that by overusing swear words, they lose this power and become more like non-swear words: still useful, perhaps, but not uniquely so. Is there substance to this worry?

Well, yes and no. It's certainly true that the shock power of individual swear words rises and falls. Part of that has to do with context: as Lawson notes, one important difference between the Sex Pistols' sweary TV interview in 1976 and John Lydon's 2004 outburst is that the former occurred during a teatime broadcast whereas the latter took place almost ninety minutes after the 9 pm watershed—the time after which, in the UK, TV shows may contain material that is not suitable for children—and so even ignoring the twenty-eight-year gap between them, we could expect the former to be more shocking than the latter.

Broadcasting restrictions on swearing are often viewed as the outcome of a tug-of-war between those who value freedom of expression and conservatives who want to keep the airwaves clean—but, at least in one instance, swearing's power to offend has been put to humane use. British comedy duo Mel and Sue (Mel Giedroyc and Sue Perkins) found an ingenious way to use the rules against swearing on air to protect the privacy of overemotional contestants while co-hosting the baking competition series *The Great British Bake Off*. In an interview with *The Guardian* in 2013, Perkins explained, 'if we see [a contestant] crying or something, Mel and I will go over there and put our coats over them or swear a lot because we know then that the film won't be able to be used' (Carpenter 2013).

The measure of swearing's capacity to offend, however, does not depend solely on who the audience is and how accepting they are of offensive language in general. The power of individual swear words to shock and offend changes over time too. That's just what happens with swear words, and explains why *damn* is not as shocking a word today as it once was. Swear words tend to track wider cultural values: the words that we find most shocking and offensive are those linked to the things we value the most. So, as society has become more secular, the shock value of *damn* has receded; and in the last couple of decades, the offensiveness of slurs relating to ethnicity, sexual orientation, and disability has increased. I don't think we need worry that we're going to run out of ways to shock, offend, express strong emotion, cope with pain, and so on. But what's interesting about the worry that we might, is that despite being often expressed by people who disapprove of swearing, it reveals a recognition that swearing is valuable, and that it performs an important function that can't be performed using other words. On this view, swearing is a linguistic superpower that must be respected and used with care—otherwise we squander its precious gifts.

Swearing and intimacy

There is something to this worry—even if it's unlikely that we're going to run out of ways to do the things that we do with swearing. Much has been written on the good things that swearing enables us to do. Michael Adams—whose discussion of the intimacy-fostering *cunt* in *Six Feet Under* readers will recall from Chapter 12—has argued that far from being simply a crass way to upset people, there are many overlooked uses to which we put swearing; uses for which other words are no good (Adams 2016a). Part of this relates to breaking the rules of politeness in a particular, calculated way—something that is illustrated by the anecdote above about Noël Carroll.

The point is this: while, in most circumstances, politeness is important in oiling the wheels of our social interactions, sometimes impoliteness plays the same role. Trusting another person to recognise when our impoliteness is done with love, and to react warmly to it, can be an effective way to increase intimacy. Perhaps you have close friends with whom you don't think twice about swearing, and never worry about them taking offence. Imagine it's the first time you casually swear in this way with a new friend: often, there's a brief moment of *Can I say this? Can I trust them not to take offence?* In those situations, an analogue of offence escalation can occur—an analogue that we might call *trust escalation*. We take a risk and decide to trust a new friend to react positively to our swearing; they, recognising the risk we have taken and the trust we have placed in them, react in exactly the way we hoped they would and match our casual swearing with their own; we recognise and are encouraged by their positive response; they recognise that we have reacted in this way; and the friendship increases in intimacy. In this way, swearing—and other breaches of etiquette, like Carroll's dirty joke—can be an effective way to support intimacy and connection. The link between swearing and intimacy has been noticed by scientists: in a 2004 study, psychologists recorded the conversations of workers in a New Zealand soap factoryand found that good-humoured swearing was common between workers who knew each other well but absent in conversations between workers who were not part of the same group (Daly et al. 2004). Michael Adams, too, draws on examples from literature, politics, blogging, and beyond to argue that swearing—and profanity more widely—plays an important role in 'marking and developing intimacy' (Adams 2016a, 59).

Not unrelated to all of this is a 2017 study entitled 'Frankly, we do give a damn: The relationship between profanity and honesty', which found that profanity is associated with honesty and integrity (Feldman et al. 2017). This article opens with the quotation alluded to in the title: 'Frankly my dear, I don't give a damn'. The authors go on to remark: 'Profane as it is, this memorable line by the character Rhett Butler in the film *Gone with the Wind* profoundly conveys Butler's honest thoughts and feelings' (816). The role that swearing can play in establishing intimacy, along with its link with honesty, indicates that much as we might value good manners, we also view them as introducing distance between ourselves and those with whom we interact—distance that it can be satisfying to close so that we get a better look at what sort of person we're dealing with. Something like this satisfaction perhaps underpins the glee with which news stories about swearing (and other etiquette breaches) by royalty and other upstanding figures are reported and consumed. Many layers of tradition, ceremony, and ritual separate these people from the rest of us; but when they swear inappropriately, it turns out that in this one respect at least, they are not so different from the people we work and socialise with.

Swearing as a pressure valve

In *Swearing Is Good for You*, Emma Byrne runs through a range of swearing's benefits. Among the ones described above, she also argues that swearing 'forestalls violence'. Byrne explains: 'Without swearing, we'd have to resort to the biting, gouging, and shit flinging that our other primate cousins use to keep their societies in check' (2017, 203). She points, for support, to the work of Professor Roger Fouts, who adopted chimpanzees, taught them sign language, and studied how they communicate. It turned out that the chimps would use the sign for shit in much the same way that we humans use the word *shit*; in other words, not just to refer literally to shit, but also non-literally as an insult and to express emotion. 'Unlike their wild cousins', Byrne remarks, 'these chimpanzees would throw the notion of excrement instead of throwing the stuff itself' (2017, 204). If this is right, then our capacity to swear functions as an emotional pressure valve and enables us to express the anger and frustration that we might otherwise vent through violence. Disapproving of angry swearing, in this case, is short-sighted: you might not like to hear a shouty *Fuck you!* but you'd probably enjoy a fistfight even less.

This pressure-valve view of swearing might seem at odds with the idea that swearing can constitute fighting words; that is, the idea that swearing can make subsequent violence *more* likely, rather than less likely. However, it could be that both are correct. According to the pressure-valve view, when a speaker uses swearing to vent their anger, they are less likely to use violence themself. But if their swearing constitutes fighting words, then it is more likely that *others* will turn violent. This makes intuitive sense: if you're feeling angry and you're allowed to yell swear words at someone who just stands there and takes it, you can probably expect to run out of steam pretty quickly. But as self-calming measures go, it's a risky strategy, since you're reasonably likely to find yourself on the receiving end of your interlocutor's own sweary outburst (if not their fist)—which is likely to send your stress levels up rather than down.

The examples of swearing's positive side that we've considered in this chapter all have something in common: they tell us that if we were tempted to dismiss swearing as nothing more than offensive language, we have underestimated it. Sure, swearing offends people—but look at all the good things it can do too!

16

The value of offensiveness

Throughout this book, I've been taking for granted that it's pretty easy to offend people. Too easy, perhaps. So easy that we need strategies to avoid inadvertently offending people even when we're just trying to communicate with them. But what if things were different? What if we struggled to cause offence even when we wanted to? What if we could throw out as many *cunts* and *motherfuckers* as we liked, as repetitively and directly and aggressively as we could manage, and all we'd get in response were indulgent smiles and perhaps comments about how adorable we are? What, exactly, would we *lack* in that case—and is it something worth having? In this chapter I want to show you that there are some people who lack something important through their inability to cause offence by swearing, and that by lacking it, they are victims of a moral wrong.

Swearing and disability

Feinberg makes a pretty strong claim about swearing. He writes:

> By virtue of an almost paradoxical tension between powerful taboo and universal readiness to disobey, the words acquire their strong expressive power. The utterance of one of these words for any purpose in an inappropriate social context is sure to produce,

> as if by magic, an extraordinary emotional response in one's listeners, most of whom treat the word with a kind of exaggerated respect, anxiety, and even fear. (1985, 190–91)

He's wrong, unfortunately. It's not the case that swearing inappropriately 'is sure to produce' the 'extraordinary emotional response in one's listeners' that we associate with saying the wrong thing at the wrong time. Only certain speakers can reliably offend people with swearing, by which I mean that some speakers can utter swear words as disrespectfully and aggressively and directly as they can and yet still not manage to produce a feeling of offence in those around them.

The late Mel Baggs, an American disabled activist and blogger, highlighted this issue in a blog post, and explained why it is a problem. Baggs used a computerised communication device to express what they were 'unable to say in real time'. One page of their communication software was devoted to asserting boundaries with other people, and featured sentences that they could utter by tapping a picture. The sentences varied in forcefulness, ranging from the relatively polite *Leave me alone* and *You're too close to me* to assertions like *Get out of my face* and *Fuck off*. On their blog, Baggs described a distressing encounter with a woman who tried to force Baggs to converse and make eye contact with her, and who became patronising and abusive when Baggs tried to make it clear that they didn't want to interact. Baggs explained the importance of being able to treat people rudely:

> It is absolutely vital that people who use communication devices, have ways to respond to violations of our basic boundaries. Disabled people are far more likely than others to have others behave invasively with us, ranging from subtle to violent. People teach us from our earliest years onward that such invasion is normal, natural, and something we should accept without complaint. We *have* to have the means to say no.

> And we have to have the means to say no forcefully, even rudely. We need to be *able* to use cuss words, even if we have the kind of personality that would never use them. Sometimes the only reason that we appear unnaturally even-tempered is because we've never been allowed to be otherwise. We have the right to say *fuck off*, but people don't always give us the *ability* to do so.
>
> Of course, even if we say things like that, there's no guarantee anyone will listen. Some people's reactions when I get mad, remind me of the way people giggle at my cat when she swipes someone who touched her in a way that hurts her. It's like she and I aren't *real* enough to them, so our anger is cute and funny.
>
> I'll also never forget the time someone made an asinine comment when I was out in public. I typed a response and stuck the speaker up to his ear so he could hear it. All his friends burst out laughing. One of them said 'Dude, that guy's cussing you out using a machine!' Which is . . . so much not the response I was going for. (Baggs 2012)

When Baggs tells us that 'people don't always give [them] the *ability* to' say *fuck off*, what they mean is that while they can (with the help of their communication device) utter the words, those words fail to impact their listener in the way that they would had another person uttered them. Baggs simply wasn't recognised—or, perhaps, given permission—by others as someone who could swear offensively. Their comment that their anger is regarded by others as 'cute and funny' provides us with a clue about why their attempt to cause offence with swearing didn't come off: the sorts of speaker emotions that, as we saw in Chapter 6, typically make swearing more objectionable, failed to do so when Baggs swore angrily, because those around them either didn't notice the anger or, if they did, were not affected by it in the usual way. Saying *fuck off* to another person, in a polite context, ought to shock and offend them—but Baggs found themself unable to produce this effect by uttering the words.

Swearing in a foreign language

People with disabilities aren't the only ones who may find it difficult to shock and offend people through swearing. People for whom the language in which they are swearing is their second (or third, fourth, fifth . . .) language—for brevity, *LX users*—also experience a bumpy ride with swearing.

As far as I can tell, there has not been any published research on how people for whom the language in question is their first language—*L1 users*—view swearing by LX users. Research on swearing and multilingualism has tended to focus on how LX users view swearing, rather than how their swearing is viewed by others. This research has found that LX users view swear words in the LX to have less 'emotional force' than swear words in their L1 (Dewaele 2010b; Gawinkowska et al. 2013), or as being 'weaker' (Dewaele 2010a), or even 'fake' (Dewaele 2010c). LX users also tend to have a reduced understanding of exactly what LX swear words mean and how strong they are, compared to L1 users (Dewaele 2016). This is a predictable consequence of the fact that students of foreign languages tend not to be taught by their instructors how to swear—an oversight that Geraldine Horan has argued needs to be corrected (Horan 2013).

Jean-Marc Dewaele—a multilingual researcher who has published extensively on LX users and swearing, and whose scholarly articles include the wonderfully named '"Christ fucking shit merde!" Language preferences for swearing among maximal proficient multilinguals'—has remarked that 'LX speakers may not realise that their swearing in the LX might be interpreted differently by L1 users compared to the same words used by L1 speakers in an identical situation' (Dewaele 2017, 2). When I emailed him to ask him for his thoughts on this, he was kind enough to elaborate further, with the comment that 'L1 users may react more diversely to swearing by LX users than by fellow L1 users'. On the one hand, L1 users, detecting a foreign accent or some other sign that the LX speaker is not part of the in-group, may judge swearing by a LX speaker more harshly, because they view swearing in the L1 as a privilege open only to L1 speakers. But on the other hand, L1 speakers, sensing that LX speakers do not fully grasp the meaning and the strength of L1 swear words, often view swearing by LX speakers as less offensive than swearing by L1 speakers.

Children, again

Something similar is true of children. We understand that, as Timothy Jay and Kristin Janschewitz put it, children 'acquire the knowledge that some words are taboo before developing a nuanced understanding of how and when to use taboo words' (Jay and Janschewitz 2008, 275). Sometimes, swearing by children is more shocking and offensive than swearing by adults, although much of that turbo-charged shock relates to the fact *that* a child swore, rather than to the specific term that they used. Other times, swearing by children is funny—and again, this is often due to the shock of hearing a child swear. If a child's sweary outburst happens to be caught on camera, then so much the better. This is what happened a few years ago with a twenty-five-second video clip of a smartly dressed toddler standing in a garden as some bubbles float past her. When she spots them, she calls, 'Come back, bubbles! Come back!'—before turning back to the potted plant she had been examining and muttering, 'Fuck's sake'. Predictably, the clip became widely shared on social media, where the reaction was hilarity rather than offence. That sweet little girl in her shiny shoes, and her *Fuck's sake*. How incongruous!

Toddlers are unlikely to lose much sleep over the fact that they face difficulties being taken seriously when they swear—they do, after all, have more effective weapons in their arsenal for upsetting people, like throwing tantrums, inflicting sustained sleep deprivation, covering entire rooms with Vaseline (as my daughter once did), and using a rock to wash their mother's car (as my son once did). But as Mel Baggs's account illustrates, being incapable of causing shock and offence by swearing can be a real problem. People with disabilities and foreign speakers of our language lose out on an important aspect of communication by not being able reliably to cause offence. It happens because they are not part of the 'in-group.' In other words, their difficulties with causing offence reveal them not to be part of the group whose opinion most people care about, and whose validation and respect matter.

In some cases it is appropriate not to treat people as members of the in-group, but in other cases it reflects unjust attitudes. To see this, imagine, first, how you might react to another adult who takes offence at a toddler's *Fuck's sake* in the same way that they'd take offence at the same utterance by an adult. I expect you'd view them as overreacting. You might say to them something like, 'Hey, it's just a little kid, don't take it so seriously'. You'd say that because you think it's a mistake to include a toddler in the group of people who are capable of offending you by swearing. By contrast, imagine urging someone not to take seriously swearing by a person with a disability. The latter would be outrageous. Having a disability ought not to disqualify a person from being recognised as a member of the in-group.[1]

This is what Baggs complained about when they wrote that people with disabilities 'have the right to say *fuck off*, but people don't always give us the *ability* to do so'. Their point is that people with disabilities ought to be capable of producing the same effects with *fuck off* that (almost) everyone else is able to produce, but they aren't, because they are inappropriately excluded from the in-group—or, as Baggs puts it, they aren't considered '*real* enough'.

[1] What about cases where someone swears involuntarily, as people with Tourette's syndrome do? There *is* a case here for not reacting with offence, but not because the swearer does not belong to the in-group. Rather, this sort of swearing can be viewed as inoffensive because there is no question of it expressing the sort of disrespect that we associate with inappropriate swearing.

Swearing on the outside

In fact, the group of people who are excluded from the in-group, and who consequently lose out on being able to offend by swearing, is much bigger and diverse than I've suggested so far. People who are unusual in any way risk not being able to use swearing effectively. If you're very small; if you're unconventionally dressed; if you speak with a high-pitched voice, a strong accent, or some other unusual way of speaking; if you're very old; if you're recognisably *other* in some way, then your ability to produce certain effects in other people by swearing is less reliable and predictable than it is for other people. In certain cases—especially those where you are viewed as unusually strong or powerful—your swearing might cause *more* shock and offence than other people's swearing. But for the most part, you might find that you're not '*real* enough' to cause offence.

This is a form of inequality that most of us don't consider. When we think about the norms around swearing, what's most likely to spring to mind is the widespread thought that swearing is in some sense impermissible, and it's impermissible because it's offensive, or at least potentially offensive. For most people, most of the time, normative issues around swearing focus on how to mitigate the risk of offending people. How to deal with the risk of *not* offending people when we swear is something we don't think about, because we don't have to. Most of us enjoy sweary privilege.

All this raises a normative question about swearing that we haven't yet considered. We've seen that sometimes, the right thing to do might be to avoid swearing, in order to avoid causing offence. But perhaps we ought also to consider that sometimes, the right thing to do might be to feel offended by someone else's swearing. Because not being offended by another person's swearing could be a sign that something is awry in the way that we relate to that person, and in some cases, that could be cause for ethical concern. If you're completely unconcerned by someone telling you to fuck off, ask yourself why. Would you have been offended had someone else said the same thing to you? Would you have been offended if the speaker had been a different gender, nationality, age, physical size, or if they had sounded or looked or behaved differently when they spoke? Concluding that you would have felt offended had someone else told you to fuck off is not necessarily a red flag: we've seen that there is a complex combination of factors that contribute to how offensive a particular instance of swearing is. But reflecting on our attitudes and patterns of offence in response to swearing can help us spot influences that ought not to be there. If we find that we're less offended by the swearing of—say—people with disabilities, small people, or bizarrely dressed people than by the swearing of abled people, average-sized people, and conventionally dressed people, something is wrong. This does not mean that we do something wrong—immoral, unethical, rude—by failing to be offended by the swearing of a particular person. But it might mean that, for no good reason, we care less about that person's attitude towards us than we do about other people's attitudes towards us. That is a moral issue: it reveals that we're not respecting them as we should. Even people who are very unlike us are capable of spotting a twat when they see one.

Conclusion

You're all fucking superheroes

Swearing, in its own modest way, is a superpower. Understanding it—and I hope you're ending this book feeling that you understand swearing better than you did when you started it—is a rewarding process that reveals to us some of the vast complexity and richness in the way we use language to relate to each other. Language is, of course, a tool that enables us to communicate information to one another; but the way we swear reveals that language also enables us (among other things) to express and communicate how we feel, to fast-track trust and intimacy with others, to cause shock and upset, to create and reinforce shared values, and to defuse or escalate tension and conflict. And, incredibly, most of this stuff is going on between and behind the words that we actually utter: it happens through the inferences that we make about each other when we interact, inferences that we generally don't even realise we're making. There's some comfort to that, especially in a world that has social conservatives shaking their heads and moaning about how society is falling apart because young people today are more connected to their smartphones than they are to each other. It turns out that even while we're screaming sweary abuse at each other, we understand each other more than we think. Even a snarled *Fuck you!* is a rich and complex form of connection. (It is, of course, a form of connection that most of us would rather pass on—so, keep that in mind before you say it to your boss or your prospective in-laws.)

It's precisely because swearing is so powerful that we are faced with some of the dangers that we've looked at in the course of this book. Our knee-jerk response to swearing can be so dramatic that we take leave of our senses and unreflectively judge those who swear inappropriately to have done a Bad Thing. These automatic responses can conceal bias and prejudice, which is a big problem when they are fast-tracked into law or other formal regulations. We've seen that, if we can slow down and reflect on the way we respond to swearing, then not only can we reduce the influence of bias and prejudice, but we can also use the power of swearing to reflect and reinforce social values in order to create a more just society. Of course, sensible decisions about swearing alone aren't going to lead us to Utopia, but they can be one tool in the armoury we use to fight injustice.

Embrace your superpower, friends. Use it wisely. Just don't pull on your underpants over your tights, superhero style. You'll look like a fucking knob.

Acknowledgements

I'm approaching this acknowledgements section with more anxiety than I've approached any other part of the book, because so many people have contributed in various ways to creating this book, and I would be mortified to forget to mention any of them. Very early in the project—as in, during the first few days—I received encouragement from Jennifer Saul and Nigel Warburton. I was invited to give a St Cross Special Ethics Seminar at the University of Oxford in early 2015, which the university advertised on the main page of its website (I still have the screenshot somewhere) and which quickly became fully booked. I'm embarrassed at the half-baked ideas I shared during that talk, but the enthusiasm and engagement of the audience members were inspiring, and I'm especially grateful to Roger Crisp for his generous and thoughtful write-up of the talk on the university's Practical Ethics blog.

Nigel Warburton opened my mind to the possibility that there may be more mileage in this topic than a couple of articles in a scholarly journal, and he pushed me to write this book, as well as invited me to record an interview on swearing for *Philosophy Bites*, the podcast he hosts with David Edmonds. I had such an inspiring and interesting conversation with them, both during the interview and behind the scenes.

My agent, Peter Buckman, was supportive and encouraging throughout and kept up a patter of swearily good-humoured emails even while the three months he initially expected I'd need to write this book (dream on, Peter) turned into seven years. I am, he has told me, his slowest ever client, living or dead. Towards the end of the process he even threatened to die before publication if I didn't get a bloody move on. Equally lovely, encouraging, and patient is Lucy Randall, my editor at Oxford University Press. She has been kind and understanding as one deadline after another whizzed by with no sign of a finished draft. Her approach to editing the draft has involved ten parts enthusiastic compliments to one part helpful criticism, which I appreciated very much especially as I've spent most of the process worrying that I've written a laughable pile of junk. I'm sorry, Lucy, that I didn't quite manage to remove all the funeral-related examples in the text (I used to be a goth, it's in my DNA now). Lucy also came up with the title of the book, after I'd spent years puzzling about it. Yay, Lucy!

While I'm on the subject of my publisher, the entire team at Oxford University Press has been wonderfully enthusiastic and supportive. Everything they've done has exceeded my expectations, from the beautifully designed and barely-censored cover to the mind-bogglingly detailed publicity plan.

Someone else who took a wonderfully encouraging and thoughtful approach to providing feedback is Karen Stohr, who reviewed the draft for Oxford University Press, initially anonymously (to me). I was so worried about receiving the review that I didn't open it for a few days, and eventually got a fellow academic in another discipline to read it for me and report back (thanks, Marcus Munafó). I needn't have worried: the review combined extremely sensible criticism with plenty of praise, in a masterclass of how reviewing other people's work does not need to be the painful and combative process it often is. I was delighted to find out the identity of the reviewer, since I am a big fan of Karen's work and had already quoted it in the book.

Aside from my woeful smattering of Welsh, I am embarrassingly monolingual and could not have written about swearing in other languages without help from other people. I appealed for help via Philos-L, an email list for philosophers that has been going for so long that I hear Aristotle used it in his research for the *Nicomachean*

Ethics. I asked my fellow subscribers to email me about the most offensive words in their first language. Plenty of people took the time to respond, and the replies were incredibly interesting and entertaining. The examples of swearing from around the world in Chapter 2 are mostly thanks to these people.

This section is already pretty long, so let me just reel off an alphabetised list of names of some of the people whose advice, feedback, and ideas have helped me develop my ideas at various points, and who I haven't mentioned yet either in this section or in the main text: Andrew Bowie, Matthew Broome, Nick Davis, Ed Lake, Gail Leckie, Neil Levy, Hannah Maslen, Jonny Pugh, Clemens Setz, Nick Shea, Josh Shepherd, Mark Silcox, and Malcolm Voyce.

I've given more talks and interviews on this topic and written more articles than I can remember (and I'm not great at keeping records). I'm so grateful to those who invited me, and to those who attended, for their interest and thoughtful comments and questions. Off the top of my head, these have included audiences at Oxford, Royal Holloway, Nottingham, Warwick, St. Andrews, and the Hay-on-Wye. I've also taught this topic to third-year philosophy undergraduates as part of my Philosophy of Language module at Royal Holloway, and the class discussions have been unfailingly fascinating and lively. It's difficult to spend seven years writing a book without getting bored of the topic, but the wonderful audiences I've shared my work with have buoyed me up and helped me rediscover my interest in swearing again and again at times when I'd rather have stuck pins in my eyes than encountered another *fuck*.

Finally, the process of writing this book has been fraught with difficulty unrelated to the subject matter. When I started, I was in dire personal circumstances, which were nevertheless way better than they had been a few years previously. If you want details, look up the 'Why I took SO BLOODY LONG to write my book' episode of my podcast, *The Academic Imperfectionist*. I've reached the end of the process battle-scarred and with an ADHD diagnosis and a lot of insight about myself that I've gained largely thanks to my therapist, Sanchia Barlow, and my coach, Rumbi Moyo. For my next trick, I'm going to write another book and complete it in a sensible amount of time, like a normal person. There, I've written it down, so now I have to do it.

References

Académie Française. 2019. 'Salop ou Salaud?', June 6. Available at http://www.academie-francaise.fr/salop-ou-salaud.

Acocella, Joan. 2017. '"Fuck"-ing Around'. *The New York Review*, February 9. Available at https://nybooks.com/articles/2017/02/09/f-ing-around/.

Adams, Michael. 2016a. *In Praise of Profanity*. New York: Oxford University Press.

Adams, Michael. 2016b. 'Making Friends with "Cunt"'. *Strong Language*, October 28. Available at https://stronglang.wordpress.com/2016/10/28/making-friends-with-cunt/.

Allen, Keith, and Kate Burridge. 2006. *Forbidden Words: Taboo and the Censoring of Language*. Cambridge: Cambridge University Press.

Anderson, Luvell. 2018. 'Calling, Addressing, and Appropriation'. In *Bad Words: Philosophical Perspectives on Slurs*, edited by David Sosa, 6–28. Oxford: Oxford University Press.

Anderson, Luvell, and Ernie Lepore. 2013. 'Slurring Words'. *Noûs* 47, no. 1: 25–48.

Anderson, Nick. 2020. 'A Stanford Law Professor Read a Quote with the n-Word to His Class, Stirring Outrage at the School'. *The Washington Post*, June 4. Available at https://www.washingtonpost.com/education/2020/06/03/stanford-law-professor-read-quote-with-n-word-his-class-stirring-outrage-school/.

Andersson, Lars-G., and Peter Trudgill. 1992. *Bad Language*. London: Penguin.

'Argentine Mothers Hold Mass Breastfeeding Protest'. 2016. *Deccan Chronicle*, July 24. Available at https://www.deccanchronicle.com/world/america/240716/argentine-mothers-hold-mass-breastfeeding-protest.html.

Atta, Dean. 2013. *I Am Nobody's Nigger*. London: Westbourne Press.

Austin, John L. 1962. *How to Do Things with Words: The William James Lectures Delivered in Harvard in 1955*. 2nd ed. Edited by J. O. Urmson and Marina Sbisà. Oxford: Clarendon Press.

Baggs, Mel. 2012. 'Communication Page I Used to Handle That Invasive Woman I Met'. *Ballastexistenz*, June 25. Available at https://ballastexistenz.wordpress.com/2012/06/25/communication-page-i-used-to-handle-that-invasive-woman-i-met/.

Banks, Clive. 2005. 'An Interview with Oliver Postgate'. Available at http://www.clivebanks.co.uk/Oliverpostgateinterview.htm.

Bet, Martina. 2019. 'Royal RAGE: How "Bossy" Prince Philip Was Heard SWEARING at Queen Elizabeth II'. *Express*, January 8. Available at https://www.express.co.uk/news/royal/1068345/royal-news-queen-elizabeth-ii-prince-philip-buckingham-palace-spt.

Bianchi, Claudia. 2014. 'Slurs and Appropriation: An Echoic Account'. *Journal of Pragmatics* 66: 35–44.

BlackTree TV. 2018. 'Kendrick Lamar Stops White Fan Rapping n-Word Onstage, Is He Wrong?' YouTube, May 21. Available at https://youtu.be/KEcugkqcHO8.

Bloom, D. 2014. 'Swearing Is Emotional and Creative Language Say Researchers Who Claim It Is GOOD for You'. *Daily Mail*, May 11. Available at http://www.dailymail.co.uk/news/article-2625581/Swearing-emotional-creative-language-say-researchers-claim-GOOD-you.html.

Bowers, Jeffrey, and Christopher W. Playdell-Pearce. 2011. 'Swearing, Euphemisms, and Linguistic Relativity'. *PLoS One* 6, no. 7: e22341.

Brontë, Charlotte. 1850. *Two Short Pieces* (Project Gutenberg). Available at https://www.gutenberg.org/files/771/771-h/771-h.htm.

Brophy, John, and Eric Partridge. 1930. *Songs and Slangs of the British Soldier: 1914-1918.* London: E. Partridge Ltd., at the Scholartis Press.

Brown, Lee. 2022. 'University Issues "Trigger Warning" for Mark Twain's "Huckleberry Finn"'. *New York Post*, August 25. Available at https://nypost.com/2022/08/25/university-gives-trigger-warning-for-huckleberry-finn/.

Bruggeman, Lucien. 2018. 'Melania Trump Says She Is One of the Most Bullied People in the World; Distrusts Some in the West Wing'. *ABC News*, October 13. Available at https://abcnews.go.com/Politics/melania-trump-bullied-people-world-distrusts-west-wing/story?id=58419018.

Burgess, Anthony. 1992. *A Mouthful of Air: Language and Languages, Especially English.* London: Hutchinson.

Buss, Sarah. 1999. 'Appearing Respectful: The Moral Significance of Manners'. *Ethics* 109, no. 4: 795–826.

Butler, Carly. W., and Richard Fitzgerald. 2011. '"My F***Ing Personality": Swearing as Slips and Gaffes in Live Television Broadcasts'. *Text & Talk* 31, no. 5: 525–51.

Byrne, Emma. 2017. *Swearing Is Good for You: The Amazing Science of Bad Language.* London: Profile.

Carey, S. 2016. 'Book Review: "In Praise of Profanity" by Michael Adams'. *Strong Language*, October 6. Available at https://stronglang.wordpress.com/2016/10/06/book-review-in-praise-of-profanity-by-michael-adams/.

Carlin, George. 1972. 'Seven Words You Can Never Say on Television'. In *Class Clown.* Santa Monica, CA: Little David/Atlantic.

Carpenter, Louise. 2013. 'Behind the Scenes at The Great British Bake Off'. *The Guardian*, July 20. Available at https://www.theguardian.com/tv-and-radio/2013/jul/20/bake-off-behind-the-scenes.

Carter, R. 2020. 'Young People in the Time of Covid-19: A Fear and Hope Study of 16–24 Year Olds'. *HOPE Not Hate Charitable Trust*. Available at https://www.hopenothate.org.uk/wp-content/uploads/2020/08/youth-fear-and-hope-2020-07-v2final.pdf.

Cavazza, Nicoletta, and Margherita Guidetti. 2014. 'Swearing in Political Discourse: Why Vulgarity Works'. *Journal of Language and Social Psychology* 33, no. 5: 537–47.

CBC News. 2015. 'Taber Bylaw Bans Public Swearing, Spitting and Yelling in Alberta Town'. March 10. Available at https://www.cbc.ca/news/canada/calgary/taber-bylaw-bans-public-swearing-spitting-and-yelling-in-alberta-town-1.2988992.

Channel 4. 2013. *Was It Something I Said?* series 1, episode 4. Clip available at https://youtu.be/r-X4K0D38zQ.

Cherry, Myisha. 2021. *The Case for Rage: Why Anger Is Essential to Anti-Racist Struggle*. New York: Oxford University Press.

Cohen v. California, 403 U.S. 15. 1971.

Copeland, William E., Dieter Wolke, Adrian Angold, and E. Jane Costello. 2013. 'Adult Psychiatric Outcomes of Bullying and Being Bullied by Peers in Childhood and Adolescence'. *JAMA Psychiatry* 70, no. 4: 419–26.

Cornell, D. 1990. 'Doubly-Prized World: Myth, Allegory, and the Feminine'. *Cornell Law Review* 75, no. 3: 643–99.

Crown Prosecution Service. 2022. *Nudity in Public—Guidance on Handling Cases of Naturism*. Available at https://www.cps.gov.uk/legal-guidance/nudity-public-guidance-handling-cases-naturism.

Crystal, David. 2003. *The Cambridge Encyclopaedia of the English Language*. Cambridge: Cambridge University Press.

Daly, Nicola, Janet Holmes, Jonathan Newton, and Maria Stubbe. 2004. 'Expletives as Solidarity Signals in FTAs on the Factory Floor'. *Journal of Pragmatics* 36, no. 5: 945–64.

Davidson, Donald. 1979. 'Quotation'. In *Inquiries into Truth and Interpretation*, 79–92. Oxford: Oxford University Press.

Dearden, Lizzie. 2014. 'WTF? Australian Police Raise Fines for Swearing to $500 in New South Wales'. *Independent*, February 8. Available at https://www.independent.co.uk/news/world/australasia/wtf-australian-police-raise-fines-for-swearing-to-500-in-new-south-wales-9116636.html.

Dewaele, Jean-M. 2010a. 'Christ fucking shit merde!' *Sociolinguistic Studies* 4, no. 3: 595–614.

Dewaele, Jean-M. 2010b. 'The Emotional Force of Swearwords and Taboo Words in the Speech of Multilinguals'. *Journal of Multilingual and Multicultural Development* 25, no. 2–3: 204–22.

Dewaele, Jean-M. 2010c. *Emotions in Multiple Languages*. London: Palgrave Macmillan.

Dewaele, Jean-M. 2016. 'Thirty Shades of Offensiveness: L1 and LX English Users' Understanding, Perception and Self-Reported Use of Negative Emotion-Laden Words'. *Journal of Pragmatics* 94: 112–27.

Dewaele, Jean-M. 2017. 'Self-Reported Frequency of Swearing in English: Do Situational, Psychological and Sociobiographical Variables Have Similar Effects on First and Foreign Language Users?' *Journal of Multilingual and Multicultural Development* 38, no. 4: 330–45.

Dhal, Sharmila. 2013. 'Why Using the "F-Word" Is a Crime'. *Gulf News*, November 6. Available at https://gulfnews.com/uae/why-using-the-f-word-is-a-crime-1.1252234.

Dong, Quang P. 1971. 'English Sentences without Overt Grammatical Subject'. In *Studies Out in Left Field: Defamatory Essays Presented to James D. McCawley*, edited by Arnold M. Zwicky, Peter H. Salus, Robert I. Binnick, and Anthony L. Vanek, 3–20. Edmonton, Ontario: Linguistic Research.

Donnella, Leah. 2017. 'This Halloween: What Does It Mean to Call Something "Spooky"?' *NPR Code Switch*, October 24. Available at https://www.npr.org/sections/codeswitch/2017/10/24/559502238/this-halloween-what-does-it-mean-to-call-something-spooky.

Eckert, Penelope. 2006. 'Communities of Practice'. In *Encyclopedia of Language & Linguistics* (2nd ed.), edited by Keith Brown, 683–85. Oxford: Elsevier.

Fairman, Christopher M. 2006. 'Fuck'. *Ohio State Public Law Working Paper No. 59, Center for Interdisciplinary Law and Policy Studies Working Paper Series No. 39.*

FCC v. Pacifica Found. 1978. 438 U.S. 726, 749.

Federal Communications Commission. 2004. *Complaints against Broadcast Licensees Regarding Their Airing of the 'Golden Globe Awards' Program.* Memorandum Opinion and Order, File No. EB-03-IH-0110. Available at https://transition.fcc.gov/eb/Orders/2004/FCC-04-43A1.html.

Feinberg, Joel. 1983. 'Obscene Words and the Law'. *Law and Philosophy* 2: 139–61.

Feinberg, Joel. 1985. *Offense to Others: The Moral Limits of the Criminal Law.* Oxford: Oxford University Press.

Feldman, Gilad, Huiwen Lian, Michal Kosinski, and David Stillwell. 2017. 'Frankly, We Do Give a Damn: The Relationship between Profanity and Honesty'. *Social Psychological and Personality Science* 8, no. 7: 816–26.

Fox, Kate. 2004. *Watching the English: The Hidden Rules of English Behaviour.* London: Hodder & Stoughton.

Fox News. 2020. 'America Together: Returning to Work Town Hall with President Trump'. Part 2, May 3. Available at https://youtu.be/6HDUYiyF_DQ.

Friedman, N. 2021. 'You Bet Your Asterisk!' *Strong Language*, February 16. Available at https://stronglang.wordpress.com/2021/02/16/you-bet-your-asterisk/.

Fry, Stephen. 1994. *The Hippopotamus*. London: Random House.

Fry, Stephen. 2010. 'Interview with Craig Ferguson'. *The Late Late Show*, February 23. Remarks on swearing available at https://www.youtube.com/watch?v=n1nL-Q2iwyI

Furness, Hannah. 2015. 'Joanne Harris condemns Clean Reader app for Replacing Swear Words in Novels'. *The Telegraph*, March 24. Available at https://www.telegraph.co.uk/news/celebritynews/11492003/Joanne-Harris-condemns-Clean-Reader-app-for-replacing-swear-words-in-novels.html.

Galinsky, Adam D., Cynthia S. Wang, Janet A.Whitson, Eric M. Anicich, Kurt Hugenberg, and Galen V. Bodenhausen. 2013. 'The Reappropriation of Stigmatizing Labels: The Reciprocal Relationship between Power and Self-Labeling'. *Psychological Science* 24, no. 10: 2020–29.

Gander, Kashmira. 2014. 'Australia Threatens to Deport Asylum Seekers Who Spit, Swear or Spread Rumours'. *Independent*, January 30. Available at https://www.independent.co.uk/news/world/australasia/australia-threatens-to-deport-asylum-seekers-who-spit-swear-or-spread-rumours-9097152.html.

Gawinkowska, Marta, Michal B. Paradowski, and Michal Bilewicz. 2013. 'Second Language as an Exemptor from Sociocultural Norms: Emotion-Related Language Choice Revisited'. *PLoS One* 8, no. 12: e81225.

Gimbel, Steven. 2006. 'Four Letter Ethics'. *Philosophers' Playground*, May 17. Available at http://philosophersplayground.blogspot.co.uk/2006/05/four-letter-ethics.html.

Goffman, Erving. 1967. *Interaction Ritual: Essays on Face-to-Face Behavior.* New York: Pantheon Books.

Golden, Martha. 2007. *Don't Play in the Sun: One Woman's Journey through the Color Complex*. New York: Knopf Doubleday.

Grose, Francis. [1785] 1788. *A Classical Dictionary of the Vulgar Tongue*. 2nd ed. London: S. Hooper.

Grove, Thomas. 2013. 'Russian Gay Rights Activists Detained after "Kissing Protest"'. *Reuters*, June 11. Available at https://www.reuters.com/article/russia-gay-idINDEE95A09L20130611.

Haidt, Jonathan. 2001. 'The Emotional Dog and Its Rational Tail: A Social Intuitionist Approach to Moral Judgment'. *Psychological Review* 108, no. 4: 814–34.

Hall, Melanie. 2015. 'Swiss Artist Arrested in Front of Eiffel Tower for "Naked Selfie Performance"'. *The Telegraph*, July 6. Available at https://www.telegraph.co.uk/news/worldnews/europe/france/11720839/Swiss-artist-arrested-in-front-of-Eiffel-Tower-for-naked-selfie-performance.html.

Hartzer, Cleo. 2018. 'Punching Up, Punching Down: Why Melissa Wolf Is Right and Matt Groening Is Wrong'. *The Good Men Project*, May 2. Available at https://goodmenproject.com/featured-content/punching-up-punching-down-phtz/.

HG.org. 2022. 'Nudity and Public Decency Laws in America'. Available at https://www.hg.org/legal-articles/nudity-and-public-decency-laws-in-america-31193.

Higgins, Colin. 2012. 'Cannes: Ken Loach Brands BBFC Hypocritical over Cuts to the c-Word'. *The Guardian*, May 22. Available at https://www.theguardian.com/film/2012/may/22/ken-loach-bbfc-hypocritical.

Hodgkinson, Mike. 2019. 'The Slants: Asian-American Band Who Took the Fight for Their Name to the US Supreme Court'. *Post Magazine*, March 24. Available at https://www.scmp.com/magazines/post-magazine/long-reads/article/3002529/slants-asian-american-band-who-took-fight-their.

Holt, Richard, and Nigel Baker. 2001. 'Indecent Exposure—Sexuality, Society and the Archaeological Record'. In *Towards a Geography of Sexual Encounter: Prostitution in English Medieval Towns*, edited by Lynne Bevan. Glasgow, Scotland: Cruithne Press.

hooks, bell. 2003. *Rock My Soul: Black People and Self-Esteem*. New York: Atria.

Horan, Geraldine. 2013. '"You Taught Me Language; and My Profit on't/Is, I Know How to Curse": Cursing and Swearing in Foreign Language Learning'. *Language and Intercultural Communication* 13, no. 3: 283–97.

Humber, James M., and Robert H. Almeder, eds. 1976. *Biomedical Ethics and the Law*. Boston, MA: Springer.

Ipsos MORI. 2016. *Attitudes to Potentially Offensive Language and Gestures on TV and Radio*. Ofcom-commissioned research report. Available at https://www.ofcom.org.uk/__data/assets/pdf_file/0022/91624/OfcomOffensiveLanguage.pdf.

Iricibar, Valentina. 2016. 'Mass Breastfeeding Protest Organised after Woman Is Banned from Publicly Doing So'. *The Bubble*, July 19. Available at https://www.thebubble.com/mass-breastfeeding-protest-organized-after-woman-is-banned-from-publicly-doing-so.

Jackson, Hughlings. [1866] 1958. *Selected Writings of Hughlings Jackson*, Vol. 2. New York: Basic Books.

Jay, Timothy B. 2009. 'Do Offensive Words Harm People?' *Psychology, Public Policy, and Law* 15, no. 2: 81–101.

Jay, Timothy B., and Kristin Janschewitz. 2008. 'The Pragmatics of Swearing'. *Journal of Politeness Research* 4, no. 2: 267–88.

Jeshion, Robin. 2013. 'Expressivism and the Offensiveness of Slurs'. *Philosophical Perspectives* 27, no. 1: 231–59.

Jeshion, Robin. 2018. 'Slurs, Dehumanization, and the Expression of Contempt'. *Bad Words: Philosophical Perspectives on Slurs*, edited by David Sosa, 77–107. Oxford: Oxford University Press.

Keveney, B. 2018. '"*The Simpsons*" Exclusive: Matt Groening (mostly) Remembers the Show's Record 636 Episodes'. *USA Today*, April 27. Available at https://eu.usatoday.com/story/life/tv/2018/04/27/thesimpsons-matt-groening-new-record-fox-animated-series/524581002/.

King, Martin Luther, Jr. 1963. *Letter from a Birmingham Jail.* The Martin Luther King, Jr. Research and Education Institute, Stanford University. Available at https://kinginstitute.stanford.edu/king-papers/documents/letter-birmingham-jail.

Laërtus, Diogenes. c. 300. 1972. *Lives of Eminent Philosophers*, edited by R. D. Hicks. Cambridge, MA: Harvard University Press. Available at http://www.perseus.tufts.edu/hopper/text?doc=urn:cts:greekLit:tlg0004.tlg001.perseus-eng1:1.

Lanfranc of Milan. c. 1400. 1894. *Lanfrank's 'Science of Cirurgie'.* Edited by Robert Von Fleischhacker. Early English Text Society 102. London: Kegan Paul, Trench, Trübner.

Laws, Mike. 2020. 'Why We Capitalise "Black" (and Not "white")'. *Columbia Journalism Review.* June 16. Available at https://www.cjr.org/analysis/capital-b-black-styleguide.php.

Lawson, Mark. 2004. 'Has Swearing Lost Its Power to Shock?' *The Guardian.* February 5. Available at https://www.theguardian.com/media/2004/feb/05/broadcasting.britishidentityandsociety.

Lefevre, Romana. 2011. *Rude Hand Gestures of the World.* San Francisco, CA: Chronicle Books.

Lizzo. 2022. Instagram post, June 13. Available at https://www.instagram.com/p/Cew0HrlPhEq/.

Lowe, Adrian. 2013. 'Cane Looms for Aussie Swear-Accused in Singapore'. *The Sydney Morning Herald*, January 23. Available at https://www.smh.com.au/lifestyle/cane-looms-for-aussie-swearaccused-in-singapore-20130123-2d5vi.html.

MacKinnon, Catherine A. 1989. *Toward a Feminist Theory of the State.* Cambridge, MA: Harvard University Press.

Marsh, David. 2012. 'The Risks of Using Asterisks in Place of Swearwords'. *The Guardian*, July 22. Available at http://www.theguardian.com/media/mind-your-language/2012/jul/22/mind-your-language-asterisks-swearwords.

Marsh, David, and Amelia Hodsdon, eds. 2021. *The Guardian and Observer Style Guide.* Available at https://www.theguardian.com/info/series/guardian-and-observer-style-guide.

McGowan, Michael. 2017. 'Man Convicted of Swearing Was Illegally Arrested in First Place, Court Hears'. *The Guardian*, November 2. Available at https://www.theguardian.com/australia-news/2017/nov/02/man-convicted-of-swearing-was-illegally-arrested-in-first-place-court-hears.

McWhorter, John. 2021. 'How the N-Word Became Unsayable'. *The New York Times*, April 30. Available at https://www.nytimes.com/2021/04/30/opinion/john-mcwhorter-n-word-unsayable.html.

Mendoza-Denton, Rodolfo. 2010. '"Spook Drop Parachuters": Racism or Halloween Spirit?' *Berkeley Blog*, October 1. Available at https://blogs.berkeley.edu/2010/10/01/spook-drop-parachuters-racism-or-halloween-spirit/.

Mill, John S. 1978. *On Liberty*. Indianapolis, IN: Hackett.

Millwood-Hargrave, Andrea. 2000. 'Delete Expletives?' *Advertising Standards Authority, British Broadcasting Corporation, Broadcasting Standards Commission*, and *Independent Television Commission*. Available at http://www.biblit.it/wp-content/uploads/2014/08/ASA_Delete_Expletives_Dec_2000-2.pdf.

Molyneux, Wendy. 2021. 'Oh My Fucking God, Get the Fucking Vaccine Already, You Fucking Fucks'. *McSweeney's Internet Tendency*, December 31. Available at https://www.mcsweeneys.net/articles/oh-my-fucking-god-get-the-fucking-vaccine-already-you-fucking-fucks.

Morris, Chris. 1997. 'Sex'. *Brass Eye*, Channel 4.

Morris, Desmond. 2005. 'Desmond Morris on Symbolic Gestures'. *Forbes*, October 24. Available at https://www.forbes.com/2005/10/19/morris-desmond-gestures-culture-comm05-cx_lr_1024morris/?sh=741def1528ff.

Motley, Mary P. 1975. *The Invisible Soldier: The Experience of the Black Soldier, World War II*. Detroit, MI: Wayne State University Press.

Nasaw, Daniel. 2012. 'When Did the Middle Finger Become Offensive?' *BBC News Magazine*, February 6. Available at https://www.bbc.co.uk/news/magazine-16916263.

National Association for the Advancement of Colored People. 2023. *Criminal Justice Fact Sheet*. Available at https://naacp.org/resources/criminal-justice-fact-sheet.

Nunberg, Geoffrey. 2008. 'Fleeting "Fucking": Original Sinn'. *Language Log*, November 6. Available at https://languagelog.ldc.upenn.edu/nll/?p=814.

Nunberg, Geoffrey. 2012. 'Swearing: A Long and #%@&$ History'. *NPR*, July11 . Available at https://www.npr.org/2012/07/24/156623763/swearing-a-long-and-history.

Nunberg, Geoffrey. 2018. 'The Social Life of Slurs'. In *New Work on Speech Acts*, edited by Daniel Fogal, D., Daniel W. Harris, and Matt Moss. Oxford: Oxford University Press.

Olad, Mahad. 2019. 'Who Gets to Say the N-Word'. *The Ithacan*, February 5. Available at https://theithacan.org/columns/who-gets-to-say-the-n-word/.

Omidi, Maryam. 2014. 'WTF? Russia Bans Swearing in the Arts'. *The Guardian*, July 1. Available at https://www.theguardian.com/world/2014/jul/01/russia-bans-swearing-arts.

Oxford English Dictionary. 'Swearing'. Available at https://www.oed.com/view/Entry/195610.

Oxford Learner's Dictionaries. 'Swearing'. Available at https://www.oxfordlearnersdictionaries.com/definition/english/swearing.

Parliament of Kurdistan-Iraq. 2011. *The Act of Combating Domestic Violence in Kurdistan Region—Iraq*. Act No. 8. Available at http://www.ekrg.org/files/pdf/combat_domestic_violence_english.pdf.

Perraudin, F. 2014. 'Bob Geldof Cut Off by Sky News for Saying "Bollocks"—Twice'. *The Guardian*, November 17. Available at https://www.theguardian.com/media/mediamonkeyblog/2014/nov/17/bob-geldof-cut-off-by-sky-news-for-saying-bollocks-twice.

Perry, Douglas. 2015. 'Clean Reader App Scrubs Sex and Profanity from E-books, Causing Authors to Fight Back'. *The Oregonian*, March 31. Available at https://www.oregonlive.com/books/2015/03/clean_reader_app_scrubbed_sex.html.

Philipp, Michael C., and Laura Lombardo. 2017. 'Hurt Feelings and Four Letter Words: Swearing Alleviates the Pain of Social Distress'. *European Journal of Social Psychology* 47, no. 4: 517–23.

Pinker, Steven. 2007a. *The Stuff of Thought: Language as a Window into Human Nature*. London: Penguin.

Pinker, Steven. 2007b. 'What the F***?' *The New Republic*, October 8. Available at http://www.newrepublic.com/article/politics/what-the-f

Quote Investigator. 2016. 'When You're Accustomed to Privilege, Equality Feels Like Oppression'. October 24. Available at https://quoteinvestigator.com/2016/10/24/privilege/.

Rachels, James. 1976. 'Active and Passive Euthanasia'. In *Biomedical Ethics and the Law*, edited by James M. Humber and Robert H. Almeder. Boston, MA: Springer.

Rawlinson, Kevin. 2014. 'Farage Blames Immigration for Traffic on M4 after No-Show at UKIP Reception'. *The Guardian*, December 7. Available at https://www.theguardian.com/politics/2014/dec/07/nigel-farage-blames-immigration-m4-traffic-ukip-reception.

Read, Allen W. 1935. *Lexical Evidence from Folk Epigraphy in Western North America: A Glossarial Study of the Low Element in the English Vocabulary*. Paris: privately published.

Renner, K. Payton. 2015. 'Girl Raps Onstage with Kendrick'. YouTube, June 2. Available at https://youtu.be/c_2z_jGZjqw.

Rini, Regina. 2021. *The Ethics of Microaggression*. Abingdon: Routledge.

Roache, Rebecca. 2015. 'Are There Any Powerful Swearwords Left?' *The Ethics Centre*, November 4. Available at https://ethics.org.au/are-there-any-powerful-swear-words-left/.

Romano, Aja. 2019. 'Gina Rodriguez Apologizes, Amid Backlash, for Saying the N-Word on Instagram'. *Vox*, October 16. Available at https://www.vox.com/culture/2019/10/15/20916272/gina-rodriguez-n-word-apology-backlash-history.

Rosewarne, Lauren. 2013. *American Taboo: The Forbidden Words, Unspoken Rules, and Secret Morality of Popular Culture*. Santa Barbara, CA: Praeger.

Sagarin, Edward. 1962. *The Anatomy of Dirty Words*. New York: Lyle Stuart.

Santiago, Esteban. 2018. 'Rohan Ghosh: 5 Fast Facts You Need to Know'. *Heavy*, May 22. Available at https://heavy.com/news/2018/05/rohan-ghosh-5-fast-facts-you-need-to-know/.

Saucier, Donald A., Derrick Till, Stuart S. Miller, Conor O'Dea, and Emma Andres. 2015. 'Slurs against Masculinity: Masculine Honor Beliefs and Men's Reactions to Slurs'. *Language Sciences* 52: 108–20.

Scarsi, A. 2020. 'Royal SHOCK: How Queen Turned Air Blue Using F-Word in Front of Stunned Guest'. *Express*, March 23. Available at https://www.express.co.uk/news/royal/1258974/queen-news-queen-elizabeth-ii-brian-blessed-royal-family-royal-news.

Shriver, Lionel. 2015. 'Why Filthy Literature Should Not Be Cleaned Up'. *The Guardian*, March 27. Available at https://www.theguardian.com/commentisfree/2015/mar/27/filthy-literature-clean-reader-app-profanities-ebooks.

Simon, Herbert. 2015. 'Obama Didn't Use the N-Word: A Distinction with a Difference'. *Huffpost*, June 30. Available at https://www.huffpost.com/entry/obama-didnt-use-the-nword_b_7658416.

Smitherman, Geneva. 2006. *Word from the Mother: Language and African Americans*. New York: Routledge.

Stephens, Richard, and Olly Robertson. 2020. 'Swearing as a Response to Pain: Assessing Hypoalgesic Effects of Novel "Swear" Words'. *Frontiers in Psychology* 11: 723.

Stephens, Richard, and Claudia Umland. 2011. 'Swearing as a Response to Pain—Effect of Daily Swearing Frequency'. *Journal of Pain* 12: 1274–81.

Stephens, Richard, John Atkins, and Andrew Kingston. 2009. 'Swearing as a Response to Pain'. *NeuroReport* 20, no. 12: 1056–60.

Stohr, Karen. 2012. *On Manners*. New York: Routledge.

Tatlow, Didi K. 2013. 'Fault Lines Laid Bare in Hong Kong'. *The New York Times*, August 7. Available at https://www.nytimes.com/2013/08/08/world/asia/08iht-letter08.html?_r=0.

Theoharis, Mark. n.d. 'Disorderly Conduct Laws and Penalties'. *Criminal Defense Lawyer*. Available at http://www.criminaldefenselawyer.com/resources/disorderly-conduct-utah.htm.

Thoms, Gary, and E. Jamieson. 2018. 'If Anycunt Says It, Will Everycunt Accept It?' *Strong Language*, December 18. Available at https://stronglang.wordpress.com/2018/12/18/if-anycunt-says-it-will-everycunt-accept-it/.

Todd, Carolyn L. 2017. 'Oprah Responds to Bill Maher's n-Word Controversy'. *Refinery29*, June 13. Available at https://www.refinery29.com/en-us/2017/06/158950/oprah-winfrey-against-the-n-word-bill-maher-controversy.

UK Government. 2022. 'Arrests'. Available at https://www.ethnicity-facts-figures.service.gov.uk/crime-justice-and-the-law/policing/number-of-arrests/latest.

Vandeveer, Donald. 1979. 'Coercive Restraint of Offensive Actions'. *Philosophy & Public Affairs* 8, no. 2: 175–93.

Van Lancker, Dian R., and Jeffrey L. Cummings. 1999. 'Expletives: Neurolinguistic and Neurobehavioral Perspectives on Swearing'. *Brain Research Reviews* 31: 83–104.

Van Mill, David. 2015. 'Freedom of Speech'. In *The Stanford Encyclopedia of Philosophy*, edited by Edward N. Zalta (Spring ed.). Available at http://plato.stanford.edu/archives/spr2015/entries/freedom-speech/

Visconti, Luke. 2020. 'Why Capitalising the "B" in Black Still Matters for Cultural Competence and Accurate Representation'. *DiversityInc*, August 18. Available at https://www.diversityinc.com/why-the-b-in-black-is-capitalized-at-diversityinc/.

Warwick, Kate. 2015. 'What Gives "Cunt" Its Offensive Power?' *Strong Language*, February 6. Available at https://stronglang.wordpress.com/2015/02/06/what-gives-cunt-its-offensive-power/.

Wei, Lo. 2013. 'Most Teachers Support Curbs on Swearing'. *South China Morning Post*, September 23. Available at https://www.scmp.com/news/hong-kong/article/1315411/most-teachers-support-curbs-swearing.

Wickman, Forrest. 2013. 'Rhymes with *Runt*'. *Slate*, February 26. Available at https://slate.com/human-interest/2013/02/quvenzhane-wallis-and-the-onion-tweet-why-is-the-c-word-so-offensive.html.

Willgress, Lydia. 2015. 'M&S Bans Customers Using the Words "Christ" and "Jesus Christ" in Messages When They Are Ordering Flowers Online—But Jihad Is Okay'. *Daily Mail*, March 1. Available at https://www.dailymail.co.uk/news/article-2974554/M-S-bans-customers-using-words-Christ-Jesus-Christ-messages-ordering-flowers-online-jihad-okay.html.

Williams, Archie. F. 1992. *The Joy of Flying: Olympic Gold, Air Force Colonel, and Teacher.* Berkeley: Online Archive of California. Available at http://www.oac.cdlib.org/view?docId=hb3779n9gv&query=&brand=oac4.

Wilson, John P., Kurt Hugenberg, and Nicholas O. Rule. 2017. 'Racial Bias in Judgments of Physical Size and Formidability: From Size to Threat'. *Journal of Personality and Social Psychology* 113, no. 1: 59–80.

Wittgenstein, Ludwig. 1970. *Zettel*. Edited by G. E. M. Anscombe and G. H. von Wright, trans. G. E. M. Anscombe. Berkeley: University of California Press.

World Economic Forum. 2019. *Global Gender Gap Report 2020*. Available at https://www.weforum.org/reports/gender-gap-2020-report-100-years-pay-equality.

Wyatt, Daisy. 2015. 'Kendrick Lamar: I'm Not Ready to Stop Using the N-Word in My Music'. *Independent*, July 16. Available at https://www.independent.co.uk/arts-entertainment/music/news/kendrick-lamar-i-m-not-ready-stop-using-n-word-my-music-10392610.html.

Zaltzman, Helen. 2015. 'Allusionist 4: Detonating the C-Bomb'. *The Allusionist*. Available at https://www.theallusionist.org/allusionist/c-bomb.

Index

D0623122

CHANGING THE GUARD: CANADA'S DEFENCE IN A WORLD IN TRANSITION

HOWARD PETER LANGILLE

Changing the Guard: Canada's Defence in a World in Transition

UNIVERSITY OF TORONTO PRESS
Toronto Buffalo London

Toronto Buffalo London
Printed in Canada

ISBN 0-8020-5870-1

Printed on acid-free paper

Canadian Cataloguing in Publication Data

Langille, Howard Peter
Changing the guard: Canada's defence in a world in transition

ISBN 0-8020-5870-1

1. Canada – Military relations. 2. Canada – Military policy. I. Title.

UA600.L35 1990 355'.033071 C90-094546-X

'Complexity is not inherent in any phenomenon; it is relative to the conceptions with which we approach reality. It is the task of those who want peace to identify causes and to clarify them to the point of action ... Programs require that next steps be reasonably linked with principled images of a goal. To act toward goals requires that the step be consciously worked out in terms of its consequences, and that these consequences be weighed and valued in terms of the goal.'

C.W. Mills, *The Causes of World War Three* (1958)

For Mom, Dad, David, Lesley, Megan, Julie, and common security

Contents

Acknowledgments

The origins of this book go back to the early 1980s and an earnest attempt to understand better international security affairs. Much of chapters 1–4 appeared in two previous research essays I wrote in 1985 and 1988 while studying at Carleton University and the Norman Paterson School of International Affairs. Chapters 5 and 6 also draw on research I carried out with the Group of 78's Alternative Defence Project and while attending the Department of Peace Studies in the University of Bradford, England.

The prospects for peace were not encouraging at the beginning of the last decade. The election of Ronald Reagan and his loose talk of limited and protracted nuclear war prompted a return to university and ended a life-style that centred around professional ski-racing and tree planting. Until then, about the nearest I had come to conflict resolution and the real affairs of peace and security were odd jobs in juvenile detention centres, bars such as Diamond Tooth Gertie's, and the oilfields. A few of these early experiences provided helpful lessons, but I quickly came to learn that international security is a much messier business.

This book draws heavily on a number of military sources. The research included interviews and discussions with several generals, admirals, deputy ministers, chiefs of defence staff, and a minister of national defence. (For career and social reasons, many of these people requested anonymity.) However, I would like to thank Admiral Robert Falls (ret.) and Major-General Leonard Johnson (ret.). They helped many Canadians to understand better our security and defence requirements at a time when quite a number of their old colleagues were 'crying wolf,' warning of 'the overwhelming threat,' and flocking to lucrative careers as consultants in the defence industry.

A few critics have charged that I am 'anti-defence' – a unique position for one who has committed several years to researching defence options. Some confusion may be inevitable, because I share in the belief that the institutions of war must be controlled better and eventually put behind us if we are to make the next great jump in civilization. But I also share great respect for the majority of Canada's armed forces who consistently display professionalism and competence when faced with limited budgets and extended commitments. Moreover, they are hardly responsible for our security problems. More often than not, it appears to have been their political masters who 'departed their posts' or 'slept on duty.' But the intent here is not to ascribe blame to anyone; it is simply to draw attention to several problems and clarify appropriate courses of action.

While 1989 and 1990 were wonderful years in heralding the end of a dangerous cold war, the pace of change was enough to grey the hair of anyone writing on international security and defence relations. After nearly forty years of confrontational politics and the 'sure-thing' style of analysis, the new adage appeared to be 'here today – gone tomorrow.' As is the norm in any discipline undergoing serious revision, one can already anticipate an element of the conclusion: further research will be required.

It is hoped that this book also represents an evolution in my thinking since commencing studies on international relations and writing that mind-numbing paper on 'Why the West Needs the B-1 Bomber.' A special thanks is due to several excellent professors who shared their thoughts and helped to prompt the appropriate questions: Dr Michael McGuire, Dr Harald von Riekhoff, Dr John Sigler, Dr Leo Panitch, Dr Nigel Young, Dr Dietrich Fischer, and Dr Paul Rogers.

Throughout these learning endeavours, I was a very privileged student to have wonderful colleagues in Joanne Ursino, John Alerton, Carleton Hughes, Gloria Shalay, Kristen Ostling, Jillian Skeet, Axel Dorscht, Marja Ten Holder, Greg Albo, Bill Robinson, Jim Hammond, Robert O'Brien, and Alan and Cathy Bloomgarden. Among others who provided encouragement and help at critical times were Amy Bartholomew and Patrick Redgrave, Ian and Elin McLaurin, Harold and Ruth McCormick, Fred and Eleanore Barret, and Melvin and Rosie Smith. A special note of appreciation is reserved for Julie Scott whose inspiration and support helped to overcome many of the day-to-day hurdles.

Over the past four years, I have been very fortunate to enjoy the friendship of Jim Lee, Tina Viljoen, and Gwynne Dyer. Aside from their assistance and sense of fun, their knowledge and clarity of thought on the subject-matter repeatedly proved invaluable. They deserve considerable credit for contributing to chapter 3 and provoking chapter 6. I am also indebted to Robert Winters of the Montreal *Gazette* for several helpful tips on using the Access to Information Act and for providing hundreds of pages of material on cruise missile testing released through the act.

At the University of Toronto Press, Virgil Duff and John St James combined editorial skill and patience in managing a rough text and an over-extended author through tight schedules. Emur Kileen, now with Studies in Political Economy, was very helpful with comments and initial edits on the first four chapters. Leslie Silver also provided excellent advice on an earlier draft of chapter 2. Many thanks!

The Canadian Institute for International Peace and Security enabled me to carry out this research and writing. I am most grateful to the Institute and their graduate scholarship program for helping to fund these studies.

Finally, it must be acknowledged that this book has been a family effort. James Howard Langille assisted with several proof-readings, Marion Langille prepared the index, and David Langille helped to edit several drafts and offered numerous insightful observations on the content. Their patience and kindness provided the appropriate environment; their many personal sacrifices and enduring commitment to peace work and the pursuit of common security provided the lead.

Any errors or omissions in this work are, nevertheless, the author's.

Howard Peter Langille
June 1990

CHANGING THE GUARD: CANADA'S DEFENCE IN A WORLD IN TRANSITION

Introduction

As we enter the 1990s, there are new hopes and opportunities for moving well beyond the Cold War to a new era of common security. At this critical juncture, a changing of the guard is essential. How it is changed will no doubt structure Canada's potential for contributing to a just and long-term peace.

Defence issues were a continuing source of controversy in the 1980s. The testing of the air-launched cruise missile, participation in the U.S. Strategic Defense Initiative, NATO membership, and the renewal of the NORAD agreement all prompted serious debate. Canadian governments explained their defence decisions in terms of commitments to our allies, the Soviet threat, or the imperatives of job creation, collective security, and deterrence. Viewed in isolation and often from a short-term perspective, many of these decisions appeared quite rational and necessary. Yet very little attention was paid to non-strategic factors and the underlying structural determinants of defence policy.

The 1987 publication of *Challenge and Commitment: A Defence Policy for Canada*, the first defence white paper in over sixteen years, justified a reassessment of the factors that influence Canadian defence relations. The new defence policy represented a shift in emphasis towards preparations for a long war, formal integration within a North American Defence Industrial Base

(NADIB), and a strengthening of Canada's commitment to NATO's Central European Front.[1] At the time, it was suggested that there were no alternatives.

These developments prompted several questions. What are the internal and external forces that constrain and determine Canadian defence relations? To what extent is the security decision-making process in Canada influenced by our allies? Should we consider other factors such as the growth of the defence industry, further bilateral economic and military integration, and the emergence of a military-industrial complex? Does defence-policy planning reflect long-term continuity, or can it be adapted to changes in the political and strategic environment? Were Canadians caught in a 'defence trap' that limited their policy options? If so, what is required to improve upon this state of affairs?

In 1985, an American defence analyst portrayed Canada's complex and interdependent defence relationship using a particularly apt metaphor. Tryping to decipher it all, he suggested, 'was like peeling away the skin of an onion – layer after layer. But there is no centre, each layer raises and exposes new agreements with new questions.'[2] Experience suggests that one can 'get bogged down' and overwhelmed in the technicalities and details of Canadian defence relations. But the 'centre' alluded to may not be all that elusive. This analysis will attempt to clarify some of the complexity by pulling back a few more 'layers of skin,' first, to reveal the determinants of Canadian defence relations, and, second, to identify defence options that would help to promote a transition to common security in the 1990s.

For the purpose of this analysis, *defence relations* may be understood as the wide range of interests, developments, procedures, and arrangements that combine to influence defence decisions. These relations cannot be understood when viewed in isolation or as the outcome of an independent variable such as strategic necessity. It is increasingly apparent that defence-planning and policy-making are subject to an array of complex and often conflicting interests. In order to analyse 'defence relations' one has to examine a wider range of determinants – including bilateral, multilateral, and domestic factors.

It is time to develop a political economy of Canadian defence relations. The 'realist' paradigm orienting most of Western strategic analysis has structured both the context within which defence policy is assessed and the questions that are asked about Canada's defence policy. Within this paradigm, nuclear and conventional deterrence are accepted as unavoidable; Canada's membership within military alliances is imperative; a capacity for protracted warfare is required; and Canada is thought to have few if any options. Not only has this approach to the study of defence relations been incapable of generating alternatives, it has often limited the scope of analysis and debate, leaving aside many important questions.[3] For instance, it places an undue emphasis on conformity with our allies and with the orthodox assumptions of military tradition. The emphasis on comformity risks encouraging an anti-intellectualism in Canadian defence analysis – favouring a technical rationality oriented to short-term cost-benefit analysis and the study of strategic weapon systems.

To date, there has been a dearth of critical work assessing the underlying determinants of Canadian defence policy. Many of the security debates in this country have focused on the military and strategic merits of different policy options. It has been assumed that these are the central determinants of defence policy. While at times these factors are important, such a narrow focus has tended to obscure the importance of political factors and economic interests.

In 1972, Colin Gray, then a Canadian defence analyst, noted that 'the scholars and not-so-scholarly who have been filling the library shelves with tomes on defence policy and strategic theory have lacked both the time and the incentive to provide the conceptual frameworks that might advance the art of defence policy analysis.'[4] Since that time there have been few attempts to develop concepts that might contribute to our understanding of Canadian defence relations. By drawing upon contributions from peace research and political economy, it is possible to introduce concepts that shed fresh light on several relatively unresearched determinants of Canadian defence policy. Concepts such as 'leverage and linkage,' 'dependency and integration,' the 'military-industrial complex,' and the 'defence trap' are relevant to an understanding of Canadian defence relations.

Over the last forty years, Canadian governments have found it difficult to pursue independent defence initiatives. They have been confronted with domestic constraints as well as bilateral and multilateral impediments. The analysis begins with a short review of the political, economic, and strategic developments that structured Canadian defence relations in this period. The ensuing three chapters seek to identify the determinants of several Canadian defence decisions: the agreement to test the U.S. air-launched cruise missile; the attempt to withdraw Canadian forces from NATO's Central European Front; and the shift to a long-war policy entailing defence preparedness, industrial mobilization, a total-force concept, and formal integration within the North American Defence Industrial Base.

In 1979, speaking to the First Special Session on Disarmament at the United Nations, Prime Minister Pierre Trudeau promoted a Canadian 'strategy of suffocation' that called for, among other things, an end to the flight testing of new strategic delivery vehicles. Within four years, however, the Trudeau government agreed to assist in testing a new generation of strategic delivery vehicles – the air-launched cruise missile. Was the government's capacity to implement an independent security initiative constrained by the extent of Canada's military and economic integration with the United States?

In 1985, Canadian defence officials attempted to withdraw all Canadian forces from Europe so as to attain greater strategic flexibility. Within two years, however, a decision was made to double Canada's troop commitment to NATO's Central European Front and to relinquish the military commitment to Norway. Do Canada's military allies constrain the government in pursuing defence initiatives that they deem to be necessary for Canadian security?

After the Korean War, Canada adopted a short-war policy that minimized the requirements of the armed forces and the need for defence industrial preparedness. In the 1987 defence review, the Canadian government implicitly endorsed a long-war policy which entailed that the armed forces and the defence industrial base be prepared to sustain protracted conventional war-fighting. Was this decision, or those in the two previous cases, influenced by the emergence of a military-industrial complex? In summary, how can we explain these decisions, and what do these cases have in common?

A central point here is that Canadian governments have at times been trapped into defence arrangements by political and economic concerns. While some of these concerns may be unwarranted, they are, nevertheless, influential and can be self-fulfilling when accepted over an extended period. The three cases reviewed reflect a wide range of pressures and constraints arising in Canada's domestic, bilateral, and multilateral defence relations.

Canada has risked being caught in a 'defence trap,' a trap that would limit our autonomy and threaten our long-term security. The risk was compounded by the success of the defence industry in the early 1980s, its reliance upon foreign demand, and the perception that this sector of the economy would engender technological take-off and industrial growth. These factors in turn contributed to the emergence of an influential military-industrial complex – a coalition of interests active in promoting rearmament. Alliance commitments, perceptions of economic and political vulnerability, and a host of bilateral agreements combined to subordinate Canadian defence policy to a range of short-term commercial, bureaucratic, and military interests.

Chapter 5 reviews many of the domestic and international developments that have occurred since the release of the defence white paper *Challenge and Commitment*. It is apparent that several of the factors that influenced the formulation of the 1987 policy may still constitute powerful impediments to progressive change.

Understanding the relations that have an impact on the Canadian state should help to provide directions when planning future security policies. Canadian leaders are now confronted with several difficult security decisions. Defence options that were previously considered inappropriate for Canada are slowly becoming the focus of national debate. Since the three cases examined in this book dealt with an alternative security policy, this review may impart some useful guidelines to those currently involved in the search for means to promote common security.

1989 and 1990 were watershed years heralding revolutionary developments in political, economic, and military affairs. The international security environment is in a period of transition. A range of unanticipated events have provided Canada with an opportunity to move beyond the defence trap. In such a period, good ideas may be capable of moving events.

At this time, there is an urgent need for an open defence review and a public debate over the policy options that are to ensure our security well into the twenty-first century. The Conservative government's 1987 defence policy is unlikely to be effective in dealing with future security challenges: it is fixated on outdated commitments and methods, and it is too expensive to implement. There is widespread consensus that Canada's defence posture will have to be restructured.

In the final chapter it is argued that new priorities and new methods will be necessary if we are to help an improving international situation improve further. In the 1990s, defence policies can and should be designed to civilize international relations and to complement efforts to abolish war as a phenomenon. The objective of common security now provides an excellent basis upon which to develop consistent and coherent defence policies. Canada could once again play an important role in safeguarding international peace and security.

A 1989 report from a special committee of the Senate on national defence recommended that 'Canada should seize this window of opportunity and thrust it open to new concepts for its armed forces both in Canada and abroad.'[5] Greater attention will likely be paid to several of the ideas developed in the field of peace research. Concepts such as non-offensive defence and dissuasion, security buffers and demilitarized zones, neutrality and semi-alignment are all relevant to the study of Canadian defence options in the 1990s.

It is time for a changing of the guard. An outline of a new defence is proposed. By emphasizing the maintenance of a security buffer, a non-offensive defence posture, a strategy of dissuasion, and greater support for the United Nations, Canada's armed forces, resources, and territory could be effectively utilized to promote common security.

If one is to understand contemporary Canadian defence relations, to assess how these relations affect the formulation of defence policy, and, ultimately, to provide guidance in the search for defence options that would help to promote common security, it is appropriate to begin with a short review of the developments that have structured these relations, a review that relates these developments to the other political, economic, and geostrategic forces involved.

CHAPTER ONE

Background to Canadian Defence Relations

Canadian defence relations have long been predicted on the assumption that our security could not be guaranteed without foreign assistance. Rather than pursue an independent defence posture, Canadian governments have sought security via collective military arrangements with other friendly powers. The extent to which Canada developed in close alliance with and dependency upon Britain, and then the United States, has had a profound influence on our defence relations.[1] As Stephen Clarkson writes, 'While imperial centres have waxed and waned and while technologies have changed dramatically, the constant fact of Canadian military history since the first white settlements is Canada's status as a defended country – the military corollary of its colonial position as a political and economic extension of an imperial power.'[2]

With Britain's decline from great-power status providing the impetus for a shift away from the old empire, Canadians turned south towards the powerful neighbour with whom they shared the longest undefended border in the world. Canada and the United States developed a 'special relationship' based on common international goals and mutual economic needs. Recognizing the high costs required to defend a nation the size of Canada, policy-makers favoured a relationship with the United States that would guarantee sovereignty and security at what was assumed to be a low cost, and also provide the opportunity for enhanced trade.

The importance of Canada's geostrategic position was magnified by East-West tension and the development of long-range weaponry. Situated between the two superpowers, Canada could not be isolated or immune from external conflicts. After 1949, the threat of nuclear attack reinforced the conviction that some form of continental defence was necessary. Canadian territory had come to represent the strategic fore-field of the United states – a fact that was clearly recognized in both Ottawa and Washington. As the world polarized into hostile camps, a close continental relationship appeared to be both the safest and also the most profitable option for Canada to adopt.

The relationship between the two countries, although important to both, was far from symmetrical. The United States was the pre-eminent superpower of the period; Canada at best was an emerging middle-power.[3] To offset some of the continental military and trade imbalance, Canada sought membership in the North Atlantic Treaty Organization. Since the 1950s, Canadian governments stationed forces in Western Europe to assist in the defense of our allies and to retain a political counterweight to the American presence on the home front. Apart from the danger implicit in East-West hostility, Canada faced few military threats. However, given our political, economic, technological, and military interdependence, the Canadian government assumed a wide range of defence commitments.

The Canadian economy in the post–Second World War period remained heavily reliant upon trade in staples and semiprocessed goods. Difficulties were encountered in the development of an industrial and technological base. Efforts to expand this base and diversify trade relations were often frustrated. In defence production, however, Canada obtained a sectoral trade agreement with the United States that enhanced access to American markets.

Attempts to diversify defence relations encountered problems similar to those experienced in the economic sector. There were no easy options. Immediate interests tended to be furthered by the process of military and economic integration. In Canada's defence and trade affairs, multilateral relations involving Western Europe were important. But maintaining a smooth bilateral relationship with the United States was often conceived to be an imperative.

THE BILATERAL IMPERATIVE AND THE MULTILATERAL COUNTERWEIGHT

The continental defence relationship was initiated with an exchange of promises between U.S. President Roosevelt and Canadian Prime Minister Mackenzie King. According to Desmond Morton, the Canadian government initiated the relationship by sending senior officers to establish contacts in Washington. At the time, King was discouraging similar contacts with the War Office in London.[4] Shortly thereafter, in August 1936, Roosevelt spoke of a commitment to the defence of Canada at Chautaqua, New York. Two years later in Kingston, Ontario, he stated: 'The people of the United States will not stand idly by if domination of Canada is threatened by any other empire.' Within the week, Mackenzie King responded with a statement of Canada's commitment to continental defence: 'We, too, have obligations as a good friendly neighbour, and one of these is to see that, at our own instance, our country is made as immune from attack or possible invasion as we can reasonably be expected to make it; and that, should the occasion ever arise, enemy forces should not be able to pursue their own way by either land, sea, or air to the United States across Canadian territory.'[5] These now classic exchanges helped to set the precedent for a long series of binding commitments – more than seventy treaties and at least twenty-five hundred documents covering bilateral defence matters.[6]

Concerns related to the Second World War led to the discontinuation of high-level consultations on defence matters. In August 1940, bilateral discussions over defence co-operation resulted in the Ogdensburg declaration. This declaration, which has since become the basis of the defence relationship, directed that 'studies should commence immediately, relating to land, sea, and air problems.' The Permanent Joint Board on Defence (PJBD) was established to co-ordinate bilateral defence affairs.[7] The board, which was strongly influenced by the military authorities, formulated the plans for defence integration with the United States.[8] The Canada–United States Military Co-operation Committee was also formed in 1945 to prepare the initial plans for joint air defence of the continent. As such, it represented the first move towards a post-war alliance.[9]

Co-operation was ongoing, but political leaders at this time were not insensitive to the overpowering capability of the United States.[10] A 1945 government policy document expressed concern over the substantial pressure which might be brought to bear by the United States if Canada appeared reluctant or refused to co-operate in continental defence.[11] According to Michael Tucker, 'It has been axiomatic in Canadian defence thinking since at least the 1930s that if Canada did not participate with the United States in the defence of North America, and allow that great power some degree of access to Canadian territory, then it would assume for itself the burden and the responsibility for the defence of this continent.'[12]

Since the end of the Second World War, Canadian territory has been of considerable geostrategic importance to the United States. As Colin Gray writes, 'It has become axiomatic to assert that the defence of North America is indivisible, and brutally, that North America constitutes a single target system.'[13] John Honderich also notes: 'There is a fundamental U.S. strategic belief that defence of all of North America represents defence of the U.S. heartland. One senior Pentagon official put it this way: "I don't look at it as defence of Canada, I look at it as defence of two alliance members, collectively joined in defending a common treaty area. Yes by all means, defence of Canada is virtually defence of the American homeland."'[14]

Within this context Canadian territory and military support became strategically important to Americans in at least three respects: intelligence-gathering; access to Canadian facilities for forward basing, that is, locating elements of the Strategic Air Command closer to their targets in the Soviet Union; and continental early warning and air defence.[15] James Littleton writes that 'each of these has at times assumed critical importance in the mind of U.S. strategic planners. Generally, as that importance increases, successive Canadian governments have had less room to manoeuvre.'[16] The desire to gain some manoeuvrability prompted Canada's pursuit of a multilateral counterweight.

Following the Second World War, Canada worked in concert with other nations to develop the United Nations as a successor to the League of Nations. It was partly as a result of the frustrations stemming from this second effort at co-ordinating collective security that Canada pursued an alternative alliance. In September 1947, Canadian Prime Minister Louis St Laurent suggested in his 'frozen in futility' speech that Western nations might have to look to regional defence arrangements for their security. St Laurent's proposal for a single mutual defence system coincided with a number of initiatives then under way to organize a Western European alliance.

On 4 April 1949, after participating in the negotiation process, Canada joined the North Atlantic Treaty Organization (NATO).[17] Along with the United States, Britain, and nine other nations, Canada entered into a multilateral alliance devoted to ensuring the security and sovereignty of its members. If it was not the embodiment of liberal internationalism, NATO was apparently conceived as the best collective-security alternative given the disturbing international environment. It was clear at the time that Ottawa was consciously linking the defence of Canada to the defence of Europe; in essence pursuing an 'Atlanticist' partnership based on common interest. As former NATO Ambassador John Halstead says, 'Canada became a founding member of NATO with the conviction, borne of the experience of two world wars, that North American security and European security were indivisible.'[18]

As a multilateral counterweight to any act of aggression against members, NATO was perceived as a better option than isolationism. North America would henceforth constitute a NATO region and, regardless of any defence activities pursued on this continent, fellow members would be expected to respect and abide by the provisions and articles of the treaty. A concern shared by those Canadians involved in the negotiation of NATO was that it should help to offset and control the two superpowers.[19] In this respect, it was assumed that participation and the provision of arms brought influence – influence with the European governments and influence in Washington.[20] As previously mentioned, decision-makers in Ottawa had a particular interest in arranging a counterweight to the American presence on the continent. Ernie Regehr suggests that the pursuit of collective defence stemmed from a concern that unless Canada joined others in common defence arrangements, the influence of the United States would be so strong as to imperil and finally erode Canadian sovereignty.[21] NATO was an appealing option: decisions were to be made by consensus; each nation was to have complete freedom of decision.

In effect, however, as another former NATO ambassador, George Ignatieff, noted, NATO became 'a military partnership in which one of the players held all the trump cards.'[22] While the United States held the trump cards when issues related to their particular concerns, NATO remained a multilateral affair that was neither wholly defined nor directed at their behest. Although they were hardly in the same league as the United States, Britain and West Germany also became alliance powers – powers with influence over the formulation of NATO and Canadian defence policy. Canada and the other NATO allies were involved in a collective defence arrangement which was often (but not always) co-ordinated by Americans. Jockel and Sokolsky concede that 'the United States largely sets the strategic context in both North America and in Europe, to which Canada must by and large, as an alliance partner, accommodate its defence policy.'[23]

Thus, in a rather ironic twist, the 'counterweight' fell somewhat under the control of a member whose influence it was partly intended to offset. NATO's general reliance upon the U.S. strategic deterrent would leave alliance members dependent upon American leadership. In return, Canada and the other allies could 'shelter' under the U.S. nuclear umbrella. At times, it was thought that the 'shelter' was a relatively cheap guarantee of security. But in turn, there was little question that it provided the United States with a powerful lever with which to pressure allies into support for American policies. Protection entailed some long-term obligations.

Canadian defence roles and requirements would, therefore, come to be defined largely in response to the superpower rivalry. Political and military leaders could not ignore American strategic perceptions or requirements. In many respects, they constituted a primary determinant of Canadian defence relations. There was little doubt that Canadian and American leaders tended to agree in the view that the policies of the Soviet Union constituted a serious threat to the West. But strategic planners in Ottawa also assumed that they had little choice but to accept and conform to whatever strategic policy the Americans pursued in consequence of this view. This state of affairs led David Cox, a Canadian defence analyst, to testify in 1984 that 'what is important to Canadians is not what we think the Russians will do; it is what we think the Americans think the Russians will do, because our strategic doctrine is essentially one of trying to accommodate ourselves to American strategic doctrine.'[24]

There is also little doubt that the extended effect of accommodating American strategic perceptions limited the scope of official Canadian defence analysis. Stephen Clarkson suggests that 'the conventional wisdom of the military and diplomatic bureaucracy considers that Canada has no autonomous defence option.'[25] Retaining trade and defence contacts with Western Europe might provide a counterweight to the American presence, but it would not offset the U.S. requirement for access to their strategic fore-field and for defence assistance. While political leaders in Canada were generally inclined to 'stand on guard' against the diminution of national sovereignty, the pursuit of an independent defence policy would have been difficult given the emergence of new threats as well as an array of powerful political, economic, and military interests.

The defence and economic contacts that were established between Canada and the United States were multiplied and strengthened by the Cold War and the Korean War. The outbreak of the latter had a profound effect upon Canadian defence policy. Under the leadership of C.D. Howe, Canada was quick to mobilize its military and industrial resources. Recognizing that Canada was initially unprepared for the war, officials felt that, in future, a much larger peace-time military establishment should be maintained with commitments of regular forces-in-being rather than depending upon the mobilization potential of reserves or industry.[26] NATO commitments were also strengthened in this period as its leaders concluded that there was a need for a standing alliance force in Europe to defend the continent. And, as Jockel and Sokolsky attest, 'Canada all but rebuilt its army, navy and air force to meet NATO's needs. Most important, it sent nearly 10 thousand troops and 12 air squadrons to Europe.'[27] The results of these two trends, as the historians R.D. Cuff and J.L. Granatstein observe, were costly: 'Astronomical defence budgets, the arms race, arms sales, and a permanent military-industrial complex all became characteristic of the post Korea institutional setting. These were among the most obvious ramifications of America's imperial power, and they underscored the utility for Canada of securing a continuing and co-operative economic relationship with the United States.'[28]

While external pressure (from the United States and NATO) helped to harmonize Canada's defence policy with those of the allies, complementary pressures were being brought to bear form within. Sectors within the Canadian Armed Forces, particularly the RCAF, tended to favour a close working relationship with their counterparts in the United States. Their rationale was simply that co-operative arrangements made it easier to defend the continent.[29] That they would bolster their influence and position in an integrated alliance, receive support, training, intelligence, and the latest in advanced technology, was undoubtedly a considerable influence on their willingness to participate. Moreover, the roles and requirements associated with a partnership in both the continental and collective defence of the 'West' were attractive to the professional soldiering orientation. Canada's armed forces assumed a particular relevance within the 'big league' structures of an East-West conflict.[30] As Jockel and Sokolsky write:

> Without Canadian-U.S. defence co-operation and NATO, not only would Canada's military leaders have had a hard time justifying expenditures in the nuclear age, they would have been excluded from joining with the larger and more sophisticated forces of the allies. Apart from any consideration of specific Canadian national interests, it is in the professional interest of the armed forces to be involved in the land and air defence of central Europe, the maritime defence of the Atlantic, and the air and maritime defence of North America. Historically, Canada's forces have always fought alongside and against those of the great powers. This has been integral to Canada's military heritage. The postwar alliances allowed the military to continue this tradition. NATO and co-operation in North American defence gave the Royal Canadian Navy, the Canadian Army and the Royal Air Force their raison d'être in the nuclear age ... Membership has been retained in NATO and NORAD – and therefore the world class roles for the forces.[31]

If isolated from participation within these structures, it was apparent that the armed forces would be relegated to relatively boring 'civilian' defence tasks.[32]

Continental defence, thus, provided an important opportunity to the Canadian forces, but especially to the RCAF. At first U.S. requests for Canadian assistance in the continental air-defence effort were simply territorial. In response to a perceived threat from Soviet intercontinental bombers, capable of carrying nuclear weapons, the United States began to erect a continental system of air defences in the early 1950s. At the time it was thought that part of the system would have to be placed on Canadian territory. In August 1951, it was agreed that the United States Pinetree Radar Line should be extended into Canada. On 27 September 1954, it was announced that agreement had been reached on the subject of a Distant Early Warning (DEW) Line, the major part of which was to be deployed in Canada's North.[33]

On 12 May 1958, Canada and the United States formalized air defence co-operation with the NORAD agreement. Only after considerable pressure from the Royal Canadian Air Force and their colleagues in the U.S. Air Force, did the Diefenbaker government, albeit reluctantly, endorse the idea of an integrated command system for North American air defence. The necessary groundwork for the arrangement had been well prepared within the Department of National Defence. As J.T. Jockel attests, 'The RCAF and the USAF constituted the driving force behind the incremental integration of the two national air defence efforts into a single operating system. They initiated all of the proposals for cross-border tactical co-operation and shepherded them all through the process of obtaining approval from the national political authorities.'[34] A host of bilateral accords and arrangements for bilateral defence co-operation were pursued in this period.[35] The implications of these integrated defence systems were not seriously considered until the Cuban missile crisis of 1962. That experience would impart a discomforting lesson. Any previously held illusions as to the benign nature of defence integration were shattered.

When warned of the crisis, Prime Minister John Diefenbaker attempted to resist American pressure to place Canadian forces on a war-time alert pending further verification of Soviet missiles being stationed in Cuba. Contrary to the explicit orders of the prime minister, the minister of national defence waited only one day, then ordered the armed forces on to war-time alert. Canadian forces, however, had already taken their cue from an earlier Washington request; they had shifted to the war-time alert status at approximately the same time as the U.S. forces.[36] Canada had obviously lost some measure of control over determining whether or not (and when) Canadian forces would be committed to a conflict. Brian Cuthbertson acknowledges that 'in the Cuban crisis Canada found that continental defence, because of its relationship to United States offensive power, could be used for purposes not only with which Canada disagreed but which were also inimical to Canadian interests.'[37]

It was clear that Western security decision-making would not be constrained by the 'last minute' concerns of nervous allies.[38] As one senior Canadian defence official observed, 'The Cuban missile crisis demonstrated to the Canadian government then in office, and perhaps to any acute observer outside the office, that the military fate of Canada, inevitably, was going to be determined by the United States.'[39] In a period of crisis, the process would be open only to senior American political and military élites and even trusted allies such as Canada would be expected to fall in line when told.

The Cuban 'experience' was not considered, however, to be an anomaly. As a former Canadian ambassador to NATO put it, 'The American failure to notify Canada about the Cuban missile crisis is unfortunately characteristic of how Americans work. The danger with the U.S. is not isolationism, it is unilateralism.'[40] While there is no doubt that Canadians did share a common interest with Americans in defending the continent, both the Cuban crisis and the process by which NORAD came into being also demonstrated the extend to which common interests were developing within and between the defence establishments of both countries.

Canada was caught in a unique conundrum. There was little doubt that the underlying rationale for a wide range of Canadian defence activity related to the fear of losing sovereignty and control. Stephen Clarkson is quite correct when he suggests that 'Canada participates in NATO to spread its bilateral dependence; it participates in NORAD to maintain some national control over how the Americans defend it.'[41] Canadian political and military leaders assumed that their neighbours on the continent would take whatever steps were necessary to ensure their own defence. It was thought that Canada's 'room to manoeuvre' was very limited. Accordingly, they saw few options: Canada could attempt to secure the continent's 'back door' on its own, at considerable expense; it could do so in alliance with the United States; or it would have to allow the United States to pursue its defence requirements unilaterally without regard for Canadian political sovereignty. At a minimum, it was understood that Canada would have to defend itself so that the Americans did not assume that it had become their right to do so. The rationale for this strategy was articulated by Nils Orvik as 'defence against help.'[42]

'Defence against help' implied a Canadian commitment to help ensure adequate surveillance and early warning for the protection of the U.S. strategic deterrent. Canada, it was understood, would have to remain relevant to the defence of the continent if it were to retain control over its northern half. An example of this argument was reflected in the 1984 testimony of John Anderson, then an assistant deputy minister of national defence: he argued that Canada must adopt a posture that makes it important to the Americans. Unless Canada were to remain important to the United States in a military sense, access to information vital to its own fate would become restricted and its influence would become negligible.[43] Canada could either play the game, according to rules defined by the United States, at a relevant level of competence, or the game would be played without Canadian participation in a manner that might undermine its security and sovereignty. Given the various roles and requirements involved, the notion of 'defence against help' led, paradoxically, to the relinquishing of some control over Canadian territory and armed forces. This dilemma is explained by Michael Tucker:

> If Canada did not participate in the air defence of North America this role would be performed solely by American forces. To have opted out of these alliance relationships, or not to have entered into the latter, would have meant, in effect, a reduction of Canadian sovereignty; thus the perplexing paradox facing a lesser power neighbour to a super power, that alliance commitments have been as much a source of as a derogation from its sovereignty.[44]

In the short term these were acceptable conditions that could be managed with diplomatic finesse and an appeal to the spirit of common cause and co-operation. Americans were not interested in running roughshod over the short-term political sensitivities of their northern neighbours.

In 1968, NATO's Harmel Report called forth a new period of détente. Security would remain premised upon deterrence but with greater East-West co-operation to reduce tension. Fears of a bomber attack on North America also subsided as the advent of intercontinental ballistic missiles ushered in the era of 'mutually assured destruction.' Credible ballistic-missile defences were beyond the technological reach of either superpower. As Cold War tensions relaxed, the Soviets and Americans negotiated an agreement to limit the development and deployment of anti-ballistic-missile defences. The importance of continental air defence and NORAD declined in the period between the mid-1960s and the mid-1970s.

Détente was short-lived, however, as a new era characterized by a search for counterforce offences and strategic defences ensued. The Cold War was back in the aftermath of a Western economic recession and the Soviet invasion of Afghanistan. So, too, was the issue of continental air defence.

In 1979, a joint U.S.-Canada study (JUSCADS) concluded that there were significant gaps in radar coverage and interceptor procedures. Two years later, the Reagan administration, in consultation with the Canadian government, developed the Air Defence Master Plan to improve continental air defences. It called for new radar systems (ground-based and airborne) and for more modern interceptors.

To reflect an expanded mandate, NORAD was renamed the North American Aerospace Defense Command in 1981. A previous clause restricting participation in anti-ballistic-missile defences was deleted from the agreement. These were decisions made without parliamentary or public discussion.

Shortly after agreeing to an American request to test a new air-launched cruise missile over Canadian territory (under the framework provided by the CANUSTEP agreement), Canadian defence officials agreed to co-operate in the development of a new North Warning System to defend against a future 'air breathing' threat from Soviet bomber and cruise-missile deployments. Consultations culminated in an agreement on the modernization of North American air defence that was concluded at the 1985 Quebec City summit.[45] In June 1987, Canada made a commitment to participate in researching the U.S. Air Defense Initiative – an initiative related to the Strategic Defense Architecture 2000 program, which envisaged active air defences to support the 'walls' of a potential strategic defence 'ceiling.'

An array of political and strategic developments in the 1980s prompted a reassessment of Canada's defence posture.[46] In terms of the technology, factors such as new cruise missiles deployed on bombers and submarines, the demand for strategic defences and active air defences, and the refinement of anti-submarine-warfare capabilities all pointed to a resurgence in Canada's geostrategic importance.[47] Canada appeared to be in the process of being drawn back from the periphery of world strategy to the centre.[48]

While the geostrategic importance of Canadian territory remained somewhat unclear, and its definition vulnerable to political currents and emerging technology, Canada was unprepared militarily or politically for a role at this centre. Canada's reliance upon multilateral (NATO) and bilateral (NORAD) defence arrangements had led to a high level of defence integration and dependency. An independent military posture had been ruled out. While over-extended in other military commitments, Canadian leaders had not pursued an independent capacity to monitor, patrol, or control peace-time developments on their own territory. Whether as reserves on NATO's Central European Front, in anti-submarine warfare on the North Atlantic, northern surveillance, or early warning, Canada eschewed a national strategy in favour of performing roles assigned by allies.[49]

Asserting control over Canadian territory has not been a high government priority. In 1986 the government's lack of concern in this respect prompted Michael Tucker to warn that Canada's political leaders were effectively passing the buck on defence decision-making back to military and national defence authorities.[50]

Since Prime Minister Mackenzie King's initial trepidation (over continental defence co-operation), attitudes have changed: defence integration and dependency now appear to have become politically acceptable. In the minds of Canada's current leaders, this dependency is to be nurtured. In the fall of 1987, Prime Minister Brian Mulroney and his minister of national defence, Perrin Beatty, made overtures to the United States for a bilateral naval accord – ostensibly a 'maritime NORAD' (referred to as NOMAD). This time, however, the Americans refused the invitation.[51] Apparently, Canadian participation in this regard was neither needed nor desired.

One area of defence relations that remained open to further co-operation in 1987 was the defence industrial sector. Over a period of nearly fifty years, this sector had also developed into an influential determinant of Canadian defence relations.

CO-OPERATIVE DEFENCE PRODUCTION AND DEVELOPMENT

As early as 1940, President Roosevelt and Prime Minister Mackenzie King discussed 'harmonizing' the industrial resources of North America, 'to further the common defence of the North American continent.' Defence co-operation was formally extended to the economic field by the Hyde Park Agreement of 20 April 1941. This agreement set the precedent for the integration of the Canadian defence industry into the North American defence industrial base. In time, it would become an important determinant of Canadian defence relations.

On 26 October 1950, Canada and the United States signed another Hyde Park Agreement.[52] This time it was to facilitate the co-ordination of military production in an effort to meet respective defence requirements. This second agreement was the forerunner of the Defence Production Sharing Agreement (DPSA) of 1958. One objective of the DPSA was to increase participation by Canadian industry in the production and supply of North American defence equipment requirements. This was an essential step if Canada was to be able to continue to purchase most of its defence equipment from the United States. The DPSA removed the trade restrictions on the bilateral exchange of military products, enabling the defence industries of both nations to compete on equal terms for Canadian and American defence contracts.[53]

In effect, the DPSA was a partial free-trade arrangement that served industrial and defence interests on both sides of the border. But there were political implications as well. A U.S. Defense Department directive issued in 1960 described the purpose of defence-production sharing: [To] continue the principle of economic co-operation with Canada in the interests of continental defense, and [to] stipulate the policy of maximum production and development program integration in support of closely integrated military planning between Canada and the United States.[54] It was quite clear that Americans expected defence co-operation to follow from co-operation in the area of defence production. As Gideon Rosenbluth acknowledges, 'For the Americans the rationale was co-operation and integration in military planning, while for the Canadians it was nurturing a viable defence industry.'[55] In essence, the harder-to-swallow terms of defence integration were sweetened by economic opportunities.

The Second World War had left Canada with a significant defence industry. According to Desmond Morton, 'Wartime demand had inspired the first really large scale manufacturing in Canada.'[56] The Cold War and the Korean War helped to maintain this demand. Later in the decade, however, the defence industry was rocked by the Diefenbaker government's cancellation of the Avro Arrow. The initial implication was startling to those involved in defence industries: the government was evidently unwilling to support the production of major weapon systems in Canada. Domestic demand alone could not keep the industry alive. Its survival would henceforth be reliant upon the production of components and subsystems for major weapon systems being produced elsewhere.

With the access to the American market provided by the DPSA and the 'boom' in demand generated by the Vietnam War, it was clear to those involved in armaments production that their future interests were dependent upon retaining co-operative defence relations with the United States. As a modern defence industry developed in Canada it did so as part of a North American defence industrial base. It was structured to specialize in, and focus on, supplying equipment to meet the Pentagon's demand. By 1980, roughly four-fifths of all Canadian defence production was exported.

In keeping with other continental economic trends, many Canadian high-technology firms turned quickly to the production of goods for the American military. With the guarantee of 'access,' the high-technology focus of U.S. defence systems, and an apparently unlimited source of funding, production for defence attracted considerable investment capital. As Regehr and Watkins have argued, Canadians had a strong commercial interest in entering into the Defence Production Sharing Agreement. However, these writers also indicate some of the consequences of this decision: 'The U.S. market had been a substantial one, and back in 1958 the Canadian government saw the DPSA as an opportunity to recapture some of the high-tech jobs in the aerospace industry ... The United States on the other hand sought control over continental defence policy, correctly assuming that integration of the military industries of the two countries would ultimately serve the interests of policy integration.'[57] Stephen Clarkson points out that arrangements such as NORAD and the DPSA involved a trade-off in which Canada received its security and economic rewards in exchange for political compliance.[58] The initial effect of the DPSA was the integration of a Canadian defence industry into the American military industrial base, albeit as a junior partner.

Ernie Regehr also argues that continental defence co-operation with the United States and defence-production sharing ultimately became balanced dimensions of a single policy.[59] He posits a symbiotic relationship between the industry's reliance upon its participation in the production of U.S. weapon systems for its survival and the influence of U.S. weapon systems on Canadian perceptions of security requirements.[60]

In 1963, officials of the Canadian and American governments altered the terms of the DPSA 'with the objective of maintaining reciprocal defence trade exchanges at increasing levels.'[61] This change meant that Canada would have to purchase defence products for the United States roughly equivalent in dollar value to that which it sold. Furthermore, Canada would be forced to increase defence spending if it hoped to ensure export growth in the defence industry via its access to the U.S. market. At roughly the same time, officials also agreed on an arrangement to promote bilateral defence development, the Defence Development Sharing Agreement (DDSA).[62]

Although these defence-sharing arrangements provided preferential treatment and partial 'free trade,' demands followed for unrestricted access to participate in meeting one another's defence development and production requirements. In the early 1980s, Canada's defence industry emerged as one of the leading growth sectors of the Canadian economy. With the Reagan rearmament program providing nearly 90 per cent of the demand, defence exports to the United States nearly quadrupled within the first five years of the 1980s.[63] Aside from the opportunity it offered to stimulate export trade and correct Canada's balance-of-payments deficit, the defence industry was perceived as a catalyst to bolster industrial productivity, engender technological take-off, and in turn create new employment. The defence industrial sector, which was largely foreign-owned, emerged in the 1980s as a powerful constituency, one that became very influential in the formulation of Canadian defence planning.

At the Quebec Summit of 1985, President Reagan and Prime Minister Mulroney committed their governments to remove many of the remaining obstacles to access, participation, and information-sharing in the defence industrial sector. Within three years, an agreement was reached between the United States Department of Defense and Canada's Department of National Defence for formal defence industrial integration through a jointly co-ordinated North American Defence Industrial Base Organization.

The development of continental defence integration and defence-production integration paralleled similar developments occurring in the Canadian economy.

CANADIAN ECONOMIC DEVELOPMENT

Canadian defence relations have been geared not only to external challenges but also to external demand. Canadian economic development has also had a profound influence upon the development of our defence relations.

Although Canada had the necessary resources for economic development, a variety of historical factors continued to limit the growth of a strong indigenous industrial base even after the

Second World War.[64] American investment and technology were considered essential to the further development of the economy. Both Canadians and Americans recognized the potential benefits of co-operation. The prevailing school of opinion among Canadian decision-makers was to accept a 'continentalist' approach to the development of Canada that emphasized a staples export economy, encouraged foreign direct investment, and assumed that U.S. branch plants would 'prime the pump' of Canadian industry.[65] Continental economic integration developed quickly during this period, overshadowing Canada's previous reliance on trade with Europe. In 1914 British investment accounted for about three-quarters of all foreign capital in Canada. By the end of 1954, the proportion had fallen to less than one-fifth.[66] Whereas in 1939 the United States absorbed about 40 per cent of Canada's exports and furnished about two-thirds of Canadian imports, by 1957 the United States was buying about 50 per cent of Canada's exports and providing 75 per cent of Canada's imports.[67]

Apart from the interdependence brought about by increasing trade, the Canadian economy was also subject to growing penetration by foreign capital investment. In the post-war period U.S.-based corporations considerably expanded their branch-plant operations so as to take advantage of Canadian markets and resources. Many Canadian firms proved incapable of competing in domestic markets, let alone exporting internationally.[68] As a result, several sectors of the Canadian economy fell under the control of American corporations. In many respects, this investment served to perpetuate Canada's traditional status as a staples-producing economy. As Hugh Aitken pointed out in 1959, 'The selective influences of the United States market and of United States investment work in the same direction: capital inflows from the United States since World War II have been heavily concentrated in areas of the economy that contribute directly to exports in the United States ... A similar pattern is evident in the distribution of U.S. ownership and control in the Canadian economy.'[69]

Instead of spurring the development of an industrialized economy, American investment contributed to extending

Canada's historic role as a supplier of unprocessed or semi-manufactured resources. The few exceptions to this pattern of development lay in those sectors of our economy that complemented American interests.[70] The relations and structures which consolidated this dependency upon exports of unprocessed resources prompted one Canadian economist to comment that Canada was caught in a 'staples trap.'[71]

To offset the negative implications of a staples-based economy reliant on the export of Canadian resources to the United States and the purchase of American processed goods in return policy-makers in Ottawa made a deliberate effort to encourage the development of a Canadian manufacturing industry. The industrial base that had developed to support the war effort in the 1940s was in serious difficulty; Canadian defence needs alone could not sustain it in a period of relative peace. At the same time, the non-defence sector of the manufacturing industry faced enormous competition from foreign imports.

In order to ensure long-term success of the industrial base, it was imperative that Canada develop its own technology. By broadening the base of the economy with modern competitive industries with a high-technology component, it was assumed that Canada would have more leverage and independence vis-à-vis the United States. This strategy was undermined by several factors which left both state and industry even more reliant on the United States. A Canadian 'high technology industry' could not be developed without costly investment in research and design. Nor could such new industry be sustained for long without access to larger markets. The result was to force Canadian industry to become even further integrated into the American economic orbit.

Seldom were the detrimental effects of the bilateral trade relationship questioned by Canadian policy-makers. However, in 1971, without warning, President Richard Nixon signalled the demise of the 'special relationship' by introducing measures to protect the ailing American economy from increased foreign competition. Canada was not exempt.[72] The impact of the new U.S. legislation immediately aroused Canadian concern.[73]

The response in Ottawa was cautious. Secretary of State for External Affairs Mitchell Sharp presented the Third Option strategy in an effort to reduce the vulnerability of the Canadian economy. Far from being a concrete plan with unanimous endorsement, the 'third option' only sought to investigate the potential for increasing trade ties with countries other than the United States. However, no alternative counterweight to offset the reliance on the United States could be found.

When attempts were made to establish links with Europe, the Trudeau government discovered it had not won the favour of Canada's other NATO allies when it decided to withdraw half its troops from Europe. Canadian diplomats quickly learned that their allies would not be willing to come to Canada's aid at a time when Canada was reducing its contribution to their defence. It was apparent that the European allies perceived Canada had violated an unwritten contractual agreement, one that linked Canada's commitment to their defence to future political and economic support for Canada. As Stephen Clarkson observed, 'When it tried to establish a contractual link with the European community in 1974 to implement the foreign policy diversification promised by the Third Option of Mitchell Sharp, Ottawa discovered that its paltry military contribution had been noticed. Canada was given to understand that establishing a contractual link required in return making a serious military contribution to European defence.'[74] The message was clear: Canada would not find support from the allies until the defence relationship was firmed up with a more substantial commitment. The third-option attempt revealed that the NATO allies, who had been cultivated largely to provide Canada with a counterweight to the United States, could only be counted on for support when Canada was forthcoming with what they deemed to be an appropriate European-based military contribution.

Policy-makers in Ottawa had good reason to worry about the possibility of being isolated from the fold of Western industrialized countries.[75] The tripling of oil prices by the OPEC cartel after 1973, combined with Nixon's 'currency dumping, burden-sharing policy to cover the costs of the Vietnam War, contributed to the economic malaise of 'stagflation.' While the shocks of 'Nixonomics' destabilized the 'special relationship,' the ensuing administrations led by Gerald Ford and Jimmy Carter were quick to mend some of the fences. Nevertheless, some sectors of the Canadian decision-making community were very alarmed over the extent of our vulnerability to U.S. actions.[76] While this was certainly not the first impetus towards economic nationalism in Canada, it was significant because it coincided with the increased competition and insecurity being experienced at all levels of the Canadian economy as a result of the changing international division of labour, the increased mobility of capital, and the radical restructuring of Western economies.

Over the course of the next decade, the Liberal government attempted to reassure the NATO allies that Canada would be providing additional military support. It also attempted to assert more control over Canadian economic relations. A National Energy Program and a Foreign Investment Review Agency were prominent among a number of measures designed to diversify and nationalize sectors of the economy.

The 'third option' and the hastily aborted efforts to offset Canadian economic dependency provided minimal returns. For Canadian decision-makers, military and civilian dependence on the American market was reconfirmed. As an External Affairs official later put it, 'it is on the basis of a North American economy that the private sector [in Canada] makes its growth plans.'[77] Canadian business and political élites thus had reason to worry about the rising tide of protectionism in the 1980s. Their interests were tied to an export-oriented economy that was directly dependent upon maintaining preferential access to the American market. In such an atmosphere, Canadian leaders assumed that it was important that Canada be perceived as a reliable and trustworthy ally.

In 1985, the Conservative government of Brian Mulroney began negotiations that would lead to a continental free-trade arrangement with the United States – thorough integration of the North American economies. As Maureen Molot and Brian Tomlin commented, Canada's economic eggs would be laid into the American basket.[78] Although the Mulroney government was the first to formalize and openly pursue military and economic integration, this process was not a new development. As far back as 1961 Hugh Aitken noted that 'defence and development have combined in the post-war years to reinforce tendencies towards continental integration whose origins can be traced far back into the nineteenth century. Economically, the ties between the two countries are close and becoming closer. On defence matters, their policies and resources are virtually completely integrated.'[79] It would be misleading to suggest that economic or defence integration occurred as a result of conscious imperialist motives or conspiracy. In fact, perceived mutual interests tended to be more decisive than the projection of a foreign will onto the Canadian public.

The two nations share many basic goals and values. Since both are liberal democracies founded on capitalist economies, it was natural that capital would be invested where the returns were the highest. The impetus towards continentalization can be partly explained by a focus on the short-term priority of growth and profits. The arguments in favour of further economic integration were generally premised on the assumption that it would prime the pump of the Canadian economy, thus providing greater wealth and independence. Long-term national interests tended to be regarded as a secondary by-product of free-market development.

Similarly, there is also little doubt that Canadian officials initially assumed defence integration and alliance participation were necessary if we were to avoid losing control of Canadian territory.[80] Relative to other industrialized nations, Canada attained security and retained sovereignty at a rather inexpensive short-term price. Once again, it was the easiest solution – politically, economically, and militarily expedient in relation to the alternatives. Moreover, an increasingly interdependent international order made it virtually impossible for Canada to adopt a 'go it alone' economic or defence strategy.

The emergence of the Soviet Union as a rival superpower contributed to a bipolar system of power blocs. Canadian threat assessments tended to reflect the general level of East-West tension. For example, in 1971 – during a period marked by détente and co-operation – the Department of National Defence (DND) identified 'the only major military threat to Canada ... is a catastrophic war between the great powers.'[81] In 1987, in the aftermath of a long Cold War, DND stressed that 'the principal threat to Canada continues to be a nuclear attack on North America by the Soviet Union.'[82] In this respect, the Soviets were an important determinant of Canadian defence relations. NATO and NORAD symbolized a common determination to defend the 'Western World.' Under these circumstances, it would have been very difficult for Canada to attempt complete neutrality or independence. Some interdependence and a degree of integration were inevitable.

THE DEFENCE TRAP

Canadians have long faced particular difficulties in determining national-defence affairs. Whether in trade, defence production, Canadian, European, or North American defence, the governments of the 1950s and 1960s were proceeding down a military-industrial path from which they saw few exits.[83] The governments of the 1970s and 1980s made several half-hearted attempts to restructure Canada's economic and defence posture. But these attempts were frustrated by a pervasive network of relations and arrangements that had cumulated incrementally over the past fifty years. Once again, the 'exits' were not sufficiently attractive to risk jeopardizing short-term political and economic interests.

Since 1945, Canada's choice of defence policy has been circumscribed by numerous 'invariants' or relative constants that would have been difficult and costly to ignore in any calculation of defence requirements and obligations.[84] Canadian decision-makers had to consider factors such as geography, culture, the requirements of the domestic economy, and proximity to a superpower and a potential enemy.

The success of the defence industry and the credibility of the Canadian Armed Forces became intricately tied to co-operation with their allies, primarily their dominant ally, the United States. Aside from the 'Atlanticist' and 'liberal internationalist' concerns represented in NATO and Western Europe, and the 'continentalist' imperatives of bilateral trade and defence relations, Canadian governments had to be concerned with a wide range of international interests such as the United Nations, arms control, and the Soviet Union. On the domestic front, factors related to the state of military, political, and economic resources, the budget, inflation, access to markets and technology, electoral politics and ideology, a defence community, and a peace movement all impart an influence upon the formulation of defence policy. As previously mentioned, Canadian decision-makers have had few 'easy' options. As early as 1972, this state of affairs prompted Colin Gray to process that 'there is no clean slate upon which a "rational" defence policy for Canada can be written.'[85]

Nevertheless, the choices that were made, when extended over a period of time, proceeded to pose some of the problems they were intended to rectify. The incremental cumulation of defence arrangements and commitments has limited Canada's capacity to pursue an alternative defence posture.

In many respects, this dilemma can be characterized by borrowing and modifying Mel Watkins's concept of the 'staples trap.'[86] Canadians risked being caught in a similar 'defence trap.' Arrangements such as the North American Aerospace Defense Agreement (NORAD) and the Defence Production Sharing Agreement (DPSA) accelerated our decline towards this trap. Obligations to continental and European defence imposed considerable constraints on the use of military resources and on the formulation of an independent Canadian defence policy. One result is that Canadian policy-making, especially defence policy-making, became less and less tailored to national or international security requirements as it became an attempt to serve short-term political and economic interests while complying with the expectations of our dominant allies.

In some respects, Canada's dilemma was similar to that faced by other middle powers within the northern hemisphere. As part of a larger hegemonic system structured, in part, around the

East-West conflict, very few nations were capable of setting their own agenda and pursuing an independent defence. There can be no doubt that Canada's defence trap was conditioned by the tragic international security trap commonly known as the Cold War. Yet Canada's position was also unique. The pattern of economic and military development pursued since the Second World War as well as a location in the strategic fore-field of a superpower combined to nurture the perception that dependence upon the neighbour to the south was inevitable.

Many of the arrangements that bound Canada in this matter were deemed to be unavoidable. Canadian decision-makers often assumed they had no options. They were often trapped into conceding Canada's participation in activities such as the testing of the U.S. cruise missile and trapped into the extended deployment of Canadian forces to NATO's Central Front. Canada's defence relations forced numerous compromises. Yet the cumulative effect of these relations was seldom considered. Canada continued to be recognized as a distinct leader in peace-making and exemplary internationalism. But the defence trap also tied Canada to a particular trajectory. Over time, it developed a self-fulfilling momentum.

While the free-trade negotiations were under way, the government released the first Canadian defence white paper in sixteen years. This paper departed from previous statements in both its tone and style. Echoing Cold War assumptions, it warned of an ominous Soviet threat and saw no alternative but to reaffirm all of the armed forces' present roles, save for a commitment to the defence of Norway. In some respects, it paralleled the general thrust of Canadian defence policy for the past forty years. Canada would remain committed to nuclear and strategic deterrence, continental defence, NORAD and NATO, sovereignty protection, and peacekeeping. A shift was signalled, however, and it appeared that Canada would be committing the armed forces to a more active aerospace defence, a more active role in anti-submarine warfare, and a long-war policy entailing the preparation of both the forces and a defence industrial base capable of sustaining protracted conventional war-fighting. Canada's contribution to

NATO's Central European Front was to be doubled. Implicit in the presentation was a commitment to shift from a 'token' presence in continental and collective defence to a new posture – one that was deemed to be 'militarily relevant.' In the words of Lt.-Col. J.C. McKenna, chairman of the Conference of Defence Associations: 'The most important message of the White Paper is that we no longer wish to be a token player at the defence table.'[87] Another implicit message, however, was that an influential military-industrial complex had emerged in Canada, one that could no longer be seen as simply a token player in the formulation of defence policy.

There is a direct relationship between the 'staples trap' and the 'defence trap.' Whereas Watkins argued that the staples trap locked Canada into the position of a satellite of the industrial centres of the world economy, the search for 'big league' military relevance tied to defence-industry expansion was binding Canada to reactive policies and outdated military commitments.[88]

By the spring of 1989, however, the white paper would be undermined by a range of unanticipated political, economic, and military developments. The rearmament program would encounter a resource crisis and a thaw in East-West relations. A decision had been made to increase Canada's military contribution to the larger Cold War contest at the very time that several of the major players decided to leave the game. With limited public or political support, many of the major capital-acquisition plans would be cancelled or deferred. Confusion and uncertainty now dominate the defence policy-making process.

At the turn of the decade, it is clear that Canada will be pursuing a new course in defence matters. That course has yet to be determined. At such a critical juncture, it is imperative to recognize those relations that have influenced defence policy. The security environment is changing rapidly. New ideas are helping to overcome previous obstacles. In the near future, Canadians may be presented with a unique opportunity to influence the formulation of a new defence posture. The defence trap that has limited Canada's options in the past is neither irrevocable nor inevitable. Traps, after all, are much easier to avoid and to depart from once they are recognized.

The following three chapters will review the political, economic, and strategic determinants of three Canadian defence decisions. These decisions reflect the pressures and constraints that arose in and between Canada's bilateral, multilateral, and domestic defence relations in the 1980s.

CHAPTER TWO

Cruise Missile Testing in Canada

Speaking to the United Nations Special Session on Disarmament in 1978, Prime Minister Pierre Trudeau stressed that the long process of bringing new weapon systems from the initial development stages through to eventual deployment often made it difficult to alter national plans once commitments to produce such systems had been made. He warned of the blind and unchecked momentum of the ensuing arms race and acknowledged the risk that 'foreign policy can become the servant of defence policy which is not the natural order of policy-making.'[1] The prime minister's conclusion was that 'the best way of arresting the dynamic of the nuclear arms race may be by a strategy of suffocation, by depriving the arms race of the oxygen on which it feeds.'[2] One of four measures that Trudeau proposed was an agreement to stop the flight-testing of all new strategic delivery vehicles.

Within the next two years, however, arrangements would be made between Canadian and American officials to flight-test a new strategic delivery vehicle, the American air-launched cruise missile, over Canadian territory. The Canadian government's decision to go ahead with cruise-testing would become one of the most controversial issues on the domestic political agenda in the early 1980s. To many Canadians, this decision appeared to violate the spirit of the prime minister's call for a 'strategy of suffocation.'

This chapter will focus on the circumstances that contributed to the government's agreement to allow testing of the cruise missile in Canada. It will examine the political and economic pressure, and the underlying logic which compelled the government to sign this agreement.[3]

THE GLOBAL GEO-POLITICAL SITUATION

A series of events in the last months of the 1970s precipitated an ominous shift in East-West relations. Rocked by war in Afghanistan, hostages in Iran, the recognition of a Soviet military build-up, soaring inflation, and an ailing industrial base, U.S. President Carter agreed to a more militant and assertive foreign policy in an effort to bolster his sagging popularity. The era of détente was finished. The swing to the 'right' was marked by a level of rhetoric and political posturing reminiscent of the previous Cold War years.

Ill at ease over the increasing number of Soviet SS-20 missiles, German Chancellor Helmut Schmidt requested an allied commitment to offset what he perceived to be an imbalance in the European nuclear deterrent. But he did not request Pershing II or cruise missiles.[4]

Amidst renewed tension, the NATO allies agreed to accept the U.S. 'Twin Track' proposal of December 1979. This proposal was initially accepted on the grounds that the United States would seek to negotiate the removal of the SS-20s while preparing for the deployment of Pershing II and cruise missiles in Europe in an effort to pressure the Soviets towards serious negotiations. However, while the 'twin track' policy laid the groundwork, the alliance agreed to the deployment of ground-launched cruise missiles (GLCM) and Pershing II missiles only if the first-track negotiating process failed to bring the desired result.[5] On 8 December 1979, the Canadian secretary of state for external affairs, Flora MacDonald, gave Canadian endorsement to the 'twin track' policy.

Shortly thereafter, Canadians experienced a temporary upsurge in economic nationalism as the Liberals under Trudeau's leadership campaigned to regain power. During the 1980 election campaign they promised several measures to offset foreign control of the economy, including plans to strengthen the Foreign Investment Review Agency and to introduce a National Energy Program. The timing of these policy initiatives, however, proved to be inconvenient given the aggressive new stance in American foreign policy.

Ronald Reagan was elected president of the United States on 4 November 1980. His promise was to 'restore the American dream' by revitalizing the economy and rebuilding its military strength. Economic recovery would follow naturally from deregulation, tax cuts, and other measures to ensure free trade on American terms. Reagan was elected on a Republican party platform calling for 'the achievement of overall military and technological superiority over the Soviet Union.'[6] A five-year, $1.6 trillion dollar defence budget was to provide a stimulus for investment and to ensure that the United States had the military superiority to promote its influence.[7] Reagan's administration adopted a straightforward approach in keeping with its strong business orientation and its marked antipathy towards Soviet or socialist governments. Either a nation was pro-American or it would risk possible repercussions.

It was in the context of this changed attitude on the part of American policy-makers that the Canadian decision to allow cruise-missile tests was taken. To understand the reasons underlying Canada's decision, it is necessary to look first at how the process was initiated and developed.

ORIGIN OF THE PROPOSAL

American interest in testing several new weapon systems in Canada first came to the attention of the Canadian Defence Liaison Staff in June 1978 when they were approached by a representative of the United States Office of the Director of Defence Test and Evaluation.[8] By August 1978, research and development officials of the two defence departments began to discuss the possibility of expanding co-operation to include the testing of an electro-optical guided weapon such as the cruise missile in an unrestricted environment 'which Canada's geography and climate could provide better than that of the U.S.'[9] Testing arrangements were subsequently discussed during a number of meetings of the Canada-U.S. Permanent Joint Board on Defence.[10] The Strategic Air Command of the U.S. Air Force presented the Canadian Department of National Defence with the first cruise-testing proposal in late 1979.

The Canadian public first heard of the possibility of Canada's direct involvement with the cruise missile in October 1980, when Dr William Perry, the Pentagon's senior scientist, told the press that Canada could be helpful in providing space for the testing of this weapon.[11] According to U.S. Air Force officials, 'the terrain and climatic conditions in Northern Canada would offer a good opportunity to test the inertial guidance system of the cruise missile under conditions similar to those in the Soviet Union.'[12] Shortly thereafter the Carter administration presented a formal cruise-testing proposal to the Canadian government.

By November of 1980, Department of National Defence officials had recognized the political significance of testing the cruise missiles. An internal DND memorandum stated that 'the proposed activities may be politically sensitive and thus require consideration by other departments.' Other DND documents indicated that 'the potential benefits to Canada from testing were not so clear'; that 'unusually high hazards may be associated with particular tests'; and that 'politically sensitive issues would undoubtedly occur in this program.'[13]

Anticipating the potential for a 'political storm' over the initial cruise request, Department of National Defence officials developed a two-prong strategy in an effort to ensure acceptance of the American proposal. Although the United States had originally requested one overall 'umbrella' agreement, the Department of National Defence asked the Pentagon to first agree on a framework accord, entitled the Canada-United States Test and Evaluation Program (CANUSTEP), with the understanding that this approach would defuse political opposition to a subsequent cruise testing agreement.[14] The CANUSTEP agreement was not considered to be as politically sensitive as an initial cruise-testing agreement, thus allowing DND more time to influence public opinion and secure cabinet approval.

American officials were anxious to secure a favourable decision from Canada. There was, in fact, considerable support for DND's efforts from their counterparts in the Pentagon. On 12 December, R.R. Ledesma, U.S. undersecretary of defence, research and engineering, wrote to Dr G.T. Pullan, a DND official, offering to repeat briefings in Ottawa 'if there were sceptical individuals within other Canadian agencies' involved with the CANUSTEP agreement.[15] According to General Thériault of DND, it was the skill and effort of the U.S. Air Force negotiating team that was 'the influential contribution toward securing a favorable decision on a Draft Project Arrangement from the Canadian Government.'[16]

The Department of National Defence also developed a communications plan to shape public opinion and defuse opposition to the testing agreements. Internal correspondence reveals the existence of a 'public relations campaign for cruise tests' to be co-ordinated by DND headquarters so as to ensure a 'consistent response.' An 'ALCM response cell' and two briefing teams were established to handle inquiries and represent the department's position. According to a departmental memo, 'a speakers' resource book has been distributed to military speakers and other influential and well disposed persons who comment publicly. The spread of understanding is planned through the provision of argumentation to opinion moulders.'[17]

It is apparent that the initial decision to proceed with the American proposal to test the ALCM was made by research and development officials within the Department of National Defence. As the lead department in the negotiating process, DND was able to refine and pursue the American proposal prior to political consultation. With DND's assistance, the testing process was set in motion before an effective opposition could be organized. By the time that testing became a controversial issue the groundwork had been established to counter resistance to the cruise proposal.

Given the close ties that exist between the Canadian and American defence establishments, and previous bilateral co-operation in weapons-testing programs, it is understandable that the cruise proposal was accepted within DND.[18] As Major-General Sturgess, a Canadian military attaché in Washington, put it: 'We have for years co-operated, and perhaps for that reason we weren't so politically sensitive ... It's not some plot, it's just that you develop a bond between the two countries at a general officer rank. We have developed essentially a corporate interface with U.S. Commanders, and our relationship with the Air Force is probably the closest. Regardless of the ups and downs in the political relationship, the military just grinds along.'[19]

Cruise testing also offered an opportunity for Canadian defence personnel to gain experience with a new 'state of the art' weapon system. This sort of 'positive contribution' would also help to bolster their prestige and enhance their credibility with their NATO and NORAD counterparts. Nevertheless, DND's efforts in support of the American proposal point to a disjuncture between military and political authorities in Canada. The internal conflicts within the state were publicly expressed when the prime minister suggested a 'strategy of suffocation' which would halt the flight-testing of all new strategic-delivery vehicles, while the Department of National Defence was willing to 'pave the way' for further tests of these weapon systems. However, while DND officials certainly helped to facilitate the testing of the cruise missiles, the final decision was not theirs to make.

Unlike previous tests of allied weapon systems in Canada, cruise-missile testing quickly ascended the hierarchy of decision-making in both Canada and the United States.[20] As the proposal attracted controversy, it gained symbolic importance in both countries and became a high-priority issue both for President Reagan's administration and for Prime Minister Trudeau and his cabinet.

At a meeting in Ottawa on 15 April 1981, U.S. Defense Secretary Caspar Weinberger presented the cruise proposal to the Canadian minister of national defence, Gilles Lamontagne.[21] The proposal was then discussed in the Cabinet Committee on Foreign and Defence Policy during July 1981, and in the Cabinet Committee on Priorities and Planning during October and November 1981.[22]

The first news to filter back to the Canadian public of the government's commitment to test the cruise was obtained on 10 March 1982 by a Canadian journalist working in Washington.[23] An unintentional leak from a U.S. Air Force officer in the Pentagon scuttled Canadian government plans to 'keep a lid on' what they knew to be a controversial issue. When questioned in the House of Commons, the secretary of state for external affairs, Mark MacGuigan, acknowledged that a framework agreement had been negotiated with the United States. Although many of his colleagues, including the prime minister, denied the existence of any such agreement,[24] an internal government memorandum subsequently revealed that 'the Canadian agreement in principle, permitting the secretary of state for external affairs to negotiate and conclude a bilateral agreement on the matter, was transmitted to the United States during December 1981 in a letter from Prime Minister Trudeau to President Reagan in response to a letter from the President supporting the proposal.'[25]

It was over a year later before the new secretary of state for external affairs, Allen MacEachen, and the minister of national defence, Gilles Lamontagne, were ready to make public the 'Agreement with the United States of America on Test and Evaluation of U.S. Defence Systems In Canada' (CANUSTEP).[26] However, this agreement, announced on 10 February 1983, did not specifically commit Canada to allow testing of the cruise missile.[27] On 24 March and again on 1 June 1983 the prime minister told the House of Commons that his government would be judging the success of the arms-control negotiations in Geneva before making a decision on cruise-testing.[28] Despite this statement, however, within a short period of six weeks and well prior to the cessation of talks in Geneva, Lamontagne and MacEachen announced an agreement to test the air-launched cruise missile in Canada.[29]

On Tuesday, 6 March 1984, the first test of this weapon was carried out over Canadian territory. Since that time there have been fifteen cruise-missile tests conducted over northwestern Canada. Testing has continued even after the Intermediate Range Nuclear Force (INF) agreement was signed by the two superpowers. Although the INF agreement successfully concluded negotiations to remove cruise, Pershing II, and SS-20 missiles from Europe, effectively removing the weapons from any direct link to NATO, Joe Clark, the secretary of state for external affairs, told the House of Commons that Canada would continue to test the cruise missile. Clark's stated rationale was that 'Canada did not want to weaken the solidarity of the Western alliance.'[30] It was subsequently revealed that, contrary to Liberal and Conservative government statements, Canada would likely be testing the new AGM-129 advanced stealth cruise missile.[31] The first Canadian test of this advanced cruise missile took place on 2 March 1989.[32] In the same year, the testing agreement was renewed for a period of five years.

THE POLITICS OF CRUISE TESTING

The Canadian government could not cover up or control all of the information regarding the cruise missile. In many respects, its efforts only served to arouse suspicion that Canada was naïvely supporting what many considered to be a dangerous American foreign policy. Prime Minister Trudeau's public comments that cruise-missile testing would contradict his own 'strategy of suffocation'[33] and that 'there is some justification for public fears that President Reagan is warlike or so hostile that he cannot be trusted to look for peace'[34] left many Canadians with the impression that American cruise missiles were being forced on their government. Within months the 'cruise missile issue' generated significant public concern and outright opposition to Canadian participation in the testing of the weapon. A Gallup poll on 17 January 1983 indicated that roughly 52 per cent of the Canadian population were opposed to permitting the cruise-testing program.[35] However, the minister of state for external affairs, Allan MacEachen, had stated that regardless of the amount of public opposition to the cruise missile, the government would not be changing its plans.[36]

It is apparent that the forces in favour of testing outweighed the opposition in influence if not in numbers. Very few people within the government were willing to speak out or vote against the test agreements. However, within the Canadian cabinet, six ministers were publicly on the record as being opposed to the tests. On 14 June 1983, members of Parliament voted 213 to 34 not to oppose the testing of cruise missiles in Canada.[37]

CRUISE TESTING: AN ALLIANCE OBLIGATION?

Why was the Canadian government willing to accept the American test proposal? The prime minister's initial rationale for allowing the tests was that his government was obligated by its commitments to NATO and by NORAD decisions which the government had previously endorsed. While there was no specific article within the NATO constitution that bound Canada in this fashion, it was apparent that credibility within the alliance would be questioned if the testing proposal was refused. Canada had not won the favour of European or American governments with its relatively low defence expenditures during the early 1970s. At a time when the solidarity of Western governments within NATO was being put to the test by their respective peace movements and opposition parties, many government leaders had become obsessed with maintaining credibility and demonstrating political determination in support of alliance policies.

As internal correspondence within External Affairs indicated in 1983:

> Both the Minister of National Defence and successive SSEAS (Secretary of State for External Affairs) have assured their counterparts that we would be concluding the agreement. Ministers have also taken credit at NATO meetings for our prospective involvement in the testing program for cruise missiles. European members of the alliance would therefore also have reason to question our reliability if we reversed our decision at a time when many of them are under attack from members of their opposition over the two track decision.[38]

It may have been, as Senator Michael Pitfield argued, that Canada really committed itself to testing the cruise many steps previously, well prior to a final decision by the cabinet.[39] Moreover, having previously committed the nation to the NATO and NORAD alliances, and having recently endorsed the NATO 'twin track' agreement, Canadian officials may have felt there was an underlying, if not explicit, political obligation to support these institutions.

But while cruise-testing did serve some interests within NATO, it was not conducted at NATO's request. Moreover, it was not a NATO obligation or commitment that prompted the Canadian government to accept the American testing proposal. Prime Minister Trudeau offered a more candid explanation when he said that 'it is hardly fair to rely on the Americans to protect the West, but to refuse to lend them a hand when the going gets rough.'[40]

Throughout the controversial cruise debate the Canadian government maintained that they were under some obligation to allow testing because Canada had a responsibility to support the policy of deterrence and the institutions which upheld Western security. The government never referred publicly to the economic costs or other negative impacts involved if it were to refuse the American request.

It we are to understand the factors that compelled the Canadian government to test the cruise missile, it is imperative that the analysis go beyond the political rhetoric in search of the larger context and underlying rationale. Borrowing a famous aphorism from Karl Marx, James Eayrs points out that 'foreign ministers make their own foreign policy; but they do not make it just as they please.'[41] While the prime minister was often portrayed as playing an influential role in Canadian policy formulation, it would be misleading to assume that he alone determined these policies. As with other decision-makers, his capacity to develop policy was circumscribed by numerous structural constraints. These constraints limit not only the personal influence of the prime minister but also the collective authority of the government. The latter's capacity to influence policy is often determined by its position relative to other forces, both within Canada and in the larger international system.[42] In an increasingly interdependent world there are a wide range of bilateral, multilateral, and domestic factors that limit a nation's freedom to choose policy. In bilateral defence affairs, perceptions of American security requirements have been very influential in defining the limits to which Canadian policy is tailored.

CRUISE TESTING: A BILATERAL IMPERATIVE?

Officials in Ottawa have assumed for some time that it would be exceedingly awkward and perhaps impossible to refuse to co-operate with an American proposal that was related to their defence or security concerns. James Eayrs has suggested that the real issue would be the terms on which Canadian co-operation would be forthcoming.[43] As early as 1953, Canada's minister of national defence, Brooke Claxton, acknowledged this dilemma in a memorandum. As he wrote:

> If the United States government policy develops as forecast, it will, of course, create many serious problems for Canada. The Canadian government may or may not be convinced, when United States projects are proposed, that they are reasonably necessary when weighed against global strategic factors and political obligations overseas ... However, it may be very difficult indeed for the Canadian Government to reject any major defence proposal which the United States Government presents with conviction as essential for the security of North America.[44]

While there is little doubt that difficulties might arise from refusing to participate in an important continental defence initiative, it should be noted that the Department of National Defence also assumes that it is in their interest to accommodate American requests whenever possible. Once again, such proposals tend to be interpreted as offering an opportunity to retain relevance in continental defence. As one Canadian Air Force officer involved with the Permanent Joint Board on Defence stated, 'It isn't really a question of influence so much as it is one of relevance. If you want to influence then you become a bigger player. Officials here are concerned about becoming marginalized. How would we get back in if we said no to these requests? If we don't do more, we won't be relevant.'[45] James Littleton has argued that Canada's previous experiences in this respect have had a powerful effect on conditioning Ottawa's response to requests from Washington. As he says, 'The experience of the Bomarc missile, and the destabilization campaign that ensued, made it quite clear that even a component of continental defence that is of secondary importance can be trifled with by Canadian politicians only at their peril ... When American military priorities have serious implications for this country, the inclination of Canadian leaders is to acquiesce while finding ways to save face.'[46]

In response to Canada's approval of cruise-missile tests, Johann Galtung, a Norwegian peace researcher, warned that Canada's policies were being determined by long-distance telephone calls from Washington.[47] Yet while one might be initially inclined to posit that Canada's reliance on the United States forces it to act at the 'whim and behest' of Washington, it would be negligent to overlook all of the other factors which help determine defence issues. Moreover, it would be overly simplistic at this point to claim that the United States is capable of literally dictating Canadian policy. Bilateral defence affairs are seldom dictated by direct demands. Systemic and structural factors often combine to provide the Americans with sufficient leverage to determine the outcome of issues within the relationship. As a senior civil servant working in the Department of National Defence stated, 'They are not so blunt as to say "do X or we will do Y to you in return." They will let you know how important an issue is to them, and if necessary they may reinforce their point indirectly.'[48] Canadian decision-makers are largely governed by what Abraham Rotstein calls the 'law of anticipated reactions vis-à-vis the United States.'[49] As a result, decisions by Canadian leaders take account of American and allied interests to avoid conflict and potentially wide-ranging implications.

Moreover, it should be noted that the bilateral defence relationship is seldom strained by conflict. Co-operation is the usual norm and both parties tend to assume an identity of interest. Writing in 1972, Colin Gray suggested:

> The multiple links between Ottawa and Washington are the 'reality.' Each has a set of expectations concerning behavior appropriate to the

other, stemming from a period wherein a community of interest was widely assumed, more often than not it should be noted, by Americans than Canadians. The formalities between the two countries in defence matters are important foci of attention both for those approving and for those disapproving of current arrangements. But these arrangements are just the most prominent landmarks on a landscape sculptured by day-to-day relations that are pervasive and very close.'[50]

It should not be forgotten that the Canadian government also had a vested interest in the cruise-missile program dating back to 1979. The Department of Industry, Trade and Commerce began negotiations with Litton Systems (Canada) to provide public funds to support the company's bid to supply the guidance system for the cruise missile before NATO had even endorsed the deployment of the weapon in December 1979. As Regehr points out, 'In the three fiscal years from April 1979 to March 1982, the company received a total of $43,435,142, in D.I.P.P. funds. Of these grants at least $26.43 million are directly related to cruise missile production, and an additional interest-free loan has also been provided for the same purpose.'[51] At the time, Litton was expecting to supply $1.2 billion worth of navigation systems to the United States over the next twelve years. Defence Industry Productivity Program (DIPP) grants are often speculative grants that rely for their full pay-off on the extensive deployment of the product or weapon being funded. It would appear that the Canadian government had a strong incentive to encourage the further production of cruise missiles.

But whatever opportunity there may have been to resist President Carter's request that Canada test the cruise certainly diminished with the election of Ronald Reagan. According to Stephen Clarkson, the state of Canadian-American relations had never been worse.[52] The tension between Ottawa and Washington in 1980 was reflected in a statement by External Affairs Minister Mark MacGuigan when he warned that 'normal relations between the two countries may no longer be possible.'[53] It was soon apparent that the 'get tough' onslaught of the Reagan administration was too heavy for Canadian policy-makers to withstand.

While the new president sought a North American accord, it was an accord premised on 'America first' – of greater military strength and the protection and expansion of U.S. business interests. Canada's National Energy Program, the Foreign Investment Review Agency, and especially the take-over of several U.S. corporations by Canadian firms helped spark a period of severe tension between the two neighbours. As Bromke and Nassal point out, 'While the Carter Administration greeted the economic measures adopted after Mr. Trudeau's return to power in 1980 with initial protests, these were continued "fortissimo" by the Reagan Administration, which immediately set about to protect American interests in Canada by reversing Canadian policy.'[54]

There was also considerable acrimony over the future of a fisheries treaty that had been accepted by the Carter administration but that the Senate refused to ratify. As well, Canadian policy-makers were frustrated by the lack of action over the problem of acid rain. The list of prominent issues also included the Garrison Diversion Project in North Dakota, the Alaska Gas Pipeline, the automotive agreement, legislation restricting the import of Canadian lumber, and trucking and overland transport regulations.[55]

The efforts of the new administration were not enough for a considerable number of American senators and congressional leaders who condemned Reagan for being too lenient with Canada.[56] Nevertheless, it is important to note that in Reagan's first term as president, he retained unprecedented control over Congress. This control was largely attributed to his success at linking diverse issues together within the same proposed bill so as to ensure that opposition would be politically costly. The use of this tactic was not confined to American domestic policies. As we shall see, at the time, it could determine the outcome of Canadian policies that infringed on American concerns. The number of outstanding bilateral issues provided this administration with considerable leverage over the Canadian government.

In fact, the concepts of linkage and leverage were overriding factors in the decision-making process leading to the final weapons-testing agreement. According to a senior policy adviser in the Prime Minister's Office, 'Trudeau considered the testing agreement to be indirectly linked to a number of implied American commitments.'[57] The Liberal government was apparently hoping to gain some concessions through the leverage that cruise-testing might offer. At the same time, it was becoming increasingly aware of the retaliatory measures that the Reagan administration was capable of enacting. As the PMO official went on to state, 'While the U.S. definitely deny any linkage, there is a good chance it would happen. Some day in the future there would be a good chance we would just not be able to get a deal. We are dealing with a harder-nosed bunch with Reagan; people who clearly mean what they say. They would have considered us entirely unsound if we decided otherwise, and they take seriously people who try to thwart them. They were pounding the shit out of us.'[58]

There was a perception within the Canadian state that a U.S. weapons-testing agreement would serve some Canadian interests, whereas refusing to accommodate the Americans would jeopardize a much wider range of interests. Whether an implicit trade-off or deal was struck at higher levels of policy-making prior to signing the CANUSTEP agreement remains unclear. An official from External Affairs who was a participant in the decision-making process reiterated the government line, saying, 'It was a high level political and defence issue debated at length in Cabinet. The agreement itself fell into the general kettle of defence co-operation. The main concerns were not nitty gritty.'[59]

However, according to congressional sources in the United States, the weapons-testing negotiations may have been linked to the deal over F-18 fighter aircraft.[60] MP Pauline Jewitt tried to confirm this possibility during Question Period in the House of Commons by asking Secretary of State for External Affairs Mark MacGuigan 'if the U.S. Government was forgiving the cost of research and design for the F-18s purchased by Canada, in exchange for our agreeing to the cruise and other weapons testing?'[61] MacGuigan did not give an answer. When the same question was put to another senior source in External Affairs, he replied that 'Perhaps directly within the bureaucracy of the

Canadian Department of National Defence and the U.S. Department of Defence a deal was made.'[62]

By the beginning of 1983, the government felt it had little option but to give the United States permission to test cruise missiles over Canada. A memo dated 24 January 1983, which outlined the proposed cruise-test agreement, contained a handwritten note from an External Affairs official asking: 'Have we ever asked the Americans what was the next best thing to our (testing) conditions? What would they do if we said no?'[63] In answer, a memo from Ross Francis of External Affairs' Defence Relations Bureau stated that (after a deleted section) 'Canadian Government actions since then have ensured that a negative decision now would have much more serious consequences than it would have had 18 months ago.' The memo suggests the possibility of U.S. economic sanctions against Canada if it refused to test the cruise, adding: 'While it is difficult to indicate what the (U.S.) Administration would do, there is no doubt that its disappointment would colour the relationship (with Canada) in all its facets, including trade and economic.'[64] This point was directly reinforced in March 1983 by the published statement of U.S. Ambassador Paul Robinson who claimed that 'Canada would risk a row with the United States if it refused to test the cruise missile.'[65]

In a previous letter to a member of Parliament, Prime Minister Trudeau made a rare departure from the standard government line regarding cruise-missile testing when he allowed that there were economic considerations of particular relevance to the Canadian defence industry. Besides considering membership in NATO and NORAD, the prime minister pointed out that 'there are also considerations which related to our Defence Production Sharing Agreement with the U.S.A., to defence procurement in Canada, and therefore, to jobs for Canadians.'[66] It is apparent that Trudeau had some foreknowledge of American intentions.

Two months before cabinet was to make a final decision regarding the U.S. cruise-missile proposal, the Reagan administration unloaded a 'bargaining chip' that must have shaken many of the political and economic élites in Canada. According to congressional and Pentagon sources, the United States was about to break a forty-year tradition of Canada-U.S. participation in shared defence production that would deny Canadian weapons-makers access to a new $2 billion U.S. defence-industry development program.[67] Richard E. Donnelly, the Pentagon's director of defence industrial resources, was quoted as telling a receptive House Subcommittee on Economic Stabilization that the new scheme 'would help only domestic U.S. firms.'[68] As one congressional source predicted, 'Under this policy, Canadian firms would suffer a slow but steady slippage against their American competitors over the next few years.'[69] When asked for an explanation of this 'protectionist aid program,' a Pentagon source stated that 'Canada, with its small military budget of about $7 billion, has been given a free ride on U.S. military research and development projects and therefore is vulnerable to U.S. action.'[70]

The message must have been quite clear to all government departments and corporate powers with a vested interest in the Canadian defence industry. In the fall of 1982, U.S. Defense Secretary Caspar Weinberger intervened directly to forestall passage of a bill that would have placed restrictions on U.S. purchases of specialty metals from foreign sources – a measure that would have disqualified millions of dollars' worth of Canadian military sales to the United States.[71] By 1983, American administration officials, who had previously lobbied in Congress on behalf of Canada to prevent passage of legislation restricting Canadian industrial access to the U.S. market, were beginning to question our trading relationship – just two months before the Canadian cabinet was to make a final decision regarding the cruise.

When the Federal cabinet met on 20 June 1983 to consider the cruise-testing agreement, there was probably little if any discussion on questions of the East-West strategic balance or military requirements. In all likelihood, discussions focused on our relationship with our allies, particularly the United States, the possibility of trade concessions from the Reagan administration, and how best to deal with the Canadian electorate. It is doubtful whether much time was spent debating the options and costs of not complying with the cruise-missile request.

Johann Galtung described the testing of America's cruise missiles in Canada as 'a test of your liberal subservience ... If you don't accept it, it is an insubordination which would be followed by threats, by blackmail.'[72] However, in this case it appears American officials took prior action to ensure that Canadian decision-makers were well aware that there might be costs involved if they were to refuse this request.

CONCLUSION

Canadian leaders were unwilling to 'risk a row' with the United States over the cruise missile even though a majority of Canadians were not in favour of the agreement. As a source in the Prime Minister's Office said, 'We would have had to deal with the afterwash of not testing for a long time.'[73] Aside from the fact that some commitments had been made prior to the final decision, there were substantive economic and political considerations. Canada's subservient economic position relative to the United States was compounded by an economic crisis which left it reliant upon 'American goodwill,' especially when an increasingly important sector of the Canadian economy was at stake.

Any threat to the competitive position of the defence industry would have been taken seriously by decision-makers in Ottawa. Finding an alternative market that would generate an equivalent demand was impossible. It was assumed that there was a risk to jobs, profits, industrial growth, technology, government and commercial investment, off-sets, the potential for export surpluses, and a host of other factors directly related to the defence industry and to worsening economic and diplomatic relations with the United States.

The final decision to test the cruise missile, it may be argued, was made in the best interests of domestic economic, corporate, and political security, and not necessarily in the interests of 'western security,' as the government itself had consistently argued. In many respects, the government had been trapped into testing the cruise missile. Canadian leaders assumed that they had no options. An array of bilateral, multilateral, and domestic interests were thought to be at stake. Within a period of several years, many of these interests would combine to exert a profound influence upon the formulation of Canada's new defence policy.

The decision to proceed with the CANUSTEP and cruise agreements was not without consequence. As Joey Slinger warned, 'such developments seldom happen in isolation.'[74] Shortly after the Canadian government approved cruise-testing, Department of National Defence officials warned that a new North Warning System would be required to defend against the anticipated development of a refined Soviet cruise missile – their response to the U.S. cruise-missile threat. Rather than help to suffocate the flight-testing of a new strategic vehicle, Canada had facilitated another round of the action-reaction process propelling the arms race.

Whereas the INF agreement imposed some sanity and pulled NATO's cruise and Pershing missiles out of Europe, the Conservative government pushed the ante up another level in February 1989 when they approved the testing of the AGM-129A advanced cruise missile in Canadian airspace. The new version incorporating greater range, accuracy, and stealth technology exceeds the requirements of deterrence and assured retaliation. As David Cox writes, 'Much about the advanced cruise missile is shrouded in secrecy, but enough is known to suggest it has hard-kill capabilities that, when combined with stealth characteristics, give it a first-strike utility against command and control facilities.'[75] Simply put, the new advanced cruise missile represents the refinement of an offensive weapon suited for nuclear war-fighting.[76]

The cruise missile decision cannot be considered as being an anomaly, or even a unique development within the bilateral defence relationship. Throughout the 1980s, Americans were very influential in determining Canadian security policy. As Brian Mulroney's ambassador for disarmament, former Conservative MP Douglas Roche, acknowledged in 1989, 'I suppose the biggest shock that I got was to learn the influence, the pressure, that the United States government has on the Canadian government on the issues of disarmament and security. That influence,' he said, 'operates in varying degrees, from subtlety and politesse to crude threats.'[77]

As Roche wrote, 'Does anyone think that Trudeau actually wanted to let the U.S. test cruise missile delivery systems in Canada? He succumbed to Washington. So did John Turner who, during his few months as Prime Minister, cancelled the presentation of a Canadian study paper opposing the building of anti-satellite weapons because U.S. Secretary of State George Schultz personally phoned him to object ... Again, the Mulroney government did not actually want the U.S. to test the new stealth cruise here; it was relentlessly hammered by Washington for more than two years.'[78]

The Canadian government has yet to make a concerted effort to have cruise missiles included in the arms-control talks. As we enter the 1990s, it is ironic that a major security concern of the government is the threat posed by air- and sea-launched cruise missiles and the alleged need for more comprehensive air defences.

CHAPTER THREE

In Pursuit of Strategic Flexibility: Attempting a Return from NATO's Central European Front

Canadian forces fought on European soil throughout two world wars. At varying levels of strength, they 'stood guard' there throughout most of the ensuing period. This 'devotion' to European security has been a constant of Canadian defence policy. At times, Europe has even been regarded as Canada's main front. Nevertheless, defining an appropriate military role and level of commitment has been difficult.

In 1987, the Conservative government stated in its defence white paper that 'consolidation in Southern Germany is the best way to achieve a more credible, effective and sustainable contribution to the common defence of Europe.'[1] The government was planning to phase out Canada's previous commitment to Norway and NATO's Northern Flank and to double the forces committed to NATO's Central European Front. The CAST brigade and the two fighter squadrons which had been assigned to go to Norway in a crisis were to be reassigned to bring both the army and air-force groups based in West Germany up to divisional strength in a crisis.[2]

But this was not the initial plan or intention of either the previous minister of national defence, Eric Nielsen, or the chief of defence staff, General Gérard Thériault. In fact, they made a bold effort to restructure Canada's NATO commitment and bring the armed forces home from Europe. Canada was 'trapped,' however, into retaining a military presence near NATO's Central Front in West Germany. For our purposes, it is important to understand the structures and context in which this initiative was presented.

BACKGROUND

Canadian leaders pushed for the creation of NATO in 1949. Since then, a principal goal of Canadian defence policy has been to guarantee North American security by maintaining peace in Europe. While participation in NATO inevitably entailed making a voluntary contribution to the defence of Western Europe, Ottawa also saw it as an opportunity to cultivate a multilateral counterweight that might help to offset Canada's dependence on the United States. It was hoped that NATO would provide both a security and a sovereignty guarantee. NATO was certainly intended to be more than a military alliance.[3] Political and economic objectives were incorporated in the North Atlantic Treaty. In fact, Canada insisted that the treaty make reference to the importance of economic co-operation among the allies. Article 2 of the treaty became known as the 'Canadian' article. By its terms, the allies pledged themselves to 'eliminate conflict in their international economic policies and ... encourage economic collaboration.'[4] Membership in NATO was thought to provide Canada with access to, and influence within, the higher councils of Western political, economic, and military planning.

As the Korean War erupted, Canada and the other NATO allies proceeded to station forces in Europe. Canada dispatched the 27th Infantry Brigade to West Germany in the autumn of 1951. At the time, this response was widely perceived as necessary to counter a Soviet threat. Harald von Riekhoff noted that this decision was made without notable controversy. Writing in 1967, he observed that 'politically and psychologically this commitment has been rendered more tolerable to Canadian opinion by the fact that it constituted an identifiable role under multilateral assignment which was neither wholly defined nor directed by the United States.'[5]

The government assumed at the time that they were offering a short-term contribution to collective security; it was not conceived as a long-term treaty obligation.[6] NATO and Warsaw Treaty defences developed apace with a heavy concentration of forces deployed along a narrow corridor dividing the two Germanys: the Central European Front. Within a short period, the Central Front had developed into a pivotal structure of the Cold War. Not only was it significant in terms of its strategic importance; this structure represented an important ideological and political symbol of the East-West conflict.

With concerns related to a Soviet nuclear capability and the need for greater conventional defences, Supreme Allied Commander General Dwight Eisenhower pressed the NATO members to increase their military commitments. Between 1952 and 1954, NATO forces jumped from twelve to ninety-six divisions, with twenty-five of these at battle readiness on the Central Front.[7] With a Canadian force of nearly ten thousand troops and twelve air squadrons stationed near this front, Ottawa signalled its commitment to participate in NATO primarily through the defence of West Germany.

Participation on the Central Front provided Canada's forces with an additional opportunity to plot and plan with the big players in the NATO club. These were the 'real soldiering' professional roles that Colin Gray alluded to in 1972.[8] For its part, Ottawa was slow to recognize that these deployments would constitute a contractual link, tying European economic and political support to the permanent stationing of Canadian forces in West Germany. As one senior Canadian diplomat referred to it, Canada's commitment to maintaining troops on Europe's Central Front was really 'the Canadian key to the club.'[9] But as several Canadian governments have learned, there were some serious costs and consequences associated with the 'key' and the 'club.' The alliance had become focused primarily on military affairs.

The Pearson government was the first to seriously consider pulling the Canadian Army's armoured brigade group in Germany back from its forward position on the Central Front. They intended to restructure this force into a lightly armed mobile force with no nuclear tasks, available to serve on the flanks. In the government's 1963–4 reassessment of defence policy, it was recognized that the new force should be versatile and capable of peacekeeping, internal security, and highly mobile light-armoured support. But as Joseph Jockel notes, 'In the wake of unease in the alliance with the proposal nothing came of it during the Pearson years.'[10] While it proved difficult for the government to reduce its commitment to the Central Front, it assumed a new responsibility in 1967 – a commitment to reinforce Norway in the event of a crisis with the Canadian Air Sea Transportable Brigade (CAST).

In 1969, the Liberal government of Pierre Trudeau initiated a defence review. It arose partly out of concerns that Canadian policy had become 'Euro-centric'; that it was placing undue emphasis on NATO and allowing defence policy to circumscribe foreign policy.[11] The Liberal government contemplated pulling Canada's armed forces out of Europe. It was no secret that the prime minister was sceptical about the necessity of this NATO commitment. Prior to launching the review of defence policy, he remarked that 'our defence policy now is more to impress our friends than frighten our enemies.'[12] Writing shortly thereafter, Colin Gray suggested that 'the Government feels that it is an absurdity for Canada to continue to deploy Forces in Europe in the 1970's, given the economic strength of Western Europe, given the fundamental shift in threat assessment from 1951 to 1971 and given Canada's somewhat amorphous, growing domestic defence needs.'[13]

On this basis, the government pursued an initiative to reduce Canada's military contribution to NATO's Central Front. Although consideration was given to complete withdrawal, a compromise was made, and the contingent on this front was halved from 10,000 to 5000 troops. 'In continuation of the direction pursued since 1964, the brigade in Germany was to be pulled back from the front and stripped of both its armour and its capability of using nuclear weapons.'[14] The reductions were also intended to complement a new emphasis on the defence of Canada. Sovereignty protection had become the government's number-one defence priority and it was assumed that these resources would be better spent on meeting 'national' defence requirements.

This limited withdrawal from the Central Front was, nevertheless, interpreted as a signal of Canada's declining interest in European security. External Affairs Minister Mitchell Sharp attempted to assuage allied concerns when he stated, 'We're still members of NATO and it really doesn't matter how many Canadian troops are in Europe – 5,000 commit us just as much as 10,000.'[15] But this was not how it was perceived in Europe. As Pratt and Keating write:

> The Europeans took great exception to Canada's new NATO policy and let their views be known to Defence Minister Leo Cadieux at a NATO ministerial meeting in May 1969 with what the American ambassador to NATO later described as the toughest talk I have ever heard in an international meeting. Germany was concerned about Canada's reliability in times of crisis. Britain feared that it would be called upon to replace the Canadians ... British Defence Secretary Denis Healey complained that Canada is 'passing the buck to the rest of us' and argued that the withdrawal of Canadian forces would lower the nuclear threshold.[16]

Two years later the political and economic implications of this initiative would surface with the 'Nixon Shock.' Canada recoiled when her major trading partner imposed an import surcharge. In an effort to recoup, proposals were made to restructure trade policy and to seek other trade alliances; this was known as the 'third option.' The restructuring of the NATO commitment coincided roughly with this 'third option.' The government was beginning to seek opportunities to offset Canada's extensive dependence upon the United States, but given the circumstances it was very bad timing. This ill-fated (and only partially endorsed) attempt to secure European support for Canadian access to the common market was a bleak failure.

Canadian diplomats soon realized that they could not count on European support for diversifying Canadian trade relations. 'When Canada approached Germany with the request for a contractual link with the European community, Chancellor

Helmut Schmidt allegedly told Prime Minister Trudeau bluntly, "No tanks, no trade," a reference to Canada's reluctance to outfit its forces in Germany with German tanks and, more generally, to make the point that Canada could not expect to obtain special standing within the community while reducing its commitments to NATO.'[17] The message was clear: if Canada reduced the number of soldiers standing on guard in Europe then it could not expect political and economic support from some of the European powers.

The Canadian initiative to reduce its troop commitment had broken the contractual link between military and political influence. Once the government recognized that they had misunderstood the terms of commitment, they set about buying back their 'key to the club.' As Clarkson says, 'Demonstrating a renewed commitment to NATO was an important factor in the decision to buy $200 million worth of German Leopard tanks and the decision to spend $1.5 billion on 18 long-range patrol aircraft with sophisticated anti-submarine warfare capability.'[18] At the NATO summit conference in Brussels in May 1975, Mr Trudeau indicated that Canada did not intend any further reduction of the 5000-man force then stationed in Europe. It was reported that the meagreness of our contribution to the common cause had been criticized at the preceding meeting of NATO defence ministers.[19] Canada's acceptance in 1977 of the NATO Defence Planning Committee's target of a 3 per cent annual real rate of growth of its defence expenditures signalled the Trudeau government's belated conversion back to support for the counterweight.[20] As Michael Tucker writes, 'In the main, all of these measures derived from a heightened appreciation by the Trudeau government of the political and possible economic benefits that might flow from alliance collaboration. The principal rationale for Canada's "return" to NATO was to help strengthen transatlantic economic ties in the hope of re-establishing a Western European counterweight to an unconcerted but real American challenge to Canadian economic integrity.'[21]

The central dilemma remained, however: Canada was stuck in a problematic role on NATO's Central Front. Questions continued to be raised about the military, economic, and political implications of this commitment. This front has been costly in terms both of the resources expended and of the opportunities forgone to assert sovereign control over Canadian territory. According to Donald MacDonald, a former defence minister, 'This massive spending has distorted our priorities, our force structure and probably led to a misallocation of our resources.'[22]

CANADA'S CONTRIBUTION TO THE CENTRAL EUROPEAN FRONT: MAINTAINING THE BALANCE OF POWER?

Since the early 1970s, Canada has had approximately 6500 troops and airmen stationed on NATO's Central Front. Within the context of 800,000 other NATO troops in West Germany and the nuclear infrastructure of the Central Front, Canada's contribution is seen as politically symbolic and militarily irrelevant.[23] For some time, it has been difficult to argue that Canadian forces were essential to the maintenance of European security or a balance of power. As early as 1974, the highly respected Canadian diplomat John Holmes stated that 'military arguments for the stationing of Canadian forces in Europe are hard to support.'[24]

Canadian forces have been stretched and over-extended in numerous roles. A perennial concern of military and political leaders over the past fifteen years was the extent to which Canada suffered from a commitment-capability gap. The armed forces were left with insufficient resources to perform in the various roles to which previous governments had committed them.[25] Allan Mackinnon, one of Canada's more recent defence ministers, acknowledged this dilemma when he stated, 'I do not believe for a minute we can carry out the commitments we have made.'[26]

The options in dealing with this problem were clear: either the commitments must be reduced or the resources for defence increased.[27] Something needed to give. Reflecting the solution shared by the chief of defence staff and several senior military planners, Jockel and Sokolsky argued that 'the most logical candidates are the militarily least important contributions, the 4CMBG and the 1CAG, which constitute CFE.'[28] It was widely recognized that the withdrawal of this largely symbolic contribution would not leave a significant gap in West German defences.[29] It was also recognized that they might make a significant contribution elsewhere.

Questioning this commitment publicly, however, creates significant anxiety for Ottawa and the allies. Neither are comfortable openly debating the merits of Canada's presence on this front. Suggesting withdrawal threatens to create both domestic turmoil and a conflict within the alliance. And, it is conceivable that those responsible for such a move might be punished for their initiative. Once again, it becomes a question of leverage and linkage. There is little incentive for politicians and bureaucrats to make significant changes if they risk provoking a harsh national and international reaction. Decisions tend to be weighted in favour of maintaining the commitment. As John Honderich attests, 'Part of the reticence in trying to redefine a new role stems from a Canadian fear of rocking the NATO boat too much. Mention the need for change in many external and defence circles in Ottawa, and the automatic response will be: "but what will our allies think?" or "we might lose our seat at important tables," or "what will the Europeans do in retaliation?"'[30]

Suggestions for change often tend to be perceived as an ideological challenge to the central principles of the Cold War.[31] The Central Front is central in another respect: it provides the clearest example of 'West' standing on guard against 'East.' Thus, it becomes very difficult for any participant, especially one heavily dependent upon a superpower, to challenge this key structure of the Cold War and one of the central organizing principles revered by the alliance leader. Withdrawal then becomes not simply a military affair, but a step that appears to be in the direction of ideological and political neutrality. As Jockel attests, three objections tend to be raised whenever a restructuring of the Central Front commitment is proposed:

First, irrespective of strengthening other Canadian roles, any restructuring is deemed to undermine Canada's ties to NATO and signal a retreat from collective security. Second, it is feared that by shifting priorities back to Canada and continental air defence, Canada will further undermine the alliance by drawing more sharply the division between European and U.S. interests. Third, if Canada is allowed to redefine its European commitment, other NATO allies, including the United States, may be tempted to do the same. This is the so-called slippery-slope argument. It has less to do with Canada's role in the alliance or the effect on NATO of Canada's withdrawal from West Germany than it has with the precedent that might be set.'[32]

STRIKE TWO: A 'SECOND SWING' AT WITHDRAWAL

In 1985, sixteen years after the Trudeau review, in the midst of another struggle between those calling for non-alignment and disengagement, on the one hand, and alliance solidarity and resolve, on the other, Major-General Leonard Johnson (ret.) articulated a position that appears to have been shared by other senior officers. As he wrote, 'Collective defence would be better served if Canada looked first to her own needs and then improved her ability to go to the assistance of Norway, where her help would be needed ... The real culprit is the continual misallocation of resources to a symbolic military presence in the Central Region of NATO.'[33]

As if on cue, Deputy Prime Minister/Defence Minister Erik Nielsen and Chief of Defence Staff General Gérard Thériault attempted a more radical departure from this thirty-five-year-old military commitment.[34] The first public news of change was signalled by the *Financial Post*, which noted that 'Defence Minister Erik Nielsen appears ready to begin revamping some of Canada's military roles in Western Europe ... Nielsen is also thought to be examining Canada's multiple military roles with a view to making them more manageable.'[35] It was wrongly assumed, however, that the thrust of Nielsen's mission was to discuss expanding Canada's troop commitment to West Germany. In fact, the proposal being discussed was the withdrawal of all Canadian forces from Europe.

The rationale for such a change was premised on many of the same assessments that had motivated the Conservatives' Liberal predecessors. In the face of over-extended military commitments and limited capabilities, they perceived that the commitment to the NATO alliance had to be restructured.

First, it was assumed that within the present military context, Canada's commitment of forces to Europe was insignificant. General Gérard Thériault, then chief of defence staff and a principal architect of the plan, later defended the initiative on the grounds that 'our forces in Central Europe mean next to nothing in military terms.'[36]

Second, a number of senior military planners considered this commitment to be somewhat of a trap, which unwisely tied Canada to involvement in any future crisis or war in Europe.[37] Withdrawing Canadian forces from Europe was deemed to be one way of asserting more independent Canadian control over any decision to participate in a conflict. In the words of one senior defence official, 'The architects of the plan saw it as the posture that gave Canada the maximum of strategic flexibility. Our forces would be based here, and they could be deployed or not as the strategic situation dictated. We would basically be in charge of whether or not that happened. Thus the Canadian government gains a degree of strategic flexibility that it doesn't have with the in-place commitment of forces in Europe.'[38]

Third, when the commitment was initially made over thirty-five years ago, there were fears that Europe could not afford to defend itself against the Soviet Union. Since then, Europe's NATO members have recovered. They have the capacity to mount their own defence.

Fourth, the peace-time defence of Europe was an expensive endeavour. All indications pointed to increasing costs.[39] Without a convincing capacity to monitor, patrol, or control Canadian territory, there was a concern that the military resources that had been devoted to the Central Front might be better deployed elsewhere.

While some analysts maintained that the 'ominous' Soviet threat to Europe persisted, few believed that the Soviets would consciously accept the risks associated with an attack on the continent. There were new concerns, moreover, related to Canadian territory. As one very senior source involved in planning the proposal stated, 'Canada's geography is now very important. Space is not the priority that many had earlier assumed would bypass the need for a greater Canadian military presence on this Continent. The new evolution in thinking is going to make us very important. We have a responsibility to secure our periphery.'[40]

A PROPOSAL FOR WITHDRAWAL

Having made a commitment to present the first defence white paper in fourteen years, Nielsen and Thériault met in secret deliberations with a select group of senior National Defence officials. 'Those involved in the planning were ordered not to report their work to superiors.'[41] The initiative to withdraw from the Central Front would have caused serious concern, if not an uproar, in both the army and External Affairs. The army's primary raison d'être would be discarded; its relevance and share of the budget would be in jeopardy. For its part, External Affairs would find itself in the midst of a crisis of uncertainty.

After some study, the DND group came to the conclusion that it was time to present Canada's allies with a proposal to withdraw both the Canadian Air Group and the Mechanized Brigade Group from West Germany. Included in the proposal were plans to restructure the commitment so as to provide additional assistance to Norway. According to one official involved in the planning, 'The Mechanized Brigade Group's heavy equipment was to be pre-positioned in northern Norway and a promise would be made to fly over the troops and three squadrons of F-18s in the event of an emergency. Provision was to be made for a transit base in Scotland.'[42] This plan would do away with the need for a dubious sea-lift across the Atlantic and Norwegian Sea, leaving only an airlift for the personnel who could be in Norway in a few days. The Air Transport Group's tasks would be simplified with the termination of the Canada–Germany runs, leaving for NATO purposes only those between Canada and the Northern European Region.[43]

Aside from the merits of shifting out of a troublesome commitment, Canada would achieve more independent control of its forces and greater strategic flexibility, effectively opening up a wider range of options for the pursuit of European and North American security.[44]

Canadian forces were far better suited to serve a role in Norway than they were on the Central Front. They were well trained for the conditions in northern Norway. In this rugged environment, with pre-positioned equipment and an airlift capacity, they would constitute a serious commitment to NATO security – not simply a token presence in an overly militarized region. Moreover, given the Norwegians' concern for maintaining cordial relations with their Soviet neighbours, they are wisely inclined to rely upon non-provocative arrangements for the defence of their territory – no foreign-based military presence in peace-time. In this respect, Canadian forces would tend to pose less of an offensive threat and offer less escalation potential (in the initial stages of any conflict) than the U.S. Marines who might end up fulfilling this role.

It should be acknowledged, however, that some defence analysts and some sectors within the military considered the Norwegian commitment to be untenable. They feared that it might lead to a 'Hong Kong' situation wherein troops were not deployed until it was too late to be effective, and then thrust into a dangerous situation, or else were not deployed at all for fear of escalating a crisis.[45] It was assumed by some to be a question of Canada's making a sufficiently credible commitment to deterrence – backed not only by a declaration of support, but also by an effective coupling – the stationing of Canadian forces in the region.

Many Canadians would, nevertheless, prefer an arrangement that maintained a commitment to defending Norway without the risks of entrapment in a region as heavily militarized as the Central Front. There is some truth to Peter Newman's suggestion that 'the defence of Norway is a cause Canadians could believe in.'[46] Canada and Norway are both Nordic nations with similar security interests. There is already a history of Canadian-Norwegian co-operation in both NATO and the United Nations. As the ex-chairman of NATO's Military Committee and the ex-chief of defence staff, Admiral Robert Falls (ret.), told the Special Committee of the Senate on National Defence: 'We are naturally allied as a Northern country to Norway, and if we have common ways of thinking, common problems and solutions, I think we would be well advised to be closer to Norway rather than farther away.'[47] Moreover, such a role would ensure that Canada was not entirely alienated from the European community or NATO. As Falls put it, 'If you think of it as a deterrent role, and of how best you could make it into a deterrent role – and what it does in effect, for our contribution to Europe – it is far more important to the Europeans, and the influence we might have in NATO, than would be the doubling of our forces in the central front.'[48]

There might also be substantial savings to be gained by restructuring Canada's commitment in this manner. Freedom from the Central Front would free Canada from the expense of maintaining a heavy armoured brigade. For the new role, Canada would only require a capacity to reinforce Norway with relatively light-armed infantry. Canadian forces would henceforth be based in Canada.

These plans were formulated with a conscious effort to appease American strategic concerns. The CF-18s based in Europe were to be reassigned to NORAD duties and the money that had been allocated to the Central Front commitment was to be spent upgrading Canadian air defences with additional long-range maritime patrol aircraft and the acquisition of AWACS (airborne warning and control aircraft).[49]

THE POLITICS OF WITHDRAWAL IN 1985

With the prospect of some additional support for Continental air defence, the Nielsen-Thériault proposal received initial approval from U.S. Secretary of Defense Caspar Weinberger. The Americans had long been pressing the European allies to shoulder a greater share of the collective defence burden and they may have seen this proposal as an opportunity to assess the response to a future troop withdrawal of their own – 'to test the water without getting their own feet wet.'

Nielsen and his senior group of advisers had made plans to sound out the proposal in Washington, London, Bonn, and Oslo. They never made it to Oslo. Once again, the timing of the initiative was not good; the powers that be in the European defence community had reason to be worried about further schisms developing in the Atlantic defence relationship. Opposition to NATO policies had coalesced and grown into significant political movements calling for arms control, détente, and disarmament. The merits of non-alignment and neutrality were being debated as an option to the politics of alignment and the risky competition for military advantage. It was a time of uncertainty. The Reykjavik summit had aroused concerns that the American resolve to defend the continent might not be as solid as some European leaders desired. Consensus within the alliance had been fractured.

Although Canada's military contribution to NATO's Central European Front is of little more than token value, it represents a significant political commitment. This commitment to maintain forces in Europe effectively couples Canada to any conflict in the region.[50] The departure of a long-standing ally from the defence of Europe would be perceived as signalling chaos in the fold. Moreover, it might establish a precedent for the departure of American troops. As their contribution was often argued to be crucial to the defence of the Continent, the expense, if not the risks, associated with decoupling and going it alone would be assessed as significant.

Certainly the departure of their allies would pose some economic problems for the Europeans, particularly the West Germans. Not only would they have to spend more on their own defence, they would also be forced to get by without the income derived from hosting a multinational military presence. While the West Germans pay for some of the NATO infrastructure, the nearly half-million foreign troops based on this front spend a good deal of money in Germany. It constitutes a 'tourist/troop trap' of grand proportions.

In the face of numerous concerns related to the domestic, political ramifications as well as the military and alliance response,

Defence Minister Erik Nielsen presented the proposal for Canada's withdrawal from NATO's Central Front to British Defence Minister Michael Heseltine and then to West German Defence Minister Manfred Woerner. Their response was harsh.

It had been assumed that the British might be attracted to the prospects of rebuilding the previous association between Canadian and British forces. However, Heseltine 'was under pressure and encouraged to call back or to reduce British forces in Germany.' His reaction on hearing the proposal was to say, 'Mr Nielsen, no way!'[51] After voicing his concern, Heseltine apparently 'tipped off' the West Germans to ensure the initiative would not succeed.[52]

In the words of one defence analyst privy to the consultations, German Defence Minister Manfred Woerner 'just went crazy.'[53] His immediate response was, 'No! We don't want anyone withdrawing forces from Central Europe at the moment.'[54] Canadian defence analyst Gwynne Dyer explained that the West German refusal was related to a fairly common phenomenon in NATO affairs: 'The problem was the habitual German paranoia about North American allies not automatically backing them in a crisis, which can only be assuaged by having American and Canadian troops in West Germany who will get killed very early in a war.'[55] One senior military source agreed: 'Their refusal reflected a selfish inward-looking Central European view. They are extremely paranoid about the Americans and assume they are wholly dependent upon the U.S. guarantee. They try to establish linkage between Canadian support and the American guarantee – a link that just doesn't exist.'[56] According to another defence analyst, the Germans were also worried that a Canadian withdrawal would set a bad precedent for smaller allies like Belgium and the Netherlands. With their own troops on German soil, they might have considered following the Canadian example.[57] Once again, it was the 'slippery slope' concern. And, with the U.S. Congress making demands for greater 'burden-sharing' while questioning their own level of future commitment, the European allies were nervous.

The British and German allies whom Nielsen had consulted

apparently got together to apply indirect pressure on Canada through senior NATO channels. According to one senior source, 'The West Germans contacted U.S. Ambassador Burt in Bonn and he called back to the U.S. State Department with a very strong message. It was the State Department that put the pressure on Jack Vessey and Cap Weinberger. Weinberger was forced to support the European concerns to keep peace in the family.'[58] The initial objections to the Canadian proposal were soon backed up with leverage. As one insider put it, 'The heavy pressure came back directly from the Americans.'[59] Gwynne Dyer commented that 'the Americans joined the Germans and British in leaning on Nielsen – and the Norwegians, who had been delighted by his proposal, just kept their heads down: They didn't want to be seen as stealing Canadians from the Germans.'[60]

As Jockel wrote, 'To the United States and Germany, Canada was playing a "shell game": withdrawing forces from Germany to Canada whence they might or might or not be sent to the Northern European Region. Better, the allies felt, a physical Canadian presence on West German soil ... It even seemed, as one allied official put it, that Canada might be "back to the old tricks of the Trudeau days."'[61]

In the end, Nielsen concluded that the further pursuit of the initiative 'was politically just not on.'[62] The proposal would not be thwarted because of any strategic shortcoming but by a combination of foreign and domestic political and economic considerations. Even Caspar Weinberger had initially agreed that the proposal made military sense. As an official involved in the deliberations reflected on Nielsen's final decision, 'He didn't think it would fly in Canada either – because it wouldn't fly internationally, i.e., he would get criticized internationally. Canadians would see the reason for that instinctively and would back the international criticisms.'[63]

The American, British, and German reactions were so harsh that the government and the Department of National Defence were quick to cover up the proposal.[64] Questioned later during House of Commons hearings, the new chief of defence staff, General Paul Manson, and the assistant deputy minister of national defence, Robert Fowler, denied having ever heard of or seen a paper on the 'Thériault plan.' General Manson responded, however, saying, 'If we were to do that, there would be, in my estimation, a very serious reaction on the part of our NATO allies. The signals that would be sent by Canada withdrawing her stationed forces in Europe, when because of the INF agreement and other NATO developments, NATO is attempting to strengthen its conventional forces in the central region, would be quite unacceptable for Canada, militarily and perhaps diplomatically as well.'[65] Ironically, two months later American defence officials criticized Canada for putting a higher priority on our commitment to West Germany and neglecting Norway.[66] Apparently, Washington expected Canada to bolster its contribution to both the Central and Northern fronts.

Soon after the U.S. State Department contacted Ambassador Allan Gotlieb and External Affairs, word spread to members of the defence community interested in maintaining our forces' existing role on the Central Front. One senior insider acknowledged:

> There is opposition in Canada from a rather parochial community of communities that have deep emotional commitment to the Army and the role on the Central Front. They have a vested interest here and they looked upon how it would affect them institutionally. We have had no land threat in Canada. The only way the land forces can justify their existence is through the Central Front. They are overly concerned about maintaining this commitment and they have a very real network to harmonize their voice in the community to achieve their particular purpose. If you didn't have missions in Europe, they wouldn't be going where they are.'[67]

Nielsen and Thériault had apparently overlooked the interests of a powerful constituency that was emerging on the 'home front.' Shortly after the government learned about the initiative, the cabinet was reshuffled. Eric Nielsen retired without an explanation. This had been a secretive venture. Although the proposal incorporated sound military and strategic planning, there was insufficient political preparation. Nielsen had not discussed the proposal with the cabinet's powerful Priorities and Planning sub-committee.[68] He had not marshalled strong domestic support before discussing the initiative in Washington, Bonn, and London.

The long-awaited defence white paper would be put on hold for two years. In the late summer of 1986, Nielsen's successor as minister of national defence, Perrin Beatty, gave the order to proceed with Operation Brave Lion, which was to assess the armed forces' capacity to deploy and support the Northern Flank. Whether the operation was legitimately pursued or structured to fail from the start remains unclear. However, it was already clear that Canada's armed forces would not be leaving the Central Front.

Restructuring would have been a long-term process. Without the support of the NATO allies, it would have been a risky political venture. In the midst of negotiations over free trade, the Conservative cabinet would have been quite reticent to pursue any initiative that would 'draw fire' from either the U.S. State Department or the Pentagon.

As their Liberal predecessors had done, the Conservative government quickly set about to buy their way back into the NATO club. Their defence white paper announced that Canada's commitment to the Central Front was to be renewed with more 'muscle': three hundred new tanks, new air-defence systems, and a doubling of the troop strength, bringing both the air and land forces up to divisional strength in a period of crisis.[69] The 5 Groupe-brigade du Canada previously assigned as part of the CAST commitment to Norway was to be re-equipped for a heavy-armour role. Overall, the equipment program was described as 'the largest army project ever undertaken.'[70]

'Unfortunately,' as one very senior military source noted in 1988, 'no Canadian government has had the courage or the strength to revise this commitment accordingly ... The situation is not going to be helped by the recent proposals.'[71]

CONCLUSION

NATO did not always function as a multilateral counterweight for

Canada. The 'Canadian clause' stipulating the need for economic co-operation among the allies had come to mean very little. The NATO members would link military and economic co-operation when it suited their national interests.

In many respects, the NATO 'counterweight' had become an additional burden, tying Canadian forces to an antiquated role on the Central Front. It furnished the allies with a mechanism with which they could influence Canadian defence policy. With its range of policy alternatives further limited, Canada was, to all intents and purposes, trapped into the commitment.

At a time when other allied nations were reassessing their NATO obligations and defence spending in the wake of a thaw in East-West relations, Canada appeared trapped by an outdated military commitment and, in turn, by an outdated interpretation of the Cold War. The promised level of commitment could only be rationalized in the government's defence white paper by promoting it as a necessary response to an irreconcilable East-West conflict and an 'overwhelming Soviet threat.'

Neither the allies nor Canadians were ready for a restructuring of this commitment. One senior official noted that 'we could have prepared the groundwork a lot better.'[72] Rather than attempt to explain their defence initiatives to the public, however, Canadian governments have always fostered the impression that 'all is well' within the alliance. Having obfuscated the issues in deference to alliance solidarity, there was little chance that a government could rely on an informed public for support. As it was, Canadians might have had difficulty understanding why the Conservative government, which had just campaigned on a defence platform of 'honour thy commitment,' were about to challenge a central structure of the Cold War.

Moreover, a small group of officials attempting such an initiative without the support of the government, the opposition parties, or widespread domestic support was running a considerable political risk. Canadians would have to expect resistance from some allies. That there would be short-term political and possibly even economic consequences could not be ruled out. But seriously debilitating retaliation was unlikely to ensue from a

Canadian attempt to restructure (or even opt out of) its alliance commitments.[73] The political fallout from any 'rough and tumble' attempt to punish a Canadian government might itself have serious implications for Western security. Canada is just too important politically, economically, and strategically to be sacrificed as an example. It is difficult to imagine an American or West German crusade that jeopardizes relations that are of greater importance than Canada's military commitment to NATO's Central Front.

In an earlier period, Harald von Riekhoff noted that 'the purpose of alliance reform might perhaps be served if it were accepted that certain conflicts of interest and incompatibilities, as derived from NATO's basic structural design, are beyond solution and might best be made more tolerable through adjustment and compromise.'[74] Within the last decade, however, serious questions have been raised not only over strategy and appropriate commitments, but also over NATO's structure and decision-making process. In 1985, two of Canada's most senior officers lamented their experience with NATO's Military Committee and with what they described as the alliance's 'outdated' and 'rigid' decision-making process. Regarding NATO force proposals and funds allocated, General Maurice Archdeacon and Admiral Robert Falls wrote that 'the bottom line in both cases is determined more by financial and economic than by military considerations, and the decisions are taken on the political rather than the military side of the alliance.'[75] They concluded that the decision-making structure and process reflected 'an image many people now have of NATO: that of an organization which represents its own corporate view of the world rather than representing, as it once did, the ideas of the vast majority of its 500 million citizens.'[76] The important questions that must now be asked are whether this alliance can compromise to save itself from internal conflict and, if not, how Canada might pursue an alternative arrangement.

For NATO to have remained a relevant mechanism for coordinating international security, it would have had to be much more tolerant of its members' regional security interests. A rigid alliance structure is unlikely to survive in today's rapidly changing political environment. Lacking the flexibility to accommodate the legitimate restructuring proposals of its members, the current structure has contributed to its own demise. When reform is ruled out on the basis of tradition or particular vested interest, then over time members will pursue alternative arrangements. Several years back, John Honderich warned that, 'while belonging to the club is one thing, performing outmoded and impossible tasks is quite another. For Canada to continue to be dedicated to roles that relate more to a war that terminated four decades ago just doesn't make sense. For us to persist in those roles is to perpetuate contradictions that should have been resolved long ago.'[77]

A number of unanticipated opportunities to effect change have surfaced within the past four years. Both NATO and the Warsaw Treaty alliances are in a period of transition and crisis. In contrast to the early 1980s, when conformity and alliance solidarity appeared to dominate the alliance decision-making process, the last three years have been marked by a fracturing of consensus and by dissent. Increasingly, the rationale for maintaining a commitment to the Central Front and NATO is being questioned.

If the latest attempt to restructure Canada's commitment away from this front had been successful, it would have had a significant impact upon Canada's defence policy. As one senior military source noted:

> This option had a number of virtues. It would allow us to clean up the whole defence posture and consequent policy. As it is we are spread all over the map, doing everything in slip-shod fashion. Time has overtaken a situation conceived in the 1950s that is now fundamentally different ... Our present commitment is redundant and rather silly and it is recognized as such by our allies. We were presenting the allies with a much more rationalized posture entailing a degree of concentration that had military credibility.'[78]

The initiative itself provides another sobering glimpse of the bilateral, multilateral, and domestic pressures that have constrained Canadian defence policy. Even with a high-level initiative, backed up by strongly positioned senior political and military officials, it is difficult and politically risky to restructure alliance commitments and alter defence posture. As we shall see in the next chapter, the failure of this initiative would have a profound impact upon the formulation of defence policy in 1987. Nielsen and Thériault may have overlooked a number of interests within Canada that were merging to form a powerful constituency.

CHAPTER FOUR

Industrial Mobilization and the Shift to a Long-War Policy: The Emergence of the Military-Industrial Complex in Canada

A long 'declared' objective of Canadian defence policy has been to maintain peace and security at the lowest level of forces. Since the 1950s, Canadian defence policy has been oriented to a short-war scenario entailing limited defence preparedness. Further preparations were deemed to be unnecessary. Until recently, it was assumed that there were neither strategic nor economic justifications for shifting away from the short-war orientation.

In 1987, however, the Conservative government's white paper *Challenge and Commitment: A Defence Policy for Canada* signalled the convergence of military and industrial efforts to achieve a higher state of defence preparedness.[1] With the costs and implications of nuclear-powered submarines capturing the news, relatively little attention was paid to this seemingly unrelated endorsement. Nevertheless, it is clear that high-level authorization was given to a shift in emphasis from preparations for a short war to preparations for a long war; with the adoption of a new level of defence preparedness entailing industrial mobilization, a total-force concept, a tripling of Canada's reserve force (up to 90,000), and a major rearmament program. Shortly after the white paper's release, the minister of defence, Perrin Beatty, announced the formation of a new Defence Industrial Preparedness Advisory Committee and the organization of a joint Canada-U.S. committee to formalize an integrated North American Defence Industrial Base.

The white paper and subsequent speeches of the defence minister argued that the policy was in Canada's best economic and security interests. Although the relationship between these interests was not made entirely clear by the government, the official acknowledgment in itself raises some important questions over both the substance and process of recent defence decision-making. Was the Department of Defence influencing economic policy? Were particular sectors of the Canadian economy influencing defence policy? Is there a complex of interests structuring both economic and defence policy? Whose interests were to be served by the aforementioned initiatives? How will the formulation of defence policy be affected in the future?

There was a close relationship between the shift to a long-war policy, defence preparedness, industrial mobilization, a total-force concept, the reserves, and the planned acquisition of new equipment. These seemingly diverse defence policies were integral components of a new strategy that sought to prepare the armed forces and a defence-industrial base for protracted conventional war and to build support for military-industrial interests. The formulation of defence policy in 1987 reflected the culmination of efforts on behalf of sectors within the defence industry, recent Liberal and Conservative governments, the Department of Defence, the federal bureaucracy, and the various interests represented under the umbrella of organizations such as the Business Council on National Issues, the American Defense Preparedness Association (Canadian chapter), the Canadian Institute of Strategic Studies, and the Conference of Defence Associations. Close relations have developed between these sectors and organizations. Their relations are based upon common interests. The formulation of the 1987 defence white paper implicitly signalled the emergence of the military-industrial complex into the Canadian political process.

This chapter will focus first on the developments that preceded these policy shifts; second, on the domestic interests at stake; third, on the initiatives taken by several Canadian organizations to effect these changes; and fourth, on explaining the military-industrial complex and some of the implications for Canadian defence relations and future defence policy.

BACKGROUND

Since the 1950s, it has been widely recognized that a war between the superpowers would be of short duration, that a direct military conflict would either be quickly resolved in political forums after a conventional attack was slowed or that there was high probability it would escalate to nuclear war and mutually assured destruction. Defence preparedness came to be viewed according to the requirements of nuclear deterrence. To retain a relevant role in the nuclear age, conventional military forces would have to be ready and deployed at all times, a condition known as 'forces in being.' This was a new scenario with marked differences from the period preceding both world wars. There would be very little time for the extensive mobilization of troops or industry, and it was recognized that reserve forces would be unlikely to contribute to any conflict. Rather than prepare for sustaining a long war, planners concentrated on the lesser requirements of augmentation. Given the implications of nuclear war, 'war avoidance' became a declared, if not operational, priority. At the time, it was clear that total war was an irrational prospect.

In Canada, acceptance of the short-war thesis was sufficient to stem an active search for a protracted war-fighting capability. A long war was not expected nor would it be necessary to prepare for one. In contrast to the costly mobilization required for a long war, the new scenario entailed much less expense. The level of forces, equipment, and sources of resupply could be radically reduced. Paul Hellyer, the minister of national defence, stated: 'Forces in being which traditionally have been low priority are at the top of our list and reserve forces which have been the backbone of our mobilization in two world wars, are moved down the scale proportionately.'[2] Accordingly, Canadian governments restructured the armed forces to prepare for the limited range of activities required by the short-war scenario. As Dan Middlemiss attests:

From the mid-1950s on, DND has adhered firmly to a forces-in-being military doctrine. This approach, which corresponded to United States military doctrinal preferences, emphasized the need for operationally ready forces rather than manpower or industrial mobilization potential. For Canada, this meant that the regular forces were to have preference over the reserves in both manning and equipment; indeed, the 1971 white paper noted that the Reserves had been designated as part of the 'forces in being.'[3]

Within a short period, however, it was recognized that the political endorsement of the short-war thesis would have a profound impact on the military, altering its traditional role and challenging its relevance, and an equally profound effect on the industries involved in arms supply. If there was no need to maintain forces over an extended period of combat operations, then there would be little sense in supporting the type of defence industrial base capable of the timely resupply required for protracted fighting. Moreover, the role of the armed forces, particularly the army stationed in Europe, would be largely to act as front-line hostages to a nuclear trip-wire. Once the line had been crossed, alliance leaders would have to assess whether to negotiate or to escalate. For the armed forces this was a new and somewhat discomforting role. It was not easily supported within services that had been oriented by military tradition and training towards the pursuit of victory.

The Trudeau government's defence white paper of 1971 gave a strong endorsement to the short-war strategy. It stressed the need to prevent war between the superpowers and to promote political reconciliation so as to ease underlying tensions. Endorsing the pursuit of a non-offensive defence posture, the 1971 white paper challenged the wisdom of basing security on a policy of deterrence; it noted the limited relevance of Canadian forces in defending against a massive attack; and it argued in favour of reducing Canada's troop commitment to NATO's Central European Front so as to foster economic growth and better safeguard Canadian sovereignty and independence.[4]

Acceptance of the short-war thesis and the possibility of

mutually assured destruction certainly reduced military requirements. According to William J. Yost, director of operations for the Conference of Defence Associations and a brigadier-general in the Canadian Armed Forces until 1980: 'The short-war policy hurt the Armed Forces and the defence industry.'[5] Military-industrial interests were set back. As might have been expected, there was resistance to this type of force posture.

Economic and strategic relations would also be affected by factors such as emerging Western economic crisis and the growth of Soviet military power. At the NATO summit meeting in Washington in 1978 it was agreed that the allied nations would endeavour to increase their defence budgets 3 per cent annually, and bring their war-reserve holdings up to thirty combat days.[6] This was one of the first shifts towards defence preparedness and force sustainment. Several explanations were given.

A STRATEGIC REQUIREMENT?

With a new interest in 'escalation dominance' and preparations for protracted nuclear and conventional war-fighting arising in the late 1970s, industrial mobilization and preparedness resurfaced as an American strategic and industrial priority.[7] Some analysts have suggested that this was a belated response to the requirements of NATO's flexible-response strategy, which had been developed in the 1960s to provide decision-makers with a wider range of military options in a crisis.[8] U.S. General Bernard Rogers, NATO's Supreme Allied Commander Europe (SACEUR), offered another rationale for the long-war policy and industrial mobilization when he announced in the mid-1980s that the alliance would need a major conventional rearmament to accompany any nuclear disarmament in Europe. Rogers maintained that a significant buildup was necessary in order to counter an alleged Soviet conventional superiority. It was also argued that the shift to a long-war policy and defence preparedness would raise the nuclear threshold. Perrin Beatty, Canada's defence minister, explained that 'In the 1970s, strategic thinking changed. Détente and the prospect of nuclear arms control combined with the horrors of the prospects of nuclear war meant that a protracted non-nuclear conflict would be possible without an escalation to a nuclear exchange. Conventional forces became more important in this new scenario, in which the nuclear threshold would be raised. This in turn meant that the sustainability of a nation's forces once again became important.'[9]

However, in an uncharacteristic departure from his department's explanation, Lieutenant-Colonel Douglas Bland acknowledged that the change in strategic thinking was unlikely to have been the primary motive for the current interest in mobilization and preparedness. According to Bland, that argument 'is not entirely convincing, for the need for a modern defence industrial policy has been clear since at least 1967.'[10]

Contrary to Beatty's statement, strategic thinking in the 1970s had little influence on the NATO alliance's operational doctrine – the risks of accidental or inadvertent escalation from conventional to nuclear war were assumed to remain very high; NATO retained its nuclear first-use policy; and neither the Americans nor the alliance had endorsed a strategy that envisaged a protracted non-nuclear war (long-war) or one that necessitated a high level of continuous 'near-war' defence industrial preparedness.[11] Canadian forces were only asked by NATO to be prepared for thirty days' sustainment.[12] Few serious analysts saw a conventional war as imminent or probable.[13]

As Dan Middlemiss and Lieutenant-Colonel Bland acknowledge, the interest in defence preparedness dates back to an earlier period.[14] Faced with the prospect of a commitment-capability gap in the mid-1970s, the Trudeau cabinet authorized a Defence Structure Review to assess the tasks, effectiveness, and appropriate funding levels for the forces. According to Bland, 'pressure from NATO and national groups ... compelled the government to organize' this review in 1975.[15] In order to meet Canada's defence commitments and appease allied concerns, cabinet instituted a long-term re-equipment program. It was widely recognized that Ottawa would have to purchase some major systems if the Canadian Armed Forces were to retain relevance in the roles to which they had been committed. But as Middlemiss notes, 'while the review initiated the process of rectifying the force structure deficiencies of the CF, it did so primarily in the context of the Forces' peacetime, rather than wartime, requirements.'[16] For those who believed that Canada had to maintain a war-fighting capability to ensure 'credible' deterrence, this program was unacceptable. At the time, Canada's military credibility in this respect was a low priority for the government. Other considerations were predominant.

AN ECONOMIC REQUIREMENT?

The Defence Structure Review was not entirely convinced that the strategic situation justified a major rearmament. A number of other non-military objectives were being considered. As David Leyton-Brown and Brian MacDonald acknowledge:

> The approval by Cabinet in 1975 of the Department of National Defence long-range re-equipment programme had a number of additional objectives: to stimulate production and employment especially in high-technology industries; to improve the international competitive position of Canadian industry by encouraging technology transfers to defence and non-defence firms; to contribute to Canada's balance of trade; and to achieve a number of other economic objectives (assisting small business, alleviating regional disparities, and rationalizing and restructuring certain segments of Canadian industry).[17]

A conscious effort was under way in the mid-1970s to merge both strategic and economic objectives. But Ottawa's capacity to pursue this goal was circumscribed both by financial constraints and by the structure of the defence industry.

After the Korean War, it had become exceedingly expensive to equip the armed forces and to sustain an indigenous defence industrial base. The complexity of modern weapons technology and the fast rate at which they became obsolete entailed rapidly escalating costs. The high cost of research and development, as well as the production of armaments, forced many industrialized nations to specialize in a few areas of expertise and move into the arms export trade.

With significant demand generated by the Korean War, the Vietnam War, and the Cold War, Canada's defence industrial base became increasingly export-dependent and reliant upon access to the U.S. market. Since the cancellation of the Avro Arrow, it had not been geared to serving the needs of Canada's armed forces. As Ernie Regehr has argued, the defence industry's first priority was to achieve its own economic objectives rather than to satisfy Canadian defence requirements.[18] Dan Middlemiss explains that, even within the government, 'while there remained a concern to preserve the nucleus of a domestic defence industry in Canada, the military rationale for an industrial mobilization capacity was being subordinated to, if not entirely supplanted by, the more pressing economic and political considerations relating to balance of payments, employment, and the maintenance of an important sector of the Canadian manufacturing industry.'[19] When the re-equipment program was authorized in 1975, this sector began to attract attention.[20] For a short period, there appeared to be interest in developing an indigenous defence industrial base. The re-equipment program coincided with the Trudeau government's attempts to attain greater national control of the economy. But efforts to develop an indigenous defence industry were initially frustrated. The defence industrial base in Canada produced few complete systems. It had long been conceived in a North American context as a component of the American defence industrial base. By 1980, however, the government reaffirmed its intention to combine military and economic objectives within a new industrial strategy. The Throne Speech of April 1980 confirmed this commitment, and the intent to use procurement policies to advance these interests.[21] In 1980, John Shepherd, the former head of the Science Council of Canada, wrote: 'The appropriate strategy will be to use defence spending to intensify research and development in Canada, to build up Canadian-owned industry, and to build up a systems capability that in turn influences sources of production. These objectives must be imposed and planned across the entire span of defence purchasing, and over a decade or more of activity ... No military program of any substance should be approved which does not contribute to these industrial goals.'[22]

There remained, nevertheless, a concern that the defence industrial base would only be able to supply a small percentage of the armed forces' equipment requirements. In a Conference of Defence Associations publication, *Industrial Mobilization in Canada* (alleged by insiders to have become a very influential book), Brigadier-General Yost (ret.) argued that 'with the odd exception, such as Arsenals Canada Ltd., our industrial base for defence is part of a U.S.-dominated continental weapons industry. It is suggested that we take a pragmatic approach and determine how this situation can be further developed to improve our national security, and in so doing improve NATO's conventional deterrence.'[23]

Government support for the defence sector may have been intended to develop an indigenous defence industrial base, but these industries remained closely integrated within the larger North American defence industrial base. Canadians did not even own or control most of the defence industries in Canada. In 1986, approximately eighteen of Canada's top twenty-five military contractors were branch plants of foreign-based multinational corporations.[24] This was by no means a unique phenomenon within the Canadian economy. Concerns about growing trade dependence upon (and vulnerability to) the United States led cabinet in 1981 to consider moving towards a formal bilateral trade deal with the United States.[25]

The official confirmation of the shift to a long-war policy and the need for increased defence preparedness was given by Liberal Defence Minister Gilles Lamontagne to the Conference of Defence Associations' 1983 annual general meeting.[26] He announced that the government had agreed in principle that 'the Canadian Forces should be able to meet and fully sustain their commitments in an emergency and, if so directed, further expand their capabilities.'[27] The long-standing reliance upon 'forces-in-being' was no longer sufficient.

A flurry of high-level activity followed the defence minister's endorsement. A Department of Supply and Services document dated July 1984 urged that the federal government must take extraordinary measures to encourage the growth of a domestic defence industry as a source of high technology, jobs, and export income.[28] In the same month, a report from the Ministry of State for Science and Technology provided some indication of the future agenda. As it stated:

> It is no coincidence that some of this century's most awesome scientific achievements have been made in times of war. Military requirements create an immense demand for scientific innovation, and a state of war makes it urgent that these demands be fulfilled.
>
> We do not advocate the creation of a Canadian military-industrial complex as a means of stimulating technology development. But we do advocate it's peacetime equivalent: a policy that would effectively utilize the federal government's immense purchasing power to promote private sector innovation.

However, the report goes on to point out that

> the U.S. experience offers grounds for supposing that technology development can effectively be encouraged through government procurement practices. In the course of our research, we were especially impressed by the activities of the U.S. Defense Department. The Defense Advanced Research Procurement Agency (DARPA), alone spends out $880 million on state-of-the-art R & D and technology development. DARPA's sponsorship of hundreds of risky, state-of-the-art projects – many of which never result in useable products – has resulted in the creation of literally thousands of innovative companies and tens of thousands of new jobs.[29]

By 1985, a Defence Industrial Preparedness Task Force (DIPTF) was organized by the Department of National Defence. Its official purpose was 'to define the approach DND must take to ensure the industrial sustainment of the Canadian Forces in all operational tasks.' Unofficially, however, they were on a different mission. As officials on the task force explained, 'The DIPTF is working closely with U.S. Department of Defense industrial preparedness planners in studying ways and means of enhancing the integration of the North American Defence Industrial Base.'[30] The report of the task force concluded that 'the North American defence industrial base approach [i.e., integrated defence industrial preparedness planning with the United States Department of Defense] is the most viable from both economic and security perspectives ... Defence Industrial preparedness would serve to enhance both NATO's and Canada's war-fighting potential.'[31] In March 1987 a charter was signed to formalize defence industrial preparedness co-operation between Canada and the United States and establish a North American Defence Industrial Base organization (NADIB).[32]

Advocating industrial mobilization, defence preparedness, and a NADIB served a number of military and economic objectives and attracted a much wider range of interest. To effect political change and shift the military-industrial agenda in Canada, it was understood that diverse interests had to be aligned to support the common objective. As Brigadier-General W.J. Yost (ret.), director of operations for the Conference of Defence Associations, acknowledged, 'We decided to get people tied in with the U.S. [defence] industry and then have them develop a base of operations in Canada. I knew they could help us be more effective and we needed their co-operation. They could help us to get industry on side here.'[33] This sort of coalition-building in military-industrial relations is not uncommon. As Lieutenant-Colonel Bland writes, 'Rarely has defence policy for the sake of defence been motive enough to generate new defence policies in Canada or, indeed, within the defence establishment. Most successful policy initiatives have depended upon a harmonizing of the interests of officials and interest groups inside and outside of the defence establishment. The defence industrial base is an issue that developed a constituency.'[34] This constituency of military-industrial interests within both the Canadian state and the United States was able to mobilize numerous organizations and interest groups. It became a powerful proponent not only of a NADIB, but also of a long-war policy, defence preparedness, a total-force concept, and a wide range of acquisition programs. In short, the military-industrial complex emerged in Canada in the 1980s as a powerful determinant of Canadian defence policy.

If we are to understand the factors that compelled the government to pursue these initiatives, the analysis must go beyond a cursory review of developments and official explanations. A review of the interests related to these changes and this constituency is necessary.

THE DEFENCE INDUSTRY: IN SEARCH OF OPPORTUNITY

The manufacture and trade of weapons and military-related products has become a multi-billion-dollar international business.[35] A report on the armaments industry prepared by the Ontario Legislative Research Services states that 'although Canadian arms merchants – a term that includes both government and industry – have established a firm place for themselves among the global arms dealers, efforts to encourage further development of this profitable venture are setting the pace for industrial and technological goals of the eighties and beyond.'[36] As one senior official in the Department of National Defence stated, 'We want to get as big of a piece of this pie as we can.'[37]

The Canadian defence industry's share of this pie grew rapidly in the 1980s. Whereas in 1974 Canada exported $280.4 million worth of military products, by 1985 these exports increased to $1.903 billion.[38]

Several developments within the last decade drew considerable attention and investment to this sector of the economy. First, it was not a coincidence that the Canadian defence industry's success over the last eight years paralleled an increase in international tension and a major American arms buildup initiated by the Carter administration. The rapid growth in arms exports to the United States, according to officials of the Defence Programs Bureau of the Department of External Affairs, was attributable simply to the rapid growth in demand.[39] In the first two years of the Reagan presidency, Canada's defence exports to the United States nearly doubled from $481.7 million in 1980 to $826.6 million in 1981.[40] The opportunities arising from the Pentagon's budget were advertised in an article in a 1983 issue of *Canadian Business* entitled 'Hail to the Hawks: Ronald Reagan's $200 billion-plus defence budget is good news for Canadian business. We're selling the U.S. military everything from cruise navigation systems to snowshoes.'[41]

In 1984 Pentagon officials went on a cross-Canada tour briefing Canadian industrialists on how they might get involved in defence production.[42] The Pentagon's demand for Canadian military products contributed greatly to the growth and profitability of this industry sector. Military sales to the United States have taken place under both the Defence Production Sharing Agreement (DPSA)[43] and the Defence Development Sharing Arrangement (DDSA).[44] Since 1958, the DPSA has ensured that the Canadian defence industry can bid on many U.S. defence contracts. It guarantees access to a 'cut of the action.' The DPSA is acknowledged by government officials to constitute a 'partial' free-trade agreement. But the arrangement also has a reciprocity clause that commits both parties to purchase the equivalent of what they sell in defence products. The net effect is clear: the more defence products are exported, the more are purchased, and vice versa.

It was widely recognized that there would be significant opportunities for the expansion of the defence industry. In 1985, Robert Gillespie of the Department of Regional Industrial Expansion told the Standing Committee on External Affairs and National Defence (SCEAND) that 'the total sales of defence industries, depending upon how you classify them, are in the area of about $4 billion a year, with an annual work force in the area of 50,000.'[45] In 1986, Gordon Barthos of the *Toronto Star* claimed that the defence industry was netting $5 billion and providing 60,000 jobs.[46] 'According to the Waterloo, Ontario-based research group, Project Ploughshares, the growth is industry-wide: overseas sales in the aerospace sector doubled between 1985 and 1986; vehicle sales tripled; armaments and munition exports rose by 30%; and exports of electronic and electrical components by 50%.'[47] A poll by the Aerospace Industries Association of Canada shows that Canadian military contractors intend to boost their sales by 6 per cent a year through 1991.[48] In 1987, the Canadian Export Association noted that while defence exports were then running at approximately $2 billion they could reach $5 billion by 1995.[49] This was not simply exaggerated defence-industry hype. Two Canadian political scientists, Yves Belanger and Pierre

Fournier, wrote that 'in 1988 the total value of arms production in Canada came to more than $8 billion, and it is conceivable that production for export to world markets and for use at home could amount to between $100 and $120 billion over the next decade.'[50] Many people had great expectations that this sector of the economy would expand with continuous growth.

According to Tom Chell, director-general of the Defence Programs Bureau (the bureau responsible for marketing Canadian defence products), 'We still estimate between 30% and 40% of the U.S. procurement dollar is open to Canadian industry, which runs between $80 billion and $100 billion per year. There is a big market for our industry there, and our objective is to increase our share of that market in the coming years.'[51]

Whereas it was the external demand arising from the American arms-buildup that revitalized Canada's defence industry in the early 1980s, optimism for the future of this sector was generated by a number of developments and arrangements in the mid-1980s.

For several years, Canadian officials had been negotiating with their American counterparts in order to remove the remaining restrictions on bilateral defence production and trade. As the defence white paper stated, 'The growing importance of Canadian industry to the overall North American Defence Industrial Base and the need to enhance further Canada-U.S. co-operation were recognized at the March 1985 summit between the Prime Minister of Canada and the President of the United States. In their joint release they stated that further measures would be taken ... to facilitate defence economic and trade co-operation and joint participation in major defence programs.'[52] In March 1987, Defence Minister Perrin Beatty announced the organization of a joint Canada-U.S. organization to formalize and prepare the integration of the two defence industrial bases within a NADIB. Part of the rationale for this move was to guarantee that Canadian-based firms would retain access to (and expand their share of) the large U.S. military procurement budget.

For its part, industry was more than receptive to these initiatives. Lieutenant-Colonel Bland suggested: 'There may be significant gain for industry in general and some specific industries in particular should the defence industrial base concept take substantive policy form. Indeed, industry is keen to encourage such an outcome ... But many believe that only a demonstrated long-term commitment to continue higher levels of defence spending can convince industrial leaders to commit their time and money to a defence-industrial policy.'[53] Canadian defence industries expected to receive a substantial share of the contracts arising from the long-awaited re-equipment program of the Canadian forces. As it was, the biggest government contracts have tended to come, not surprisingly, from the Department of National Defence. In fact, as Stevie Cameron points out, 'most of the top ten contractors since 1980 have been defence contractors. Military contracting accounts for a staggering 60 per cent of the Tory government's total procurement budget. (It wasn't any different under the Liberals; between 1980 and 1984, military contracts accounted for 63 per cent of government procurement.)'[54] They saw further opportunities arising from the government's promise to bridge the commitment-capability gap. Those with a vested interest in the defence industry certainly appreciated the new emphasis on industrial mobilization and the adoption of a long-war policy. Both policies would entail support for the defence industry through government subsidies and major equipment purchases.

Moreover, the Defence Industrial Preparedness Task Force, which conducted a study in close consultation with the industry and a number of military-industry lobbies, came to the conclusion that defence industrial preparedness planners will have to identify, support, and fund 'assured' and 'strategic' sources of supply.[55] As is the practice in the United States, a select group of defence industries based in Canada will receive special inducements from the government (research and development funding, annual contracts, and so on) to ensure their production capability is maintained. In some respects this is an extension of the Defence Industrial Productivity Program and the Centres of Excellence Program by which the government had provided privileged financial and contract support to defence industries. In April 1987, Perrin Beatty announced that the government would proceed with a new Defence Industrial Research program that would transfer military research to the private sector by increasing the funds available to Canadian industry for military research and development. Canadian companies can now qualify for grants covering up to 50 per cent of the total cost of applied research projects relevant to defence.[56] Part of this initiative involves a new Defence Science Advisory Board, a private-sector body to be chaired by John Sheppard, now chairman of Leigh Industries, a defence contractor.

Many defence contractors in Canada adopted a consortia approach – a division of labour by which they could merge capabilities with other defence contractors under one umbrella firm so as to produce complete weapon systems.[57] It was assumed that with government funding for the development of a defence industrial base, these firms would be well positioned to develop longer production runs of complete weapon systems. Government support for the defence sector would not be jeopardized by free trade or American protectionist sentiments, particularly after integration within the NADIB. Further development of this sector was to be encouraged by both the Canadian and American governments. With multilateral defence trade arrangements, alliance weapons standardization, the consortia approach, and the transfer of technology arising from Canada's rearmament, it was thought that the defence industry would be in a competitive position to shift into long production runs of complete weapon systems both for Canada's armed forces and for export abroad. As a representative of one Canadian firm specializing in defence products explained, 'In order to arm ourselves, we must arm the world. That is the reality of the Canadian defence industry.'[58]

Another development that affected both the armed forces and the defence industry was the success of the recent U.S.-U.S.S.R. arms-control agreement to eliminate intermediate-range nuclear forces. As one defence contractor put it, 'We expect tremendous expansion. The superpower treaty to ban intermediate range nuclear weapons means there must be a buildup of conventional forces in Europe.'[59]

The prospect of profitable opportunity strengthened this

sector of the economy. In 1987, Martin Shadwick, a Canadian defence analyst, wrote that 'Canada's defence industrial base has undergone a dramatic transformation. Paced by the re-equipment demands of the Canadian Forces (CF) and abetted by new government approaches to defence industrial development, the Canadian defence industry is today considerably larger, more diverse and more capable of meeting domestic requirements than it was a decade ago.'[60] The profits of the military industry were expected to soar as a result of the opportunities arising from the 1987 defence white paper, *Challenge and Commitment: A Defence Policy for Canada.* As Edgar Dosman acknowledged:

> The stakes involved for Canadian business are significant now and for the foreseeable future. Megaprojects such as the CF-18 program (and even the maintenance contract), new patrol frigates or nuclear-powered attack submarines inevitably involve major regional and industrial considerations. But a host of smaller and less dramatic, but sometimes exceptionally attractive, capital projects are in the works which (as for example, in space research) may have potential billion dollar procurement applications. Major export contracts (the Oerlikon ADATS defence system, for example) are also involved. In short, the re-equipment program initiated under Trudeau and continued under Mulroney has achieved momentum, with the latter the beneficiary of a wave of defence contract-letting and procurement decisions unprecedented since the Korean war.[61]

In the words of the minister of national defence, Perrin Beatty, 'This modernization and improvement program will involve hundreds of projects and although spread over a period of fifteen years or more, will present unparalleled opportunities and challenges for Canadian industry.'[62]

Although the government made a commitment to spend $183 billion on defence over the next fifteen years, with approximately $58 billion allotted to the acquisition of new equipment, the cost of the total package was seen by many analysts to be considerably higher. Some business and defence sources predicted that 'the scope of expenditures the Canadian government has in mind will require annual after-inflation increases in the defence budget of up to 6.5% – which would almost double military spending over the next 15 years.'[63]

It was hardly surprising that three months after the release of the white paper, one of the defence industry's trade newsletters appraised Defence Minister Perrin Beatty in the following terms: 'This man is our champion.'[64] Four months later it wrote: 'It (1987) was a remarkable year and the start of something big. The arms industry, both Canadian and international, is delighted.'[65]

Therefore, it is understandable that debates about Canadian security often take on distinct economic overtones. It should also be easier to understand why Canadian governments acceded to cruise testing, to industrial participation in the Strategic Defense Initiative, and to unconditional NORAD renewal. Over the past seven years, the Canadian defence industry effectively became a 'trump card' that Americans and Canadians both used when they wanted to influence defence decisions. This pattern of influence was possible primarily because the defence industries became of increasing political and economic importance to the Canadian state.

Much of the debate over Canadian participation in the American Strategic Defense Initiative focused on the economic consequences and political impact of refusing the American request. In the hearings that preceded the government's final statement, numerous representatives of the 'defence' industry (from military and business associations and private corporations) pleaded their case for participation on the grounds that it was necessary to counter the Soviet threat; to maintain respect in Washington; and, most important, to take advantage of the opportunities open to the defence industry and the economy in general.[66]

NORAD renewal was argued on a very similar basis. All industry submissions before the standing committee favoured a continuation of the agreement.[67] John H. Simmons of Canadian Marconi gave what the committee reviewing NORAD considered to be 'a summation of the general feeling among industry representatives' when he testified that 'it is vital to Canada that the defence industrial base survives and grows, and it is vital to the defence industry that it retains its access to the U.S. defence market and continues to be considered as part of the U.S. defence industrial base. To achieve both of these goals, it is therefore vital that Canada continue to co-operate with the U.S. in defence areas generally, and in NORAD in particular.'[68] The final report of the standing committee indicated that 'the representatives of defence and other industries ... raised concerns over the possible impact of non-renewal of NORAD on Canada-U.S. relations.' They feared retaliation might take the form of protectionism and a curb on the flow of information as had happened to New Zealand. Conceding the probability of such linkage, the standing committee noted that 'senior U.S. officials confirmed that the DD/DPSA (Defence Development / Defence Production Sharing agreements) could also be seriously jeopardized.'[69]

There is little doubt that the military industry had a lot at stake in industrial mobilization, defence preparedness, and a long-war policy.[70] But the defence industry was certainly not alone in this respect. It is apparent that the federal government had its own vested interest in the continued success of this industry.

A FEDERAL GOVERNMENT IMPERATIVE: JOBS, HIGH-TECH, AND ALLIANCE CREDIBILITY

The defence industry has been perceived by the past two Canadian governments as a means to stimulate export trade, bolster industrial productivity, and create employment. Improving Canada's technological base and innovative capability became increasingly important priorities in the 1980s. The defence industry was thought to be a catalyst to provide research and development programs, foreign technology, and technical assistance – all necessary to compete in modern high-technology trade sectors.[71]

'The intention,' said Bill Laycock, director of planning and analysis in DRIE's Aerospace Defence and Industrial Benefits Branch, 'is to transfer something to Canada that has long-term business potential ... We're looking for benefits that will be good for Canadian industry. We're looking largely for high technology, and beyond that it basically comes out the way it comes out.'[72] According to a former minister of the Department of Industry, Trade and Commerce, support for the defence industry is seen as the only hope for Canadian manufacturing. He acknowledged that the businessmen are after the research and development funding and the prospects of spin-offs and subsidies. Defence expenditures were seen as a way of subsidizing industry, as an industrial strategy along the American model.[73] In essence, it was assumed that the military-induced demand for armaments could be used to further develop the industrial base.

Moreover, as David Leyton-Brown and Brian MacDonald noted, 'while defence spending does not form a large proportion of overall GNP, it has a strong potential impact upon certain highly desirable industries.'[74] Roger Voyer of the Ministry of State for Science and Technology testified to the SCEAND that

> Canada's defence industry is important, not only because it supports Canada's defence missions but also because the sector has a high proportion of leading edge technologies such as aerospace and electronics technologies. In view of Canada's serious and growing trade deficit in high technology, which reached $12 billion in 1984, all opportunities to develop what we call 'dual technologies' – that is, technologies which can be applied to both military and civilian needs – should be exploited. Like all high technology industries, Canada's defence industry has to be export oriented.[75]

Aerospace and defence were assessed as the second most important group of high-technology companies, after telecommunications, in the country. Electronics and shipbuilding are emerging as important sectors of the economy. Many of these industries argued that their long-term viability is dependent upon military production.[76]

According to Robert Gillespie of the Department of Regional Industrial Expansion, 'There has been a lot of effort of late in improving government-industry co-operation in the defence industry sector.'[77] Recent Liberal and Conservative governments deserve a large part of the credit for the success of this industry.

Government assistance has included the funding of research, development, and production and the co-ordination of marketing.[78] As the defence industry grew, federal financial assistance and subsidization of the industry increased commensurately.[79] The Department of National Defence has been steadily increasing the funds for research and development contracts in Canadian industry. While he was minister of national defence, Perrin Beatty boasted that 'In the last ten years, the expansion has been almost sevenfold.'[80]

Whereas the Mulroney government inherited many of the defence problems and plans initiated within the Trudeau era, they made a conscious effort to distinguish themselves from their Liberal predecessors by actively promoting defence issues.[81] The Conservatives promised to make defence a priority in Canadian public policy. During the 1984 campaign, the prime minister trumpeted the Soviet threat and his determination, if elected, to 'honour the commitment.' A white paper would be forthcoming with additional resources for defence and the armed forces (DND) would be going 'first class' – in pay, training, weapons, and equipment.[82] Edgar Dosman notes that 'a distinctive Conservative approach did take shape, with five principal elements':

- the raising of DND's interdepartmental and Cabinet profile;
- a new policy framework to streamline commitments;
- a determination to deliver the resources required for their effective implementation;
- a long-term procurement strategy for ensuring a militarily credible force structure; and finally
- the nurturing of a defence constituency in Canada for sustaining defence policy in the long haul.[83]

It was clearly acknowledged that the Conservatives would be putting special emphasis on strengthening not only the armed forces, but also the military industry. As the report of the Defence Industrial Preparedness Task Force states, 'For the first time in over 20 years, the peacetime preparation of industry in support of the operational requirements of the Canadian Forces is a priority of Canadian defence policy.'[84]

This 'peace-time' preparation of industry was based on two assumptions: first, that the defence industry would retain, and where possible expand, its share of the U.S. defence procurement budget and of those of its other NATO allies, and second, that it would benefit from increased capital spending by Canada's armed forces. If Canada's defence industry received a significant share of the re-equipment program, it would help pay for these acquisitions by becoming a more competitive exporter in the international arms trade.

Industrial mobilization and defence preparedness were part of an economic strategy premised on 'military Keynesianism' – using federal spending to 'prime the pump' of the economy so as not only to generate military demand and production, but also to foster the growth of other high-technology industries.[85] Attempts were made to justify new defence initiatives and higher defence expenditures as being in the interests of regional development, industrial development, and the Canadian economy in general.[86]

Nevertheless, officials recognized that such a strategy had to be explained as an initiative that was prompted by an external stimulus and one that would provide greater national security. Therefore, they explained their strategy as a response to the imminent threat posed by the Soviet Union.

While the government anticipated an economic and military return from re-equipping the armed forces, it also expected to bolster its political stature among the allies, particularly the United States. It should be noted that the prevailing wisdom in Ottawa considers Canadian diplomatic influence to be directly related to the extent to which this country is prepared to 'carry its weight' in Western collective defence arrangements.[87] Since the early seventies, Canada had been under pressure from both the European allies and the United States to increase defence spending.[88] In order to garner American support for a free-trade agreement, the Conservatives governed as if willing to 'bend over backwards' to accommodate American concerns. While the Foreign Investment Review Agency and the National Energy Program were the first significant bilateral irritants to be cancelled, American representatives were confident, even before the election, that the new government would be assuming a greater share of the defence 'burden.'[89] It would not be long before the government pursued a free-trade agreement and military Keynesianism. On both issues they had a powerful ally in the Department of National Defence.

CANADA'S ARMED FORCES: IN SEARCH OF RELEVANCE

Defence preparedness and industrial mobilization were priority issues on the agenda of the Department of National Defence (DND). After a period of relative budgetary neglect and social alienation during the early years of the Trudeau government, departmental morale and capabilities declined to the extent that fears were expressed on the inside as to whether the armed forces would remain relevant to the defence of Canada.[90] Although military commitments had not been cut back, there were recurrent complaints about the armed forces being emasculated by the lack of resources and modern equipment. It was frequently pointed out that Canada had been among the lowest contributors to the alliance in terms of military expenditures relative to GNP. The defence constituency projected the impression that Canada was shirking its responsibilities and taking a free ride on the defence efforts of the allies.[91]

Desmond Morton writes that 'in few countries have military and naval leaders enjoyed less prestige in peace or war.'[92] The armed forces were frustrated without adequate resources to monitor, patrol, or control Canadian territory, or to carry out their 'big league "real soldiering" alliance duties.'[93] As one insider put it, 'With frozen defence budgets, little support from the Trudeau government, and unprecedented inflation rates, DND and the CF adopted a survival mentality, and cut almost all operational planning in order to concentrate on a few basic operational capabilities.'[94]

The cutback in reserves meant that the armed forces lost a strongly supportive constituency within Canadian society. Without a significant acquisition program, it was difficult to sustain the respect of the allies and the support of the defence industry. In this respect, a total-force concept, tripling the reserves, and a long-war policy with industrial mobilization were particularly appealing as measures that would strengthen not only the department but also the larger defence community. Organizing a capacity for protracted conventional war-fighting was clearly going to require a level of forces and equipment unheralded in Canada's peace-time history. Cabinet only had to be assured that these shifts could be tied to further economic and political opportunities.[95]

'In military affairs as in economics, underdevelopment means dependency.'[96] Canadian military dependency led to what might be described as a 'search for relevance, wherein career and bureaucratic interests depended upon developing support from the larger defence community.[97] Apparently the armed forces felt so psychologically and materially deprived that they assumed their only option was to seek a broader and more powerful coalition of allies.[98] Edgar Dosman writes that 'by 1984, it was abundantly clear that unless National Defence could create a stronger base of support in the defence constituency, it would be at a comparative disadvantage in the political competition for scarce resources.'[99] The Pentagon, NATO, the military industry, and a number of defence and business associations feature prominently as friends and allies who champion the interests of the Canadian Armed Forces.

At stake were the interests of the armed forces; their access to a share of the budget that would narrow the commitment-capability gap and begin to restore relevance – credibility at home and among allies.[100] With the long-war policy, industrial mobilization, and an expanded constituency, the interdepartmental status of Defence was expected to increase appreciably. The Defence portfolio had a substantial $11.2 billion budget, consuming half of the overall federal capital outlays and some 40 per cent of discretionary funding.[101] Dosman wrote that the 're-equipment programs have become very big business. It is no longer a loser department.'[102]

The morale and resources of the department were further buoyed by the release of the 1987 white paper. As one headquarters general noted, 'There is a psychological aspect to the White

Paper that people overlook. It's that the government has finally recognized the problems we have and has made a commitment to do something about it. That's very important for morale.'[103]

For sectors within DND, however, it was also a strategy to reduce political control over the department and assure higher defence spending in the future. Lieutenant-Colonel Douglas Bland acknowledged that 'the military leadership by and large embraces defence industrial preparedness as a cornerstone of national defence.' However, he candidly attests that there were a number of underlying motives within the defence establishment:

> Some senior public servants in DND see the industrial base policy as an outgrowth of government needs to spread defence expenditures into all regions of the country and into 'winning' technologies. Within this context DND has been expected to play its part. The most obvious way for DND to do this is through its procurement network by encouraging 'centres of excellence' and industries already supporting DND. 'Political and bureaucratic if necessary, but not necessarily for defence,' seems to be a maxim that provides an opening to increased funding for DND. If this emphasis coincides, or can be made to coincide, with defence needs so much the better ... Not surprisingly, some see the industrial base as an aid to long-term procurement plans. It is viewed as part of an ongoing plan to gain control of the Defence procurement program so that DND can better direct where, how, and to what purpose 'our money will be spent'. By identifying and encouraging specific industries, it is hoped that DND may be able to resist some of the arbitrariness of previous decision-making. It is argued, for example, that a strong DND/industry relationship with the aircraft sector might deflect the temptation of politicians to divert defence dollars from DND to other departments or sectors of the economy.[104]

While all three services favoured the shift to a long-war policy and defence preparedness, it appears that the army stood to gain the most. 'The Army, for instance, is strongly dependent on mobilization and doctrinally committed to the notion that campaigns once begun can have no predictable conclusion, and therefore, sustainment in war is a primary assumption for Army planners.'[105] With these new policies the army would expand considerably. As Major-General Terry Liston stated, 'the Army stands to double in size, while there will be a significant increase in the reserves from today's 30,000 to 90,000 by the year 2000.[106]

Given a renewed and strengthened commitment to NATO's Central Front, the army was in a position to have the CAST Brigade re-equipped for a heavy-armour role, which entailed the acquisition of some very expensive new equipment.[107] As Perrin Beatty, then minister of national defence, told the Senate Committee on National Defence, 'I should also note the complexity of the overall re-equipment program for the total force army. Over 130 projects, of which 30 are major Crown projects, must be implemented to provide the army with the mobility, firepower and communication it requires to do its job in Europe and at home. These projects are complementary parts of a system; they are not options from which a choice can be made. The pivotal project in this system is, of course, the main battle tank.'[108] The Canadian defence industry expected to supply a good share of this equipment. Rear-Admiral T.S. Allen, president and chief executive officer of EH-Industries (Canada) Ltd and president of the Canadian Defence Preparedness Association, suggested that 'our association's focus in the next few years will be upon strengthening the Army.'[109] The army and the defence industry had their hopes tied to NATO's Central Front. It would be very difficult to justify the additional equipment, the long-war policy, or industrial mobilization if they were relegated to a role in Canada. Furthermore, such a role might be perceived as a signal that the Soviet threat did not require a higher level of defence preparedness.

Considerable support for the long-war policy and industrial mobilization was forthcoming from a wide base of organizations and departments which shared similar interests.

BUREAUCRATIC INTERESTS

There are at least five departments and numerous other agencies within the Canadian state that have programs directly or indirectly promoting the Canadian defence industry and higher defence expenditures. For example, senior representatives (ADM-level) from some twelve government departments and agencies were involved in planning Canada's integration into the North American Defence Industrial Base.[110]

In the Department of External Affairs, the Defence Programs Bureau works as a highly specialized industry and trade promotions group with a mandate to develop and promote Canadian 'defence' products for export to Canada's allies and other friendly nations.[111] There is also a Defence Relations Bureau that works 'hand-in-hand' with the Department of National Defence's director-general of international programs and with foreign governments to co-ordinate Canada's role in defence arrangements such as NATO and NORAD.[112]

Another state agency involved with the military is the Canadian Commercial Corporation (CCC), which does most of its trading in Canadian-made military products. This Crown corporation is administered by the Department of Supply and Services to assist Canadian manufacturers in marketing their products abroad. According to an official of the CCC, approximately 90 per cent of their transactions with the United States in the years 1980–4 were in military products.[113]

The Department of Supply and Services (DSS) also handles the armed forces' contract work, which accounts for roughly half the contract activity of the entire federal government.[114] DSS had a very strong interest in matters of defence preparedness and industrial mobilization. As Lieutenant-Colonel Bland notes, 'In the long-term, DSS officials believe that the goal must be to develop a military, political, public, and industry caucus of informed individuals to sustain a truly national defence industries policy.'[115]

The Department of Regional Industrial Expansion (DRIE) has a mandate to promote the industrial-benefit opportunities in all major defence acquisitions. It is responsible for the administration and success of the Defence Industry Productivity Program. As Bland attests, DRIE 'is an obvious constituent of the defence industrial base process.'[116] The Ministry of State for Science and

Technology also has a particular interest in the development of advanced technology for defence purposes.[117]

In 1985, John Treddenick, a defence economist at the Royal Military College of Canada, wrote about a 'neat coincidence of interests forming among several federal bureaucracies.' As he says:

> On the one hand, the military is able to use the argument of economic benefits to support funding of its programs; on the other, those bureaucracies concerned with trade, industry, technology and regional development are able to shape a large expenditure block in support of their own program interests. This common interest in military procurement has the potential to generate considerable mutual support for continuing and increasing military expenditures; at the very least, internal opposition to such expenditures is considerably weakened.[118]

Significant momentum developed within these departments to promote defence preparedness and industrial mobilization.

THE MILITARY-INDUSTRIAL LOBBIES

In addition to the bureaucratic interests within the Canadian state, there is an expanding defence lobby in Canada comprising influential non-governmental organizations such as the Business Council on National Issues, the Conference of Defence Associations, the Federation of United Military Services, the Canadian Defence Preparedness Association (formerly the American Defense Preparedness Association, Canadian chapter), the NATO Industrial Advisory Group, the Canadian Institute of Strategic Studies, and the Aerospace Industries Association of Canada.

As early as 1982, Kim Richard Nossal, a Canadian political scientist, wrote of 'a well organized military lobby' in Canada numbering somewhere between 500,000 and 3,000,000 members.'[119] In a 1985 study of Canadian interest groups, Elizabeth Riddell-Dixon also noted that 'Canadian veteran and military interest groups comprise a large, well organized lobby which makes representations to government on matters pertaining to national defence and to the health of the defence establishment in Canada.'[120] Over the last eight years, numerous financial and industrial interests merged with these military interest groups to form a stronger coalition. Together, they played an influential role in determining the government's decisions on defence-related issues.

In 1981, the Business Council on National Issues (BCNI) launched a Task Force on Foreign Policy and Defence. BCNI's interest in defence affairs coincided with a major shift of transnational capital into Western military industries.[121] There was a growing recognition of the financial opportunities arising from heightened Cold War tensions and the American arms buildup. Of the eleven chief executive officers on the BCNI task force, six represented corporations engaged in defence contracting: CAE Industries, ITT Canada, Control Data, Honeywell, EH-Industries, and the SNC Group.[122] Taking advantage of their extensive contacts within government and cordial relations with several ministers of defence, their task force received high-level briefings at NATO and NORAD headquarters.[123] In their publications and presentations, the BCNI emphasized the Soviet threat and the need for a Canadian military buildup.

The BCNI is a powerful organization, and has become the senior voice of business in Canada since it was founded in 1976. It is composed of the chief executive officers of 150 major companies operating in Canada – most of which are multinational corporations – representing assets of $750 billion dollars and employing over 1½ million Canadians. This stature has enabled them to exert an enormous influence over government policy in the last decade. To cite one example, the Business Council was the chief architect and the major proponent of the Canada-U.S. 'free' trade agreement.[124]

The Conference of Defence Associations (CDA) was established in Ottawa in 1932 to study problems of defence and security and to promote the efficiency and well-being of the Canadian Armed Forces. It is now composed of twelve member associations representing various branches of the Canadian Armed Forces, as well as a number of associate members. The CDA represents some

300,000 serving or retired military personnel. Each of its twelve member associations is a national group with regional branches. According to an in-house information sheet, the CDA, which comprises 'leaders in governments, business and professions, should be viewed as a highly motivated, competent, independent spokesman for National Defence.'

The CDA is not as independent as it suggests. With funding and organizational support from the Department of National Defence, it is the only directly funded lobby for a department in Ottawa. With direct access to both the prime minister and the minster of defence, its influence has been undeniable. The CDA has been recognized by the federal government as the 'voice of defence,' and is accorded treatment consistent with that recognition.[125]

In response to urging by the minister of national defence, the CDA opened an institute in 1987 to bolster its profile and to begin public education on defence issues. In the past five years the CDA has published several books on issues such as defence industrial mobilization and the Soviet threat to Europe and started its own magazine, *Forum*, which is circulated to approximately 12,000 readers.[126] In the words of past Associate Defence Minister Harvie Andre: 'The Conference of Defence Associations is a nation-wide organization which also has important connections with corporate, government and academic structures. It is truly a bridge to important sectors of the public. By exploiting your full potential you could expand and co-ordinate the defence information work done by all the agencies ... and above all effectively convey it into the public domain.'[127]

The Canadian Institute of Strategic Studies (CISS) was initially founded by Brigadier-General George Bell. The majority of its more than six hundred members are either serving in or retired from the armed forces. The business community and the general public are also represented in the Institute. The CISS is an associate member of the Conference of Defence Associations. As with most other Canadian military, strategic-studies, and international-affairs institutes and schools, a significant percentage of CISS funding has been derived from the Department of

National Defence.[128] The Donner Foundation and Litton Industries were also major financial supporters of the CISS in 1987.[129] Elizabeth Riddell-Dixon notes that a 'particular area of interest to the Institute has been Canada's inability to mobilize for anything beyond a very limited short war. A further source of concern is the fact that both Canada and its NATO allies have focused on nuclear weapons, for economic reasons, and let their conventional capabilities slide. In addition, the Institute recognizes the importance of Canada's industrial strategy to it's national defence.'[130]

According to their own literature, the Canadian chapter of the American Defense Preparedness Association (ADPA) was formed in November 1983 in order to

- improve communication within the Canadian-U.S. Defence Community (i.e. Canadian Defence Industry, Canadian Government Departments involved in defence and their U.S. counterparts);
- work with the Canadian government to increase opportunities for Canadian Defence exports;
- provide a collective voice within ADPA for Canadian corporate and individual members of the Association.

This organization grew from an initial membership of 160 to over 400 individual and 27 corporate members within three years.[131] The chapter was renamed the Canadian Defence Preparedness Association (CDPA) in 1987. In its own words, it provides 'a vital liaison among science, industry, and government on an array of subjects affecting national defence preparedness,' and 'strengthened ties among all elements of the defence community ... in a mission to promote public awareness about national defence needs.'[132] As CDPA's president, Rear-Admiral Dudley Allen (ret.), says, 'This association is about communication; between government and industry executives, and between military users and the industry that must support them.'[133] The CDPA is an associate member of the Conference of Defence Associations.

PROMOTING THE NEW AGENDA

As previously noted, military-industrial interests were set back by the short-war thesis and the low level of attention accorded to defence preparedness. These associations were at the forefront of an effort to change these policies. They adopted a loose division of labour in order to organize, lobby, publish, recruit, support, and develop a stronger defence constituency. Their seemingly unrelated initiatives all contributed to reversing the short-war policy. In the course of the last decade they have had a profound effect on changing Canadian defence policy.

Realizing that the support of an organized industrial lobby was needed to offset the short-war policy, William J. Yost, director of operations for the Conference of Defence Associations, decided in the early 1980s to contact military-industrial representatives in Washington for assistance.[134] Shortly thereafter, the American Defense Preparedness Association decided to organize a Canadian chapter based in Ottawa.[135] Since then, the ADPA (Canadian chapter) and the conference of Defence Associations have been at the forefront of efforts to formalize the North American Defence Industrial Base. In September 1988, the Canadian and American Defence Preparedness associations joined the Department of National Defence and U.S. Department of Defense in co-hosting the ninth conference on the integration of the North American Defence Industrial Base.

Aside from promoting defence preparedness and industrial mobilization, the CDA was also active in arranging Canada's integration within a North American Defence Industrial Base.[136] In 1983 Yost wrote about a number of agencies and departments interested in improving Canada's defence capability. He suggested a need for greater co-ordination and stressed that 'a closer military-industrial capability should be forged through these agencies.'[137] Among the list of supportive agencies mentioned were provincial governments, the Senate, the NATO Industrial Advisory Group, the Canadian Institute of Strategic Studies, and the American Defense Preparedness Association.[138] He also mentioned that 'there are a large number of industrial associations which have a close interest in specific aspects of Defence Industry Preparedness.[139]

Also in the early 1980s, Brigadier-General George Bell (ret.) a fellow member of the CDA and director of the Canadian Institute for Strategic Studies, was hired by the Business Council to co-ordinate their Task Force on Foreign and Defence Policy and to help organize the draft of their defence position paper, entitled 'Canada's Defence Policy: Capability Versus Commitments.'[140] According to an informed source, the paper was actually contracted out to two American researchers at Georgetown University in Washington.[141] Their first paper pointed to the 'overwhelming military strength of the Soviet Union,' the necessity of improving Canada's armed forces, and the inherent economic opportunities for Canadian industry in so doing. It called for an 80 per cent real increase in military spending over the next ten years, while stressing the importance of defence industrial preparedness.[142]

As previously mentioned, this BCNI task force was largely made up of chief executive officers of multinational corporations, many of which were engaged in defence contracting.[143] In their deliberations and testimony before various government committees, they brought in spokespersons who were also active in the CDA, the CISS, and the ADPA/CC. Among their advisors were Brigadier-General George Bell (ret.); John Halstead, Canada's ex-ambassador to NATO; and C.R. Nixon, a past deputy minister of defence.[144] The Department of National Defence assisted the BCNI task force with planning, travel arrangements, and briefings. In a speech to the annual general meeting of the Conference of Defence Associations, Tom d'Aquino, president and chief executive officer of the BCNI, boasted: 'Only two months ago, on a second visit to NATO by Business Council members, General Bernard Rogers, among others, praised the council's initiative and said that it was a model for the involvement of non-military organizations in NATO countries.' d'Aquino went on to stress that 'Canadians will need to be convinced that greater sacrifices in the bolstering of our defences will contribute to maintaining peace, and ultimately to reducing the chances of war. If we fail in communicating this idea, do not be surprised if the support the government is seeking for its new defence policy does not materialize ... You have a stake, we have a stake, in making sure the momentum continues.'[145]

In 1985, the BCNI helped ensure that the representatives of the military-industrial associations would obtain a greater say in the security decision-making process. They proposed to the minister of national defence that 'measures to improve the effectiveness of the Canadian Defence Industrial Base should be developed in full consultation and co-operation with industry.'[146] The BCNI asked that 'a forum be established through which the private sector could advise the Minister on matters of mutual concern.'[147] In response, Erik Nielsen, the minister of national defence, replied that 'it may be well to Canada's advantage to have a parallel group such as Mr. Weinberger's Defence Policy Advisory Group.'[148] Nielsen's successor, Perrin Beatty, formalized the arrangement in 1987. As he put it, 'To create a partnership with industry, the principal vehicle will be the Defence Industrial Preparedness Advisory Committee (DIPAC). This committee, which I established last year, brings together a small group of chief executive officers and others with whom I can discuss policy issues ... This non-partisan group, with its wealth of experience and knowledge, will be an invaluable source of advice and innovative proposals.[149] Peter Cameron, who originally chaired the BCNI Task Force on Foreign and Defence Policy, was chosen to co-chair the DIPAC along with Beatty. According to Tom Savage, the current chair of the task force, the DIPAC was also co-ordinated to raise the visibility of armed-forces issues; make credible the need for greater defence spending; and organize the international consortia necessary if Canada was going to develop a defence industrial base.[150]

The BCNI, the ADPA (Canadian chapter), the CDA, and the Department of National Defence maintained a close working relationship. They consulted with the minister of defence and with one another over a variety of issues such as the content of the government's defence white paper, the promotion of a North American Defence Industrial Base, and the formation of a Defence Industrial Preparedness Advisory Committee.

For example, the BCNI Task Force on Foreign and Defence Policy asked officials in the Department of National Defence to comment on the draft of their position paper and to advise about an appropriate time to schedule release of the paper.[151] On previous occasions, the defence department requested assistance from the Business Council, the American Defense Preparedness Association, and the Conference of Defence Associations.[152] According to the BCNI chairman, David Culver: 'It is not an accident that we had a lot of help from Defence Department people in making our Task Force report ... The same experts were working on both sides of the street.'[153]

Such close collaboration with private industry and industrial associations was inevitable when the government undertook its review of Canada's defence industrial base in 1984.[154] When the Defence Industrial Preparedness Task Force was established it continued to consult with the military-industrial lobby on an ongoing basis. This DND task force sought not only input and advice from the private sector but also active political support to sell defence preparedness in what they described as an 'adverse government / public environment.'[155]

It was hardly surprising, then, that the report of the Task Force on Defence Industrial Preparedness 'advocated a stepped-up cooperative (government/private sector) effort, with a national advisory committee to strengthen planning within a single-market Canadian-U.S. continentalist framework.'[156] Edgar Dosman wrote that 'National Defence, in its own way, is also cheering on free trade.'[157]

It became common practice for the Conservative government to request private-sector support for its defence policies. In a speech to a Montreal audience, Defence Minister Perrin Beatty exhorted business leaders to participate: 'We will require industry's support to help us make the policy work. Indeed, we will need the support of the whole business community as we move forward with the many defence projects necessary, over the years, to meet the requirements of the new defence policy.'[158] Dosman indicates that the systematic courting of regional and corporate support became a more specialized aspect of DND's public-relations campaign.[159] Certainly this was not the first time that a minister of national defence had requested the support of the business community. In 1979 Barney Danson, the Liberal defence minister, attempted to recruit business support. Although his efforts appeared unsuccessful at the time, his request may have caught the attention of business leaders and inspired their subsequent involvement. According to James Fleck, a chief executive who sits on the Business Council of National Issues, the BCNI became involved in defence policy owing to 'the interests of a small number of BCNI members, some of whom were supplying the defence industry, and a request from government to do something in that area.'[160]

The thrust of the defence white paper was strongly endorsed by the Business Council on National Issues, the Conference of Defence Associations, the American/Canadian Defence Preparedness Association, and the Canadian Institute of Strategic Studies. With the release of the white paper, there was a tendency to defend it as a bold initiative on the part of the government, but one that may yet be insufficient to meet Canadian defence requirements. Writing on the need to consolidate the North American defence industrial base and acquire the 'defence equipment programmes set out in the White paper and others, though unannounced, that are needed,' Brigadier-General Bell warned:

> Success will depend on concerted action by government, business associations and defence-related associations and institutes to ensure that the necessary public and political initiatives are undertaken and maintained ... But we must realize that this is only phase one of what will be a long and difficult campaign. Those of us in the defence, international relations, industrial preparedness and strategic studies communities who have been pressing, for almost fifteen years, for a more realistic approach to defence and security policy cannot afford to 'rest on our oars.'[161]

According to Brigadier-General Yost (ret.), 'Every one of the recommendations made in the book, *Industrial Mobilization For Canada*, was adopted by the Government.'[162] He acknowledged that 'Doing away with the short-war policy was a long struggle that took a lot of effort and over 10 years. It was finally accepted that we need a long-war policy with defence forces and a defence industrial base to support it. We now see a radical change of heart in this government in favour of it. It has been endorsed in the new White Paper and they are pursing it energetically.'[163]

Partly in response to pressure from these organizations as well as in an effort to promote the new white paper, the Department of National Defence expanded the Directorate of Information and created a new Directorate of Public Policy. A Department of National Defence Speakers Bureau (complete with media consultants) was organized to help promote the white paper and explain the Soviet threat.[164] The Canadian Institute of Strategic Studies was hired by the DND to train officers for the speakers bureau. Over three hundred officers were trained in the first quarter of 1988. The CISS, which had its own speakers bureau and a high-school curriculum program developed to counterbalance the peace movement, also had agreements with NATO's Information Service to conduct a national/regional speakers tour.[165] As Edgar Dosman observed, 'DND-financed programs developed momentum, particularly the Canadian Institute of Strategic Studies (Toronto) and the Military and Strategic Studies (MSS) program which underwent a 50 per cent expansion.'[166]

Throughout this 'campaign,' representatives of the military-industrial lobby were conscious of the need to stress international tensions and the existence of an overwhelming Soviet threat. A shift to defence preparedness, industrial mobilization, and a long-war policy depended upon their ability to mould public opinion. Repeatedly, organizations such as the CDA and the BCNI stressed the importance of getting the message of the Soviet threat out to Canadians.[167] In turn, the government and the Department of National Defence presented an inflated threat assessment in the defence white paper – exceeding those of the Pentagon and the International Institute for Strategic Studies.[168] Defence Minister Perrin Beatty and his assistant deputy minister for policy, Robert Fowler, repeatedly warned of an overwhelming Soviet threat that jeopardizes Canada's security. They complained that the Warsaw Pact had a 3:1 superiority in military divisions and weapon systems such as tanks and attack-helicopters. They also pointed out that the West no longer had an edge in technological superiority.[169]

The figures that Perrin Beatty and his staff presented were even questioned by retired senior officers who attested that there was a sufficient balance of forces between NATO and the Warsaw Pact. Admiral Robert Falls, previously chief of defence staff and chair of NATO's Military Committee, noted in testimony before the Senate Standing Committee on National Defence that there is internal pressure to inflate the threat assessment and that it is 'usually performed by people who work for people who are trying to get increases in their defence budgets.'[170] It is clear that a number of individuals, organizations, and departments were going to great lengths – often far beyond accepted political norms – to promote these new defence initiatives.

In their efforts to deliver the message of 'defence' to Canadians, DND and the military-industrial lobbies were counting on support from politicians, universities, and groups such as the Canadian Legion.[171] The total-defence concept was proposed as a measure that would win over more public support.[172]

Whether out of desperation or as a marketing tactic the defence agenda of 1987 was often portrayed as the only option open to Canadians. The address of Colonel H.A.J. Hutchinson, former chairman of the Conference of Defence Associations, to the CDA's 1985 annual meeting is typical:

> I would say that the Total Defence of Canada requires much more than just the support of the Canadian Armed Forces, it involves the organization of our total economy, our industrial base, towards a single objective – the defence of this country. And implicit in that concept is the commitment to a willingness to accept whatever sacrifices in our lifestyle and the way we do business and the way we operate that may be required to go along with that to achieve that goal. It therefore follows that such a commitment can only be made if the Canadian people perceive that it is necessary and that, in fact, it is the only course of action that is open to them.[173]

In January 1984 the CDA made the first proposal to the government for the adoption of a Total Defence concept. It stated that warfare has become a struggle in which the total resources of nations are committed and are vital to victory.[174] Essentially, however, the goal was to develop a broader base of support for increasing defence spending. As Brigadier General Yost (ret.) notes, 'There is a need in Canada to have a Total Defence approach to national security matters – without this we will never get an informed, supportive public.'[175]

Perrin Beatty conceded that a similar rationale was behind the proposal to triple Canada's reserve force. In a letter to BCNI President Thomas d'Aquino, he wrote, 'As you and other Business Council members obviously appreciate, one of the very real ways National Defence can gain public support is by the Reserves resuming their traditional place in the community.'[176] This idea was first suggested in a pilot-scheme prepared for the Department of National Defence by Major John Hasek in 1976. Hasek proposed recruiting large numbers of unemployed young Canadians to serve both as a reserve force and as a means by which the military might be reintegrated into Canadian society.[177] Stressing the public-relations potential of a large war-ready reserve force to 'familiarize the population with arms and armies,' Hasek notes that for the military, 'the biggest problem is to generate the right climate of opinion in which the necessary changes become politically feasible. Only then will it be possible to overcome all the entrenched resistance to change.'[178] Hasek's idea was initially supported by the Conference of Defence Associations. As early as 1977, the CDA recommended that the government should begin developing mobilization plans for several levels of forces – 150,000, 200,000, and 250,000.[179]

The business community strongly endorsed the proposal to expand the reserves. Following the release of the white paper, Peter Cameron of the BCNI task force told the Standing Committee on National Defence that 'reserves play a significant role in generating public understanding of, and support for, Canadian defence and security policy ... We are pleased by plans to expand the reserves to some 90,000, but more needs to be done.'[180]

In the words of BCNI Chairman David Culver: 'The BCNI has yet to do a job on selling that defence paper to the public; we have been so busy selling our version of the trade deal. As soon as the trade deal is out of the way, I think our number one effort will be on defence in 1989.'[181]

THE EMERGENCE OF THE MILITARY-INDUSTRIAL COMPLEX IN CANADA?

The shift to a long-war policy, industrial mobilization, and a total-force concept marked the culmination of efforts exerted by an alliance of five influential constituencies: the defence industry, the Department of National Defence, other elements of the state bureaucracy, the military-industrial lobbies, and the government. The Conservatives inherited an agenda that already had considerable momentum behind it. They gave it a further boost. This alliance was bound together by a common interest in the promotion of the defence industry and the re-equipment program of the armed forces. The process which led to these shifts in Canadian defence policy was long and complex, engaging many organizations, military services, industrial interests, and governmental institutions – as groups and individuals – all engaged in a search for solutions that would best serve their economic, political, and bureaucratic interests, as well as their personal career and corporate ambitions.

Back in 1972, Colin Gray wrote that 'the parliamentary system of government effectively precludes the formation and more sinister activities of any military-industrial complex (MIC), while the scale of defence expenditure in Canada is too limited for it to have gained a total number of constituents that would be politically very significant. Unlike the situation in the United States, Canada's legislators are very seldom in a position to influence major procurement decisions.'[182] In the intervening period, Canadian academics and defence analysts have tended to discount the possibility that Canadian policy might be unduly influenced by a military-industrial complex. The concept of such a complex has either been considered too 'radical' or inappropriate in the Canadian context. However, it is worth noting where and how this concept originated.

The term was first associated with President Eisenhower who, in his celebrated farewell address, warned against the danger of unwarranted influence, whether sought or unsought, by the military-industrial complex. As a former general and army chief of staff, he was concerned about the economic and political power that developed when military and industrial interests converged.[183] 'The total influence – economic, political and even spiritual – is felt in every city, every state house, every office of the federal government.'[184] Although Eisenhower felt that his country had been compelled to create an immense military establishment and a permanent armaments industry of vast proportions, he was worried about the implications:

> We recognize the imperative need for this development. Yet we must not fail to comprehend its grave implications. Our toil, resources and livelihood are all involved; so is the very structure of our society. In the councils of government we must guard against the acquisition of unwarranted influence, whether sought or unsought, by the military-industrial complex. The potential for the disastrous rise of misplaced power exists and will persist. We must never let the weight of this combination endanger our liberties or democratic processes. We should take nothing for granted. Only an alert and knowledgeable citizenry can compel the proper meshing of the huge industrial and military machinery of defense with our peaceful methods and goals so that security and liberty may prosper together.'[185]

Eisenhower was pointing to a phenomenon that troubled him and one which others have seen developing in many other countries.[186] This phenomenon was the development of a co-operative relationship between the armed forces, the defence industries, and related associations, a relationship based on compatible and often common interests, which provides sufficient political and economic power to influence the formulation of national policy.[187]

As Marek Thee cautions, such a complex should not be oversimplified and seen as a monolithic, like-minded entity in pursuit of power, privileges, and profit.[188] Within any such complex there are a wide variety of concerns ranging from electoral politics to inter-service rivalry to profit maximization. But as Ball and Millard suggest, the interpenetration and interdependence between the political, the economic, and the military spheres tends to create a cohesive complex whose undoubted tensions seldom override common interests.[189] Although there are various conceptions of a military-industrial complex, it can be seen as a natural association based on a perception of common interests in national security and economic gains. Dan and Ron Smith point out that 'the military-industrial complex, in general, functions not on the basis of conspiracy (though that happens) nor on the basis of bribery and corruption (though they also happen, especially if one recognizes that not all bribery is legally corrupt). Rather, it functions on the basis of a structural pairing that inevitably develops into mutual interests.'[190]

Modern industrialized states have large military establishments, whether measured in terms of manpower, weapons, or defence expenditure.[191] Canada obviously has neither the immense military establishment nor the vast armaments industry referred to by Eisenhower. But one cannot dismiss the existence of a military-industrial complex simply on the basis of relative size. Similar interests exist in every nation with armed forces and a military industry. The extent to which these interests become influential is determined not only by size but also by factors such as the extent of public awareness and political control. After Canada cut back on its defence effort in the early 1970s, it appears that public awareness and political control of these relations were assumed to be unnecessary. In any case, regardless of how the proponents of the aforementioned policies label themselves – as an alliance, a constituency, or a network – it is clear that they came to form a powerful (albeit smaller) military-industrial complex. Although the various components – the armed forces, the military industry, the bureaucracies, allies, politicians – have long had some harmony of interests, it is really only within the last six years that this entity has become a recognizable force in Canadian politics. As one retired senior officer noted, 'This close association between DND and the businessmen was not previously a normal practice. We are definitely seeing a military-industrial complex.'[192]

The relationship between institutions such as DND, DOD, NATO, DSS, DRIE, and External Affairs; associations such as BCNI, CDA, C/ADPA, and CISS; and the government is based on their common interest in promoting industrial mobilization and defence preparedness. Structural linkages have developed between the defence, industrial, bureaucratic, and political sectors. Their relationship is one of reciprocity, as each side needs what the other has to offer. Lieutenant-Colonel Bland acknowledges that 'the careful blending of objectives and procedures must be of prime concern to those who are attempting to operationalize the defence-industrial concept as policy, because they will need the widest possible constituency to achieve this aim. That constituency cannot hope to remain cohesive if the objectives of all its constituents are not well served.'[193]

As the preceding pages document, numerous vested interests are at stake within this constituency. While they may differ to the extent that some are related to career, financial, or perceived national interests, they are united by broadly compatible goals, the operation of informal cross-institutional linkages, frequent contacts, and structural interpenetration. In some cases, the structural pairing may develop as a result of a common appreciation of a perceived problem. As one senior business council executive expressed it, 'those of us in the business community just tend to see eye-to-eye with the military on Canadian defence issues.'[194] None the less, one can hardly dismiss the fact that the multinational corporations which the BCNI represents share certain interests with the armed forces.

The structural pairing that underlies the military-industrial complex is important in another sense. Canada and its allies, particularly the United States, have developed defence relations that are also based on mutual interests. Canada's complex is a far smaller version, or branch plant, of the U.S. military-industrial complex. As Ernie Regehr writes, 'In Canada the whole enterprise operates on a somewhat different scale, but the principles are similar.'[195] Given the advanced process of military and economic integration between Canada and the United States, it was probably to be expected that a similar pattern of military-industrial relations would develop. But it is important to note that other NATO nations were also pursuing similar patterns of military and industrial development.[196]

The origins of the military-industrial complex in Canada

pre-date events occurring in the last decade. It has developed over time as a result of the process of military and economic integration; the high level of Canadian military dependency; the rapid restructuring and alienation of the armed forces in the 1960s and 1970s; the retention of significant military commitments in the face of declining capabilities; the lack of a coherent long-term industrial strategy; and the dependence of the Canadian economy on access to the American market.

However, several relatively recent domestic and international developments have also contributed to the influence of this complex: the revitalization of the Cold War in the late 1970s; the shift of transnational capital into the defence sectors of the economy; the ascendance of neo-conservatism; the Reagan administration's rearmament program; the ensuing export success of the Canadian military industry; pressure from allies, particularly the United States, to assume a larger share of the defence burden and engage in conventional rearmament; the extension of the U.S. military-industrial complex into Canada; the rapid organization of a co-ordinated network of business, defence, and defence-industry lobbies; bureaucratic momentum; and the Conservative government's endorsement of a shift to a long-war policy entailing defence preparedness and industrial mobilization.

Canada's situation has obviously changed since Colin Gray made his observations in 1972. Certainly, the stakes have increased. In the last seven years there has been a steady stream of senior defence officials and military professionals leaving the Department of National Defence for lucrative careers as consultants to defence contractors.[197] As one senior officer lamented in 1988, 'All my old colleagues are now out selling weapons.'[198]

The Conservative cabinet was particularly enthused about using defence procurement as an industrial stimulus and a means of regional development. Some cabinet members used defence spending more crudely to bolster support within their constituencies.[199] Non-strategic reasons have come to play an increasingly significant role in both the selection and location of defence production.[200]

The competition for Canadian defence contracts has been quite unprecedented. Once a contest between a few international bidders, it now involves members of Parliament, federal bureaucracies, provincial governments, and municipalities. As Edgar Dosman states:

> Procurement has been marked, not by long-term planning, but by increasing politicization. Moreover, it has become more sophisticated – more 'Americanized' one might say. While pathetic examples of Latin American–style corruption (such as land-flipping) make headlines in the media, the far more dangerous tendency has been the deepening of clientelism, or 'whirlpools' of government–DND–private sector influence that make a mockery of defence industrial base planning. The fact is that each case is decided individually, with political competition built into the process at every level.[201]

The military-industrial complex has become a visible and active participant in the policy-making process.[202] In 1988 Dosman suggested that 'as the defence constituency broadens, there can be some confidence that defence issues will not sink out of sight again as they did in the 1970s.'[203] Having won the government's commitment to defence preparedness, it was thought that this constituency would become even more influential.[204] Dan Middlemiss wrote that 'in the long run, renewed interest in preparedness could have far-reaching consequences for the Forces' military doctrine, for the structure and orientation of Canada's defence industry, for the level and allocation of defence expenditures, for the role of government in industrial and emergency planning, and for Canada's relations with its principal military allies in the North Atlantic Treaty Organization (NATO).[205]

CONCLUSION

There were some common factors involved in the decision to pursue defence preparedness, industrial mobilization, a total-force concept, a long-war policy, a Defence Industrial preparedness Advisory Committee, an expansion of the reserves, and integration into the North American Defence Industrial Base.

Various interests were at stake. There were pressures arising in and between Canada's bilateral and multilateral defence relations. But the change that was of real significance for defence policy stemmed largely from domestic pressure. The convergence of military, economic, political, and bureaucratic interests constituted a power bloc strong enough to alter Canadian defence policy.

The process of defence decision-making in the 1980s and the substance of the Conservative government's 1987 defence policy are both disturbing. Were the military-industrial complex to consolidate power and influence, it would be all the more difficult to pursue a new defence agenda. The symbiotic relationship that has developed between these sectors could yet present a formidable obstacle impeding Canada from adopting independent peace and common-security initiatives.[206]

Developing a potential capacity to wage protracted conventional war would have entailed the militarization of Canadian economic, social, and foreign relations. A policy of 'military Keynesianism' designed to serve military and industrial interests would not bode well for the long-term interests of the Canadian public.

CHAPTER FIVE

Beyond the Defence Trap?

The 1987 defence white paper Challenge and Commitment signalled the extent to which domestic, non-strategic factors such as industrial policy and vested interests could combine to distort defence planning. In conjunction with the pressures arising from multilateral and bilateral defence relations, these interests were not only helping to limit Canada's defence options but fostering a dependence upon international tension to maintain the demand for Canadian-made defence products.

Yet a host of political, economic, and military developments combined to undermine several of the government's plans for economic and defence policy. The Cold War era was concluding just as Canada was preparing to play an expanded military role.

As we enter the 1990s, the international security environment is in the process of a radical transformation. Accordingly, there is a considerable crisis of uncertainty. We are at an important juncture and it remains to be seen which of several trends will determine our future.

Canada could develop policies to promote a new era of common security. However, in order to better understand our options in the 1990s, it is important to recognize those factors that influenced Canadian defence relations in the 1980s, many of which will continue to impede progressive change.

As the past three chapters have demonstrated, the defence policy-making process needs to be reviewed. Many recent developments have provided new hope and new opportunities for moving well beyond the defence trap. The important first step in devising a defence posture that will be relevant to the requirements of the 1990s is to modernize not the weapons but our thinking. We are now in a period in which good ideas may be capable of moving events.

NATIONAL DEFENCE LOSES ITS COMPASS

By the spring of 1989, Canada's defence agenda was marked by confusion and uncertainty. Political, economic, and military developments, at home and abroad, had combined to challenge the policy and the assumptions underlying the defence white paper of 1987. The *Toronto Star's* editorial caption 'National defence loses its compass' reflected the disarray in defence planning.[1]

Alarmed over the slow pace with which cabinet was approving spending for major defence projects, a representative of the defence industry warned in February 1989 that the nation's industrial strategy was being put on hold. The industry's concerns were reflected by a Senate committee on national defence that recommended an 18 per cent hike in defence spending, the acquisition of $9 billion worth of state-of-the-art weapons for the army, and the investment of $25 billion to rebuild the three branches of the armed forces by the year 2001.[2]

Shortly thereafter, however, Finance Minister Michael Wilson's spring budget of 1989 called for a cut of $2.74 billion in defence spending over the next five years. Several of the major capital-acquisition programs were cancelled. The government would not be proceeding with plans to acquire a fleet of ten to twelve nuclear-powered submarines; the decision to purchase Leopard II battle tanks and expand a heavy-armour capability would be deferred; plans for additional CF-18 Hornet jet-fighter aircraft and Aurora long-range patrol aircraft would be cancelled, as would the proposed buildup of reserves and expansion of regular forces.

The government appeared to be reconsidering its plans for defence and industrial policy. Although the more ambitious and high-profile rearmament projects were to be scaled back, the new minister of national defence, William McKnight, maintained that Canada's defence effort would continue to be guided by the 1987 defence white paper. According to McKnight, 'We started in 1984 to rebuild the Canadian Forces. There will be a pause in those plans, but they will continue.'[3] Yet to 'honour the commitment,' as the Conservatives had repeatedly promised, increases in defence spending would drop from the promised 6 per cent a year to 4.4 per cent annually over the next five years.

While the budget axe fell rather heavily on several defence acquisition programs, the rumours of 'massive' and 'savage' cuts to the defence budget were largely exaggerated. Overall defence spending would increase, but not as rapidly as projected in the 1987 white paper. Within six months of the April budget, the Department of National Defence awarded $1.2 billion in contracts for new equipment and was proceeding with other programs in modified form.[4]

Over the past five years, defence spending had already grown by 34.6 per cent, the highest single category in the federal budget save for debt carrying charges. By 1989, Canada had moved up to the rank of fifth in total defence spending among NATO's sixteen members. The latter had agreed in 1978 to maintain a 3 per cent real increase in defence spending each year, but the Stockholm International Peace Research Institute reported in 1987 that 'the 3 per cent goal was followed with some consistency by only four NATO countries: Canada, Italy, the U.K and the USA. The latter two have now, in practice, abandoned it.'[5]

The limited cuts that were made in defence spending can be explained as a response to a number of political, economic, and military developments. First, the high rate of growth in defence spending that would be required to pay for the major acquisition programs outlined in *Challenge and Commitment* was not compatible with the government's new emphasis on fiscal restraint and deficit reduction.

Second, the white paper and proposed rearmament program

received little public or political support. Perceived by many observers as a one-sided, 'cold warriors' interpretation of world affairs, the new policy did little to reduce international tension. Several of the weapon acquisition programs were not regarded as being conducive to arms control or 'constructive internationalism.'[6]

Despite dire warnings about the Soviet threat, Canadians were increasingly reluctant to pay for the controversial and costly 'big ticket' systems like tanks and submarines. Polling results showed a dramatic decline in support – while 40 per cent of Canadians were in favour of defence spending increases in 1985, by 1989 only 23 per cent supported such increases.[7]

There was particular opposition to the government's plan to acquire a new fleet of nuclear-powered submarines. Polls taken prior to the 1989 budget suggested that almost 70 per cent of Canadians were opposed to the purchase. As David Langille noted, 'The nuclear-powered submarine program had to be sacrificed after it became a political liability that threatened to undo the whole program of deficit reduction. The Conservatives would not have been able to justify large cuts in unemployment insurance, day care or other social programs if they were to spend billions on submarines.'[8] Within Ottawa, many officials had already questioned the wisdom of the program. It was rumoured to have caused a serious rift in cabinet, with several powerful ministers voicing strong opposition. A number of American senators had also expressed concern over the government's decision to acquire nuclear-powered attack submarines. Considerable apprehension trailed the program from its conception to its conclusion, in part because the Department of National Defence failed to provide a realistic cost assessment. Although their estimates were pegged rigidly at $8 billion, other analysts projected that the subs would cost between $10 and $20 billion. There were legitimate fears that the program might turn into a 'sink-hole,' drawing resources away from the army and the air force. Finally, in response to the sinking of a similar Soviet vessel, MP Fred Mifflin, a former admiral and deputy commander of Maritime Command, acknowledged that 'it was one more red flag amongst many' that signalled against purchasing the nuclear-powered submarines.[9]

While the lack of public support and the concern for fiscal restraint undermined the government's plans for industrial and defence policy, an array of changes occurring in the international environment ensured a temporary pause, it not a change in direction.

ON THE EVE OF A NEW ERA

Change has become the dominant characteristic of the international environment as we enter the 1990s. Although there are great challenges ahead, many developments are likely to be for the better.

A new era of détente appeared on the horizon in the late 1980s. While it may be premature to suggest that peace has broken out and that co-operation has replaced confrontation as the new norm of international conduct, there are encouraging trends. In November 1989, Presidents George Bush and Mikhail Gorbachev accepted that the Cold War was officially over and that it was time to begin the difficult task of building a coherent peace.

The threat of war, particularly that of premeditated attack, has been reduced. The INF (intermediate-range nuclear forces) agreement of 1987 set an important arms-control precedent. Aside from the immediate benefits of withdrawing SS-20s, cruise, and Pershing missiles from forward deployments in Europe, it demonstrated that by agreement an entire category of offensive weapons might be dismantled. By popular demand, disarmament was back in vogue. Progress is now expected from the CFE (Conventional Armed Forces in Europe) and CSCE (Conference on Security and Cooperation in Europe) talks in Vienna, as well as the Geneva-based START talks (Strategic Arms Reduction Talks). Members of the Warsaw Treaty Organization (WTO) and NATO alliances are now engaged in discussions that may lead to a restructuring of their armed forces and military doctrines.[10]

In the WTO, *glasnost, perestroika*, and the ensuing process of democratization and reform have provided member states with the freedom to radically restructure their political, military, and economic relations. This monolithic bloc has melted. Aside from the Soviet Union itself, Poland, Hungary, East Germany, Bulgaria, Czechoslovakia, and Romania are all engaged in the very uncertain process of transformation. Alliance members are openly discussing their aspirations for independent non-offensive defence postures and even the possibility of military neutrality. To all intents and purposes, the WTO is no longer a cohesive military alliance.

The pace of radical change in the USSR, even in the face of enormous challenges, was unanticipated. British historian Sir Michael Howard commented in early 1989 that 'there seems good reason to suppose that what we are witnessing in the Soviet Union are events no less fundamental and far-reaching than those which occurred in France in 1789. We are seeing a genuine revolution.'[11]

Mikhail Gorbachev's repeated unilateral gestures to trim Soviet force levels have lowered international tension and fear. Along with attempts to restructure the Soviet economy, political process, and armed forces, there has been a marked willingness to compromise and accept NATO arms-control proposals. In effect, the leadership in Moscow has started to fulfil one of the worst scenarios ever anticipated by many Western defence planners – they are slowly denying us an enemy.

Both superpowers overstretched their military and political resources in the 1980s. The West is slowly coming to terms with its own economic and environmental crisis. After a decade of unprecedented military buildup, the United States moved from being the world's largest creditor to the world's largest debtor. The massive deficit in the United States, coupled with the relative decline of its competitive position and economic base, prompted a reassessment of American defence spending. Plans have been drawn up that would entail cutting the size of U.S. forces in Europe from 320,000 to 100,000 troops.[12] A study by the Brookings Institution concluded that the United States could slash defence spending by 50 per cent and still meet its security commitments, trimming spending from the present $300 billion to as low as $160 billion by the turn of the century.[13]

Unfortunately, the widespread hope of acquiring an immediate 'peace dividend' was dashed by U.S. President George Bush's fiscal 1991 budget, which provided the Pentagon with a \$3.7 billion raise. Having previously acknowledged that the Cold War is over, the president proceeded to slash spending on health, housing, and education to provide additional funds for the Strategic Defense Initiative and development of new nuclear weapons and Stealth bombers.[14]

While the United States and the Soviet Union will likely remain great military powers, their capacity to influence, let alone mould, the world in their image has declined. The prospect of more diverse and multipolar security arrangements appear inevitable.

European post-war recovery is complete. The old artificial political divisions imposed on the continent by Allied powers at Yalta in 1945 are coming apart. Long-standing and understandable concerns over the prospect of one Germany are not slowing the process of reunification. New linkages in this respect will no doubt draw the larger regions of Eastern and Western Europe into closer relations. In the words of NATO Secretary-General Manfred Woerner, the promise of 'an end to a divided Europe, and with it an end to the division of Germany, has never been brighter.'[15] Western trade with the East has just begun to take off, fuelled by the prospect of approximately 365 million new customers in the Soviet Union and Eastern Europe. It is already apparent that the integration of the European Economic Community in 1992 will signal the rise of a new political and economic force. As Richard Gwyn says, 'As goes trade, so will go the political and diplomatic flags.'[16] A new superpower is in the making.

In light of these developments, the alliance structures that co-ordinated defence relations for forty years are now in a period of transition. The consensus in Western security planning has been fractured. A 'nuclear allergy' struck most of Europe in the 1980s. NATO's flexible-response strategy and the Reagan administration's loose talk of limited nuclear war created a ground swell of opposition to alliance plans. NATO's strategies were widely assessed to be neither credible nor safe. According to an opinion poll conducted in January 1989, only 9 per cent of the West

German public still accepted nuclear deterrence as the proper basis of NATO strategy. While France and Britain remain exceptions for the time being, other West European governments are facing a crisis over military strategy and training exercises. Governments in Spain, Denmark, Greece, West Germany, Norway, and the Netherlands have voiced strong opposition to alliance plans. Whereas alliance solidarity within NATO dominated the first eight years of the 1980s, a conditional and certainly less scripted 'flexible semi-alignment' appears to better describe current member relations.[17]

The realities of hegemonic decline, a diffusion of power, and an increasingly expensive and risky military competition have prompted a world-wide reassessment of the international security system. The sterile arguments and orthodox assumptions that contributed to the security log-jam of the early 1980s are being gradually replaced by the new thinking associated with common security, alternative defence, and sustainable development.

There is also renewed interest in the United Nations. With recent successes in Namibia, Afghanistan, and the Iran-Iraq war, the UN is once again seen to be providing vital services to the international community. Not only are past dues being paid, but the prospects of strengthening the organization, which seemed so bleak in the mid-1980s, have not looked better since its inception. The United Nations' renaissance is hardly coincidental.

At the international level there is a considerable crisis of uncertainty. We are at an important juncture and it remains to be seen which of several trends will determine our future course. On the one hand, it is possible to foresee the emergence of a new order premised on a mature recognition of interdependence and the need to engage in a co-operative search for common security.

On the other hand, there is always the danger during a period of hegemonic decline, with all of its attendant instability and risks, that we might experience a degenerative shift back to an arms race in ever more advanced technologies. The rise of new continental trading blocs will intensify economic competition and protectionism, possibly prompting new military rivalries. It is conceivable that we could find ourselves in an isolationist, and less safe, system. The importance of avoiding this scenario cannot be overstated. The potential sources of future instability are numerous: accidental or inadvertent war, political upheaval, regional conflict, widespread economic collapse, the proliferation of nuclear and other offensive weapons, underdevelopment, environmental catastrophe, and resource depletion. Many of the positive developments in recent years rest upon fragile relations within a volatile environment. As Ken Booth warns, 'Although the Cold War might be brain-dead, its powerful muscles can still twitch dangerously.'[18] In any era of profound transformation, there are considerable risks. As one recent international report cautioned: 'Without decisive action in the next few years, the constellation of international events, inspired leadership, and political, military and economic circumstances which have made the current opportunity feasible may be lost.'[19]

A previous generation of Canadians earned a unique reputation on the world stage as honest brokers and helpful fixers; a reputation built upon decisive leadership and a long-standing commitment to constructive internationalism. More recently, there have been legitimate concerns that Canadian policy and Canadian leadership have less and less to offer.

THE DEFENCE TRAP: IDENTIFYING THE CONSTRAINTS

Canada is also approaching what has been described as a 'watershed' or turning-point in matters related to sovereignty and security. The 1987 defence white paper provided neither the guidance nor the means with which to address Canada's security requirements in the 1990s. In such a state of rapid and radical change it is understandable that the Conservative government found little support for their defence policy.

Canada's defence relations have forced numerous compromises. On several occasions, Canadian leaders attempted to pursue distinct approaches to defence and security issues. Trudeau's strategy of suffocation was intended to help stem the flight-testing of strategic delivery vehicles. Nielsen's attempt to withdraw Canadian forces from Europe was meant to reduce

Canada's defence commitments and provide the government with greater strategic flexibility.

Yet Canadian governments were trapped into participating in the testing of the U.S. air-launched cruise missile and trapped into maintaining a military commitment to NATO's Central European Front. Anticipating the possibility of external pressure and linkage, Canadian officials assumed that there were no viable options. The frustrations arising from such failed initiatives reinforced those assumptions and the arrangements that foster economic and military integration. These initiatives, as well as the shift to a long-war policy and industrial mobilization, reflect a wide range of political, economic, and military pressures arising in Canada's bilateral, multilateral, and domestic defence relations. Canada's allies, the defence industry, and the emergence of a military-industrial complex have had a significant influence upon the formulation of Canadian defence policy.

Canada's current defence posture certainly reflects the importance accorded to our bilateral and multilateral relations. For nearly forty years, a priority has been placed upon providing support to the United States for the defence of North America and to the other NATO allies for the defence of Europe. While Canada's geostrategic position may have necessitated some defence co-operation, particularly to ensure the United States of adequate surveillance and early-warning, the ensuing process of military and economic integration structured defence decisions into a pattern of subservience and conformity. Canada became a follower in this respect, generally adopting NATO and U.S. strategic priorities. For example, when External Affairs Minister Joe Clark was questioned in January 1990 as to whether the government would be changing its defence policy and reconsidering cruise-missile tests, he responded: 'As a NATO member, Canada cannot and will not make unilateral decision without the unanimous support of other alliance nations.'[20] While a number of our allies are pursuing independent initiatives to improve the international environment, Ottawa appears steadfast in its support for NATO leadership and Western solidarity. Apparently, the government has accepted its lack of control over these collective defence arrangements, assuming either that they serve common political, economic, and strategic interests or that they are simply inevitable. The cumulative effect of these defence decisions is unlikely to serve Canada's long-term interests or a government's capacity to determine defence policy.

These external determinants of Canadian policy are reinforced by a number of important internal factors. Electoral concerns encourage governments to adopt policies that are deemed to be politically and economically expedient. In the words of General Gérard Thériault, former chief of defence staff, 'these are complex national issues that have to be addressed with some sense of long-term relevance and it's just not the way that government business is being transacted in Ottawa now.' In the general's opinion the Conservative government 'lacks leadership and operates on the principle of expediency.'[21] Unfortunately, Canadian governments have tended to avoid controversial initiatives or to drop them at first hint of adverse publicity. A restructuring of Canada's defence posture is assumed to jeopardize numerous important vested interests. Without a domestic consensus in support of such restructuring, however, a government is politically vulnerable to foreign pressure.

In the last decade, several groups assumed new prominence in the defence decision-making process. The government had always accorded considerable influence to its defence establishment because of its particular expertise and knowledge in this field. The military bureaucracy has been understandably anxious to obtain modern equipment and fulfil roles that would advance the interests of the armed forces and ensure their relevance in the larger Western defence community. Accordingly, the army will oppose any shift away from NATO's Central European Front and the air force will resist any move that would jeopardize its close relationship with the U.S. Air Force.

Business leaders, particularly those from the defence industry, also became influential in the defence decision-making process. They were granted special access to this process on the basis of their interest in maintaining a healthy indigenous defence production sector, an interest shared by the government and the

Department of National Defence. There was an underlying assumption that the corporate community had a clear understanding of Canadian defence and economic requirements. It also had a vested interest in arranging a growing demand for defence products, privileged access to Canadian and American markets, and state assistance so that it might better compete in the international arms trade.

Ottawa was anxious to encourage an expanded defence constituency and defence industrial sector. In many respects, the government's efforts were successful. The 1987 defence white paper had generated great expectations and attracted considerable investment. By 1989, the United States Defense Authorization Act defined Canada as part of the U.S. domestic defence industrial base. Several months after the release of the 1989 Wilson budget, *Saturday Night* ran a feature which suggested that 'the emphasis on making an industrial policy out of military spending is likely to increase.'[22]

Yet the adoption of a military-Keynesian outlook – and all it implied in terms of promoting a large defence industry as a means of engendering technological take-off, employment, and industrial growth – occurred at a time when the international demand for armaments was subsiding. According to a U.S. Library of Congress report, although military spending world-wide exceeded $1 trillion (U.S.) for the first time in 1987, the rate of defence spending has slowed significantly.[23] In the near future it is difficult to foresee the United States, Europe, or developing nations making large-scale purchases of Canadian defence products. This short-sighted economic strategy was prone to a boom-bust pattern of development. It had very limited potential for long-term growth.

The unanticipated thaw in East-West relations diminished Western perceptions of the Warsaw Pact 'threat' and undermined much of the proposed rearmament program for Canada's armed forces. It also reduced the international demand for Canadian defence products. Canadian defence exports began to plummet in 1988.[24]

The defence industry in Canada was shocked and naturally

disappointed by the Wilson budget of 1989. It meant not only less money in the short term but also contradicted the promise of secure funding for the future. Although the minister of national defence, Bill McKnight, declared that the government was still committed to the enhancement of the defence industrial base and the pursuit of a total-force concept, it was apparent that the 'gravy-train' had dried up considerably.[25] The defence industry has been left to anxiously await news of the scaled-down armed-forces replacement programs. Yet as noted in the *Financial Post*, 'the future amid military cutbacks looks bleak for U.S. and Canadian defence contractors who rely almost entirely on war and insurrection.'[26]

Although previously dismissed as a non-entity in Canada's defence decision-making process, the military-industrial complex had come to constitute a powerful and active coalition of political, economic, military, bureaucratic, and academic interests. The lack of responsible political oversight and public awareness of Canadian defence relations made it possible for this complex to exercise unwarranted influence. As a result, the 1987 defence white paper had presented an inflated threat assessment, confirmed outdated commitments, and distorted both defence and economic planning to serve vested interests.

Faced with an apparent set-back in Wilson's 1989 budget, the military-industrial complex mobilized to recoup its losses and counter the impression that defence spending could be further reduced. Members of this 'defence constituency' were quick to criticize the cancellation of the large acquisition programs and to warn of the damage they alleged had been done to Canada's international credibility, sovereignty, and security.[27] Martin Shadwick admonished the government to 'move aggressively to restore the constituency for defence in this country.'[28] Mike O'Brien gave some indication in the *Wednesday Report* of how this complex viewed the recent changes and how they might respond:

> This time will pass ... Ironically, if not dangerously, the First Secretary of the Soviet Union currently retains control over the way the world

formulates security policy. This time must pass. It is refreshing to note that numerous organizations have emerged in Canada from within the defence community, and most if not all of them, advocate a stance that reads like the credo of the Defence Associations National Network: '... to improve public debate on Canadian security policy' and 'to coordinate support for defence policies which reflect the need for modern and effective Canadian Armed Forces and to educate those who advocate otherwise.' These organizations fully recognized the nature of the weapon which has been used against them. The weapon is deception, which has distracted us from thinking about our sovereignty and lulled us into a false sense of security. How do you cope with the prevailing, pessimistic outlook? ... dealing with the obstacles anticipated for the 90s seemingly can only be done from a united front.[29]

In addition to the Defence Associations National Network, a new Defence Industry Association of Canada was organized, allegedly 'to fight peace groups in order to win public support for defence.'[30] Keith Davies is to lead a million-dollar-a-year campaign to promote militarization and higher defence spending.

As mentioned in chapter 4, representatives of the military-industrial complex have argued on numerous occasions that, if a Canadian government refused to participate in an important NATO or NORAD initiative, it would risk retaliation and the defence industry's access to foreign defence markets. The Defence Production Sharing Agreement (DPSA), which helps to facilitate most of the defence trade, was cited as an arrangement that might be cancelled if the government were to pursue an independent defence option that offended the U.S. administration.

Although the possibility of retaliation cannot be entirely dismissed, the defence industry is a very unlikely target for any such punishment. This industrial sector is mostly foreign-owned. Since most of the enterprises involved are branch plants of multinational corporations based in the United States, Britain, and West Germany, it is difficult to foresee any of these countries retaliating against their own defence contractors, who are for the most part awarded privileged treatment. Whatever veiled threat might be forthcoming, few governments are so inept as to 'shoot themselves in the foot' by targeting their own corporate citizens. It is also quite unlikely that retaliation would be directed at Canada's Department of National Defence. There are elements within this department who have assumed that it is their role to voice the Pentagon's interests.

If retaliation were to occur, it would most likely be directed at the government responsible for initiating a provocative shift in policy. While there is little likelihood of a massive campaign of economic or political destabilization, a government might find itself faced with an array of orchestrated embarrassments. It is highly unlikely, however, that Canada would be seriously threatened. As we have seen, such threats tend to be exaggerated by those with a vested interest in maintaining a wide array of defence commitments and increases in defence spending.

The Conservative government provided further cause for concern in 1989 when it signalled a revised approach to security issues. Defence Minister McKnight evoked outrage when he acknowledged that Canada would be placing even greater reliance upon its allies for the protection of Canadian sovereignty and security.[31] The anxiety generated over the prospect of contracting-out Canadian defence responsibilities to our allies increased when it was learned that the government would begin to transfer some of the armed forces' roles in coastal air patrol and surveillance to the private sector. Canadian Forces Tracker aircraft are to be grounded, resulting in the loss of 50 per cent of Canada's fixed-wing Maritime patrol aircraft. Plans to acquire a Polar 8 icebreaker were cancelled. The net effect was to reduce Canada's capacity to monitor and patrol its own territorial waters and airspace.

The cancellation of the major acquisition programs announced in the 1987 white paper prompted the Canadian Institute of Strategic Studies to warn of a move towards 'fortress North America' and to suggest that 'the Canadian military may swiftly atrophy into an adjunct to U.S. continental defence.'[32] Although the institute's alacrity to question any measure that jeopardizes defence spending or the defence industry is to be expected, there is a serious risk that Canada will be drawn into tighter continental defence arrangements.

In November 1989, on his first visit to the Soviet Union, Prime Minister Mulroney acknowledged that his government's defence policy was outdated. As he put it, 'There's been a revolution that's taken place, in thinking, in lives of nations in the last months. Times change, events change and attitudes have to be tempered.'[33] Yet four months later, with the release of the government's budget, it was unclear whether there had been any reassessment of the new environment or the revolution to which the prime minister had referred.[34] The government continued to accept the orthodox assumptions and levels of defence spending characteristic of the earlier Cold War era. Although the budget announced a 'cap' on increases in defence spending, in fact defence spending would continue to grow 5 per cent annually. John Lamb writes: 'The government's spin doctors have tried to convey the impression that the military did get cut, pointing out that 1990–92 defence spending plans will be $480 million below previously projected plans. But bringing a wish list into line with reality hardly amounts to a genuine cut.'[35] As happened in the United States, the prospect of a 'peace dividend' was denied. In the defence-spending estimates, a Soviet nuclear attack on North America was again cited as the most serous direct threat to Canada. It was also suggested that conventional forces must be able to sustain a prolonged fight if the use of nuclear weapons is to be avoided.[36] In the absence of any strategic justification for a long-war policy, especially in this new environment, one can only assume that those with vested economic and departmental interests were still in a position to exert unwarranted influence upon the defence decision-making process.

Unfortunately, it is the armed forces that are, once again, left in a state of confusion, with too little money to do too many jobs. The commitment-capability gap is a perennial problem that cannot be solved simply by raising defence spending. Unless the government finds the political courage to undertake a fundamental restructuring of Canada's defence posture and cancel commitments that it cannot meet, the burden of the commitment-capability gap will continue to fall on the armed forces.

There can be little doubt that the cuts announced in the Wilson budget of April 1989 had a demoralizing effect on the military. Their search for an expanded military role and greater relevance in the East-West conflict was abruptly set back. As one young officer lamented, 'We used to be little guys trying to play with the big kids on the block. Now we can't even do that.'[37] Yet by resolutely holding on to 'big league' soldiering roles and outdated commitments, the Department of National Defence exacerbated an already difficult situation.

The Conservative government committed both the armed forces and important sectors of the economy to a pattern of development that, in the past, has only served to reinforce the subordination of Canadian policy to foreign commercial and strategic interests. This subordination helps to explain why previous Canadian initiatives to restructure defence policy were largely unsuccessful. While arrangements such as NATO, NORAD, and the DPSA led Canada towards a defence trap, new defence arrangements such as formal integration into the North American Defence Industrial Base (NADIB) and the creation of a Defence Industrial Preparedness Advisory Committee (DIPAC) will further circumscribe the autonomy of a Canadian government. The recent move to privatize the armed forces' surveillance roles and the transfer of further security responsibilities to Canada's allies will likely compound this dilemma. Many of these developments are difficult to justify. They will undoubtedly impose an array of new obligations and constraints that limit the government's political, economic, and strategic flexibility. Coinciding with the Canada-U.S. free-trade agreement and the clearance sale of national assets, the government's defence policy is contributing to the process of continentalization.

The consequence of surrendering economic and military control is a loss of political autonomy. Such a loss diminishes Canada's capacity to pursue policies of 'constructive internationalism' or 'common security.' As Ernie Regehr warns: 'The loss of independence is to be lamented because it saps the strength and confidence of those Canadian initiatives which, in appealing to a not yet destroyed sense of identity and purpose, seek to impose political limits on the hegemonic ambitions and competitions of the superpowers.'[38]

To simply ignore this problem or try to sweep it under the carpet is to perpetuate Canada's subordinate status. The government's capacity to determine defence policy will depend in part upon how well it is apprised of its constraints and opportunities. Unfortunately, the current preoccupation with rationalizing policy so as to ensure conformity and maintain credibility in the councils of power leaves little space for constructive thought. The assumption that Canada's security is inevitably dependent upon NATO, NORAD, and the American 'nuclear umbrella' prevents the assertion of a distinct Canadian stand on issues of vital importance. These problems are not new. As Dalton Camp acknowledged in 1969, 'The critics of Canadian defence policy have been too bland, too sweetly reasonable, too lacking in outrage.'[39]

Compounding the problem, in recent years the analysis of Canadian defence relations has been unduly confined within a narrow interpretation of strategic studies and the associated paradigm of international realism.[40] The result has often been 'worst-case analysis,' exaggerated threat assessments, and the seldom-questioned advancement of American strategic ambitions. In 1986, similar concerns led a group of young Canadian academics to warn:

> This realist or neo-realist view is largely a product of the US-dominated discipline of international relations. The view of Canadians of the international system is deeply influenced by this dominant American paradigm. Canadian universities aid the socialization of policy-makers and the public into a role as guardians of US global interests which are then adopted as our own through the dissemination of a US worldview ... This view tends to narrow the consideration of alternatives and to heavily influence definitions of the national interests of Canada used by academics, policy practitioners and by society at large.[41]

Aside from the pressures arising through Canada's formal alliance and defence arrangements, there is little doubt that the 'defence trap' is buttressed by the traditional assumptions of Canadian security planning.[42] Sacred status is all too often accorded to the requirements of nuclear deterrence, a balance of power, and alliance commitments. The cumulative effect has led many to assume that Canada's defence relations are inevitable and that the nation has few, if any, independent options. For instance, when Perrin Beatty was minister of national defence, he argued that nuclear submarines were the only option to meet Canada's maritime defence requirements. Tom d'Aquino, president of the Business Council on National Issues, argued that Canada has no option but to develop closer defence ties with the United States. Colonel Cal Hegge of the Defence Industrial Preparedness Task Force has argued that Canada has no option but to integrate the defence sector into a North American Defence Industrial Base. Colonel H.A.J. Hutchinson, past chairman of the Conference of Defence Associations, has argued that Canadians must come to see that they have no option but to adopt a Total Defence approach. In 1988, Larry Pratt and Tom Keating wrote that Canada had no viable option but to reaffirm an old Atlanticism, strengthening ties to NATO with a larger military commitment to the Central Front.[43] Obviously, these are not the only options. There *are* alternatives.

Canada clearly requires independent defence analysis and strategic thinking. In the absence of such advice, a government is less likely to recognize its options. Yet efforts to support and fund this activity through the Department of National Defence's Military and Strategic Studies (MSS) program may not help. Given the structure within which funding decisions are made, it is only natural that preference is accorded to conventional wisdom, the rationalization of defence policy and the defence of departmental interests. Canada has had a number of excellent international-relations and strategic-studies schools in various universities. Nine of these universities now receive funding under the MSS program. One effect of this MSS funding has been to create a constituency of academic support for defence-department policy and objectives. Within some of these MSS-funded university programs, students have been repeatedly warned away from exploring critical analysis and alternative ideas. New thinking in defence affairs tends to be discouraged or dismissed as an unwarranted challenge.

The 1987 defence white paper confirmed that there are

entrenched interests which will attempt to hinder any progressive restructuring of Canadian defence policy. As we have seen, a return to the Cold War and an accelerated arms race will be the preferred choice of some sectors within Canada's military-industrial complex. However, these vested interests should not be allowed to compromise or distort Canada's legitimate security requirements. It is irresponsible to provide representatives of the defence industry with a privileged position in the formulation of defence policy. An unwarranted focus upon short-term interests tightened the defence trap; only long-term vision will begin to undo it.

Given the trends towards a continental trading bloc, a Canadian government could soon face a difficult decision regarding its future security options. On the one hand, it would be easiest to continue with current defence arrangements and policies. The risk of such a course is that Canada will be gradually absorbed into the larger American security infrastructure. Douglas Roche concedes that 'Canadian political and bureaucratic structures pull us ever closer to the United States at precisely the moment we need to extend our efforts outwards into the world community.'[44] Although the prospect of a future 'fortress North America' may appear remote at this time, the Canadian government should not be forfeiting its capacity to avert such a development.

On the other hand, there is the option, albeit a difficult one in such an asymmetrical relationship, of establishing a division of labour with the United States whereby the two countries would co-ordinate their defence efforts while each retained control over its national territory, armed forces, and foreign policy. Such an internationalist agenda would offer greater long-term security for all. As Douglas Roche indicates, 'Against this drift to integration, Canada must clearly articulate our own defence and defence production objectives as a primary condition of maintaining our own political and economic independence.'[45]

A total reappraisal of Canadian defence-policy and security requirements is now in order. As previously mentioned, the defence trap is neither irrevocable nor inevitable. Canada need not be confined by orthodox analysis, outdated defence commitments, or an industrial policy that leaves us dependent upon international tension and the demand for Canadian-made defence products. Traps are much easier to avoid and to escape once they are recognized. Events of the past few years have provided Canada with an opportunity to ensure that it is not confined in a defence trap.

THE 1990S: A TIME OF HOPE

We are now in a period in which ideas can move events. As previously noted, the dominant characteristic of the present security environment is change.[46] Recent developments in political, economic, and military affairs have provided new hope and new opportunities.

A new window of opportunity has been opened. Those pressures that previously impeded the pursuit of Canadian peace and security initiatives may have eased. The arms race is slowly subsiding. The Soviet Union, West Germany, and many other NATO and WTO member-states have announced defence spending cuts. Several of Canada's allies and old foes are adopting new methods to promote security and they are moving beyond previous military fixations. With the cancellation of several expensive and unnecessary armament programs, defence stocks in the West have begun to plunge. As New York money manager David Dreman noted, 'These are war stocks. What's good news for the world is bad news for them.'[47] In turn, as the rate of defence spending slows, one can expect the influence of the military-industrial complex to decline. Given the reduction in East-West tension, a subdued arms race, and a new multipolar setting, the Canadian government would appear to have a wider range of options and greater political autonomy for defence decision-making. With political will, Canada could move well beyond the defence trap.

Several official 'in-house' defence reviews are under way. With a rapidly diminishing conventional threat and very limited public support for bridging the gap between defence capabilities and commitments, Canada's current defence posture must be revised. Aside from the relatively easy reassessment of projected defence acquisition programs, the Canadian government faces the difficult task of rethinking the assumptions that have guided Canadian policy for over forty years. While it may appear easier to keep the old game alive than to confront the new circumstances, the long-term costs of this approach are unacceptable.

To date, however, there has been scant effort paid to develop new ideas on alternative security or a more comprehensive analysis of Canadian defence options. In the 1980s, a number of non-governmental organizations such as Veterans Against Nuclear Arms and the Group of 78 endorsed the concept of common security and began to explore appropriate defence options.[48] The New Democratic Party's document *Canada's Stake in Common Security* was an important contribution in this respect.[49] Although a number of proposals from journalists and non-governmental organizations encouraged a debate on new defence and security arrangements, there was little, if any, related research conducted within Canadian universities or professional institutes. As a result, there is a risk that the government's defence reviews will dwell on yesterday's problems and yesterday's methods.

Unless political energy can be mobilized and applied to overcome short-term financial interests and the institutional inertia that impedes progressive change, Canada may well continue with irrelevant policies that do little to enhance anyone's security. It is vitally important that we democratize the debate over Canadian defence policy. Better mechanisms are needed, moreover, to provide Canadians, particularly elected representatives, with a capacity to oversee Canadian defence relations.[50] The decision-making process must be reviewed and opened to public and political scrutiny. An extensive series of cross-country hearings would now seem appropriate.

It is crucial that the government establish new priorities for these defence reviews. In November 1989, General John de Chastelain suggested that the defence staff will continue giving top priority to the purchase of new equipment.[51] Obviously, the armed forces deserve the equipment and support required to fulfil their missions. Yet it would be wrong at this point to focus primarily on the acquisition of new equipment or on replacement programs for the systems that have been cancelled. That would simply lead to a weapon-driven policy. Moreover, the missions of the armed forces are likely to change. As the 1989 Special Committee of the Senate on National Defence warned, 'In these new circumstances the government should exercise caution in making new commitments of monies or equipment, and instead should seize the opportunity afforded by a period of transition to examine its options and consider new roles more in keeping with the changed realities.'[52] If we are to turn hope for a long-term peace into reality, the first step is to modernize our thinking.

It is time to focus national concerns within a transnational perspective. Canada's objective should be to help the improving international situation improve further. To this end, the government should take a much more active role in generating new ideas, formulating new plans for a relevant defence, and undertaking new initiatives to promote common security.

As the report of the Special Joint Committee on Canada's International Relations, *Independence and Internationalism*, noted, 'Unless Canada is equipped to develop new ideas and approaches, it cannot expect to be able to exert influence in Washington or in other capitals.'[53] To develop a relevant defence plan we must begin by changing attitudes as well as policies and institutions. In 1985, Canadian military historian Gwynne Dyer wrote: 'We have reached a point where our moral imagination must expand again to embrace the whole of mankind.'[54] Fortunately, there are now encouraging signs of movement in this respect. The final report of Palme Commission acknowledged:

> In the final decade of the Twentieth Century, humanity has an historic opportunity to create a less dangerous, more humane, and more peaceful world. The transformations which have taken place in the 1980s – trends in world opinion, the activation of concerned groups of citizens in many nations, major advances in the policies and positions espoused by key governments, and an apparent new willingness to use the United Nations as an effective peace-making organization – have established the pre-conditions necessary for major leaps forward.

> Humanity has the chance to move decisively away from the existing system, in which countries futilely pursue national security at one another's expense, to a system founded on an understanding that true security can only be achieved in cooperation with other states. The pursuit of common security could be the hallmark and dominant organizing principle of the international system by the dawn of the Twenty-first Century.[55]

As part of an increasingly interdependent global community, Canadians have a lot at stake. The stakes, moreover, justify a thorough reassessment of how Canada can best manage its territory, armed forces, and resources to promote common security. The armed forces in particular will require coherent guidance from a new defence policy, one that outlines viable commitments and defines roles relevant to the security environment of the 1990s.

CHAPTER SIX

Changing the Guard: From Defence Trap to Common Security

The great question is: Can global war now be outlawed from the world? If so, it would mark the greatest advance in civilization since the Sermon on the Mount. It would lift at one stroke the darkest shadow which has engulfed mankind from the beginning. It would not only remove fear and bring security – it would not only create new moral and spiritual values – it would produce an economic wave of prosperity that would raise the world's standard of living beyond anything ever dreamed of by man. (General Douglas MacArthur, 1961)

Over twenty years ago, Andrew Brewin argued in *Stand On Guard: The Search for a Canadian Defence Policy* that Canada would have to be divorced from security policies that were 'obsolete, provocative and meaningless.'[1] As we enter the 1990s, Canadian defence planners may have little choice but to accept Brewin's message. They are now confronted by a range of largely unanticipated and quite profound changes in the strategic environment. The divorce may be discomforting, but it is time for a changing of the guard.

First, the conventional military threat has subsided and is being surpassed by other challenges; second, a commitment to deterrence and refining preparation for war is neither safe nor necessary; third, Canada's continued participation in multilateral military alliances and bilateral collective defence arrangements may no longer be required or desirable; and fourth, Canada, as is the case with other nations, can no longer afford to allocate the level of resources required to maintain foreign-based defence commitments. These developments require a fundamental reappraisal of Canada's approach to international security and defence policy. As we restructure Canada's defence posture for the 1990s, the armed forces will be called upon to perform different tasks.

It is time to shift priorities from preparing to fight wars towards a force posture and strategy that focuses upon war avoidance in the short term and the abolition of war in the long term. In essence, defence in the 1990s must facilitate transition to a new era of security. It can and should be designed to civilize international relations and to complement efforts to abolish war as a phenomenon. If guided by a long-term vision of the post–Cold War era, Canada's armed forces may be well positioned to provide a safer, more reliable defence while also contributing to international peace and a just world order.

Common security provides an excellent basis upon which to develop consistent and coherent goal-oriented defence policies. It poses a refreshing alternative to the practices of 'collective security,' which have left the world in two armed camps. To complement a safe transition to common security, it is important for countries like Canada to develop policies relevant to their particular region and context.

In this chapter it will be argued that by emphasizing the maintenance of a security buffer, shifting to a non-offensive defence posture, adopting a strategy of dissuasion, and working to strengthen the United Nations Canada's armed forces, resources, and territory could help to promote common security. The roles and requirements are within our means.

This section will begin with a short review of Canada's current defence posture, noting several changes occurring in the larger strategic environment. A number of assumptions and commitments will have to be reassessed if the government is to formulate a relevant defence for the 1990s.

REVIEWING CANADA'S DEFENCE POSTURE IN 1990

For roughly forty years, a primary security concern of Canadian governments has been to support efforts to maintain international peace and stability. This was accurately perceived as the best approach by which to ensure Canadian security. Matching the ideal means to this end, however, has been somewhat difficult.

Through participation in one military alliance, the North Atlantic Treaty Organization (NATO), and in one bilateral defence partnership, the North American Air/Aerospace Defence Command (NORAD), Canada's armed forces stood guard as a part of the larger Western collective defence effort. With Canada's vast territory and limited resources, an independent defence was seen to be too difficult for Canada and of little contribution to the security of the West. Moreover, for a variety of reasons that have already been discussed, successive Canadian governments agreed to co-ordinate their defence efforts with other powers, assuming that Canada's interests would be best assured while participating in bilateral and multilateral arrangements.

Since the early 1950s, Canada's military and that of its allies were focused primarily upon deterrence and the military containment of the Soviet Union. With its forces so committed, Canada was firmly aligned in the East-West confrontation. The strategy adopted to deal with this conflict was to meet the threat as an integral part of another threat. Within NATO and the continental defence partnership, Canada provides support for nuclear and conventional deterrence in North America, Western Europe, and at sea. In North America, the armed forces work within NORAD to ensure the safety of the United States' strategic nuclear forces. They provide early-warning information and maintain a limited interception capability largely to identify unknown aircraft and, if necessary, to provide a thin line of defence against a bomber attack.

In Europe, the army and the air force join other NATO forces in defending the Central Front. A previous 'fly-over' commitment to NATO's Northern Flank and Norway was dropped in the 1987 defence review, but a similar arrangement has since been reconfirmed. At sea, the navy protects Canada's territorial waters on three oceans and the sea lanes of communication to Europe. It also has responsibility for a considerable region of the North Atlantic, which has been partitioned off between NATO allies. Canada's primary naval activity is in preparing for anti-submarine warfare.

Canadian forces are also responsible for asserting sovereignty. In this regard they attempt to maintain adequate surveillance and control of Canadian territory. In addition to these tasks, the armed forces assist in United Nations peacekeeping activities and, when called upon, they advise on international arms-control negotiations.

While Canadian governments have occasionally changed the priority accorded to these defence commitments, the NATO and NORAD deterrence tasks have generally dominated the defence agenda. Although declaratory policy emphasized the peace-time defence of Canada, operational policy reflected a somewhat different objective. The East-West confrontation was deemed to be inevitable and the military competition seen to be unavoidable.[2]

It was widely understood that a war between the superpowers constituted the worst threat, but it was also assumed that the defence of Canada required military forces capable of fighting in such a war. One of the rationales for committing Canadian forces to the conventional defence of Europe was to raise the nuclear threshold and avoid early resort to nuclear weapons should deterrence fail. It was on this basis that defence planners attempted to justify the shift to a long-war policy and the acquisition of nuclear-powered submarines and tanks, systems designed primarily for use in conventional warfare.

As previously mentioned, Canada's armed forces were inclined to seek 'big-league' professional soldiering duties and participate in the larger search for military advantage. A 1972 study by the Canadian Armed Forces on professionalism argued that the *raison d'être* of a professional military force is to apply or threaten to apply force on behalf of the state and at the lawful direction of the duly constituted government of the nation.[3] As with all forces in NATO and NORAD, Canadian armed forces are organized, equipped, and trained with the objective of being able to wage and, if possible, to win a war within the shortest possible time. The guiding principle has been to prevent war by means of deterrence based on the capability to wage war.[4] It is simply a time-honoured military tradition that armed forces prepare to fight and win a war, irrespective of whether it might be the Third World War.

Canada's armed forces have performed very well in the roles to which they are assigned. Provided with little public support and often less than state-of-the-art equipment, it is to their credit that they have maintained a competent and professional military force. However, the nature of the problem to which they were assigned has altered considerably.

Over the last fifty years, a host of changes have called into question many of the assumptions that have hitherto guided national defence planning. As early as 1945, Albert Einstein warned of the dangers of pursing security on the basis of outmoded beliefs. In his words, 'The unleashed power of the atom has changed everything save our modes of thinking and thus we drift towards unparalleled catastrophe.' Rapid technological advances, uncertainty, and old mind-sets mix in a manner that generates a particularly volatile environment.[5] Yet attitudes within Canada's defence establishment remain largely unchanged. Traditional military thinking is no longer an adequate basis for security planning. War between advanced industrial nations can no longer be considered in 'Clausewitzian' terms as the continuation of politics by other means. Nineteenth-century thinking and twentieth-century technology do not mix safely. As a report of the Palme Commission noted:

> The evolution of military technology has simply made traditional concepts of national security obsolete. The development of nuclear weapons, along with the aircraft and missiles capable of delivering them to any point in the world within minutes, or at most hours, means that war can no longer be considered a rational instrument of statecraft. It means that all nations would be threatened should a military conflict directly involving the nuclear powers ever take place. It means that national boundaries are forever permeable, that no state can guarantee the security of its citizens through military means. There would be no winner in a nuclear war.[6]

War has become just too dangerous. Scientific research in the early 1980s demonstrated that even a very limited nuclear exchange would risk creating a nuclear winter in the Northern hemisphere – an extremely hostile environment incapable of supporting human life.[7] Even in the unlikely event that escalation from a conventional to a nuclear war could be controlled, the results would be catastrophic. As the former head of West German military intelligence attests, 'Given the complex organisation of highly industralised states and their dependence on an extremely fragile global infrastructure, even a war fought with advanced conventional weapons could destroy civilisation as we know it.'[8] Moreover, there is no real or foreseeable defence against the offensive weapons that are now deployed. Irrespective of the defence posture adopted and equipment purchased, any war-time defence would be too little, too late. The controversy over the Strategic Defense Initiative has made it clear that a full defence is impossible at any price.

In the nuclear age, military force has lost much of its efficacy. As it can no longer be considered a productive instrument of statecraft, there is little to support the claim that the deployment of large forces is necessary as a means to add 'weight' to diplomacy and gain influence in world politics.

Modernizing defences accordingly has been difficult. Recognition of our mutual and inescapable vulnerability has not yet had a profound effect on military planning. It is conventional wisdom that the military prepares to fight the next war on the basis of the last. As Peter Worthington says, 'It is almost a psychological inevitability that the winners of a war concentrate on the methods that were successful for them.'[9] Yet as historians often note, no war ever shows the characteristics that were expected on the basis of previous experience.[10] Given recent advances in military technology and the overall course of socio-political change, it is unlikely that the historical record can provide any clear or accurate strategy for dealing with these new circumstances. Adhering to the practices and strategies of the past will provide no guarantee of security in the future.

Many of the assumptions that have provided the intellectual

foundation for Canadian defence analysis and the associated paradigm of international realism are breaking down. For instance, nuclear deterrence, maintaining a balance of power at higher levels of force, and the perpetual search for military advantage are increasingly regarded as unsafe and economically unfeasible. Armed conflict is no longer deemed to be inevitable nor is the pursuit of power and military force regarded as the best means to ensure security. As Carolyn Stephenson writes: 'The combination of the changes in the technology of both war and peace with the changes in communications and in socioeconomic and international interactions has weakened the central conditions of the "realist" paradigm.'[11] We are now in the midst of a paradigm shift – a period wherein old methods are seen to be unsatisfactory for the continued well-being of the system.[12] Another factor encouraging this shift is the emergence of new thinking on security and international relations.[13]

Canadians are revising their perceptions of global threats and security.[14] Analysing the results of a 1989 public-opinion survey, Don Munton writes that 'international security has come to mean something quite different to the present generation of Canadians, a set of concerns at once broader and more fundamental than physical security from military attack. The evidence suggests a declining concern with such conventional threats.'[15] Slowly, we are recognizing the implications associated with ever-increasing levels of interdependence: that major world problems may affect us all; that global security is indivisible; and that greater international co-operation will be unavoidable. In short, one could argue that we are beginning to adopt many of the same conclusions as the Palme Commission, which initiated studies on common security.[16]

COMMON SECURITY

The ideal of common security now offers an excellent basis on which to develop a coherent, goal-oriented defence policy for Canada.[17] It offers our armed forces a much-needed sense of purpose and relevance for the 1990s and beyond (much as 'constructive internationalism' does for the foreign service).

Premised on a mature recognition of the interdependence of nations and the urgency of revising current security practices, the common-security ideal is now widely perceived as a worthy objective and as an organizing principle for planning a safer and more just world.[18] The essence of common security is that security for one nation can only be enhanced by increasing the confidence and security of all. No one can gain security by making another feel insecure; similarly, nations cannot achieve security at each other's expense, or by building a fortress in a fearful world.[19] The key elements of the common-security approach are to develop international confidence; to exercise national self-restraint in military affairs; to emphasize co-operative over competitive security planning; and to promote the common good rather than the pursuit of short-term national interests.

In effect, this means that those providing for our security have to abide by the Golden Rule – one should treat others as one would wish to be treated. After two world wars and a long Cold War, we are finally learning that the failure to account for the security needs of other nations only entrenches hostilities and perpetuates the arms race.[20] We are also learning that our common security will increasingly depend upon ensuring sustainable development, a safe environment, and socio-economic justice. As the latest Palme Commission report acknowledged, security is a broader and more complex concept than protection from arms and war:

> The roots of conflicts and insecurity include poverty, economic disparities within nations and between them, oppression, and the denial of fundamental freedoms. Unless problems of social and economic underdevelopment are addressed, common security can never be truly attained. New threats are also emerging from environmental problems and the degradation of certain ecosystems. Against these threats to humanity's survival, the adversaries in the East-West conflict no longer stand on opposite sides; they often confront the same dangers – dangers they share as well in North/South relations.[21]

The interrelated problems of ensuring security and sustainable international development are complex and difficult, but they are not beyond solution. By broadening our vision we will be in a better position to manage these tasks. Thus, common security could evolve from a concept intended to protect against war to a comprehensive approach to world peace, social justice, economic development, and environmental protection.[22] The recommendations of the Palme and Bruntland commissions provide a general blueprint of transition strategies for moving in this direction.

As the Group of 78 and New Democratic Party have argued, with the ever-increasing interdependence and transnationalization of security affairs, Canadians have a significant stake in common security. For some forty years our security has been dependent upon the actions and reactions of the two superpowers, between which we are situated. The peaceful management of their relationship poses an unavoidable challenge to Canada. At the same time, Canada cannot insulate itself from the interrelated problems of global militarization, regional violence, underdevelopment, and environmental degradation. This understanding has long been reflected in Canadian foreign policy.[23] Canada's defence commitments and strategies will have to be revised accordingly. As the Palme Commission concluded: 'Security in the nuclear age means common security ... A doctrine of common security must replace the present expedient of deterrence through armaments. International peace must rest on a commitment to joint survival rather than a threat of mutual destruction.'[24]

DETERRENCE

In 1971, the Department of National Defence accepted in its white paper that 'the fearsome logic of mutual deterrence is clearly not a satisfactory long-term solution to the problem of preventing world conflict. But pending the establishment of a better system of security, it is the dominant factor in world politics today.'[25] At the time, it was well understood that the foundation of deterrence is an offensive threat, with Canadians helping to pose a threat to the security of other people – a threat that in turn provokes a reciprocal response – so that the net effect is to reduce our collective security. The action-reaction process underlying the arms race is largely propelled by such threats.

In 1987, the Department of National Defence attempted to portray this strategy as benign, claiming that 'the structure of mutual deterrence today is effective and stable.'[26] However, their assessment of the threat and demand for a major rearmament program suggested that a forty-year commitment to this strategy had, if anything, reduced stability and security, contributing more to international tension and an advanced arms race.

Given the inherent element of fear and threats, deterrence can't be non-provocative. Given economic and technological dynamics, it can't be stable. Stability is constantly undermined by the unrelenting search for military advantage. In the late 1970s and the 1980s, deterrence was expanded to rationalize 'extended deterrence,' the pursuit of escalation dominance, 'credible' war-fighting options – for limited or protracted nuclear and non-nuclear conflicts – and the search for military advantage in counter-force offences and strategic defences. It thus evolved into an even more dangerous strategy.[27] By promoting fear and threatening the destruction of all that it is intended to protect, the pursuit of deterrence continues to undermine a truly stable peace.

This is not to suggest that Canada should attempt to undermine mutual deterrence. It is vitally important to offset trends that would further endanger the retaliatory capability of either side. In the 1980s, the Canadian government wisely responded to the over-zealous strategic aspirations of several allies by repeatedly voicing its preference for a system of stable mutual deterrence.[28] Essentially, the government's problem stems from choosing between the lesser of two evils. As bad security arrangements go, the pursuit of war-fighting options is ominously worse than the pursuit of stable mutual deterrence. To further compound this dilemma, the Bush administration has signalled its intention to pursue the Strategic Defense Initiative, concentrating efforts on the development of a space-based system referred to as 'brilliant pebbles.' As Prime Minister Mulroney warned the Atlantic

Assembly in 1987, 'The great danger is that when deployed in conjunction with counter-force weapons, strategic defence will produce first-strike options.'[29] That the government's preference for stable deterrence has been challenged, and to a certain extent surpassed, by developments in military technology and doctrine now justifies assessing a wider range of options.

It is important to recognize three salient points: first, the military threat has changed; second, Canada's armed forces need not be committed to deterrence; and third, those who pursue the strategy don't need Canada to support their efforts.

The conventional military threat has subsided considerably and a new approach is now required. In a fundamental reassessment of the military balance in Europe, a 1989 report by the U.S. defence intelligence community concluded that 'for the past several years the Soviet Union and its Warsaw Pact allies have been incapable of quickly launching a massive attack against the West' – a conclusion that undermines the assumptions behind existing NATO strategy and military deployments.[30] As previously mentioned, the Soviet Union has also undertaken a number of unilateral initiatives to promote confidence and peaceful coexistence. Soviet military forces are in a process of restructuring. An emphasis in their military planning is being placed upon a number of new recommendations, several of which were initially put forth by peace researchers: relinquishing the capacity for surprise attack; shifting conventional forces to a non-offensive defence posture; and maintaining a 'reasonable sufficiency of forces.'

Contrary to the conspiracy theories claiming that it is a guise or trick intended to weaken Western resolve, the new Soviet thinking has been followed in practice.[31] Acknowledging that 'the situation is already in the process of significant change,' the International Institute of Strategic Studies' *Military Balance 1989–1990* states that 'Eastern force reductions have begun and, together with reorganization plans and reported changes in doctrine and training patterns (though the latter are difficult to ascertain with absolute assurance), do now support Soviet claims of new thinking. Even the unilateral reductions will, once complete, virtually eliminate the surprise attack threat which has so long concerned NATO planners.'[32] The WTO is rapidly dismantling. As previously mentioned, it can no longer be seen as an effective military alliance. The phased withdrawal of all Soviet forces from other Eastern European nations is now an objective of Soviet policy. The conservative historian Sir Michael Howard recently wrote: 'There is now real scope for reconsidering a defence policy based upon the kind of worst-case analysis that has governed Western strategic policy towards the Soviet Union since the days of Stalin.'[33]

Irrespective of whether these new developments are discomforting to Canada's defence and foreign-policy establishment, they do call in question the long-term viability of Canada's current defence and alliance relations. Over the past forty years, Canada's defence effort has been significantly determined by its membership in the NATO alliance. This need no longer be the case.

NATO

The world is fast becoming less polarized. Hence, there are greater prospects for a dissolution of the WTO and NATO. Members of both alliances are once again exercising their rights of national self-determination and pursuing a much more conditional alignment. Countries such as West Germany, Hungary, and Denmark have departed from the fold of alliance conformity and demanded that the larger allies pay heed to their political and regional-security concerns. A wide range of new defence arrangements are now on the political agenda. Neither of the major alliances will remain capable of dominating security relations in the 1990s. The diverse interests of member states are often incompatible and increasingly difficult to co-ordinate.

Whereas a previous consensus within NATO over military doctrine had fractured by the mid-1980s, by the end of the decade it appeared that the conflicts over burden-sharing, nuclear-force modernization, and conventional-force reductions might strain relations beyond repair. There has been discussion on the need for a new approach that would allow members to assume greater responsibility for their particular regions and involve a more feasible division of labour. The message of Senator Sam Nunn, chair of the U.S. Senate Armed Services Committee, to the International Institute of Strategic Studies is of particular relevance to Canada: 'I believe the time has come to look seriously at the opportunity for specialization through build-down. Each allied country should play the instruments it plays best rather than trying to stage an entire symphony orchestra ... H.L. Menken once said: "For every complicated question there is an answer that is simple or easy and wrong." The answers to these questions will not be simple or easy; but if NATO's answers are not to be wrong, we must think anew.'[34] Canada's defence effort has long reflected the problems inherent in attempting to stage what Senator Nunn referred to as an entire symphony orchestra. Our armed forces have been overextended in an effort to meet numerous commitments, with the Department of National Defence attempting to maintain a scaled-down version of a great power's navy, air force, and army.

One directly related consideration that has already caused great anxiety within the defence establishment is the looming resource crisis. The members of the WTO and NATO are not in a position to maintain the high levels of defence spending that characterized the 1980s. With limited resources and declining public support, the armed forces in many countries will be forced to accept a declining share of their national budgets and fewer advanced weapon systems. Hence, the recent emphasis on specialization and build-down.

Admiral Sir James Eberle's acronym 'MUD' – mutual unilateral degradation – characterizes a very possible scenario for the armed forces of the 1990s.[35] As the price of major weapon platforms soar, governments and armed forces will be faced with the choice of either restructuring their military commitments and force postures or gradually approaching 'MUD.' This warning was recently heard in Ottawa. Speaking to an audience of defence industrialists, Canada's minister of national defence, Bill McKnight, cited Norm Augustine's 'First Law of Impending Doom': 'That law states that in the year 2054, based on current price projections, the entire United States defence budget will purchase just one aircraft. This will have to be shared by the Air Force and the Navy, 3½ days each per week, except for leap year, when it will be made available to the Marines for the extra day.'[36] The cost of seeking to remain close to the leading edge of military technology is increasing and can be prohibitive.[37] But as one former chief of defence staff predicts, 'If the money runs out, the Department will give some time and consideration to the alternative defence ideas.'[38] 'Specialization' and 'build-down' will be inevitable. So, too, are changes to Canada's overseas defence commitments.

For one, there is no longer a requirement for Canada to maintain forces in Europe. In the face of a considerably reduced threat – one that is no longer capable of overwhelming Western European defences – there is simply no strategic justification for maintaining a Canadian troop presence. There is little doubt that Canadian and American forces will be reduced if not entirely withdrawn from NATO's Central Front. Neither the United States nor European members of NATO require Canadian military assistance. Irrespective of whether the initial rationale for this commitment was political or military, if it is neither needed nor desired, it is time to consider packing up.

Timing the withdrawal, however, is of considerable political importance. After over forty years of providing a military commitment to NATO's Central European Front, neither the United States nor Canada will want to be seen deserting the flag in Europe prior to 1992, when that continent assumes an integrated political and economic structure. The outgoing chief of defence staff, General Paul Manson, warned that 'Canada must not be the unraveler.'[39] Too much capital and effort has been invested to risk departing on bad terms.

Yet while Canada need not prompt the unravelling of the NATO alliance, it is now only responsible to be prepared and to ease our way towards a safe exit. Canada might help in facilitating the required transition. Negotiations to achieve greater stability at lower levels of conventional forces are now underway in Vienna. Hopefully, a withdrawal of Canadian forces in Europe will be negotiated to coincide with a withdrawal of WTO forces. Arranging some form of East-West symmetry would help to allay any fears of a unilateral move disturbing a 'balance' or stability.

In the short term, as an alternative to the deployment of Canadian forces abroad, the government might again explore the requirements of upgrading a fly-over commitment to NATO's Northern Flank. A light-armed air-transportable brigade could be based in Canada to fulfil commitments to both NATO and the United Nations.[40] It should be remembered that Canada is a NATO region and there is no NATO obligation to deploy the armed forces away from Canadian territory.

Canada's influence on the international stage need not suffer from such a troop withdrawal. After over forty years, it remains unclear whether Ottawa ever exercised the influence that was supposedly derived from committing forces to Europe. In 1984, Prime Minister Pierre Trudeau stated that he had attended four of the six summit meetings the NATO alliance had held since its foundation, and that at none of them was there any real consultation. As he said, 'Any attempt to start a discussion .. was met with stony embarrassment, or strong objection.'[41] It would appear that the multilateral counterweight was seldom used.[42] As early as 1972, Colin Gray argued that the deployment of Canadian forces in Europe was unnecessary. As he suggested: 'Possible damage to Canada's "access" to allied deliberation should be countered by a far more determined programme of domestic Canadian strategic studies / arms control / peace research cerebral activity. The path to influence and relevance in discussions of international security lies not through military tokenism, but through an endeavour to have arguments of value to contribute.'[43]

In the aftermath of the Cold War and NATO's fortieth anniversary, the lingering question is, Where do we go from here? West European post-war recover is now complete. NATO's relevance is quickly declining. This alliance was never intended to exist forever. As the old cliché goes, the rationale for NATO was to keep the Soviets out (of Western Europe), the Americans in (Western Europe), and the Germans down. Times have changed!

In the short term, NATO and the WTO may be required to provide reassurance amidst the uncertainty of revolutionary change. However, it should be recognized that these military alliances were called into being to deal with the threat of each other. They are inappropriate for dealing with conflicts or tension elsewhere in the world. These institutions have thrived upon military confrontation and it is unlikely they could be sufficiently reformed so as to promote political co-operation.[44] In the words of Major-General Leonard Johnson (ret.), 'These alliances have squandered an enormous amount of money over the years without producing a permanent form of security. They've stood in the way of detente and permanent reconciliation.'[45]

Serious thought now has to be accorded to the alternatives. As Tina Viljoen and Gwynne Dyer warned several years ago, 'We have to get ahead of events and manage the dismantling of the alliances rationally, with some agreed idea about what kind of security regime will eventually replace them. Otherwise, the whole structure will fall in on our heads one day in an atmosphere of panic and crisis.'[46] Replacing the blocs with a new security regime is now feasible. It will, nevertheless, force a reassessment of priorities and practices. There are also options in this respect.

Initially, Canada might pursue a policy of semi-alignment, a conditional alignment wherein support is provided within the NATO alliance structure for strictly defensive activities and arrangements – those deemed to be in the interests of Canadian and common security. Writing in 1971, Nils Orvik referred to the semi-aligned as practising partial participation within a formal alliance arrangement. 'They were states which are formally aligned, but which have made certain explicit reservations as to the degree of involvement in the alliance.'[47] In 1986, a group of scholars argued that substantial elements of semi-alignment within an alliance would be a favourable development, providing restraint and a moderating influence on the alliance and helping to limit rash or bellicose acts.[48] Adopting a policy of semi-alignment might put a Canadian government in a better position to decide for itself what would be acceptable defence commitments.

As the alliances proceed to unwind, there is also a good case to be made for considering Viljoen and Dyer's model of Finnish neutrality tied to a security guarantee.[49] Neutrality, however, would not be cheap. As Dyer and Viljoen acknowledged several years ago, such a policy might be harder than it looks, possibly entailing a number of costly acquisitions. Nevertheless, in this very new environment, there is likely to be more leeway and tolerance for innovative policies whether they entail semi-alignment, non-alignment, or neutrality. As we shall see, the military requirements may not be as extensive as previously projected.

Irrespective of the approach adopted, it will be hard to ignore Rear-Admiral Fred Crickard's warning that 'We can no longer afford the luxury of a defence establishment that is overwhelmingly alliance driven.'[50] As General Gérard Thériault, former Canadian chief of defence staff, testified in early 1990, 'Conceptually there has to be just a more compelling and lasting and solid basis, I would suggest, to our defence policy than what I might describe as NATO "me-tooism."'[51] For many of the same reasons, we must now also question NORAD 'me-tooism.'

NORAD

In 1991, the North American Aerospace Defence Command agreement (NORAD) comes up for renewal. William Winegard, the chairman of the standing committee that dealt with NORAD renewal in 1986, acknowledged that new technology was challenging comfortable certainties and familiar assumptions; that North American aerospace defence might be approaching a watershed.[52]

Bilateral defence co-operation between Canada and the United States is no longer a continental imperative. It is widely acknowledged that the United States will shortly have little need of Canadian support for obtaining surveillance, early warning, or any other military measure required for deterrence. In 1982, John Hamre, a professional staff member of the U.S. Senate Armed Services Committee, observed that 'today's technology provides an opportunity for long-distance detection without relying on Canadian participation. It is a cornerstone of United States relations with Canada that there should be collaboration in the defence of North America. Time and technology are making that a matter of choice, not of necessity.'[53] As the 1987 SCEAND report on NORAD stated, 'The United States will be able to rely upon its own national land-based and space-based surveillance facilities for warning and assessment of ballistic missiles, space and air-breathing threats.'[54]

NORAD has generally been recognized as a defensive arrangement, providing vital early warning and identification to both Canada and the United States. Its primary activities are in surveillance, warning, control, and air defence. In some respects, Canada has been the beneficiary of this arrangement: gaining access to strategic information; avoiding the considerable costs associated with independent surveillance and air defence; and, in part, benefiting from relatively smooth continental defence relations. However, in the 1980s many Canadians expressed concern about NORAD on account of its shift to an aerospace focus and its association with the American Strategic Defense Initiative, the Strategic Defense Architecture-2000 program, and the Air Defense Initiative (ADI). There are legitimate fears that NORAD is becoming part of a larger war-fighting infrastructure.[55]

Relations developed through NORAD have not been without cost. One result of such close military co-operation is that sectors within DND have adopted an unquestioning role as junior partners in the defence of the continent. This adoption of American strategic assumptions and priorities has certainly influenced, if not determined, Canada's defence posture. The Pentagon unilaterally determines the strategic objectives of NORAD; Canada follows. In an earlier period, Dalton Camp wrote: 'Military men are fond of saying NORAD "costs us nothing." It has already cost us a fortune in wasted time, material and manpower, self respect and national integrity ... It corrupted the Canadian people as it corrupted their political leaders, who so cheerfully allowed themselves to be employed to serve the purposes of another nation's policy.'[56] Since then, Canadian surveillance assets have become less important to NORAD and Canadian officials are receiving less access to American surveillance data. If the United States no longer requires Canadian territory or the support of Canada's armed forces to maintain surveillance, early warning, or deterrence, then it is an appropriate time to negotiate a new arrangement for managing continental defence.

Extensive bilateral defence co-operation is not essential to protect the northern part of North America. An independent defence of Canadian territory can no longer be dismissed as economically or strategically unsound. With a reallocation of resources from the other commitments that are likely to be cancelled, Canada's armed forces could be well positioned to undertake the surveillance and patrol of Canadian territory.

If Ottawa was to put a serious case to Washington for negotiating a new arrangement, it is unlikely the Americans would insist that we continue to play the old game according to their rules. There are bilateral agreements that establish the right of each nation to pursue its own approach to defence. As far back as 1947, the Canada-U.S. Joint Statement on Defence Collaboration acknowledged that 'each country retains control over military activities undertaken on its territory and is legally free to determine the extent of its military cooperation with the other.'[57] If the Brezhnev doctrine of imposing conformity on neighbouring states is unacceptable in Eastern Europe, it surely is unacceptable here in the West.

This is not meant to suggest that Canada should forsake the defence of its allies. Nor is it to imply that Canada build its own fortress and withdraw to an isolationist stance. The rationale for pursuing a new arrangement is not mean-spirited self-interest or narrow nationalism. Rather, it is the desire to encourage constructive internationalism and a commitment to multilateralism through international law and the United Nations. Such shifts are in our common long-term interest. In this period of rapid change, it will be important to reassure one's friends and allies that their legitimate security interests are not being ignored.

However, as Major-General Richard Rohmer (ret.) asked: 'Why shouldn't we be rethinking the entire raison d'etre of our armed forces, reshaping them with entirely new purposes, tasks and roles that reflect the realities of the end of the twentieth century, not those of World War II and the decade immediately following it?'[58] Our assessments are now complicated by the encouraging, yet near overwhelming, pace of change in security relations. As the Palme Commission noted: 'Military force planning should be based on a comprehensive concept of security which encompasses not only an assessment of military threats, but also an understanding of international political change and the possible outcomes of negotiations for disarmament.'[59] It is increasingly important that our defence policies are consistent with our long-term security objectives. If the defence effort is to be supported, it has to maintain domestic trust and inspire international confidence. The armed forces will need appropriate guidelines if they are to remain effective guardians of the public interest.[60]

Unfortunately, it will likely be some time before we see a universal commitment to disarmament and development. Conflict will not vanish from international life. Nor will we see political co-operation replace military rivalry until we strengthen global institutions and develop better mechanisms for ensuring the peace. In the foreseeable future, nations will continue to maintain armed forces and, when deemed necessary or advantageous, some will take action to defend their interests.

REASSESSING THE THREAT

The 1971 white paper on defence observed that 'a catastrophic war between the superpowers constitutes the only major military threat to Canada.'[61] Shortly thereafter, Colin Gray noted that 'the Canadian adversary is the system of international politics, and its military foundations, that would render Canada the recipient of nuclear spill-over from the conflict of others.'[62] There is no direct conventional military threat to Canada. Aside from the United States, no state is in a position to invade Canadian territory. We are extremely fortunate in that there are no enemy states with aggressive ambitions seeking to undermine Canadian security. The greatest immediate danger that confronts Canada and indeed the world as a whole is not deliberate Soviet or American aggression, but any activity that might lead to a war between these states. While there are risks that a crisis might inadvertently or accidentally escalate to war, few analysts believe that any of the major military powers intends or has cause to launch a premeditated assault. The threat is systemic. It is directly related to military competition, particularly the search for war-fighting options. Unfortunately, many of the strategic systems underlying this threat will be with us for some time to come. They cannot simply be dismissed or wished away.

Another threat arises from the widespread proliferation of nuclear and chemical weapons. At the beginning of the 1980s, the official nuclear club comprised the United States, the Soviet Union, France, China, and the United Kingdom. By the end of the decade, membership in the club expanded (unofficially) to include Argentina, Brazil, India, Israel, Pakistan, and South Africa. The Stockholm International Peace Research Institute has identified twenty-four countries, most in the Third World, that either have ballistic missiles or are developing long-range rockets that can be used as ballistic missiles.[63] As Douglas Roche notes, 'Such missiles can be armed with chemical or nuclear warheads.'[64] The risk of serious regional conflict has increased, fuelled by runaway population growth, environmental degradation, poverty, and access to advanced military technology. Canada can neither ignore nor isolate itself from these conflicts.

In the absence of any easily identifiable enemy, we have to revise our defence to deal with a number of new challenges. In the 1990s, our common adversary remains the system of international politics – its military and economic foundations that risk security with arms races, militarism, environmental degradation, underdevelopment, and the unequal distribution of resources.

At this time there is certainly a more relevant role for Canada's armed forces, one more attuned to the security requirements of the nuclear age than geared to fight in a major war, whether it be in Europe or in North America. As early as 1946, the influential military strategist Bernard Brodie noted: 'Thus far the chief purpose of our military establishment has been to win wars. From now on its chief purpose must be to avert them.'[65] At about the same time, Albert Einstein pointed out that we cannot simultaneously prepare for and prevent wars. In the nuclear age, there is little to be said for the old Roman dictum *si vis pacem para bellum* (if you want peace prepare for war).

One lesson of this age is that we just can't fight our way to peace. In the past, the emphasis in defence planning (and defence spending) has been largely upon military tasks. However, in the 1990s, there are certainly fewer strictly military tasks that require a capacity to apply or threaten to apply force on behalf of the state. Given the widely recognized risks associated with war-fighting, the emphasis in defence is likely to shift away from maintaining combat readiness and preparations for total war to the para-military tasks of peacekeeping, surveillance, and patrol and to the non-military tasks of arms control, conflict resolution, and mediation.[66]

If a primary objective of Canadian security policy is to reduce the risk of war, then a first task is to prevent conditions that might lead to war.[67] One popular analogy that has helped us to conceptualize the interdependence of the current strategic environment is that of two people in a canoe – one can't be secure by attempting to destabilize the other. Security, therefore, is a condition that can be found only in common. Since we Canadians are in the 'middle of the canoe,' between these military powers, it is our responsibility to manage this middle ground so as to maintain peace. Our security is inextricably dependent upon our ability to limit the potentially destabilizing activities of any power on our territory. Our location not only imposes an obligation to provide early warning of any incursion; it also offers a unique opportunity for mediating this northern relationship.

For our purposes it is important to distinguish between the threats we currently face and those anticipated in the future. Since several of these anticipated threats will arise as a result of trends in military technology and doctrine, they are not yet predetermined or beyond our capacity to avert.[68]

For some forty years it has been accepted that the threat of an attack over the Arctic is diminished by the distance between the two superpowers. The distance provides a measure of strategic comfort because it allows time for detection, warning, and, if necessary, retaliation. Coupled with uncertainties related to the performance characteristics of intercontinental weapons in the northern environment, this distance has been a stabilizing factor. Given the vast expanse and sparse population of the northern region, there were very few concerns of a conflict arising or escalating out of any military activities in the area.

The Canadian government could soon face a more difficult situation. As the conflict in Europe is resolved, special efforts may be required to prevent it from resurfacing in the North. This area has the potential to become a new focus of military rivalry. Stability in the region may be jeopardized by several disturbing trends: the development of advanced air- and sea-launched cruise missiles, aggressive anti-submarine-warfare strategies, and strategic defences. There are also fears that Ottawa may concede to U.S. pressure and participate in the development of an active air defence system. As John Lamb warned in March of 1990:

> Ironically, one serious (and expensive) military threat that Canadians will soon have to confront stems directly from the prospective conclusion of a U.S.-Soviet strategic arms reduction (START) agreement. Expected in June, that agreement will result in a major increase in the Soviet air launched cruise missile and strategic bomber forces, and Canada will come under heavy pressure from Washington (whose preference it was, by the way, to increase cruise levels) to do more on air defence. NORAD comes up for renewal in 1991 and none of this is going to result in defence savings for Canada. Far from it.[69]

Canada at present has a very limited capacity to monitor, patrol, or control activities within its territory. Although the Department of National Defence was somewhat alarmist in warning that 'Canadians cannot ignore that what was once a buffer could become a battleground,' there are valid concerns that Canadian territory, airspace, and waters may be acquiring new strategic importance.[70]

Should these trends proceed, they may reduce the time

available for early warning and decision-making, thus reducing the stability derived from the region. They pose a serious challenge to Canada in that they may promote the militarization of the northern region. As this development would stem partly from a desire to attain a wider array of war-fighting options, it could incur a higher level of fear and risk. Yet this militarization is not inevitable.

What appears to have been overlooked in the 1987 defence white paper is the possibility of resurrecting this buffer. We could use our territory so as to reduce these threats. In 1986 John Lamb also told the Special Joint Committee on Canada's International Relations that 'Canada has an opportunity to use its newly enhanced strategic importance to take a lead in shaping the strategic environment for the benefit of both Canadian and international security.'[71]

TOWARDS COMMON SECURITY: THE OUTLINE OF A RELEVANT CANADIAN DEFENCE

A Canadian Security Buffer

A government could pursue the option of using the armed forces to ensure that Canadian territory and airspace remained an effective security buffer. This approach would call for a monitored and enforced geographic disengagement, one that would provide a greater measure of distance and time between both powers, one that couldn't be exploited to any military advantage, and one that denied foreign military access (for purposes other than pre-arranged surveillance) to Canadian territory, airspace, and waters. It would help ensure that there was no risk of a threat to any party's legitimate interests emanating from within the area. Essentially, the idea is to make our territory militarily irrelevant and stem any future deployment of forward-based systems that might be used for war-fighting purposes. If effectively managed, it might build confidence, reduce American and Soviet security concerns, and, possibly, even reduce their defence expenditures.

The idea is not new. As early as 1957, U.S. Ambassador George Kennan suggested establishing buffers to make an era between potential combatants militarily irrelevant.[72] Ernie Regehr has argued that it is Canada's job to see that activity and installations within its borders serve to stabilize the international order. As he writes: 'Canadian resources should be used not to add to the burdensome inventory of weapons and new weapons technology but rather to advance the means of reducing and eliminating those weapons. To do this, Canadians must take charge of their own territory to assure both of this country's neighbours, north and south, that neither is surreptitiously using Canadian territory as a platform from which to threaten the other.'[73]

A Canadian security buffer would be a peace-time confidence-building measure. It is well understood that in the event of a major war, neither of our neighbours to the north or to the south will stop to pay any regard to Canadian sovereignty or to Canada's defence effort. In such a situation, an effective defence is neither economically feasible nor technologically possible. Yet by guarding Canadian territory and ensuring it remained a buffer in peace-time, Canadians would be taking a useful step to promote our common security interests and to avoid conditions that might lead to war.

Canada has already earned international respect for its military restraint and, in particular, its unilateral decision not to build, store, or deploy nuclear weapons on Canadian territory. An additional method for signalling Canada's determination to refuse to accept passively the unchecked militarization of this region would be to declare Canada a nuclear-weapon-free zone (NWFZ).[74]

A NWFZ is a 'defined geographic area within which the possession, deployment, storage, transit, manufacture, testing or other support of nuclear weapons and nuclear weapon systems is prohibited.'[75] Although it might be construed as a departure from the tradition of continental military co-operation, such a step would not entail a very radical change. At the present time, no nuclear weapons are stored or deployed on Canadian territory. There would, however, be a number of changes required and restrictions placed upon Canada and its neighbours. Canada would be required to deny activities such as the production and testing of the guidance system for the cruise missile; the port visits of any ships that might be carrying nuclear weapons; sea and air transport of nuclear weapons through Canadian territory; and the training or testing of nuclear-capable delivery systems on Canadian territory.

This would be a peace-time measure to restrict the spread of nuclear weapons, to withdraw political and technological support from the nuclear arms race, and to build trust between neighbouring nations.[76] Making Canada a NWFZ would also be conducive to establishing our territory as a security buffer between the two superpowers. If effectively managed, these two initiatives would represent a confidence-building measure by verifying the absence of foreign military activity; a measure of zonal disarmament by restricting nuclear weapons; and a measure of geographic disengagement through the assertion of Canadian sovereignty and the reassertion of distance and time between the military powers.

A Canadian Non-offensive Defence Posture

This country could help to shape an era of common security by devising a defence posture that is truly defensive in nature and that indicates to the rest of the world that the protection of our territory is effectively exercised in a manner that promotes the security of all nations. An option worthy of consideration is the endorsement of a non-offensive defence posture.

The rationale for a non-offensive defence posture has already been established in previous Canadian defence policy statements. In the 1971 white paper on defence it was stressed that

> a constant criterion for evaluating all aspects of policy is the determination to avoid any suggestion of the offensive use of Canadian Forces to commit aggression, or to contribute to such action by another state. Such a policy would be unthinkable and unacceptable. With a view to ensuring the protection of Canada and contributing to the maintenance of stable mutual deterrence, Canada's resources, its territory, and its armed forces will be used solely for purposes which are defensive in the judgement of the Government of Canada.[77]

A number of international security problems arise not only from the weapons that are deployed, but also from offensive military doctrines and intimidating-force postures. One of the major impediments to a durable peace stems from the misperceptions and fears engendered by respective military strategies for 'forward' and 'offensive' defence. The conditions for an arms race, and possibly even war, were fuelled by the impressions that such defence postures may not serve purely defensive functions.

Obviously, Canada's defence posture has not been noted as one that posed a major threat in this respect. Yet the solution to this larger problem is to shift, where possible, to more defensive arrangements. The recent contributions in the field of non-offensive defence have helped to set an important global standard, establishing criteria that can be applied universally.[78] In the words of Randall Forsberg, 'The concept of nonoffensive defence is central to developing a truly stable and enduring international peace, characterized by a demilitarized, democratic international system; the lowest safe levels of standing armed force and military spending; and greatly reduced nuclear arsenals – in general conditions that ultimately will make thinkable the complete abolition of nuclear weapons.'[79]

Whereas a non-offensive defence shares several of the military objectives of traditional defence – to dissuade deliberate aggression and to defend if necessary, it also has an important political element. By shifting the focus to defence rather than military confrontation and the offensive requirements of deterrence, one eliminates the basis for fear and misperception. As it becomes evident that the intent is solely to defend, one undermines the action-reaction process that sustains the arms race. As Anders Boserup writes, 'Politically, [non-offensive defence] would attempt to eliminate the sources of hostility and arms competition and build a climate of trust in which further arms reductions and detente can take place ... It is defensive only in the military sense. As an instrument of broadly conceived security policy, non-offensive defence is clearly an aggressive 'offensive' tool which each side can use to undermine militarism on the other side by denying it the benefit of a credible enemy.'[80]

Whereas many of the non-offensive defence models recently

designed for other contexts are unsuitable for Canada, the core assumptions of non-offensive defence are very appropriate. The underlying idea of a non-offensive defence is that nations should relinquish offensive capability and support for provocative strategies in order to ensure that military means conform with defensive ends.[81] Military arrangements, strategies, and weapons are structured so as to remain consistent with strictly defensive objectives.[82] Such a defence discards any association with nuclear weapons and threats. It converts conventional forces so as to better contribute to local or territorial defence. Defence and defence alone – in the narrow sense of policing, protecting sovereignty, defending from within one's own territory, and working to maintain international peace and stability – are the only justifiable rationales for military capabilities. Canada's defence could be structured accordingly without going to great effort.

A commitment of this nature would impose several constraints. Any military activity deemed to be provocative or destabilizing would have to be terminated. For example, the armed forces would likely have to forgo participation in affairs such as NATO's follow-on-forces attack strategy, the U.S. Army's air-land battle strategy, any refinement of strategic anti-submarine-warfare capabilities, and permission for testing of offensive systems such as the advanced cruise missile or for low-level bomber training.

So there are advantages to a non-offensive defence posture: first, it is conducive to good long-term relations with other countries; second, it removes any justification for being attacked or even being targeted by a potential enemy; third, it would establish firm policy criteria by which the government could forestall some of the more destabilizing trends that may arise if the strategic importance of Canadian territory increases; fourth, it is conducive to the limited defence requirements of a security buffer; and fifth, it is a defence posture compatible with the foreign-policy goals of confidence-building, nuclear disarmament, and the limitation of various kinds of offensive conventional weaponry.[83] It is now an appropriate time to renew and strengthen Canada's previous commitment to the pursuit of a non-offensive defence posture.

Within the next few years, Canadians may also have to devise a new strategy for the armed forces. They will need relevant guidelines if they are to be effective in their activities. There are options in this respect.

Dissuasion

Rather than attempt to deter aggression through participation in a strategy that relies on threats, a more appropriate strategy for Canada's armed forces might focus upon dissuasion. Whereas deterrence refers to intimidation, usually by threatening retaliation and punishment, dissuasion refers to caution and discouragement by emphasizing persuasion. Canada has no need of a confrontational strategy or one that presupposes an enemy. In the words of Rear-Admiral Elmar Schmaling of West Germany:

> War must be prevented with another kind of military – one that provides the greatest possible freedom of action during a political crisis. That is to say, defence preparations must be flexible and leave time for political decision, not create a momentum of their own that is irreversible ... In other words, whereas the objective until now has been to prevent war by means of a capability to wage war, in the future, it must be to prevent war by means of an ability to manage any crisis that may arise. This would mean an end to the predominance of military thinking in foreign relations.[84]

A general strategy of dissuasion, sharing several similar objectives, was proposed in the earlier détente period.[85] For Canadian purposes, dissuasion might be considered as those defensive military and non-military activities that promote war avoidance. Such a strategy should not be equated with pacifism. It would require a military apparatus, albeit with strong restraints, limiting defence to the resistance of aggression and stressing primarily non-lethal methods.[86] The military focus would likely be upon vigilance and the denial of Canadian territory for any activities deemed to be destabilizing. Potential intruders would have to be cautioned and persuaded that Canada had a capacity to respond. The armed forces would require a capacity to establish a presence and, if necessary, arrange an immediate controlled response.

Unambiguous rules of engagement will be necessary to ensure that any conflict (or even a violation of Canadian law) is dealt with and controlled. These rules could help to ensure that control is established at the lowest level of force. When dealing with conflicts that entail potentially serious international repercussions or the loss of life, these rules would also have to provide a considerable degree of flexibility. The intent in dissuasion would not be to intimidate or achieve a quick victory in a violent conflict.[87] In the unlikely event of an intrusion or even a small-scale hostility occurring on Canadian territory, it would be the responsibility of the armed forces to resist, to encourage de-escalation, and to impose a stalemate or pause in which diplomacy might take over. Buying time becomes far more important than striking a decisive blow. A fundamental consideration in any conflict would be to have it resolved or terminated without incurring disaster for either party.

Accordingly, with a focus on dissuasion and the peace-time defence of Canada, the means of defence might narrow in one respect (war-fighting), while expanding in several others (surveillance, patrol, peace-keeping, and conflict resolution). If properly managed, such a strategy should be considerably safer than deterrence. For one thing, there would be more room for diplomacy to enter into the resolution of conflict.[88] Dissuasion would also lend itself more readily to common security and co-existence.

Another essential task for Canada will be to revitalize the one international institution that is committed to ensuring common security.

Strengthening the United Nations and World Order

Providing assistance to United Nations' security activities is likely to be a key priority of Canada's defence effort in the 1990s. Support for this institution should be encouraged and expanded. Efforts to strengthen international law and a civilized code of international conduct will help to defend Canada and bolster common security. Canada's primary defence responsibility, as the New Democratic Party and a coalition of church leaders have argued, is to contribute to a just international order.

The United Nations is increasingly recognized as the appropriate organization for co-ordinating international order and a necessary response to the dominant security issues of the next decade. It is simply unique in this respect. No other organization has the credibility and potential capability, the experience, or the range of institutions required by this task.

With a seat on the Security Council, and expertise in the vital areas of peacekeeping and arms-control verification, Canada is well positioned to play a leadership role at the UN. Although criticized by some for not shouldering a fair share of the security burden – having been ranked sixth overall in defence spending within NATO – Canada's rank of fourth overall in contributions to the UN system suggests an exemplary record. In the UN, Canada's influence is real and its potential impact is to be taken seriously. Moreover, as NATO's relevance to European security declines, Canada's one sure option for re-establishing a multilateral counterweight is the United Nations. It may yet prove to be a more effective mechanism in this regard.

Peacekeeping has been declared a cornerstone of Canadian foreign and defence policy for over thirty years. These operations are considered to be one of the most successful innovations of the United Nations. Rod Byers notes that peacekeeping forces can contribute to international peace and stability in a number of ways: they can serve to limit conflict – both in terms of geographic scope and the number of combatants; they can perform a stabilization function, creating an atmosphere in which peacemaking may proceed; they can contribute to escalation control, ensuring that parties not directly involved in the conflict remain uninvolved; they can contribute to confidence-building and enhance the prospects for conflict resolution; and they can perform a verification function with respect to agreed treaties and arrangements between parties to a dispute.[89]

Canada has an excellent record of participation and support in this respect. Andrew Cohen writes that 'Canada is already the world's most visible peace-keeper – a member of almost every mission, a leading contributor in blood and treasure, a crusader for the cause.'[90] The record is excellent, but it could still be improved.

With a disturbing number of regional conflicts still on the agenda, the world will be calling for United Nations peacekeepers in the 1990s. Plans have already been drawn up for several new operations. Unfortunately, there have been occasions when the assistance and material requested by the UN secretary-general could not be provided. Peacekeeping could now be accorded a higher status on the list of Canadian defence priorities. It is time, as John Hay has argued, to raise the ceiling on manpower committed to this task – now only 2000 out of 87,000 in uniform.[91]

Another option that would follow in a fine tradition of support for internationalism was the recent proposal for developing a Canadian centre devoted to the training of both Canadian and foreign forces for UN peacekeeping activities. In 1986, John Sigler described Canada as having the best military peacekeeping training program anywhere in the world.[92] A Special Joint Committee on Canada's international relations recommended that Canada continue to make its peacekeeping expertise available to the armed forces of other countries.[93]

In the near future, consideration may be given to expanding the scope of peacekeeping operations. Some governments have begun to recognize that it is in their long-term interest to strengthen the United Nations' capacity to enforce international law. Other nations, especially those engaged in international conflicts, will be unlikely to forgo military solutions until they can be assured that their legitimate security interests will be defended. As early as 1963, Tommy Douglas proposed that Canada provide a conventional military force to support a permanent international police force. The objective was to develop a capacity to deal with brush fires in different parts of the world.[94] Consideration should be given to a future standing multinational brigade of peacekeepers. Johnathan Power writes that 'the Security Council needs to think about pre-emptive peacekeeping – sending UN observers and soldiers into regions of conflict which while smoking, have not yet burst into flames.'[95]

Greater efforts might be accorded to co-ordinating a new division of labour, encouraging each contributor to a UN standing brigade to specialize in a particular area of expertise, much as our own armed forces have developed special skills in the much-needed area of communications.[96] A UN peacekeeping force could even be based in Canada, ready to leave as soon as directed by the UN secretary-general. And, given the resurgence of interest in the UN, it is not inconceivable that a percentage of the funds currently being spent elsewhere in the defence portfolio could be diverted to cover UN expenses. Ensuring that peacemaking coincides with (or at east follows) peacekeeping will be increasingly important. While the immediate containment of violence is crucial, a lasting peace is likely to depend on whether or not the underlying causes of a conflict have been addressed.

For their part, a Canadian security buffer, a non-offensive defence posture, and a strategy of dissuasion would provide a model for others to emulate as well as an array of services supportive of UN security functions.

Roles, Requirements, and Other Considerations

A Canadian security buffer, an independent non-offensive defence posture, a strategy of dissuasion, and a strengthening of the United Nations are all consistent with the objective of promoting common security. While they all address a particular problem, they are mutually supportive components of a new defence for Canada. As such, many of the necessary roles and requirements overlap. Moreover, it would appear that the requirements are within our means.

Canada's armed forces must be capable of monitoring, patrolling, and, to a limited extent, controlling Canadian territory. As this task includes a mix of sea-, air-, and land-based operations, a role remains for components of the three services. Essentially, the primary tasks of Canada's land forces will focus on peacekeeping and policing sovereignty; for the navy, one can anticipate an enhanced coast-guard role and responsibility for monitoring and patrolling Canada's territorial waters; and for the air force, the job of surveillance, early warning, patrol, and the maintenance of a limited interception capability (primarily for purposes of identification). An interception capability does not necessitate active air or naval defences capable of stemming an all-out attack.

It would only imply the capacity to meet and identify a peace-time intruder as is consistent with Canada's current approach entailing passive interception for purposes of identification.[97]

Given the resource crisis and level of national debt, a new defence will have to be more cost-effective. And, where possible to this end, an effort should be made to ensure that the defence is dual-capable – in the sense of being conducive to civilian as well as defence missions. The armed forces will have no choice but to expand their support for civilian agencies in areas such as search and rescue, fighting forest fires, and environmental protection.

For reasons related partly to the budget, but more directly to strategic requirements and the 'more probable range of scenarios' anticipated, the emphasis should be upon greater mobility and very-lightly-armed units of all three services. Diversification and flexibility will likely be much more appropriate to meeting Canada's defence needs than extensive combat training and readiness. As the next ten years will be a period of transition marked by uncertainty, it would also be prudent to retain a core of soldiers, seamen, and airmen capable of training a larger force should the need arise.

New skills such as those required for conflict resolution, mediation, and arms-control verification will be increasingly in demand. If trained and equipped to perform these roles, the armed forces might enhance their peacekeeping capacity and expand their present work under United Nations auspices. Canada would be in a better position to facilitate the peaceful settlement of regional conflict. Moreover, these are the types of skills that would be required when pursuing a strategy of dissuasion.

Within a non-offensive defence posture our armed forces would be based in Canada. They would have a better capacity to monitor and patrol Canadian territory. A limited control capability would likely be necessary to offset our neighbour's apprehensions. Whereas the requirements of patrolling and controlling Canadian territory overlap, they are often considered as somewhat distinctive operational roles. To patrol Canadian territory simply requires an ongoing commitment to pass regularly over or through all regions of the country. While the effective control of

Canadian territory assumes a patrol capability, for purposes of dissuasion it also requires a capacity for a military response – mobile air, sea, and land forces capable of asserting authority over national territory. The priority is to assure others that we know what is happening within our territory and are capable of organizing a peace-time response.

As noted in chapter 1, Canadian territory and military support have been strategically important to the Americans in at least three respects: intelligence gathering; continental early warning and air defence; and access to Canadian facilities for forward-basing. U.S. advances in surveillance technology have largely overtaken the previous requirement for Canadian military support to ensure surveillance, early warning, and deterrence. Nevertheless, these developments do not obviate Canada's requirement for reliable information, surveillance, and early warning. A Canadian government must be capable of knowing what is happening within and around its territory – all the more so if we wish to assure others that we are capable of maintaining a security buffer. This capability is necessary in order to prevent misperceptions and uncertainty. There are ways, however, in which Canada and the United States might pursue independent defence postures, yet co-operate to provide for one another's common security requirements. In fact, there are now ways in which we might organize a division of labour that would help to reduce both nations' long-term defence expenditures and strategic concerns.

The 1989 'open skies' initiative of the Canadian government may yet allow participants unrestricted aerial surveillance over European and North American skies. According to the initial study drafted by External Affairs, the basic principle would be that participating nations open their skies to regular unarmed, non-combat-type aerial-surveillance flights.[98] The measure should be supported as a means to encourage transparency, reduce military secrecy, and strengthen arms-control verification.[99] Open skies appears to be an appropriate arrangement for providing our neighbours with access to Canadian territory solely for purposes of information-gathering. Signatories to the treaty will likely provide airfields and observers. American and Soviet surveillance planes could make use of the forward operating locations in Canada's North. Surveillance overflights and the occasional 'fuel-up' and 'sleep-over' of unarmed, non-combat-type aircraft would not undermine Canada's status as a security buffer. As a means to engender confidence and transparency, they would certainly help to promote common security.

Canada could negotiate a new arrangement with the United States for co-ordinating continental air defence. In order to present a credible security buffer, Canada will likely require independent ownership and control over the NORAD installations on its territory.[100] At this time, the North Warning System is the only tangible Canadian contribution to the surveillance assets reporting to NORAD.[101] The United States and Canada are already researching the development of more advanced surveillance and early-warning systems. A 1987 report from the Defence Research and Education Centre provides a response worthy of a Canadian government's consideration. It proposed the following:

> The North Warning System, Canadian interceptor aircraft, their bases and logistic support, their command, control and communication systems should be formed into a Canadian Air Defence command at the expiration of the current term of the NORAD agreement in four years' time. If it is within our financial capability, relative to our other objectives, we should at this time buy out the 60% share of the system's cost paid by the United States so that ownership as well as operation should be entirely vested in Canadian hands (apart from the portion located in Alaska). Canada would guarantee to provide to the United States full and continuing access to North Warning System information. In order to ensure that the Soviet Union had no cause to misperceive northern air activity, they should be offered provision of radar information, with appropriate communication by satellite. The United Nations should be offered the same information, should it by that time have created a Monitoring and Verification Agency.[102]

Provision of two-way information and early warning is premised on a similar rationale to the 'open-skies' initiative – greater transparency, co-operation, and confidence-building. As the report stated, 'This would assure a common picture of northern and polar traffic, a means of sorting out discrepancies and preventing surprise attack, that would be in the security interests of all.'[103] As the North Warning System was only planned as an interim response to the evolving nature of airborne threats, the United States may be quite willing to sell these assets. According to a study sponsored by the Canadian Centre for Arms Control and Disarmament, this would be a one-time expenditure of $1.236 billion ($936 million for the North Warning System, $300 million for the northern fighter aircraft bases called forward operating locations). There would also be an $81.8 million additional annual cost for operating the Northern Warning System.[104]

While the acquisition of the North Warning System based on Canadian territory would address a large share of Canadian surveillance requirements, there are concerns that the limited focus on northern-perimeter warning provides inadequate coverage of our territory.[105] A report from the Canadian Institute for International Peace and Security suggests that 'were Canada to establish a totally independent air defence system, and in the absence of U.S. continental cooperation and information sharing, some degree of additional radar coverage from Canadian territory would be necessary.[106] Aside from a limited-purpose Ministry of Transport Radar Modernization Project intended for control of compliant air traffic in specified zones, Canada will shortly be without a capacity to monitor its internal airspace.

One area that may hold promise in the near future is the development of satellite or space-based radar. The 1985 Report of the Special Committee of the Senate on National Defence noted several advantages provided by a national military space program:

> In this way, Canada could control the use of its own satellites and make sure they remained dedicated to passive detection and surveillance needs. Canadian military satellites over the North could also provide Canadian civil authorities with much useful information about activities in the Arctic and frontier regions. They could, for example, help monitor many forms of air, land and sea movements across the North,

keep track of oil spills and other dangers to the environment, or document the impact of development. They could improve communications with remote settlements and facilitate search and rescue operations, while at the same time enabling Canadian industry to aim at the forefront of world technological development in the space field.[107]

That there would be considerable costs in developing and managing such a space program is undeniable. However, it might promise the best means of assuring continuous, extensive 'area' coverage, as well as reliable early-warning information and the capacity to monitor Canadian territory. Accordingly, it would help to alleviate American security concerns. In the long term, if the system was double-tasked to civilian purposes, it might also prove to be the most cost-effective approach.

Some consideration has been given to the development of a low-powered, limited-purpose space-based radar system capable of imaging aircraft but not cruise missiles. The exact performance capabilities of these systems remain somewhat unclear. David Cox notes that an advantage of a Canadian space-based radar would lie in its ability to monitor all aircraft operating in the Canadian Arctic, and possibly off the east and west coasts. In 1986 he wrote that 'the cost of a small system, assuming a minimum of four radar satellites, might be in the vicinity of $1.5 billion, or as the leading proponent of the system has argued, $300 million per year until the system was in place, and a lesser sum thereafter for replacement satellites.'[108]

Because of the significant costs associated with a more sophisticated space-based radar system that might track cruise missiles, the government has assumed that the most feasible arrangement for project development is in a co-operative venture with the United States. Canadian officials might, however, negotiate an arrangement with their American counterparts to maintain independent signal receiver stations, allowing each party to conduct its own data analysis and interpretation. Such an arrangement might save both parties the costs associated with a go-it-alone development program while providing both with a system that could be used independently.

Canada could also explore the prospects of renewing interest in the 1978 French proposal for an international satellite monitoring agency (ISMA). Canadian scientist and Nobel prize winner John Polyani described the ISMA as a proposal for a type of peacekeeping force in space. He writes that 'the objectives would be to provide credible verification of arms control agreements (which could be simply agreements to demilitarize a buffer zone), and also to provide reassurance in some tense region of the world that forces are not being readied for attack.'[109]

As far back as 1981, a United Nations group of experts studying this proposal concluded that from a technical point of view, it was both feasible to verify the compliance with arms-control treaties and to monitor crisis areas.[110] The proposal calls for a step-by-step approach on the part of an unspecified consortium of nations linked to the UN to supplement the present bilateral U.S.-USSR space surveillance with a multilateral surveillance system. The cost of developing such a capability would certainly decline in a larger co-operative venture.[111] Moreover, the costs might decline significantly were it possible to rent time on the medium-resolution cameras that the Americans and Soviets already have in place.[112] Given the new political environment, it is conceivable that one or perhaps even both of the superpowers would consent to providing an ISMA with access to some of their surveillance technology. Many of the previous political impediments to such an initiative are slowly being overcome.[113]

Canada may shortly be in a better position to provide the United States with an assurance that we are capable of managing the peace-time air defence of our security buffer. By redeploying the thirty-six CF-18s that are now stationed in Europe back to Canada, to supplement the sixty CF-18s and fifty-eight CF-5 tactical fighters that are already deployed here, the armed forces would improve their capacity to patrol territorial airspace. To supplement the eighteen CP-140 Auroras and three new P-3C Arcturus aircraft now assigned to surveillance and patrol, consideration should be given to acquiring the Canadian-built, multipurpose Dash-8 aircraft. With these Canadian systems monitoring and patrolling the security buffer, the United States would only need forward operating locations in Canada for surveillance overflights associated with an open-skies agreement.

Over the past five years, there has also been a growing demand for the surveillance and patrol of Canadian territorial surface and sub-surface waters. A blue-water navy with extensive anti-submarine-warfare capabilities may no longer be required. In order to establish a year-round presence in Canada's territorial waters, a government might consider using the dozen frigates that are being developed as well as a combination of fast patrol boats and ice-breakers. In contrast to submarines and a larger fleet of frigates, the reduced unit costs of this latter combination would allow for a greater number of vessels, and thus for enhanced overall sustainability.[114] Barney Danson, Canada's minister of national defence from 1976 to 1979, argued that ice-breakers would be a more appropriate response than nuclear-powered submarines for meeting our sovereignty and security requirements.[115] Two Polar 8 ice-breakers at a cost of approximately $1.2 billion would provide Canada with a capability of operating in all northern waters as well as an all-season platform for the dispersal of helicopters and hovercraft.[116] Together, these vehicles and aircraft would enhance Canada's capacity to monitor and patrol territorial waters, expanding search-and-rescue abilities as well as providing better support for fisheries and environmental protection.

In 1987, it was suggested that sub-surface surveillance, especially under-ice detection in northern waters, necessitated the acquisition of nuclear-powered attack submarines. The Department of National Defence has since moved to develop an alternative underwater, under-ice surveillance capability. Passive detection systems such as sonars and fixed sea-bed acoustic surveillance systems placed at strategic locations throughout Canadian territorial waters now appear to be an appropriate, cost-effective option.[117] In a discussion of these systems in 1987, Vice-Admiral Nigel D. Brodeur, deputy chief of defence staff, stated that 'those are technologically feasible. We have proved the capabilities, but such a permanent system is not there yet.'[118] These systems would help to provide the Canadian government with an adequate knowledge of the use of Canada's ice-covered waters. Canada would have a capacity to detect intrusions.

Dissuading such intrusions might also be possible without acquiring submarines. A variety of new non-lethal weapon systems have been developed to deal with an array of similar scenarios. For example, research by the Swedish Ministry of Defence has led to the development of magnetically affixed noise and non-explosive penetrating devices that could be used for dissuading foreign submarine activity in Canadian waters.[119] They do not kill or risk the immediate loss of a crew and vehicle, but, if necessary, they have the potential to reduce operating effectiveness and comfort to a degree that would force an intruder to surface within a short period. The fact that these are non-lethal systems would not reduce their military effectiveness. To the contrary, they could be more readily activated without risking a deadly conflict or escalation. To dissuade further foreign naval activity in northern Canadian waters, such non-lethal systems might be based on an ice-breaker and, if absolutely necessary, deployed from either a helicopter or hovercraft. In the very unlikely circumstance they were required, an intruder would likely be identified, escorted away from Canadian territory, and embarrassed sufficiently to dissuade further activity in the immediate region. The important point is that the conflict would incur a relatively low level of risk to the respective forces involved, and that it could be quickly passed on for resolution at a diplomatic level before significant losses occurred. And, for Canada, this illustration approaches a near-worst-case scenario.

While systems of this nature may appear somewhat unconventional or even quite unnecessary, they force us to question how one would respond in such a circumstance. For purposes of defence and security in the nuclear age, this reassessment is vital. It is worth noting that some of the Soviet and American submarines are carrying an arsenal estimated to have over ten times the destructive power unleashed in the Second World War. Last year's officially endorsed proposal to acquire twelve nuclear-powered attack submarines would have provided the navy with a choice between bumping an intruder with an attack sub, launching a wire-guided torpedo from the same sub, or just doing nothing.

Sweden, unlike Canada, has apparently had the opportunity to use these non-lethal devices on submerged intruders. Wisely, they declined. They are still on the map enjoying neutrality, the highest standard of living in the world, and considerable influence in international forums. This should tell us something about the utility of force in the nuclear age. Dissuasion is really about the farthest any power can go if it has a sincere interest in building international confidence and maintaining a long-term peace. When pursued within an independent, non-offensive defence posture, dissuasion would appear as a safer alternative to the larger threat system of deterrence. Similarly, given the choice between facilitating an ongoing search for war-fighting options, entailing the potential militarization of Canadian territory, or a monitored and patrolled security buffer, the latter would appear to be in everyone's long-term interests.

Defence Spending

Dan Smith has written that the famous question of defence policy is 'How much is enough?' In practice, the answer has always been 'As much as you can get.' It ought to be 'As little as possible to do the job.'[120] Clearly, there is little sense in any defence effort that bolsters Canada's prestige abroad and bankrupts Canadians at home. In 1990, it is difficult to ignore an accumulated debt of approximately $354 billion and annual defence spending exceeding $12 billion. A stated goal of Canadian arms-control and defence policy is to enhance security and stability at the lowest level of forces.[121] Canada now has a unique opportunity to scale back its defence commitments and reduce manpower levels in the land forces. At a time when there is an urgent need to increase funding for overseas development assistance and foreign aid, a persuasive argument can be made for reducing Canadian defence spending. But it is equally clear that there are advantages to a defence that would offset several potentially dangerous trends as well as Canada's presumed dependency on the United States and NATO – allowing Canadians to get on with the important work of promoting common security and sustainable development.

Contrary to Conservative Defence Minister Bill McKnight's assertion that we will have to rely more on our allies, we could be well positioned within the near future to pursue such a new defence. Maintaining the present level of defence spending may be unnecessary if we reallocate some of the money that is currently being spent elsewhere within the defence portfolio.

A 1989 study estimates that Canada might save approximately $668 million per year if European-assigned units were disbanded.[122] While the CF-18s based in Germany would be redeployed to territorial-air-defence tasks, there is virtually no way to justify the maintenance of mechanized brigade groups or heavy armoured forces. In the next few years, Canada's land forces could be reduced from 22,500 regulars and 15,000 reserves to approximately 6000 regulars and 5000 reserves. As the government wisely recognized, there were big savings accrued from cancelling plans for expanding these heavy armour forces with new tanks. They alone were to have cost approximately $2.25 billion. Assuming in a very rough measure that the air forces to be redeployed to Canada account for approximately one third of the $668 million in savings projected, a government would still stand to save close to $444 million yearly by easing its way off of NATO's central front.

At this time it is difficult and somewhat risky to venture the total cost of shifting to the defence posture proposed. Yet, for purposes of comparison, if a government was to reassign the thirty-six CF-18s now in Europe to Canada, acquire the North Warning System ($1.296 billion), a limited-purpose space-based radar surveillance system ($2 billion), two Polar 8 ice-breakers ($1.2 billion), a dozen fast coastal patrol craft ($500 million), and a dozen Dash-8 multi-purpose planes for monitoring and patrolling Canadian airspace and waters ($250 million), Canada could legitimately claim to have an independent defence posture – all at a cost ($5.246 billion) considerably lower than for the previously proposed acquisition of twelve nuclear-powered attack submarines ($8–15 billion).

In the short term, the costs are considerable. Whether they could be managed by shifting spending priorities while reducing the current defence budget remains unclear. However, an independent defence would likely provide significant savings over the long term. There would be fewer pressures to acquire expensive state-of-the-art conventional weapon systems and less incentive to participate in the costly 'big-league' roles that have fostered tension and propelled the arms race.

Moreover, as previously mentioned, the government could equip the armed forces with systems that contributed to an array of functions. The merit of such a defence is partly in its compatible and mutually supportive requirements. For example, by developing a satellite surveillance system, one is in a better position to monitor the security buffer; to verify arms control agreements; to provide useful information to the United Nations and other neighbours; and to support civilian agencies. Similarly, systems such as helicopters, fast-patrol craft, and surveillance and transport planes could also be assigned to United Nations security functions and might be utilized to serve a wider array of Canadian and common security interests. Double-tasking the armed forces with both international and domestic responsibilities (in areas such as environmental protection and coast-guard work) is the only way to justify the acquisition of these very expensive systems. Given the costs involved, one is obliged to question how any proposed defence system might be developed at tolerable expense and, where possible, how the development might further Canada's long-term interests.

Two cost-saving options that are likely to become even more central to defence planning are in arms control and disarmament. It has finally been widely recognized that we can negotiate and co-ordinate security at lower levels of threat and at lower cost to all. Yet military restraint and force reductions need not always be negotiated. They should be a determinant of defence planning. In 1987, Norway wisely introduced a requirement that all new weapon systems must first be reviewed for their impact on the future of arms control and disarmament.[123] The Norwegians now stand to save considerably.

Unfortunately, while arms control was declared to be a commitment of Canadian defence policy, the Department of National Defence has tended to accord it a very low priority.[124] In fact, it is only within the last year that departmental approval was given to devote resources, personnel, and offices to this task on a full-time basis.

In this very new international environment, Canada has the opportunity to put several security concerns forward onto the negotiating table. After several generations of 'quiet diplomacy,' in the limited role of 'consensus builder,' Ottawa could take a more active role in the various confidence-building, arms-control, and disarmament forums. We should have some arguments of value to contribute. There are, after all, enormous long-term savings and security benefits to be derived from supporting initiatives to arrange a strict interpretation of the anti-ballistic missile (ABM) treaty, a stronger non-proliferation treaty, and the negotiation of a leak-proof comprehensive test-ban treaty. Canadians now have a unique opportunity to take a lead role in hosting discussions to revise military doctrine and strategy to a more defensive orientation. Many nations would also welcome an initiative from Ottawa to place air-launched and sea-launched cruise missiles on the arms-control agenda. As they are alleged to be one of the primary threats to North America, that would seem to be an appropriate response. Failing to limit the large-scale deployment of cruise missiles could well bring about a situation wherein a Canadian government was pressured to develop active air defences at a cost that might exceed $10 billion.

Another arms-control option that would help to promote common security and reduce Canada's defence spending would be to arrange the demilitarization of the Arctic region. There is already considerable support for this idea. A 1986 Report of the Special Joint Committee on Canada's International Relations recommended 'that Canada in co-operation with other Arctic and Nordic nations seek the demilitarization of the arctic region through pressure on the United States and the Soviet Union, as well as through a general approach to arms control and disarmament.'[125] In 1987, Soviet General-Secretary Mikhail Gorbachev made several proposals for Arctic arms control and called for making the region a 'Zone of Peace.' A panel of prominent Canadian arms-control and defence experts responded with a number of sound counter-proposals and recommendations in a report entitled Security Co-operation in the Arctic: A Canadian Response to Murmansk.[126] Canada is well positioned to take the lead in launching an arctic-basin regime for security and co-operation.

The inadequacy of the Conservative government's 1987 policies to enhance security and build a viable defence industrial base are increasingly apparent. Previous plans for rearming the forces by subsidizing a defence-industry boom have now gone bust. The form of 'military Keynesianism' launched by the Canadian government in the 1980s was feasible neither as an economic nor as a military strategy. Government investment in military production tends to create considerably fewer jobs per dollar spent than investment in the civilian economy. For one, military industries tend to be exceedingly capital-intensive, employing fewer people at higher cost.[127] Second, the development of advanced military technology has few civilian spin-offs.

Aside from the requirements for new surveillance and patrol equipment, the armed forces will have very little need of advanced high-technology weapon systems. Projects such as the low-level air-defence system for West Germany acquired in controversy from Oerlikon Aerospace are a huge investment ($1.1 billion) that provide very marginal returns. There is now no justification for a major program to rearm Canada's forces with state-of-the-art weapon systems.

By contrast, mid-range aerospace and shipbuilding technology is always in demand and is more appropriate for Canada's civilian and defence needs. Rather than rearm to prepare for a war that must be prevented, it would be in our economic and security interest to focus on the non-offensive and non-lethal systems necessary for monitoring and patrolling Canadian territory. Back in 1985 Stephen Clarkson had a sound idea when he argued:

> The development of medium-technology military and naval equipment adequate to this task might provide a more practical, if less dramatic focus for Canada's military-industrial strategy ... Canada still has the technical capacity to produce competitive medium-sized aircraft. It is conceivable that by developing this capacity in to a new genera-

tion of technologically unsophisticated but reliable ships and aircraft, Canada could have an export niche that did not compete with the big power weapons merchants or foster the dangerous arms race in mega-destruction.[128]

With support, Canada's aerospace and marine-shipbuilding industries might be positioned to supply Canada's new range of defence requirements. There will inevitably be international demand for such products. Export opportunities and ethics in non-offensive defence production – imagine!

For the defence industries based in Canada that are unable to shift production to meet these new requirements, conversion to civilian production is now an appropriate option. Studies already undertaken indicate that workers employed in this sector of the economy can be moved into effective civilian work.[129] As the government encouraged military production in the 1980s, they now have a responsibility to encourage conversion to civilian production in the 1990s. Canada's past disarmament ambassador to the United Nations, Douglas Roche, claims: 'No issue has such domestic political potential as conversion: converting the work-force and industrial base of military spending to the production of goods and services in the civilian sector ... The political climate in Canada is now ready for a major governmental effort to study, plan and explain conversion as a positive step in the disarmament process ... In brief, conversion ought to lead to a redirection of Canadian resources to the promotion of common security.'[130]

There can be no doubt that the new environment of the 1990s poses a rather frightening challenge to over forty years of Canadian defence relations and hundreds of years of military tradition. Obviously, within the short term, it is difficult to conceive of any government in Ottawa immediately pursuing a radical new defence agenda. The ultra-conservative nature of security planning, combined with the military prudence expected in any period of uncertainty, will tend to safeguard against governments being taken by surprise. A more serious problem is likely to arise from political and bureaucratic intransigence in the face of these changes. Old habits will be difficult to overcome.

'The great problem,' one senior officer told *Defense News*, 'is for people to come to grips with the fact the future is a very different world.'[131]

CONCLUSION

Can we change the guard? By establishing a security buffer, shifting to an independent, non-offensive defence posture, adopting a strategy of dissuasion, and working to strengthen the United Nations, Canada could effectively use its armed forces, resources, and territory to promote common security. Such an approach would be consistent with Canada's commitment to peace-making, constructive internationalism, disarmament, and the building of international trust and confidence.

This cursory review of a new defence posture is not meant to provide definitive answers. It is an outline of a new defence: an instrument for thought, not a final blueprint. All new and untried proposals, especially in defence planning, involve a great deal of speculation. One of the key points to be stressed is that there are options. Moreover, there are defence options that might serve to promote both Canadian and common security. They have yet to be critically assessed and woven into a comprehensive defence plan for the 1990s.

The process of exploration has just begun. As an initial step towards a political economy of Canadian defence relations, this study has provided some indication of how various structures and interests have combined to determine Canadian defence policy. Concepts such as leverage and linkage, the defence trap, and the military-industrial complex were relevant to the study of Canadian defence relations in the 1980s. It may be possible to put several of the problems associated with these developments behind us in the 1990s.

Canadians can expect a defence review and an important debate over the policies that will have to provide for our security into the twenty-first century. Concepts such as common security, non-offensive defence, security buffers, nuclear-weapon-free zones, and dissuasion are relevant to the study of Canadian defence options.

Shifting policy will be difficult. Although many of this century's leaders and philosophers have warned of the great risks that stem from traditional thinking in the nuclear age, the necessary changes have been rather slow in coming. A young student has drawn an apt analogy: 'It's been like stopping a supertanker in an emergency – many of those on board understand what is happening, but it takes a very long time for the ship to respond.'

It has been over twenty years since Dalton Camp suggested that Canada seek to withdraw from both NATO and NORAD and pursue an alternative defence. At that time, amongst the proposals Camp listed were the following:

– a non-nuclear role;
– a modest-sized versatile conventional force sufficient to maintain civil order if required;
– a force that could serve as a cadre to train a larger citizen-recruited force in the event, however unlikely, of a conventional war;
– one that could fight forest fires, patrol the North, provide air-sea rescue and coast guard services, build roads and airfields and perform such other tasks as may be assigned them in the national interest;
– a force that could be available for peacekeeping; and,
– one that would be trained in a new concept of peace-making duties.[132]

Camp claimed that such a 'military posture would not increase the danger to Canadian security; it would strengthen Canadian security. It would allow us to become a nation, and a people directly concerned and involved in the most meaningful problems of the world.' 'Imagine,' he wrote, 'if we were to refuse to isolate ourselves from the Third World, if we were to refuse to remain neutral in the struggle for survival of millions of human beings.'[133]

Several states that were aligned and heavily armed are in the process of shifting to independent, territorial-based, non-offensive defence postures. They are thereby helping to reduce international tension, free up valuable resources, and provide greater security. Some of the more serious military threats are being eliminated. As these threats diminish, so will the arms race.

In the next few years, it may also be possible to arrange the return of all foreign-based forces to their home nations. As the security functions of the United Nations are enhanced, there will be no justification for independent foreign military intervention. Of course, there will be risks and conflicts along the way. Yet if these processes are encouraged to continue, by the turn of the century we may truly be on the verge of abolishing war as a phenomenon and moving on to a new era of common security. Canada could play an important role in this transition. Changing the guard may take time, but it is overdue!

Notes

INTRODUCTION

1 Canada, Department of National Defence, *Challenge and Commitment: A Defence Policy for Canada* (Ottawa, June 1987)
2 See the testimony of William Arkin, 'Canadian Policy with Respect to Future Defense Co-operation with the United States,' presentation before the House of Commons Standing Committee on External Affairs and National Defence, Washington DC, 3 December 1985.
3 For elaboration of this argument see: Richard Ashley, *The Political Economy of War and Peace* (London: Frances Pinter Ltd. 1980); Carleton Hughes, 'International Relations Theory: Possible Implications for Strategic Analysis,' unpublished paper, Carleton University, May 1985; Bradley S. Klein, 'After Strategy: The Search for a Post Modern Politics of Peace,' *Alternatives* 13, no. 3 (July 1988), 293–318; Anatol Rapoport, 'Critique of Strategic Thinking,' in Roger Fisher, ed., *International Conflict and Behavioral Science* (New York: Basic Books 1964); Carolyn M. Stephenson, 'The Need for Alternative Forms of Security: Crises and Opportunities,' *Alternatives* 13, no. 1 (January 1988), 55–76.
4 Colin Gray, *Canadian Defence Priorities: A Question of Relevance* (Toronto: Clarke, Irwin & Co. 1972), 6
5 Report of the Special Committee of the Senate on National Defence, *Canada's Land Forces* (Ottawa, October 1989), 10

CHAPTER 1 Background to Canadian Defence Relations

1 Brian Cuthbertson, *Canadian Military Independence in the Age of the Superpowers* (Toronto: Fitzhenry & Whiteside 1977), 1–2

2 Stephen Clarkson, *Canada and the Reagan Challenge: Crisis and Adjustment 1981–85*, 2d ed. (Toronto: James Lorimer & Co. 1985), 251

3 As Ambassador John Halstead writes: ' While Canada's most important relationship by far in the defence field, as in other fields, is with the United States, there is a great imbalance because of the disparity of power between the two countries. In terms of population and GNP, the United States is roughly ten times Canada. In terms of the 'continental pull' which the American economic and cultural dynamo exercises, it is far more than that. More than three quarters of Canada's trade is with the United States, while less than one-fifth of U.S. trade is with Canada. A quarter of Canadian industry is American owned, but only half of one percent of American industry is Canadian owned. And in terms of military power, Canada's specific weight is miniscule compared to the United States.' 'Canada's Role in the Defence of North America,' in *NATO's Sixteen Nations*, vol. 30, no. 5, 5 September 1985, 35

4 Desmond Morton, *Canada and War* (Toronto: Butterworths 1981), 101. Morton notes: 'The fading of British power left Canada with a very much more domineering defence partner. The war had taught Canadians how swiftly the Americans could move when their minds were made up and how little weight Ottawa's appeals really carried in Washington. Canadians also knew that whatever the United States wished to do for its own security, it would do so whether or not Canada agreed' (156).

5 James Eayrs, *In Defence of Canada*, vol. 2: *Appeasement and Rearmament* (Toronto: University of Toronto Press 1965), 183

6 See William Arkin and Richard Fieldhouse, *Nuclear Battlefields* (Cambridge: Ballinger Publishing Co. 1985), 101–19

7 Mr Allan Sullivan, assistant deputy minister, Political and International Security Affairs Branch, Department of External Affairs, in Canada, House of Commons, 'Minutes of Proceedings and Evidence of the Standing Committee on External Affairs and National Defence,' issue no. 30, 1 October 1985, 7–10

8 See General Charles Foulkes, 'Canadian Defence Policy in a Nuclear Age,' in *Behind the Headlines, Minutes of Proceedings and Evidence*, no. 1 (May 1961), 2; also see the testimony of George R. Pearkes, minister of national defence, House of Commons, Special Committee on Defence Expenditures, no. 10 (8 June 1969), 251; cited in John Warnock, *Partner to*

Behomoth: The Military Policy of a Satellite Canada (Toronto: New Press 1970), 130.

9 Colin Gray, *Canadian Defence Priorities: A Question of Relevance* (Toronto: Clarke, Irwin & Co. 1972), 24–5

10 As early as May 1946, Prime Minister Mackenzie King reported some of his concerns to cabinet: 'I said I believed the long range policy of the Americans was to absorb Canada. They would seek to get this hemisphere as completely one as possible. They are already in one way or another building up military strength in the North of Canada. It was inevitable that for their own protection, they would have to do that. We should not shut our eyes to the fact that this was going on consciously as part of the America policy. It might be inevitable for us to have to submit to it.' Cited in James Eayrs, *In Defence of Canada: Peacemaking and Deterrence* (Toronto: University of Toronto Press 1972), 351

11 Cited in Ernie Regehr, 'Canada and the U.S. Nuclear Arsenal,' in E. Regehr and S. Rosenblum, eds, *Canada and the Nuclear Arms Race* (Toronto: Lorimer 1983), 102

12 Micheal Tucker, *Canadian Foreign Policy: Contemporary Issues and Themes* (Toronto: McGraw Hill-Ryerson 1980), 3

13 Gray, *Canadian Defence Priorities*, 18

14 John Honderich, *The Arctic Imperative: Is Canada Losing the North?* (Toronto: University of Toronto Press 1987), 97. As Honderich goes on to say, 'For Canada, the continental defence relationship is like a marriage with no right of divorce. Our geostrategic position makes any break-up difficult to imagine' (117).

15 James Littleton, *Target Nation: Canada and the Western Intelligence Network* (Toronto: Lester & Orpen Dennys 1986), 78

16 Ibid.

17 See General E.L.M. Burns, *Defence in the Nuclear Age: An Introduction for Canadians* (Toronto: Clarke, Irwin & Co. 1976), 34–5.

18 Ambassador John Halstead, Foreword to Joseph T. Jockel and Joel J. Sokolsky, *Canada and Collective Security: Odd Man Out* (New York: Praeger 1986), viii

19 See Escott Reid, 'Canada and the North Atlantic Treaty: More Than Just a Military Obligation,' in *Canada & the World: National Interest and Global Responsibility* (Ottawa: The Group of 78, 1985), 6–7. Also see George Ignatieff, in association with Sonja Sinclair, *The Making of a Peacemonger: The Memoirs of George Ignatieff* (Markham: Penguin 1987), 115.

20 Joseph T. Jockel and Joel J. Sokolsky, *Canada and Collective Security: Odd Man Out* (New York: Praeger 1986), 50

21 Ernie Regehr, *Arms Canada* (Toronto: Lorimer 1987), 37

22 Ignatieff, *The Making of a Peacemonger*, 116

23 Jockel and Sokolsky, *Canada and Collective Security*, 30

24 Cited in Honderich, *The Arctic Imperative*, 135–6. As Honderich says, 'Thus far, Canadian defence policy had operated in relative concert with U.S. interests. The "American factor" has been the dominant one in the evolution of Canadian security policy. Conversely, Canada has been forced to adapt itself to whatever strategic policy the United States pursues.' At the same time, Jockel and Sokolsky suggest that Canadian military leaders have been much more willing partners. As they write, 'The Canadian and U.S. strategic outlooks have been largely complementary since 1945. From the need for strategic nuclear deterrent forces to the importance of local conventional defence along the NATO perimeter, Canada has rarely questioned the assumptions which have guided the Western alliance in its efforts to maintain the peace and secure the political independence of its members.' *Canada and Collective Security*, 35

25 Clarkson, *Canada and the Reagan Challenge*, 252

26 See Dan Middlemiss, 'Canada and Defence Industrial Preparedness: A Return to Basics?' *International Journal*, 42 (Autumn 1987), 712–13.

27 Jockel and Sokolsky, *Canada and Collective Security*, 50

28 R.D. Cuff and J.L. Granatstein, *American Dollars – Canadian Prosperity* (Toronto: Samuel Stevens 1978), 175; cited in Regehr, *Arms Canada*, 42

29 As J.T. Jockel points out, 'To Canadian and United States airmen in the mid-1950s, it only made sense to provide a way whereby the various elements of their two national air defence systems could be used rationally and efficiently as part of a well designed, well executed and continent-wide battle plan.' Joseph T. Jockel, *No Boundaries Upstairs: Canada, the United States, and the Origins of North American Air Defence, 1945–1958* (Vancouver: University of British Columbia Press 1987), 4

30 The term 'big league professional soldiering orientation' is borrowed from Colin Gray, *Canadian Defence Priorities*, 201.

31 Jockel and Sokolsky, *Canada and Collective Security*, 60–1

32 For an elaboration of this perspective see Gray, *Canadian Defence Priorities*, 37–50. Gray writes: 'Canadian forces are currently faced with an increasing crisis of relevance. To surmount this crisis they must be prepared to re-examine the roots of their professionalism and to endure incomprehension from a society that sees no obvious need for their existence' (50).

33 Ibid., 25

34 Jockel, *No Boundaries Upstairs*, 123

35 Colin Gray writes: 'Bilateral Canadian–United States agreements on air defence matters succeeded each other in the early 1950s with a rapidity matched only by the pace of eager endorsement by the RCAF of the strategic views of their willing tutors in the USAF.' Gray, *Canadian Defence Priorities*, 25

36 Gwynne Dyer (Film), 'The Space Between: The Defence of Canada,' part 2 (Montreal: National Film Board 1985)

37 Cuthbertson, *Canadian Military Independence*, 267

38 George Ignatieff writes: 'When the chips were down and decisions being made that might plunge the world into a nuclear holocaust, all NATO could do was hold its breath while Washington took whatever steps the President and his military advisors deemed appropriate. For all the ringing declarations of solidarity made around the NATO table during that week when peace and possibly the survival of millions of people hung in the balance, none of the allied governments could claim to have been consulted before the Americans imposed their naval blockade, nor did we have any illusions as to the part we might have played in subsequent decision making had the Soviets refused to give way.' See *The Making of a Peacemonger*, 206.

39 Interview with senior source in the Department of National Defence, March 1988

40 As John Halstead noted, 'In the defence field we have very limited bargaining power with the Americans. But we are in a very awkward position because we can't defend our own territory with our means alone. So we need to make allies and form coalitions wherever we can and the only forum open to us is NATO.' Cited in Honderich, *The Arctic Imperative*, 121

41 Clarkson, *Canada and the Reagan Challenge*, 252

42 As Orvik says, 'The greater the small state's strategic significance for the larger, the more it will have to invest in military capabilities both to deter and to assure the neighbouring state that its military presence is not required on the small state's territory for the purpose of denying it to others.' Cited in Clarkson, *Canada and the Reagan Challenge*, 252

43 Senate of Canada, Proceedings of the Special Committee of the Senate and National Defence, issue no. 2, 22 February 1984, 9. Cited in Regehr, *Arms Canada*, 69

44 Tucker, *Canadian Foreign Policy*, 149–50. Cited in Clarkson, *Canada and the Reagan Challenge*, 252

45 Ambassador Halstead, 'Canada's Role in the Defence of North America,' 37

46 As the chairman of the SCEAND committee, which renewed NORAD in 1986, attested, 'Technology is challenging comfortable certainties and familiar assumptions. North American aerospace defence may be approaching a watershed.' Canada, *NORAD 1986*, Report of the Standing Committee on External Affairs and National Defence, February 1986

47 For several interpretations of these developments see: David Cox, 'Living along the Flight Path: Canada's Defence Debate,' *Washington Quarterly* 10 (Autumn 1987), 98–112; David Cox, *Trends in Continental Defence: A Canadian Perspective*, Canadian Institute for International Peace and Security, Occasional Papers, no. 2, 1986; Albert Legault, 'Canada and the United States: The Defence Dimension,' in Charles F. Doran and John H. Sigler, eds, *Canada and the United States: Enduring Friendship, Persistent Stress* (Englewood Cliffs, NJ: Prentice Hall 1985), 161–202; Canada, *NORAD 1986.*

48 In the government's recent defence white paper it was noted that 'Canadians cannot ignore that what was once a buffer could become a battleground.' Canada, Department of National Defence, *Challenge and Commitment: A Defence Policy for Canada* (Ottawa, June 1987), 6

49 Paraphrased from Regehr, *Arms Canada,*185

50 As Tucker writes, 'The crucial decisions which by 1985 could be seen to have tightened the web of the continental defence embrace, were not at all "made" at the political level. These and others comprised a set of discrete and in effect incremental understandings forged in seemingly routine fashion at the bureuacratic level and dealing with the testing and modernization of weapon systems and with contingency war plans. (It should be recognized that the dilemma of these agreements from the standpoint of Canadian security interests did not, and does not, necessarily lie in their substance but in the process through which they came into being.) Political leaders, it seems were not always so much myopic as they were neglectful. Military and national defence authorities did not usurp national security decision-making functions – rather political authorities abdicated their responsibility for ultimate control.' 'Canadian Security Policy,' in Maureen Appel Molot and Brian W. Tomlin, eds, *Canada among Nations 1985: The Conservative Agenda* (Toronto: James Lorimer & Co. 1986), 74

51 See James Bagnall, 'White paper wins applause despite isolationism fears,' *Financial Post*, 16 November 1987, 47.

52 The 'New Hyde Park Agreement' had its origins in a declaration between Prime Minister Mackenzie King and President Roosevelt during the Second World War by which they 'agreed as a general principle that in

mobilizing the resources of this continent, each country should provide the other with the defence articles which it is best able to produce, and above all produce quickly, and that production programs should be co-ordinated to this end.' Cited in Ernie Regehr, *Making a Killing: Canada's Arms Industry* (Toronto: McClelland and Stewart 1975), 18

53 Mr Alan Sullivan (see note 7, this chapter), 9

54 John Kirton, 'The Consequences of Integration: The Case of The Defence Production Sharing Agreements,' in Andrew Axline, ed., *Continental Community? Independence and Integration in North America* (Toronto: McClelland and Stewart 1974), 123. See also Middlemiss, 'Canada and Defence Industrial Preparedness,' 716.

55 Gideon Rosenbluth, *The Canadian Economy and Disarmament* (Toronto: Macmillan 1967), 36–7. See also Regehr, *Arms Canada*, 51.

56 Morton, *Canada and War*, 1

57 Ernie Regehr and Mel Watkins, 'The Economics of the Arms Race,' in E. Regehr and S. Rosenblum, eds, *Canada and the Nuclear Arms Race*, 70

58 As Clarkson says, 'In return for Canada's quiet and diplomatic approach to the U.S., Washington was conciliatory and indulgent towards Canada's needs, offering the Canadian military privileged access to strategic intelligence and granting Canadian industry privileged access to the Pentagon's defence contracts.' Clarkson, *Canada and the Reagan Challenge*, 6

59 Ernie Regehr, 'The Political Economy of Shared Defence Production,' unpublished paper, 5

60 Ibid., 16

61 See Frank Jackman, Office of International Special Projects, 'The Canada–United States Defence Production Sharing Agreement,' (Ottawa: Department of Industry, Trade and Commerce 1976), 4.

62 As Regehr notes, 'In 1985 government officials told the Commons External Affairs and National Defence Committee the objectives of defence production sharing are "greater integration of military production, greater standardization of military equipment, wider dispersal of production facilities, establishment of supplemental sources of supply.' *Arms Canada*, 52, 60

63 In the first two years of the new American president, Canada's defence exports to the United States nearly doubled from $481.7 million in 1980 to $826.6 million in 1981. By 1982, Canadian military exports to the United States increased to $1.028 billion; in 1983 to $1.207 billion; and up to $1.903 billion in 1985. See Canada, Defence Programs Bureau, Department of External Affairs, *Defence Trade Statistics: United States and Overseas* (Ottawa 1987).

64 Glen Williams, *Not for Export: Towards a Political Economy of Canada's Arrested Industrialization* (Toronto: McClelland and Stewart 1983). Also see John N.H. Britton and James M. Gilmour, *The Weakest Link: A Technological Perspective on Canadian Industrial Underdevelopment* (Ottawa: Science Council of Canada 1978).

65 Williams, *Not for Export*, 129–49

66 Hugh G.J. Aitken, 'The Changing Structure of the Canadian Economy with Particular Reference to the Influence of the United States,' in H.G.H. Aitken et al., *The American Economic Impact on Canada* (Durham: Duke University Press 1959), 7

67 Ibid., 8

68 While Glen Williams accepts that there is some merit in explanations that stress our advantage in resources, the unambitious character of our business élites, our small domestic market, and so on, he argues that 'instead of adopting a policy of international specialization through the production for world markets of a number of technologically innovative lines, our state and economic élites chose a much less ambitious alternative strikingly similar to that known in the contemporary underdeveloped world as import substitution industrialization.' *Not for Export*, 12–13

69 Aitken, 'The Changing Structure of the Canadian Economy,' 11

70 The exceptions included the telecommunications and the defence industries.

71 M.H. Watkins, 'A Staples Theory of Economic Growth,' in W.T. Easterbrook and M.H. Watkins, eds, *Approaches to Canadian Economic History* (Toronto: McClelland and Stewart 1967) 63

72 As Clarkson notes, 'The first shock of "Nixonomics" in Ottawa was the announcement of general measures which would have a direct impact on the Canadian economy: an import surcharge of 10 percent and a tax device called the Domestic International Sales Corporation (DISC) to encourage U.S. multinational to export from their American facilities to the detriment of their foreign branch plants.' *Canada and the Reagan Challenge*, 8

73 Colin Gray, then a Canadian defence analyst, responded by writing, 'The 10% import surcharge imposed by President Nixon in August 1971 and the later Domestic International Sales Corporation Programme (DISC) are just reminders of the real dependence of Canada on economic fair weather south of the border. Canadians must remember that official Washington is their most valuable ally against those economic interests that are not disposed to be receptive to Canadian susceptibilities.' *Canadian Defence Priorities*, 48

74 Clarkson, *Canada and the Reagan Challenge*, 250
75 See Tucker, *Canadian Foreign Policy*, 231.
76 As G.B. Doern and R.W. Phidd note, 'The mid-1970s was also a period in which debate over fundamental economic ideas was beginning to be openly readdressed, albeit in somewhat confined quarters. For example the reports of the Science Council of Canada advanced a nationalist technological sovereignty line of argument focusing ... on technology and on the obstacles of foreign ownership placed on the Canadian economy. On the other hand, the Economic Council of Canada ... expressed the more classic freer trade preferences of classic liberal economics.' *Canadian Public Policy, Ideas, Structure, Process* (Toronto: Methuen 1983), 421
77 Micheal Hart, 'Some Thoughts on Canada–United States Sectoral Free Trade' (Montreal: Institute for Research on Public Policy 1985), 7; cited in Regehr, *Arms Canada*, 117
78 Maureen A. Molot and Brian T. Tomlin, 'A World of Conflict,' in Molot and Tomlin, eds, *A World of Conflict: Canada among Nations / 1987* (Toronto: Lorimer 1987), 3
79 Hugh G.J. Aitken, *America Capital and Canadian Resources* (Cambridge: Harvard University Press 1961), 10
80 This assumption is clearly reflected in the following statement of former Defence Minister Barney Danson. As he says, 'Vis-à-vis NORAD, we have to be there to assert our sovereignty as best we can. If we're not there, they (the United States) are going to do it anyway. So we might as well be there, soak up as much as we can and keep them out of our backyard unless we say so.' Cited in Honderich, *The Arctic Imperative*, 121
81 Canada, Department of National Defence, *Defence in the 70s* (Ottawa: August 1971), 6
82 Canada, Department of National Defence, *Challenge and Commitment*, 10
83 Paraphrased from Regehr, *Arms Canada*, 49
84 The term 'invariants,' meaning slow to vary variables, is borrowed from Robert Sutherland, 'Canada's Long Term Strategic Situation,' *International Journal*, Summer 1962; cited in Gray, *Canadian Defence Priorities*, 7.
85 Gray, *Canadian Defence Priorities*, 25
86 Watkins, 'A Staples Theory of Economic Growth,' 63
87 Lt. Col. J.C. McKenna, 'Foreword,' *Forum* 3, no.1 (Ottawa: Conference of Defence Associations 1988)
88 Watkins, 'A Staples Theory of Economic Growth,' 63

CHAPTER 2 Cruise Missile Testing in Canada

1 Speech by Pierre Elliot Trudeau, prime minister of Canada, to the United Nations Special Session on Disarmament, New York, 26 May 1978, p. 6
2 Ibid., 7
3 This chapter draws upon a previous research essay. See Peter Langille, 'The Political Economy of Cruise Missile Testing In Canada: Causes and Consequences,' Honours Research Essay, Carleton University, Ottawa, April 1985.
4 As Schmidt was later quoted: 'My paternity is limited to having publicized the problem of Soviet SS-20 armaments. The (specific) concept came from [former U.S.] president Jimmy Carter as early as the beginning of 1979.' *Gazette* (Montreal), 18 May 1983, B4
5 This distinction is important partly because the GLCM that was deployed in Europe is not the same weapon as the air-launched cruise missile (the AGM-86B) that Canada was asked to test. Air-launched cruise missiles (ALCMS) would be deployed on U.S. Strategic Air Command bombers in North America, not as part of a NATO deterrent in Europe. NATO would not have control over the use of the weapons that would be tested over Canada.
6 See Robert Scheer, *With Enough Shovels: Reagan, Bush and Nuclear War* (New York: Random House 1982), 127.
7 Address of Rear-Admiral Eugene Carroll, Jr (ret.), Center for Defense Information, Guelph University, November 1983
8 Letter from Richard A. Ledesma, assistant director of research and engineering, United States Department of Defense, to L.G. Crutchlow, assistant deputy minister, Department of National Defence, Canada (Washington, DC, 11 January 1979)
9 Canada, Department of National Defence, 'Memorandum, re: Cruise Missile Testing in Canada: Historical Rationale for U.S. Request,' 2 June 1983
10 Canada, Department of External Affairs, Defence Relations Bureau, 'Canada-U.S. Agreement on the Testing and Evaluation of U.S. Defence Systems in Canada,' May 1983, 1
11 See *Ottawa Citizen*, 19 March 1982, 1, 5.
12 Ibid.
13 Canada, Department of National Defence, 'Memorandum Regarding Proposed Agreement on the Testing and Evaluation of DOD Defence Systems in Canada,' prepared by Edward J. Bobyn, 12 November 1980
14 Confidential letter from Colonel H.L. Broughton, Department of Nation-

al Defence, June 1980. As he says, 'the two proposals must be given separate consideration and staff action ... The ALCM test will certainly require Cabinet approval as a separate issue.' See also Canada, Department of National Defence, 'Memorandum regarding Proposed Agreement' (12 November 1980). This was also cited in Robert Winters, 'The Cruise: Secret files provide new data about the missile testing pact,' *Gazette* (Montreal), 18 August 1984.

In addition to the air-launched cruise missile guidance system, Canada agreed under the terms of the CANUSTEP agreement to evaluation of a number of conventional weapon-systems: the LANTIRN night navigation and targeting system, and the air-delivered Gator mine.

15 Letter from R.A. Ledesma, assistant director of research and engineering, United States Department of Defense, to Dr G.T. Pullan, Department of National Defence, Canada (Washington, DC, 12 December 1980)

16 Letter from General G.C.E. Thériault, Department of National Defence, to General C. Gabriel, chief of staff, Headquarters, United States Air Force, Washington

17 Canada, Department of National Defence, 'Memo to the Minister regarding Cruise Missile Testing in the Context of Canadian Policy on Deterrence, Defence, Arms Control and Disarmament,' prepared by D.B. Dewar, 17 October 1983. See also 'Government trying to counter cruise protests,' *Ottawa Citizen*, 12 May 1983.

18 Military aircraft from the United States and several European allies are often tested in Canada. The United States and Canada also share test facilities for the development of underwater detection and anti-submarine-warfare research. Canada, Department of National Defence, 'Confidential Memorandum re: Use of Canadian Facilities U.S. Testing and Training,' prepared by Col. H.L. Broughton, 29 August 1980. Also see Ernie Regehr, 'Canada and the U.S. Nuclear Arsenal,' in E. Regehr and S. Rosenblum, eds, *Canada and the Nuclear Arms Race* (Toronto: James Lorimer & Company 1983), 120.

19 Cited in David Macfarlane, 'The Eve of Destruction: Does the Cruise Missile Bring Us Closer to Catastrophe?' *Saturday Night* 11, no. 12 (December 1984), 27

20 In contrast, there was relatively little political or public concern over American tests of a nuclear-capable 'sleeping' torpedo at the Nanoose Bay test range on the coast of British Columbia in 1976.

21 Canada, External Affairs, Defence Relations Bureau, 'Canada-U.S. Agreement,' May 1983

22 Ibid.

23 Don Sellor, 'How Canada Took the Cruise,' in Thomas L. Perry, Jr, ed., *The Prevention of Nuclear War* (Altona: Friesen Printers 1983), 194
24 See *Hansard*, Ottawa, 18 March 1982.
25 Canada, External Affairs, Defence Relations Bureau, 'Canada-U.S. Agreement,' May 1983
26 Canada, Department of External Affairs, 'Communiqué No. 15,' 10 February 1983
27 This agreement, also referred to as the 'Umbrella Agreement,' did not stipulate any specific weapon to be tested. It was solely the framework necessary to co-ordinate further requests.
28 From Pauline Jewitt, 'Cruise Missile News,' Ottawa, 22 July 1983
29 Canada, Department of National Defence, 'Canada–United States Test and Evaluation of the AGM-86B Air Launched Cruise Missile' (Ottawa, 15 July 1983)
30 Cited In *International Perspectives* 17, no. 2 March/April 1988
31 Among a list of ministerial briefing notes for Defence Minister Perrin Beatty was a 21 April 1986 project proposal categorized as secret for a captive-carry test of the AGM-129 advanced cruise missile. This item was noted by Bill Robinson, Project Ploughshares.
32 See Bill Robinson, 'Unsafe at Any Speed,' *Monitor*, Project Ploughshares, March 1989. Also see Robinson, 'Games Air Forces Play,' *Ploughshares Monitor* (forthcoming).
33 Quoted by Pauline Jewitt in *Hansard*, Ottawa, 18 March 1982, for an article in the *Globe and Mail*
34 'U.S. ignores Prime Minister's raps at Reagan,' *Ottawa Citizen*, 17 May 1983, 3
35 'Poll shows half oppose tests,' *Ottawa Citizen*, 17 January 1983
36 *Globe and Mail*, 30 October 1982. It was indicative of how unpopular this decision was that the Liberals should make the announcement at 6:30 p.m. on a Friday evening in the middle of July. A State Department official in Washington was overheard saying, 'Our government is in favour of this agreement, and so is theirs. Only the people up there are against it.' Cited in Sellor, 'How Canada Took the Cruise,' 195
37 See *Hansard*, Ottawa, 14 June 1983.
38 Memo from J.R. Francis, director of Defence Relations Bureau, Department of External Affairs, 'Agreement for Testing U.S. Defence Systems in Canada,' 2 February 1983
39 Stated by Michael Pitfield, former clerk of the Privy Council and secretary to the cabinet, in an address to the Annual Meeting of the Ottawa Chapter of Physicians for Social Responsibility, Ottawa Health Services Centre, 12 March 1984

40 Prime Minister Pierre Trudeau, 'An Open Letter to All Canadians,' Ottawa, 9 May 1983, 3

41 James Eayrs, *Fate and Will in Foreign Policy* (Toronto: T.H. Best 1967), 1

42 See Leo Panitch, 'The Role and Nature of the Canadian State,' in Leo Panitch, ed., *The Canadian State: Political Economy and Political Power* (Toronto: University of Toronto Press 1977), 3–23. See also Ralph Miliband, *The State in Capitalist Society* (London: Quartet Books 1973), 46–62.

43 James Eayrs, *In Defence of Canada: Peacemaking and Deterrence* (Toronto: University of Toronto Press 1972), 369

44 Cited in ibid., 369

45 Interview with air-force source in office of Assistant Deputy Minister, Policy, Department of National Defence, 28 July 1986

46 James Littleton, *Target Nation: Canada and the Western Intelligence Network* (Toronto: Lester & Orpen Dennys 1986), 84, 79

47 'No ties, no holocaust,' *Ottawa Citizen*, 17 January 1983, 1

48 Interview with senior civil servant in the Department of National Defence, 9 August 1984

49 Abraham Rotstein, *Rebuilding from Within: Remedies for Canada's Ailing Economy* (Toronto: James Lorimer & Co. 1984), 24

50 Colin Gray, *Canadian Defence Priorities: A Question of Relevance* (Toronto: Clarke, Irwin & Co. 1972), 23

51 Ernie Regehr, 'Canada and the U.S. Arsenal,' in E. Regehr and S. Rosenblum, eds, *Canada and the Nuclear Arms Race* (Toronto: James Lorimer & Company 1983), 113

52 Stephen Clarkson, *Canada and the Reagan Challenge* (Toronto: Lorimer 1982), 23–49

53 'MacGuigan rakes U.S. interference,' *Toronto Star*, 9 October 1980; cited in Clarkson, *Canada and the Reagan Challenge*, 16

54 Adam Bromke and Kim Richard Nossal, 'Tensions in Canada's Foreign Policy,' *Foreign Affairs* 62, no. 2 (winter 1983/1984), 348

55 Ibid., 347

56 For example, American senators in a 'House Oversight Committee' placed a large proportion of blame on the White House for failing to act forcefully in Canadian matters. It was their opinion that the United States 'must either through persuasion or stronger measures convince Ottawa to modify its restrictive investment and confiscatory energy policies.' Furthermore, they state that 'any near-term modification to the thrust of Ottawa's protectionist policies is likely to be achieved only through highly coercive economic measures' and the 'the Administration

should not strictly limit policy review to options of retaliation in kind, but should view the Canadian actions in the total context of bilateral relations.' United States, House Subcommittee on Oversight and Investigations, Washington, DC, October 1982, 1–6

57 Interview with senior source in the Prime Minister's Office, 21 March 1984

58 Ibid.

59 Interview with a senior source in the Department of External Affairs, 19 March 1984

60 'U.S. wants missile tests over Canada,' *Ottawa Citizen*, 10 March 1982, 5. Also see Don Sellor, 'How Canada Took the Cruise,' 194.

61 *Hansard*, 18 March 1982

62 Interview with a senior source in the Department of External Affairs, 19 March 1984

63 Memo from R.P. Cameron, assistant undersecretary, Bureau of International Security Policy and Arms Control Affairs, Department of External Affairs: 'Proposed Agreement on Testing of U.S. Defence Systems in Canada,' Ottawa, 24 January 1983

64 Memo from J.R. Francis, director, Defence Relations Bureau, Department of External Affairs, 'Agreement for Testing U.S. Defence Systems in Canada,' Ottawa, 2 February 1983

65 'Canada committed to Cruise: Envoy,' *Ottawa Citizen*, 11 March 1983

66 Letter from Prime Minister Trudeau to MP Terry Sergeant, 23 March 1982

67 Don Sellor, 'Pentagon plans to bar Canada from new deal,' *Ottawa Citizen*, 23 April 1983, 1, 10

68 Ibid., 1

69 Ibid.

70 Ibid.

71 Ernie Regehr, 'Cruise Testing: An Offer We Can't Refuse?' *Ploughshares Monitor* 4, no. 4 (March 1983)

72 'No ties, no holocaust,' *Ottawa Citizen*, 17 January 1983

73 Interview with a senior policy adviser in the Prime Minister's Office, 21 March 1984

74 Joey Slinger, 'In the Shadow of the Cruise,' in *No Axe Too Small to Grind* (Toronto: McClelland and Stewart 1985)

75 David Cox, 'Mixed Signals from the North: Canada's Defence Debate,' *World Policy Journal* 5, no. 3 (Summer 1988), 477

76 See Simon Rosemblum and Bill Robinson, 'Modernizing the Cruise,' *International Perspectives*, July/August 1989, 1/3. As they write, a 1985 U.S.

Congressional Research Service study noted that stealth capabilities 'would make strategic SLCMS mush more threatening as potential first strike weapons, given their capacity for flying undetected and unimpeded to their targets.'

77 Cited by John Hay, 'Ex-disarmament envoy feels betrayed by Canada's role,' *Ottawa Citizen*, 28 October 1989

78 Douglas Roche, 'Canada is silent as U.S. escalates arms race,' *Toronto Star*, 10 November 1989

CHAPTER 3 In Pursuit of Stategic Flexibility

1 Canada, Department of National Defence, *Challenge and Commitment: A Defence Policy for Canada* (Ottawa, 1987), 61

2 See ibid., 61–3. As of November 1989, Mobile Command will no longer be committed to helping defend Northern Norway. Instead the Canadian Air Sea Transportable (CAST) brigade group – Groupe-brigade du Canada (5GBC) based in Valcartier, Quebec – will be dedicated to the defence of the Central Front, bringing Canada's European commitment up to division strength. Currently Canada's land commitment to the defence of Central Europe consists of the 4203 troops of 4 Canadian Mechanized Brigade Group. Based in the southwest corner of West Germany, in Lahr and Baden-Soellingen, these troops are the Commander of Central Army Groups (CENTAG) only in-place reserve force. See *Jane's Defence Weekly*, vol. 8, no. 20 (21 November 1987), 1194.

3 See Escott Reid, 'Canada and the North Atlantic Treaty: More Than Just a Military Obligation,' in *Canada and the World: National Interest and Global Responsibility* (Ottawa: Group of 78, 1985), 6–7.

4 Cited in Joseph T. Jockel and Joel J. Sokolsky, *Canada and Collective Security: Odd Man Out* (New York: Praeger 1986), 53

5 Harald von Reikhoff, *NATO: Issues and Prospects* (Toronto: Canadian Institute of International Affairs, 1967), 104

6 American General Dwight Eisenhower, the first Supreme Allied Commander of NATO's integrated multinational force, maintained that these initial deployments were in response to an emergency, but that on a long-term basis, each important geographical area must be defended primarily by the people of that region. Tom Keating and Larry Pratt, *Canada, NATO and the Bomb* (Edmonton: Hurtig Publishers 1988), 28

As Major-General Leonard Johnson (ret.) notes, Canada makes a voluntary contribution to the defence of Western Europe. It is not bound by a NATO treaty obligation to maintain forces in Europe. As far as Canada's obligations to the military provisions of the treaty are concerned, members are only obligated to maintain their individual and collective ability to resist armed attack. 'Canada and NATO: What Price Symbolism?' in Derek Paul, ed., *Defending Europe: Options for Security* (London: Taylor & Francis 1985), 51

7 See Keating and Pratt, *Canada, NATO and the Bomb*, 28.

8 See Colin Gray, *Canadian Defence Priorities: A Question of Relevance* (Toronto: Clarke, Irwin & Co. 1972), 201.

9 Cited in John Honderich, *Arctic Imperative: Is Canada Losing the North?* (Toronto: University of Toronto Press 1987), 151

10 Joseph T. Jockel, *Canada and NATO's Northern Flank* (Toronto: Centre for International and Strategic Studies 1986), 20

11 As Jockel and Sokolsky note, 'In 1969 Prime Minister Pierre Trudeau justified his decision to halve the size of Canada's European forces by reminding Canadians that "we're perhaps more the largest of the small powers than the smallest of the large powers." He noted the "magnificent recovery" of the European states, allowing them to provide more and more for their own conventional defence, and discounted fears that his reductions in the Canadian Armed forces would have "profound international consequences."' *Canada and Collective Security*, 40

12 Cited in Honderich, *The Arctic Imperative*, 170

13 Gray acknowledged that the political and economic costs of total withdrawal might be excessive. He wisely suggested that 'the 5,000 men and their equipment, deployed in Europe, must be versatile.' *Canadian Defence Priorities*, 203

14 Jockel, *Canada and NATO's Northern Flank*, 22

15 Cited by Gwynne Dyer in 'Operation Au Revoir,' *Globe and Mail*, 22 April 1988

16 Keating and Pratt, *Canada, NATO and the Bomb*, 34

17 Jockel and Sokolsky, *Canada and Collective Security*, 53

18 Stephen Clarkson, *Canada and the Reagan Challenge: Crisis and Adjustment 1981–1985*, 2d ed. (Toronto: James Lorimer & Co. 1985), 250

19 As General E.L.M. Burns noted, 'Mr. Trudeau had been visiting EEC countries for the purpose of gaining support for a special "contractual relationship" of Canada with the Common Market, i.e., better terms of trade. Journalists have suggested that the government's more forthcoming attitude toward NATO is related to the hope of eventual trade benefits.' *Defence in the Nuclear Age: An Introduction for Canadians* (Toronto: Clarke, Irwin & Co. 1976), 123

20 Clarkson, *Canada and the Reagan Challenge*, 250

21 Michael J. Tucker, 'Canadian Security Policy,' in Maureen A. Molot and

Brian T. Tomlin, eds, *Canada among Nations 1985: The Conservative Agenda* (Toronto: James Lorimer & Co., 1986), 73

22 Cited in Honderich, *The Arctic Imperative*, 154

23 Ibid., 154

24 Cited by Major-General Leonard Johnson (ret.), 'Canada and NATO: What Price Symbolism?' 3. Major-General Johnson also attested to the fact that 'Canada provides only one-fifth of one percent of the 2.6 million troops in NATO, about 1 percent of the 13,000 main battle tanks, and 2.7 percent of the 1,950 fighter-bombers.' As he said, 'The commitment does not make a significant contribution to the balance of forces between NATO and the Warsaw Pact.' (This is not to denigrate Canada's troops, it is simply that among so many others, their presence is militarily insignificant.)

25 Within NATO, only the United States has a comparable range of varied and geographically diverse roles. As Honderich noted in 1986, 'With only 84,000 active forces, Canada is committed not only to maintain and supply a land and air contingent on the Central Front in West Germany, send a brigade of 5,000 to Norway in times of crises (now under review), and supply a contingent of 500 to Denmark in similar times of crises, but also to patrol 2.76 million kilometres of the northwest Atlantic in times of war and ensure (with the United States) the security of 6.3 million kilometres of Canada's archipelago. Those are only Canada's NATO commitments. The list doesn't include the military's first task, the defence of Canada itself, or Canada's promise to exercise surveillance over 1.66 million kilometres of the north Pacific.' Honderich, *The Arctic Imperative*, 149

26 Ibid., 149

27 See Edgar J. Dosman, 'The Department of National Defence: The Steady Drummer,' in Katherine A. Graham, ed., *How Ottawa Spends: 1988/89* (Ottawa: Carleton University Press, 1988), 166.

28 Jockel and Sokolsky, *Canada and Collective Security*, 91

29 John Honderich was correct in stating: 'Altogether these forces are just a minuscule part of what is indisputably the greatest concentration of military might anywhere in the world.' *The Arctic Imperative*, 151

30 Ibid., 170

31 In 1972, Colin Gray commented on the limited withdrawal from the Central Front, suggesting that, 'overall, *Defence in the 70s* should be welcomed as representing a step away from the former very heavy commitment of Canada's scarce defence funds to the support of the military structure of Cold War alliances ... The most important development in

official Canadian defence thinking of recent years has been the recognition that a major proportion of Canada's defence activity should relate to quite distinctive Canadian requirements.' *Canadian Defence Priorities*, 207

32 Jockel, *Canada and NATO's Northern Flank*, 99–101

33 Major-General Leonard Johnson (ret.), 'Canadian Defence Policy: A Prisoner of Mythology,' in *Canada & The World: National Interest and Global Responsibility* (Ottawa: Group of 78, 1985), 8

34 Gwynne Dyer, 'Operation Au Revoir'

35 James Bagnall, 'Nielson's secret European trip signals change in military role,' *Financial Post*, 21 September 1985

36 Address of General Thériault to the Annual Conference of the Canadian Institute of International Affairs, Ottawa, March 1988

37 According to General Thériault, the costs in making viable this highly fragmented effort are associated with an elaborate support infrastructure that does not make military sense per se: 'I am further concerned, as the Chief military advisor to the government, that having paid this large bill and deployed much of our resources in fulfilment of these various commitments, a Canadian government would not be left with much strategic flexibility.' Address of the chief of defence staff the 48th Annual Meeting of the Conference of the Defence Associations, 11 January 1985; Conference Report, 28

38 Interview with senior source involved in Department of National Defence planning, March 1988

39 To cite one example, David Cox pointed out that to maintain an armoured role for any future European battlefield will be extraordinarily expensive – it is, as he suggests, not too far-fetched to argue that capital expenditures in the order of $10 billion will be required over the next decade. Cited in Jockel and Sokolsky, *Canada and Collective Security*, 69

40 Interview with very senior source involved in Department of National Defence planning, 12 October 1988

41 Interview with senior source involved in Department of National Defence planning, March 1988. As another planner noted, 'The proposal was dealt with only at the top level. It was handled very discreetly and contained very carefully. All correspondence and communication was carried out within one office.' Interview with very senior source involved in Department of National Defence planning, 12 October 1988

42 Interview with senior source involved in Department of National Defence planning, March 1988

43 Jockel, *Canada and NATO's Northern Flank*, 47

44 Jockel and Sokolsky suggest one of the many alternatives: 'With the substantial savings that would accrue from shedding the armoured role and closing down the expensive Canadian facilities in West Germany (coupled with increases in the defence budget), the government could then consider the modest expansion of the CAST force to 5,000 or perhaps 6,000 and the acquisition of three desperately needed systems: more airlift capability for the CAST Brigade Group, AWACS aircraft for the surveillance of southern Canadian airspace, and more maritime forces.' *Canada and Collective Security*, 86–7

45 See the testimony of Admiral Robert Falls (ret.), Senate of Canada, Proceedings of the Special Committee of the Senate on National Defence, issue no. 12, 26 January 1988, 22. Admiral Falls, who was previously chief of defence staff, elaborated on this dilemma: 'It was intended, in the event of a crisis, to prevent war from happening. It was not to go over there and start to fight. In other words, the Hong Kong syndrome comes forefront and centre in terms of people's thoughts about it. The decision will be taken at the time, and it would be a very difficult decision to take, as to whether the sending of troops to Norway would cause a heightening of a crisis or whether it would reduce it. We would not have to make the decision until the time; but it would be made before war starts. That was always the intention of the Norwegian commitment. It could be made much more credible with a very small cost of putting some equipment, prepositioning of equipment, in Norway' (22).

46 Jockel, *Canada and NATO's Northern Flank*, 45

47 Testimony of Admiral Robert Falls (ret.), Senate of Canada, p. 23

48 Ibid.

49 Interview with senior source involved in Department of National Defence planning, March 1988. As another source noted, 'When we put the proposal to Weinberger we illustrated the range of rational options. He liked it and it and was quite supportive.' Interview with very senior source in Department of National Defence planning, 12 October 1988

50 As Gwynne Dyer says, 'Like the U.S. forces in Europe, Canadian troops are "hostages" whose principal purpose is to be killed in any war there, thus guaranteeing that Canada is automatically committed regardless of how the war begins or what Ottawa's wishes are at the time.' 'Operation Au Revoir'

51 Interview with senior source involved in Department of National Defence planning, March 1988

52 Such was the opinion of one senior source who noted that 'Heseltine had never been sympathetic to Canadian concerns. The British in general

looked down on us and felt we were making a paltry contribution to their security.' Interview with very senior source involved in Department of National Defence planning, 12 October 1988

53 J.J. Jockel, cited by Gwynne Dyer, 'Europeans torpedoed Tory plan to withdraw NATO troops,' *Ottawa Citizen*, 14 March 1988

54 Interview with senior source involved in National Defence planning, March 1988

55 Dyer, 'Europeans torpedoed Tory plan.' This perspective was shared by retired Defence Minister Paul Hellyer. As he stated, 'There's no question Canada's contribution is entirely political. This is not to degenerate the force. The real reason they're there is as hostages. It's not politically so much to guarantee Canadian involvement as it is to shore up America involvement. If we pulled out, the Americans would hop on the crusade.' Cited in Honderich, *The Arctic Imperative*, 154

56 Interview with very senior source in Department of National Defence planning, 12 October 1988

57 Interview with Joseph Jockel, 25 August 1988

58 Interview with very senior source in Department of National Defence planning, 12 October 1988

59 Interview with Joseph Jockel, 25 August 1988

60 Cited by Dyer, 'Europeans torpedoed Tory plan'

61 Jockel, *Canada and NATO's Northern Flank*, 26

62 Interview with senior source involved in Department of National Defence planning, March 1988

63 Ibid.

64 As the government's popularity subsided after numerous internal scandals, it is likely that they saw little to be gained from an international scandal. Moreover, with the NDP front-running in the polls for several months, it was clear that the government intended to attack them on the basis of their initial commitment to withdraw from NATO. This would have been a difficult platform to launch any attack from if the Conservatives were being criticized by the NATO allies for withdrawal from the Central Front.

65 The Liberal defence critic MP Doug Firth, asked the chief of defence staff, General Paul D. Manson, and the DND assistant deputy minister (policy) whether a paper or a cost analysis was ever done by the department to assess Thériault's plan to withdraw the armed forces from Europe. On defence committee travels to Europe the previous year Firth had spoken with a Canadian general at SHAPE headquarters and been told that it had gone beyond just talk; that Thériault had in fact done some planning

on withdrawing the armed forces. Canada, House of Commons, 'Minutes of Proceedings and Evidence of the Standing Committee on National Defence,' issue no. 31, 28–29 March 1988

66 For example, U.S. Deputy Defence Secretary William Taft, at a special meeting at NATO headquarters, cited Canada's decision to reassign troops to West Germany that had been specially earmarked to defend northern Norway in a crisis as an example of allied shortcomings. 'NATO allies must spend more on defence: U.S.,' *Gazette* (Montreal), 4 May 1988

67 Interview with very senior source in Department of National Defence planning, 12 October 1988

68 Ibid.

69 Department of National Defence, *Challenge and Commitment*, 61

70 See Sharon Hobson, 'Army needs new material for European commitment,' *Financial Post*, 16 November 1988, 53.

71 Interview with very senior source in Department of National Defence planning, 12 October 1988

72 Ibid.

73 For an elaboration of this argument see Tina Viljoen and Gwynne Dyer, 'Neutrality: A Choice Canada Can Make,' *Compass* 5, no. 5 (January 1988), 6–10.

74 von Riekhoff, *NATO: Issues and Prospects*, 11

75 Maurice Archdeacon and Robert Falls, 'Decision Making in NATO,' in Derek Paul, ed., *Defending Europe: Options for Security* (London: Taylor & Francis 1985), 251

76 Ibid.

77 Honderich, *The Arctic Imperative*, 158

78 Interview with very senior source involved in Department of National Defence planning, 12 October 1988

CHAPTER 4 Industrial Mobilization and the Shift to a Long-War Policy

1 See Canada, Department of National Defence, Challenge and Commitment: A Defence Policy for Canada (Ottawa, June 1987). Dan Middlemiss explains that '*defence preparedness* is a catch-all phrase which may have different meanings, depending on how it is used. In common military parlance, however, it is usually associated with the concept of *mobilization* [see NATO definition below] ... *Mobilization* is itself a broad concept and encompasses several interrelated aspects of defence planning including manpower, industry, and emergency measures.' 'Canada and Defence

Industrial Preparedness: A Return to Basics?' *International Journal* 42 (Autumn 1987), 707

The NATO glossary defines *mobilization* as 'the art of preparing for war or other emergencies through assembling and organizing national resources.' Cited in W.J. Yost, *Industrial Mobilization in Canada* (Ottawa: Conference of Defence Associations 1983), 3

Colonel W.N. Russell (ret.) writes: 'The *defence industrial base* means the capability of Canadian industry to support Canada's defence undertakings in times of both peace and war. Defence Industrial Base includes the infrastructure and personnel required to produce modern weapon systems, spare parts for weapon systems, munitions, and supplies. It also includes the infrastructure and personnel to perform equipment repairs and overhauls as well as to conduct research and development.' 'The Need for a Viable Canadian Defence Industrial Base,' *Canadian Defence Quarterly*, Spring 1986, 16

Brigadier-General W.J. Yost (ret.) writes: 'The only way to respond to modern Total War is by *Total Defence* – a system which would embrace all Canadians, and most effectively direct their efforts in response to an attack on our country ... We must have plans in place which will allow us to quickly convert our peacetime Armed Forces and other national resources over to a highly regulated wartime system which suspends many of our normal democratic rights and freedoms. Total, centralized control of all the nation's resources is required in order to respond effectively and survive future wars.' *Peace through Security: A Total Defence Approach* (Ottawa: Conference of Defence Associations 1987), 9–10

A *long war policy* entails the capacity to engage in and sustain protracted conventional war.

2 Canada, House of Commons, Special Committee on Defence, Minutes of Proceedings and Evidence, 26 May 1964, 12; cited in Douglas L. Bland, 'The Canadian Defence Policy Process and the Emergence of a Defence Industrial Preparedness Policy,' in David G. Haglund, ed., *Canada's Defence Industrial Base: The Political Economy of Preparedness and Procurement* (Kingston: Ronald P. Frye & Co. 1988), 240

3 Middlemiss, 'Canada and Defence Industrial Preparedness,' 711

4 Canada, Department of National Defence, *Defence in the 70s* (Ottawa, August 1971)

5 Interview with Brigadier-General W.J. Yost (ret.), director of operations for the Conference of Defence Associations, 10 March 1988

6 As Brigadier-General Yost acknowledges, 'Outside of the United States, Canada has possibly the best record in the Alliance in meeting these

goals. This was in part forced on us because of our previous lack of spending on capital equipment – which forced a re-equipping programme on our forces – and the small size of our committed formations makes it easier for us to reach the goal.' Brig.-Gen. William Yost, 'Sustaining the Force: Industrial Mobilization in Canada,' in Brian MacDonald, ed., *Guns and Butter: Defence and the Canadian Economy* (Toronto: Canadian Institute of Strategic Studies 1984), 76

7 The U.S. program has been renamed the United States Industrial Preparedness Production Planning Program. For details, see *Production Sharing Guidebook: Canada–United States Defence Production Sharing Program* (Ottawa: Defence Programs Bureau, Department of External Affairs 1985); cited in Middlemiss, 'Canada and Defence Industrial Preparedness,' 718

8 This explanation was provided in interviews with Brigadier-General Yost (10 March 1988) and Dan Middlemiss (28 September 1988).

9 Perrin Beatty, minister of national defence, Address to the Financial Post / Air Canada Conference, Ottawa, 18 November 1987, p. 5

10 Bland, 'The Canadian Defence Policy Process,' 241

11 Both NATO's strategy of 'Follow on Forces Attack' (FOFA) and the American 'Airland Battle' strategy for a conventional war in Europe involve a short-war scenario.

12 See the testimony of Perrin Beatty before the Senate of Canada, Proceedings of the Special Committee of the Senate on National Defence, issue no. 25, 21 June 1988.

13 David Haglund assesses several of the arguments associated with the interest in a long-war policy and the defence industrial base in the Introduction to *Canada's Defence Industrial Base*, 2–3.

14 Middlemiss notes that as early as 1947 'the defence minister, Brooke Claxton, listed as one of Canada's long-term defence objectives: Close integration of the armed forces, the defence purchasing agency, government arsenals and civilian industry, looking towards standardization and industrial organization to permit the speedy and complete utilization of our industrial resources. To this end a small coterie of Canadians sought to ensure the survival of certain key sectors of Canada's defence industry and advance planning for industrial mobilization.' 'Canada and Defence Industrial Preparedness,' 711

15 Bland, 'The Canadian Defence Policy Process,' 240

16 Middlemiss, 'Canada and Defence Industrial Preparedness,' 721

17 D.L. Brown and Brian MacDonald, 'Industrial Preparedness,' in R.B. Byers, ed., *The Canadian Strategic Review 1982* (Toronto: Canadian Institute of Strategic Studies 1982), 142

18 See Ernie Regehr, *Arms Canada* (Toronto: Lorimer 1987), 68
19 Middlemisss, 'Canada and Defence Industrial Preparedness,' 715
20 John Treddenick suggests that it was the intermingling of military and economic instruments and goals that garnered increasing support. 'The Arms Race and Military Keynesianism,' *Canadian Public Policy* 77, no. 7 (1985), 90
21 Ibid.
22 John J. Shepherd, *The Transition to Reality: Directions for Canadian Industrial Strategy* (Ottawa: Canadian Institute for Economic Policy 1980); cited in Treddenick, 'The Arms Race and Military Keynesianism,' 90
23 Yost, *Industrial Mobilization in Canada*, 67
24 Interview with senior official in Defence Programs Bureau, Department of External Affairs, July 1985
25 As Stephen Clarkson writes, 'In September 1981, at the peak of the Canadian-American crisis, the Priorities and Planning Committee of the Cabinet commissioned an interdepartmental task force to do a study on Canada's trading options. The consensus that developed in the bureaucratic team after consultations with the private sector and the provinces was to bury the "third option" approach of diversifying Canadian trade away from American markets. While accepting the multilateral system as the context for Canada's trade prospects, the paper that was ultimately published by the Minister for International Trade favoured making a bilateral deal with the United States, possibly with a formal exemption from the GATT. The Cabinet had been impressed both by the growing dependence of the Canadian economy on trade with the United States and by the increasing vulnerability to unpredictable trade-restricting actions that congressional protectionism threatened.' *Canada and the Reagan Challenge*, 339
26 Interview with Brigadier-General Yost (ret.), 10 March 1988
27 Lamontagne emphasized that this was a signifiant policy shift inasmuch as it acknowledged that the previous 'almost exclusive reliance on forces-in-being ... will be insufficient in the future.' He added that the long-term ability to sustain the operations of the CF during a crisis was dependent on the state of our national industrial readiness, which obviously lies beyond the sole purview of the Department of National Defence. See Yost, 'Sustaining the Force,' 75.
28 Canada, Department of Supply and Services, *Annual Procurement Plan and Strategy 1984/85* (Ottawa, July 1984)
29 Canada Ministry of State for Science and Technology, *Report of the Task Force on Federal Policies and Programs for Technology Development* (Ottawa,

July 1984), 13–14. It is noteworthy that the authors of the ministry report argue: 'What is lacking, we believe, is an overriding mandate which legitimizes – and in fact, demands – a reasonable degree of risk taking in government procurement.'

30 Annex A (a review of background information and a list of questions) sent from the Defence Industrial Preparedness Task Force to the BCNI (Business Council on National Issues) Task Force on Foreign and Defence Policy for comments and input, November 1986

31 Department of National Defence, Executive Version of the Final Report of the Defence Industrial Preparedness Task Force, *Defence Industrial Preparedness: A Foundation for Defence*, November 1987, pp. 1-3, 2-5

32 A Directorate of Defence Industrial Resources was established shortly thereafter to 'serve as a focal point for defence industrial preparedness planning.'

33 Interview with Brigadier-General Yost (ret.), 10 March 1988

34 Bland, 'The Canadian Defence Policy Process,' 241

35 *International Defense Review* pointed out in a recent survey of 'Canada's Defence Industry' that 'the Canadian arms industry does not have a large home market on which it can rely, but Canadian companies have a perhaps surprisingly wide range of capabilities based on a mixture of indigenous development, license agreements and industrial collaboration particularly with partners in the United States.' 'Canada's Defence Industry,' *International Defense Review* 3 (1985), 347

36 Helen Fritz, 'The Armaments Industry' (Toronto: Ontario Legislative Research Service, March 1983), 1

37 Interview with a senior source in the Department of National Defence, 9 August 1984

38 Canada, Department of External Affairs, Defence Programs Bureau, 'Defence Trade Statistics: United States and Overseas' (Ottawa 1987). Canadian military exports were worth $1.8 billion in 1987.

39 Cited in Ernie Regehr, 'The Reagan Boom Years: Military Production in Canada,' *Ploughshares Monitor* 4, no. 4 (March 1983), 2

40 By 1982, Canadian defence exports to the United States increased to $1.028 billion; in 1983 these exports rose to $1.207 billion. Cited in Canada, Department of External Affairs, Defence Programs Bureau, 'Canada–United States Defence Production Sharing Procurement – 1983.' Also see 'Defence Trade Statistics: United States and Overseas' (Ottawa 1987).

It is quite possible that Canadian exports of military products exceed the figures listed by the Defence Programs Bureau. While their statistics indicate that subcontracts account for roughly 60 per cent of the military trade in the last five years, officials in both the Canadian Commercial Corporation and the Department of External Affairs attest to the fact that it is very difficult to determine military trade exchanges that are not co-ordinated by the federal government. As an official in the Department of External Affairs stated, 'We really don't know how much trade goes on between American parent corporations and their branch plants in Canada.' An address by a senor source in the Export Control Division, Department of External Affairs, to INPUT meeting, Ottawa, 2 August 1984

41 Boyd Neil, 'Hail to the Hawks,' *Canadian Business*, May 1983, 61

42 Remarks by the minister of national defence, Robert C. Coates, to the 48th Annual General Meeting, Conference of Defence Associations, January 1985, pp. 19–30

43 Since 1959, the Canadian defence industry has had access to United States defence contracts through the Defence Production Sharing Agreement (DPSA). This industry was given equal opportunity to compete with the US. armaments industry for U.S. defence contracts on the normal commercial basis of price, quality, and delivery. The Buy America Act restrictions were eliminated for Canadian defence products. Previous government regulations were changed to permit duty-free defence trade exchange through the DPSA.

44 The Defence Development Sharing Agreement (DDSA) was established in 1963 to enable a co-operatively funded approach to production of defence items that might be of mutual benefit to the United States and Canada. In essence, the DDSA established a framework for the development by Canadian industry of items that might be required for the future needs of the U.S. military, with such development costs to be paid by both governments.

45 See the testimony of Robert Gillespie, Minutes of Proceedings and Evidence of the Standing Committee on External Affairs and National Defence, issue no. 34, 3 October 1985, 19.

46 Gordon Barthos, 'Canada's arms sales worth $5 billion but buyers remain a well-kept secret,' *Toronto Star*, 22 November 1986

47 Cited in Stephen Dale, 'The Boom Bust,' *Canadian Business*, March 1988, 100

48 Jerry Zeidenberg, 'Gunning for Profits: Canadian Military Contractors Surge into Deadly Business,' *Small Business*, March 1988

49 'Ottawa forms defence industry group,' *Toronto Star*, 7 October 1987, C11

50 Yves Belanger and Pierre Fournier, 'Best Weapons to Combat a Military Economy,' *Peace and Security* 4, no. 1 (Spring 1989), 6

51 Thomas Chell, director-general, Defence Programs Bureau, Department of External Affairs, in 'Minutes of Proceedings and Evidence of the Standing Committee on External Affairs and National Defence,' Issue no. 32, 2 October 1985

52 Department of National Defence, *Challenge and Commitment*, 76

53 Bland, 'The Canadian Defence Policy Process,' 242

54 Stevie Cameron, *Ottawa Inside Out: Power Prestige and Scandal in the Nation's Capital* (Toronto: Key Porter 1989), 160–90

55 Executive Version of the Final Report of the Defence Industrial Preparedness Task Force, *Defence Industrial Preparedness: A Foundation for Defence*, pp. 3/2–8

56 See Ken Epps, 'Research Targeted,' *Ploughshares Monitor* 9, no . 3 (September 1988), 23.

57 Examples of this 'consortium' approach are: EH-Industries Canada, bringing together Bell Helicopter, Paramax Electronics, IMP Group, Canadian Marconi, and Amtek Management; and MIL/SNC, bringing together MIL Vickers, MIL Tracy, MIL Systems Engineering, Norris Warming, W.P. London Associates, LN Technologies, Securiplex, CANATOM, YARD Inc., Sandwell Swann Wooster, Alsthom, and M&M Manufacturing.

58 Cited by Wilson Ruiz, 'Canadian munitions sales to Latin America taking off,' *Globe and Mail*, 9 September 1988, B18

59 Frank Hasenfratz, cited by Paul Mooney, 'The Defence Industry,' CBC Ottawa (radio), 19 December 1987

60 Martin Shadwick, 'State of the Industry' series compiled by Sharon Hobson on 'Canada's Defence,' *Jane's Defence Weekly* 8, no. 20 (21 November 1987), 1200

61 Edgar J. Dosman, 'The Department of National Defence: The Steady Drummer,' in Katherine A. Graham, ed., *How Ottawa Spends: 1988/89* (Ottawa: Carleton University Press 1988), 180

62 Beatty, 'Defence Industrial Preparedness,' Speech to the Montreal Chamber of Commerce, 2 February 1988, 3

63 Dale, 'The Boom Bust,' 37. Another estimate is provided by Robert Fowler, an assistant deputy minister in the Department of National Defence, who indicated to *Jane's Defence Weekly* that 'with 2% real growth annually for 15 years, the DND will still fall $5–10 billion short of the money it needs. In other words, the DND will need a budget increase of at least 5% in real terms, annually.' Cited by Sharon Hobson, 'Canada's New Priorities,' *Jane's Defence Weekly* 8, no. 20 (21 November 1987), 1188

64 See *The Wednesday Report: Canada's Defence News Bulletin* 1, no. 16 (23 September 1987).

65 *The Wednesday Report: Canada's Defence News Bulletin*, 6 January 1988; cited in Dosman, 'The Department of National Defence: The Steady Drummer,' 181

66 See Minutes of Proceedings and Evidence of the Special Joint Committee of the Senate and of the House of Commons on 'Canada's International Relations,' issues no. 1–18, 1985–6.

67 Report of the Standing Committee on External Affairs and National Defence, *NORAD 1986*, February 1986, 59

68 Ibid., 60

69 Ibid., 66

70 There are well over 400 companies involved in the Canadian defence industry. On average there are 250–300 companies that export military-related products each year. This export industry provides directly some 35,000 to 50,000 jobs, typically scientists, engineers, and technicians, and indirectly (without counting commercial spin-offs) accounts for approximately 150,000 jobs. Over 75 per cent of the 'Canadian' defence industry is foreign-owned. Many of 'our' major defence contractors are just subsidiaries of United States–based multinational corporations (Interview with senior source in the Defence Programs Bureau, Department of External Affairs, June 1985). In an earlier period, Gideon Rosenbluth found that less than one-fifth of the payments to the leading defence contractors in Canada went to Canadian-controlled firms (*The Canadian Economy and Disarmament* [Toronto: Macmillan 1967]).

71 In 1981, the *Financial Post* noted: 'With U.S. defence spending heading for one of its greatest binges in peacetime, Canada faces a rare opportunity to boost its fortunes with the U.S. on the military, industrial, trade and technology fronts' (24 October 1981, 123).

Michael Tucker writes that 'political calculations about the interstate benefits to Canada from alliance military collaboration were reinforced by similar calculations about the domestic benefits from military hardware programs. Since the mid-1970s Ottawa had increasingly viewed technological innovation in the military sphere as a cutting edge for advances in Canadian civilian high technologies. Indeed, industrial and technological offsets from the military to the civilian sector were seen as a vital means for developing a new and more vibrant Canadian technological infrastructure: they were also designed in part to help mitigate untoward effects of regional economic disparities.' 'Canadian Security Policy' in Maureen A. Molot and Brian T. Tomlin, eds, *Canada among Nations 1985: The Conservative Agenda* (Toronto: Lorimer 1986), 73

72 Cited in Dale, 'The Boom Bust,' 36

73 Interview with former minister of the Department of Industry, Trade and Commerce, May 1988

74 D. Leyton-Brown and B. MacDonald, 'Industrial Preparedness,' in R.B. Byers, ed., *The Canadian Strategic Review 1982* (Toronto: The Canadian Institute for Strategic Studies 1982), 142

For an analysis that suggests the defence industry does not make a significant contribution to the Canadian economy, see R.B. Byers, 'Canadian Defence and Defence Procurement: Implications for Economic Policy,' in Denis Stairs and Gilbert R. Winham, eds, *Selected Problems in Formulating Economic Policy*, Royal Commission on the Economic Union and Development Prospects for Canada, vol. 30 (Toronto: University of Toronto Press 1985), 163–74.

75 See the testimony of Roger Voyer, 'Minutes of Proceedings and Evidence of the Standing Committee on External Affairs and National Defence,' issue no. 34, 3 October 1985, 23.

76 See Regehr, *Arms Canada*, 67–79.

77 See the testimony of Robert Gillespie, 'Minutes of Proceedings and Evidence of the Standing Committee on External Affairs and National Defence,' issue no. 34, 3 October 1985, 20. Noting the existence of a new memorandum of understanding with the Aerospace Industries Association of Canada, he pointed out that the advantages 'are seen to be, from the industry side, provision of a more stable environment within which they can address long-term business planning, and from the government side the provision of a means of developing a longer term perspective on the opportunities and prospects for the industry sector.'

78 Canadian government support is required to retain the favoured position of the defence industry. This also means political support. As Ernie Regehr writes: 'The military industry is not an industry of the free market. Its wares are purchased almost exclusively by governments, and in Canada as in other countries, its commercial success depends heavily on government administrative and political support. While individual firms advertise their products, governments are the primary arms export promoters.' *Arms Canada*, 101

79 Canada, Department of Industry, Trade and Commerce, Annual reports 1981–82. Whereas in 1978–9 the federal government authorized \$52.2 million to this sector through the defence Industry Productivity Program (DIPP), by fiscal year 1982–3, the government was contributing \$181.2 million for DIPP projects. It is also very difficult to gauge the amount of government funding that is directed to the defence industry. Frequently programs of the departments of Defence; Industry, Trade

and Commerce; Science and Technology; and Regional Economic Expansion overlap, and corporations producing military products receive funds through more than one specific government program. As a report from the Ministry of State for Science and Technology acknowledges, 'The federal government's "alphabet soup" of technology support programs has become a pervasive factor in Canadian industrial development. Very little private-sector research and development is now undertaken without some form of federal incentive' ('Task Force on Federal Policies and Programs for Technology Development,' 7).

80 Beatty, 'Effects of Advanced Technology on Defence,' Address to the Canadian Export Association, 5 October 1987, 7. The defence white paper also heralded new funding for defence-industry research and development: 'Such contracting would continue to increase. In addition, the Government is considering a Defence Industrial research program to help domestic industry establish a technology base from which to meet the Canadian Forces requirements for new equipment, resupply and life-cycle support. The program would help mobilize those areas where Canadian industry has strengths and would serve as a channel for information exchange and technology transfer between the Canadian Defence research establishments and the defence industrial community. *Challenge and Commitment*, 78

81 See for example, 'The Progressive Conservative Agenda, Honour the Commitment: National Defence and the PC Party,' August 1984 (PC campaign literature).

82 Dosman, 'The Department of National Defence: The Steady Drummer,' 165

83 Ibid., 166

84 Executive Version of the Final Report of the Defence Industrial Preparedness Task Force, *Defence Industrial Preparedness: A Foundation for Defence*, 1–3

85 Such a policy underlies the systemic difficulty in maintaining sufficient demand to match the productive capacity of the economy. John Tredenick notes that the economic policies pursued throughout the Second World War imparted the general impression that there was a direct relationship between military spending and prosperity. 'Public acceptance of this relationship has not gone unheeded by the military bureaucracy which regularly argues the merits of proposed budgets, and their content, on the basis of their stimulating economic benefits.' He also suggests that 'the resulting intermingling of economic and military policy goals and instruments may then impart an upward bias to military expenditures.' 'The Arms Race and Military Keynesianism,' 77–92

86 According to the 1987 defence white paper, 'Defence expenditures in Canada contribute economic benefits to all sectors of Canadian society. In fiscal year 1985–86, Canadian defence spending accounted for approximately $12 billion of the Gross Domestic Product. It produced $1.6 billion in taxes and generated approximately 294,000 jobs, 178,000 in the private sector ... Canadian defence spending contributes significantly to the maintenance of a robust and flexible economic environment. Defence purchases contribute to the development of internationally competitive Canadian industries. By enhancing Canadian international competitiveness, defence expenditures allow us to take advantage of economic opportunities abroad in both defence and parallel non-defence industries ... Because of the pervasive nature of Canadian defence activity, Canada has an entree into a wide variety of foreign research, development and manufacturing processes. The education and training of highly skilled workers essential to the operation of a modern economy is a further benefit of Canada's defence industrial base.' *Challenge and Commitment*, 84–5

87 See Regehr, *Arms Canada*, 72

88 Brigadier-General Yost writes: 'NATO and the Supreme Allied Commanders have stressed the need to member governments for increased defence expenditures on improvements to our conventional force capabilities to achieve increased readiness of stationed forces, the application of advanced conventional or dual weapons technology and the expansion and preparation of reserve forces. They have suggested that NATO expenditures, on average, be increased annually by four percent as agreed in 1978, and that countries like Canada, whose force structures have decreased since 1970 should expand more so that their contribution will be restored to the appropriate level.' *Peace through Security*, 96

89 U.S. Ambassador Paul Robinson, Jr, observed that the United States was in a 'no-lose' position with either Mulroney or Turner. Citing the Canadian government's increased military spending in recent years, he predicted: 'If Turner comes in, it will improve even more, and if Mulroney comes in, it will improve even more than that.' Sherri Baron, 'U.S. envoy sees closer ties with new PM,' *Ottawa Citizen*, 28 May 1984

90 This view was expressed by senior officials in the Department of National Defence in the course of interviews in April 1987. Edgar J. Dosman writes that 'the critical issues for DND related to the capital budget and continuous updating of equipment. For eight years, between 1968 and 1976, Canada did not place a single contract for a major weapon system; in 1972 the capital budget fell to eight per cent. DND is still recovering. But the capital share of the budget had rebounded to 28 per cent by 1984–85,

and a shower of major procurement projects accompanied the general election of 1984. By the end of the Trudeau period the DND rebuilding process was clearly off the ground.' 'The Department of National Defence: The Steady Drummer,' 176

91 This point should not be overstated. As John Treddenick says, 'What would appear to be more important in assessing a nation's military contribution to the alliance is the absolute level of its military expenditures. By this measure Canada currently stands a respectable sixth among the nations of the alliance.' 'The Arms Race and Military Keynesianism,' 85

92 Desmond Morton, *Canada and War* (Toronto: Butterworths 1981), 1

93 As previously noted, the term 'big-league professional soldiering orientation' is borrowed form Colin Gray, *Canadian Defence Priorities: A Question of Relevance* (Toronto: Clarke Irwin & Co. 1972), 201.

94 Bland, 'The Canadian Defence Policy Process,' 240

95 Dan Middlemiss acknowledges that, 'for DND, the strategy has undoubtedly helped to "sell" its expensive procurement programmes to cabinet.' 'Canada and Defence Industrial Preparedness,' 723

96 Morton, *Canada and War,* 199

97 Bland explains: 'All the actors within the defence establishment – politicians, bureaucrats and soldiers – have interests that they wish to protect and promote.' 'The Canadian Defence Policy Process,' 239

98 David Cox, a Canadian defence analyst, commented: 'The defence white paper illustrates once again what all experienced shoppers know: never do the grocery shopping when extremely hungry.' Cited in 'Challenge and Commitment: Comments on the Defence White Paper,' in *Behind the Headlines* (Toronto: Canadian Institute of International Affairs 1987), 3

99 Dosman, 'The Department of National Defence: The Steady Drummer,' 186

100 Major-General Leonard Johnson (ret.), who is quite familiar with this problem, maintains that 'it is an iron law of bureaucratic survival that a task once assigned must be continued at all costs, for that is how resources are justified ... Justification gets stretched to the limit of plausibility and often beyond; facts are selected and shaded to support predetermined conclusions, vested interests determine defence policy, and Canada becomes servant and victim of a defence establishment concerned only with its own survival.' In 'Military Co-operation with the U.S. and Canadian Independence,' *International Perspectives* (Ottawa), July/August 1986, 5

101 Figures cited in Dosman, 'The Department of National Defence: The Steady Drummer,' 165

102 Ibid., 165–6

103 Cited by James Bagnall, 'Beatty's Doctrine,' *Financial Post*, 16 November 1987, 45

104 Bland, 'The Canadian Defence Policy Process,' 242–3. R.B. Byers has also argued that 'explicit linkages between defence policy and Canada's defence sector can be supported on both military and economic grounds.' 'Canadian Defence and Defence Procurement' in Stairs and Winham, eds, *Selected Problems in Formulating Economic Policy*, 176

105 Bland, 'The Canadian Defence Policy Process,' 242

106 Cited by Dan Black, 'A Prescription for Vigilance,' *Legion*, May 1988

107 'When asked about the army's top equipment priority, Maj.-Gen. R.J. Evraire, Chief, Land Doctrine and Operations, told *Jane's Defence Weekly*: 'The first thing we need are three things. The reason I say that is, it's no sense in having tanks and no armoured personnel carriers for infantry; and it's no sense having artillery and no tanks. You must have an all arms combat team ... Therefore we require tanks, APC's, anti-tank weapons and communications equipment.' 'Defence of Europe,' *Jane's Defence Weekly* 8, no. 20 (21 November 1987), 1194

108 See the testimony of Beatty to Senate of Canada, 'Proceedings of the Special Committee of the Senate on National Defence,' issue no. 25, 21 June 1988, 9.

109 Interview with Rear-Admiral T.S. Allen, president of the American Defense Preparedness Association (Canadian chapter), 2 June 1988

110 As the minister of national defence wrote, 'Appropriate measures are being taken by the Departments to ensure their work proceeds in concert [on the DIP task force]. Senior representatives (ADM level) of some 12 government departments and agencies met under the Chairmanship of ADM (MAT) in November 1985, and a working level group of similar representation is now being formed.' Minister of National Defence comment to CDA Resolution 23/86

111 Canada, Defence Programs Bureau, 'Canadian Defence Products' (Ottawa 1984). The specific objectives of this bureau are to identify and follow up export opportunities for Canadian producers of defence and defence-related products; to establish and manage Canadian participation in bilateral and multilateral co-operative defence research, development, and production agreements; and to assist Canadian industry in making contacts and negotiating with foreign government agencies with respect to defence and related export marketing endeavour.

112 See Bland, 'The Canadian Defence Policy Process,' 246.

113 Interview with official from the Canadian Commercial Corporation, June 1984

114 See, for example, DSS's recent report, *The Defence Industrial Base Review 1987* (Ottawa: Department of Supply and Services 1987).
115 Bland, 'The Canadian Defence Policy Process,' 245
116 Ibid.
117 See, for example, Ministry of State for Science and Technology, *Report of the Task Force on Federal Policies and Programs for Technology Development.*
118 Treddenick, 'The Arms Race and Military Keynesianism,' 89
119 Kim Richard Nossal, 'On the Periphery: Interest Groups and Canadian Defence Policy in the 1970s,' unpublished paper presented to the Conference on Domestic Groups and Foreign Policy, Canadian Institute of International Affairs, Ottawa, 9 June 1982; cited in D.W. Middlemiss and J.J. Sokolsky, *Canadian Defence Decisions and Determinants* (Toronto: Harcourt Brace Jovanovich 1989), 122
120 Elizabeth Riddell-Dixon, *The Domestic Mosaic: Domestic Groups and Canadian Foreign Policy* (Toronto: Canadian Institute of International Affairs 1985), 32. Riddell-Dixon notes that 'the foreign policy concerns of veteran and military support interest groups encompass a wide range of issues which affect national defence. These include Canada's roles in the North Atlantic Treaty Organization (NATO), and the North American Aerospace Defence Command (NORAD), bilateral relations with allies and potential foes, Canadian imports and exports of military equipment and technology, and questions of disarmament' (33).
121 For an analysis of this shift see John Lovering, 'The Atlantic Arms Economy: Towards a Military Regime of Accumulation?' *Capital & Class* 33 (Winter 1987), 129–55.
122 See David Langille, 'Security for Whom? – The Business Council on National Issues Promote Military Spending at the Expense of Social Security,' *Compass* 7, no. 1 (January 1987).
123 See the address of Thomas d'Aquino, president of the Business Council on National Issues, to the Conference of Defence Associations, 10 January 1985, p. 71.
124 See David Langille, 'The Business Council on National Issues and the Canadian State,' *Studies in Political Economy* 24 (Autumn 1987), 41–85.
125 Riddell-Dixon, *The Domestic Mosaic,* 33
126 According to one officer in the Department of National Defence, 'the CDA sets much of the agenda to which the Department responds.' It is worth noting the themes of the CDA's recent conferences. In 1985, the focus was upon industrial mobilization; in 1986, total defence; in 1987, implementing the white paper; and in 1988, developing Canada's army.
127 Address of Harvie Andre, associate minister of national defence, to the

Conference of Defence Associations, 10 January 1986; *Report of the 49th Annual General Meeting*, 40

128 As of 1986, the Military and Strategic Studies Program of the Department of National Defence had established programs within eight Canadian universities. With a 50 per cent increase in funding designated to this program in 1987, one would expect several other Canadian universities to establish similar programs.

129 See Canadian Institute of Strategic Studies, 'Information Programmes Office Fundraising Project 1988.'

130 Riddell-Dixon, *The Domestic Mosaic*, 34–5

131 Letter to Mr D.B. Dewar, deputy minister of National Defence, from Bernard Charbonneau, president, American Defense Preparedness Association (Canadian chapter), 21 January 1986

132 American Defense Preparedness Association (Canadian chapter), 'Join the people who are part of the ADPA team!' Arlington, Virginia. According to M.S. Fleiszer, 'The first objective of the Chapter – as contained in its incorporation documents, is the promotion of awareness by all elements of Canadian society of the need for a strong defence posture, and our programs and activities are oriented toward that objective. Further, we recognize, as does your committee, that our defence planning is inextricably linked with that of the United States.' See letter to MP Erik Nielsen, minister of national defence, from M.S. Fleiszer, executive vice-president, American Defense Preparedness Association (Canadian chapter), 17 March 1986.

133 American Defense Preparedness Association, Canadian chapter, *Newsletter* 1, no. 1, March–April 1987, 1

134 Interview with Brig.-Gen. W.J. Yost (ret.), 10 march 1988. In his book *Industrial Mobilization*, Yost mentions that the DND 'maintain[s] an effective dialogue with about 40 industrial associations.'

135 As Yost acknowledged, 'We were really the founder of ADPA in Canada.' Interview, 10 March 1988

136 As subsequently recommended to the minister of national defence, the Conference of Defence Associations 'considers that the current arrangements under this treaty should be expanded with the objective of ensuring the defence industries of both countries are complementary and capable of providing both Canada and the United States with an assured source of material in any emergency.' Conference of Defence Association Resolution 18/86

137 See W.J. Yost, *Industrial Mobilization*, 67.

138 Ibid., 59–62

139 Ibid., 61

140 As David Langille notes, 'Peter C. Newman was hired to write the BCNI's first report on defence policy. His work was rejected because he argued against Cruise testing in the North – although it surfaced eventually in Newman's book True North: Not Strong and Free.' See David Langille, *Corporate Statesmen: The Business Council on National Issues*, forthcoming, Fall 1990.

141 Interview with source in the Privy Council Office, 15 August 1986

142 The BCNI paper noted: 'In view of the significant equipment acquisitions needed to bring Canada's defence capabilities up to an acceptable level, it is clear that the role of defence procurement in providing industrial and technological opportunities for Canadians must be borne in mind. For example, Canada has impressive high technology capabilities in our aircraft, computer, telecommunications, radar, laser, and simulator industries; all of these will be increasingly important as Canada and its allies move to develop more advanced conventional weaponry. Canada thus has a clear opportunity to contribute to the growth of these and other domestic industries through increasing defence spending on weapons and other capital equipment used by the armed forces. It is also important to recognize that a greater Canadian defence effort is likely to make the U.S. in particular more willing to purchase Canadian goods in its own defence procurement.' See Business Council on National Issues, 'Canada's Defence Policy: Capabilities versus Commitments' (Ottawa, September 1984), 43.

143 While many of the BCNI's arguments were premised on the need for sovereignty protection, it is interesting to note that aside from being the key proponents of free trade, they were also proposing the merging of the defence industry into a NADIB and greater defence integration with the United States. See, for example Robert Matas, 'Canadian executives propose increased ties to U.S. defence system,' *Globe and Mail*, 5 September 1988.

144 Business Council on National Issues, 'National Security and International Responsibility: A Reassessment of Canadian Defence Policy,' Ottawa, 1 June 1987

145 Thomas d'Aquino, address to the Conference of Defence Associations, 10 January 1985, 71. D'Aquino stated that, 'as a group of some 150 chief executive officers of leading Canadian companies with a broad mandate to influence public policy in a number of important areas, we felt that the Business Council was the organization best placed to address the questions of defence policy.'

146 See the minister of national defence's response to CDA resolution 22/86
147 Department of National Defence, 'Briefing Note for the Minister, Subject: Defence Industrial Preparedness Advisory Committee (DIPAC),' 17 November 1987, 2
148 Letter to Peter Cameron, chairman, BCNI Task Force on Foreign Policy and Defence, from minister of national defence, Erik Nielsen, 5 February 1986
149 Beatty, 'Defence Industrial Preparedness,' Speech to the Montreal Chamber of Commerce, 2 February 1988, 9
150 Interview with Tom Savage, president of ITT, Canada, and member of the Business Council on National Issues, 13 July 1988
151 For example, the following correspondence indicated that there was ongoing co-operation in this respect: Letter from Brian Creamer, Business Council on National Issues, to Colonel Bill Weston, Planning Guidance Team, Department of National Defence, 25 March 1987; Letter from Brian Creamer, Business Council on National Issues, to Colonel Cal Hegge, leader, Defence Industrial Preparedness Task Force, Department of National Defence, 7 April 1987; Letter from Thomas d'Aquino, president, Business Council on National Issues, to Perrin Beatty, minister of national defence, 3 June 1987; Letter from Thomas d'Aquino, president, Business Council on National Issues, to Mr D.B Dewar, deputy minister of national defence, 27 February 1987; Letter from D.B. Dewar, deputy minister, Department of National Defence to Mr Thomas d'Aquino, president, Business Council on National Issues, 1 March 1987; Annex A to CC/ADPA letter of 30 January 87 addressed to CD/DND, Response to DND Questionnaire of 18 November 1986.
152 Letter from M.S. Fleiszer, executive vice-president, American Defense Preparedness Association (Canadian chapter) to the Hon. Erik Nielsen, minister of national defence, 17 March 1986; Letter from J.C. Bond, vice-president, American Defense Preparedness Association (Canadian chapter) to Lt.-Col. E. Exley, DIPTF, Department of National Defence, 9 February 1987; Annex A to 1747–1050 (DIPTF), dated November 1986; Business Council on National Issues, Memorandum for Peter Cameron, Tom Savage, Dudley Allen from John Bemesh, Re: DND's Questionnaire on the Defence Industrial Base, 19 February 1987
153 Interview with chairman of the Business Council on National Issues, 22 July 1988
154 In 1984, Brigadier-General Yost (ret.) acknowledged that the review and examination of Canada's defence industrial base was being made in consultation with private industry and industrial associations. 'Sustaining the Force,' 79

155 In a letter from Colonel Cal Hegge, Defence Industrial Preparedness Task Force leader, National Defence, to M.S. Fleiszer, executive vice-president of the American Defense Preparedness Association (Canadian chapter), 29 August 1986, Hegge notes a U.S. Defense Department recommendation for the 'utilization of professional associations – AIA and ADPA – to market the preparedness concept to what was described as an adverse Government/Public environment.' Hegge suggests that 'a similar situation prevails in Canada and that it would be appropriate for us to consider similar cooperation.' It is interesting to note that the same letter was sent by Colonel Hegge to Ken Lewis, Aerospace Industries Association of Canada.

156 Dosman, 'The Department of National Defence: The Steady Drummer,' 184–5

157 Ibid.

158 Beatty, 'Defence Industrial Preparedness,' 14. As early as 1985, Defence officials confirmed to a parliamentary committee that the subcommittee on the defence industrial base aims 'to ensure that the North American Industrial base concept is implemented' (in other words, to maintain and increase Canadian access to the U.S. market). SCEAND, 2 October 1985; cited in Regehr, *Arms Canada*, 105

159 Dosman, 'The Department of National Defence: The Steady Drummer,' 186

160 Interview with James Fleck, member of the Business Council on National Issues, 28 July 1988. Fleck also acknowledged that some members of the Task Force on Foreign Policy and Defence would have a vested interest in increased defence spending.

161 Brigadier-General George Bell, 'Sound Beginning but an Unfinished Work,' *Forum*, Conference of Defence Associations, vol. 2, no. 3 (1987), 29–30

162 Interview with Brigadier-General Yost (ret.). In response to a question about CDA's influence on the formulation of Canadian defence policy, Yost replied, 'I think we have had a major impact. We are getting a major restructuring in NDHQ. We have a marked upswing in the defence industry. All sorts of initiatives are now being undertaken. We are getting emergency planning, a total defence approach and the return to a long-war policy.'

Yost's claim to having initiated the formation of the ADPA and the building of a defence industrial base was corroborated by his associate Rear-Admiral T.S. Allen, past president of Computing Devices Company, control Data Canada, and currently president and chief executive officer of EH-Industries (Canada) Ltd. and president of the American Defense Preparedness Association (Canadian chapter). Interview, 2 June 1988

163 Interview with Brigadier-General Yost (ret.)

164 See Canada, House of Commons, Minutes of Proceedings and Evidence of the Standing Committee on National Defence, issue no. 14, 25 June 1987, 43. Also see John Best, 'Defence headquarters wages "war about peace,"' Saskatoon *Star Phoenix*, 6 April 1988.

165 Canadian Institute of Strategic Studies, Information Programmes Office Fundraising Project 1988. Also see *Coup d'Oeuil*, newsletter of the Canadian Institute of Strategic Studies.

166 Dosman, 'The Department of National Defence: The Steady Drummer,' 186

167 For example, see the BCNI task force's testimony to the Standing Committee on National Defence, issue no. 23, 27 January 1988. As Peter Cameron stated, 'It would appear to me that the government ought to take the responsibility of telling the Canadian people, not once, not twice, but a number of times, that a very real threat exists. If the people of Canada, Canadian citizens, realize there is a threat, then I suspect their support for a national security policy would be very much greater. Until that happens, I am afraid that we will continue to struggle, bit by bit, here and there, to sensitize Canadian citizens to defence needs, and that would be my first point.'

Rear-Admiral T.S. Allen (ret.), president of the American Defense Preparedness Association, writes, 'To begin with, we must create a new business climate based on a sense of national urgency, and a set of attitudes that will allow us to marshal our resources efficiently.' 'Poised to go either way,' *Forum*, Conference of Defence Associations, vol. 2, no. 3 (1987), 16

168 For an analysis of these figures see the exchange of correspondence between Bill Robinson of Project Ploughshares and the minister of national defence, Perrin Beatty, October 1987. Also see Bill Robinson, 'Canada's White Paper Doesn't Add Up,' *Ploughshares Monitor* 8, no. 3 (September 1987), 9. Also see 'NATO and Warsaw Pact Forces: Conventional War in Europe,' *The Defense Monitor* 17, no. 3 (Washington: Centre for Defense Information 1988).

169 See the testimony of Perrin Beatty and Robert Fowler, Proceedings of the Special Committee of the Senate on National Defence, issue no. 25, 21 June 1988, 28–32.

170 See the testimony of Admiral Falls to the Senate of Canada, Proceedings of the Special Committee of the Senate on National Defence, issue no. 12, 26 January 1988. Admiral Falls noted that even the U.S. Joint Chiefs of Staff assess that they have sufficient conventional forces to withstand a

Warsaw Pact attack (p. 9). Moreover, he acknowledged that while he was chair of NATO's Military Committee he had been pressured to inflate the threat assessment: 'I was often given briefings to say those things, but I never did. I went through history to try to get the facts to match the record, and I never could. There were lots of people employed to write up on military appreciation, from which all of this starts, and I think they were trying to outdo each other in the use of superlatives year after year. It did not really bear any relationship to facts ... What you were told was what the party line was at the time ... I was not very popular even when I was in NATO for trying to put a little less enthusiasm, if you like, on this so-called imbalance' (30–1).

171 For example, see the address of Major-General Terry Liston to the Dominion Executive Council of the Canadian Legion; cited in Dan Black, 'A Prescription for Vigilance,' *Legion*, May 1988.

172 For a review of one part of DND's recent public education program see Howard Goldenthal, 'Failing Grade for Forces Kit,' *NOW Magazine*, July 1988.

173 Address by Colonel H.A.J. Hutchinson, 'A Total Defence Concept,' *Report, 48th Annual General Meeting*, Conference of Defence Associations, January 1985, 79. Another assessment suggesting that 'the only way to equip and sustain Canadian forces ... is to integrate our industry with that of the U.S.A.' was provided at the same conference by Colonel L.S. Thompson, 'A Continental Defence Concept,' 74–9.

174 Yost, *Peace through Security*, 4

175 Ibid., 142

176 Letter from Beatty to d'Aquino, 19 March 1987

177 See John Hasek, *The Disarming of Canada* (Toronto: Key Porter Books 1987), 209–23.

178 Ibid., 212–13

179 See Yost, *Peace through Security*, 90.

180 Minutes of Proceedings and Evidence of the Standing Committee on National Defence, issue no. 23, 27 January 1988, 5

181 Interview with Culver, 22 July 1988

182 Gray, *Canadian Defence Priorities*, 49

183 Andrew Cox, Paul Furlong, and Edward Page, *Power in Capitalist Societies: Theory, Explanations and Cases* (Sussex: Wheatsheaf Books 1985), 130

184 Dwight D. Eisenhower, 'Farewell Address to the Nation,' delivered 17 January 1961, in William M. Evan and Steven Hilgarnter, eds, *The Arms Race and Nuclear War* (Englewood Cliffs, NJ: Prentice Hall 1987), 210–12

185 Ibid.

186 Cox, Furlong, and Page, *Power in Capitalist Societies*, 130
187 For further analysis of the military-industrial complex see: Lt.-Gen. E.L.M. Burns, *Megamurder* (Toronto: Clarke, Irwin & Co. 1966), 178–98; Gordon Adams, *The Politics of Defense Contracting: The Iron Triangle* (New Brunswick, NJ: Transaction Books 1984), 14–43; Volker R. Berghahn, *Militarism: The History of an International Debate 1861–1979* (Cambridge: Berg Publishers 1981), 85–105.
188 Marek Thee, 'The Dynamics of the Arms Race between the Great Powers,' PRIO paper 4/85 (Oslo: International Peace Research Institute 1985), 5
189 Alan R. Ball and Frances Millard, *Pressure Politics in Industrial Societies: A Comparative Introduction* (Atlantic Highlands: Humanities Press International 1987), 249
190 Dan and Ron Smith, *The Economics of Militarism* (London: Pluto Press 1983), 74
191 Ball and Millard, *Pressure Politics in Industrial Societies*, 261
192 This was a view expressed in conversation with a recently retired very senior officer, 20 October 1988.
193 Bland, 'The Canadian Defence Policy Process,' 246
194 Interview with source in the Business Council on National Issues, July 1988
195 Regehr, *Arms Canada*, 69
196 Ball and Millard acknowledge numerous commonalities in western defence relations (*Pressure Politics in Industrial Societies*, 265). John Lovering argues that there is a global restructuring of production under way accelerated by the international concentration of capital in the arms sector. 'The Atlantic Arms Economy,' 129–55
197 The recent surge of defence bureaucrats and senior military officers into the defence industrial sector, consulting firms, and lobbies was well documented by Stevie Cameron in *Ottawa Inside Out: Power, Prestige and Scandal in the Nation's Capital* (Toronto: Key Porter 1989), 160–90. For examples of this trend see also: Stevie Cameron, 'Old soldiers often don't retire; they become private consultants,' *Globe and Mail*, 23 June 1988; James Bagnall, 'Looking at the ties that bind,' *Financial Post*, 2 February 1987; and Ron Lowman, 'Old soldiers gunning for defence contracts,' *Toronto Star*, 13 January 1984.

It should be noted that this practice is partly due to existing legislation that restricts armed-forces personnel from active service after the age of fifty-five.
198 Conversation with senior military officer, May 1988
199 Liberal Defence critic Len Hopkins charged that Beatty found an excellent election tool in the Department of National Defence. See Mark

Clark, 'The New Weapons of War,' *Maclean's*, 8 August 1988.

200 Dosman, 'The Department of National Defence: The Steady Drummer,' 182

201 Ibid., 183

202 In August 1988 a new lobby was formed to promote the acquisition of nuclear submarines for Canada. Among the members were former Liberal Defence Minister Jean-Jacques Blais, Argus Corporation Chairman Conrad Black, John Craig Eaton, chairman of T. Eaton Company, Harriet Critchley, director of Strategic Studies at the University of Calgary and Brigadier-General George Bell (ret.) of the BCNI, CDA, and CISS. Described as non-partisan, this Committee for a Sovereign and Effective Naval Defence was put together by Jean-Jacques Blais, who worked for Thomson CSF, one of the two submarine firms that submitted tenders for the project. See 'Pro-SSN Faction Forms Lobby Group,' *Canadian Defence Update* 2, no. 7 (August 1988), 5.

203 Dosman, 'The Department of National Defence: The Steady Drummer,' 187

204 Elton J. Healey, assistant deputy minister (Material), Department of National Defence, says that 'the breadth and frequency of industry contacts (with DND), at both the provincial and national levels, is certain to increase in the future as the awareness of the government's new emphasis on defence industrial preparedness begins to permeate the relationship. So too will the international relationship, as the presence of ADM (Mat.) is likely to be increasingly sought in the NATO Industrial Advisory Group and in the International Conference of Armaments Directors to enunciate that new emphasis.' In 'ADM (Mat.) Group: Maintaining the Forces in Peace and War,' *Aerospace and Defence Technology*, March/April 1988

205 Middlemiss, 'Canada and Defence Industrial Preparedness,' 707

206 Cox, Furlong, and Page comment on the implications of military-industrial complexes: 'The problem is that they are self-consciously striving to subvert the political system to enrich themselves or to strengthen their position in society. The problem is, however, compounded by the fact that the web of this disease spreads ever outward into society and incorporates many different and apparently conflictual sectors of the socio-economic and political systems such that it becomes very difficult to combat its influence ... Governments find it difficult to introduce radical change when this entails the disruption of entrenched vested interests accustomed to a particular set of relationships, especially when the short-term economic impact would be considerable.' *Power in Capitalist Societies*, 143

CHAPTER 5 Beyond the Defence Trap?

1 'National defence loses its compass,' *Toronto Star*, 15 May 1989, 16
2 Annette Keunig, '$9B military spending urged,' *Halifax Chronicle Herald*, 18 March 1989
3 Cited in Marc Clark, 'The Defence Gap,' *Maclean's*, 22 May 1989, 12
4 See Ken Rowman, 'DND carries on with some make-do spending programs,' *Globe and Mail*, 17 October 1989.
5 Cited in 'Defence Spending and the Federal Election,' Canadian Institute for International Peace and Security, *Communiqué*, 9 November 1988
6 For an elaboration of constructive internationalism see: Canada, Report of the Special Joint Committee on Canada's International Relations, *Independence and Internationalism* (Ottawa 1986), 137–40.
7 'Canadians feel defence budget too high: poll,' *Gazette* (Montreal), 14 September 1989
8 David Langille, 'Defence cuts camouflage a spending increase,' *Toronto Star*, 18 May 1989
9 Randy Jones, 'Canada should rethink sub purchase – Mifflin,' *Halifax Chronicle Herald*
10 For an overview of these discussions and trends see the newsletter *Non-Offensive Defence*, no. 10, August 1988, Centre of Peace and Conflict Research, University of Copenhagen.
11 Sir Michael Howard, '1989: A Farewell to Arms?' *International Affairs* 65 (London), no. 3 (Summer 1989)
12 John D. Morrocco, 'The Fog of Peace: Does NATO Have a Future?' *Aviation Week and Space Technology*, 18 December 1989
13 Paul Mann, 'Brookings Study Suggests Halving U.S. Defense Budget in 10 Years,' *Aviation Week and Space Technology*, 27 November 1989
14 See Bob Hepburn, 'Bush cuts spending on health, housing,' *Toronto Star*, 30 January 1990.
15 Cited by David Fairhall, 'Military plans awry as blocs fall apart,' *The Guardian*, 11 November 1989
16 Richard Gwyn, 'The Superpowers face obsolescence,' *Toronto Star*, 16 November 1989
17 Discussions on developing new arrangements for co-ordinating European defence were prompted, in part, by several clubs within the larger NATO alliance. This has raised the prospect of several distinct and potentially incompatible security agendas. For an excellent review of rapidly changing alliance relations see Robert J. O'Brien, 'Canada and a Changing NATO,' *Canadian Defence Quarterly* 18, no. 4 (February 1989).

18 Ken Booth, 'Alternative Defence,' in Ken Booth and John Baylis, *Britain, NATO and Nuclear Weapons: Alternative Defence versus Alliance Reform* (London: Macmillan 1989), 213

19 Background report prepared for the Palme Commission, *A World at Peace: Common Security in the Twenty-first Century* (Stockholm, April 1989), 67

20 Cited by Tim Harper, 'Cruise missile testing regressive, MPS say,' *Toronto Star*, 23 January 1990

21 Cited by Murray Campbell, 'Deficit, changing Europe require new roles for forces,' *Globe and Mail*, 19 February 1990

22 See Malcolm Gladwell and Bruce Headlam, 'Arms à la Carte,' *Saturday Night*, June 1989, 46–51.

23 'Defence spending slowing down,' *Gazette* (Montreal), 2 August 1989

24 The *Financial Times* (17 July 1989) reported that 'shipments fell to $500 million in the first half of the year, compared with $740 million a year earlier. And the figure for the second half dropped so sharply that External Affairs is checking its numbers to find out if any sales were overlooked.' See 'Arms makers feel the fallout as world peace breaks out.' According to figures released by the Defence Programmes and Advanced Technology Bureau of the Department of External Affairs, Canada's defence exports to the United States in 1988 dropped to a seven-year low of $920 million.

25 McKnight, 'Outlook for Canadian Defence,' speech given at ARMX dinner, 24 May 1989

26 Rod McQueen, 'Eastern Europe's transition is shaking U.S. defence firms,' *Financial Post*, 19 December 1989

27 See, for example, the articles by Iain Hunter, 'Canada written off by allies: Professor,' *Ottawa Citizen*, 6 October 1989, and 'Ex-defence official warns cuts actually far worse,' *Ottawa Citizen*, 6 October 1989. One of the more counter-intuitive suggestions was provided by John Halstead, who warned that 'Canada has almost been written off by its NATO allies' and that if it were to make a contribution to the negotiations on arms reductions in Europe, it would need to back its claim with a continued contribution to European security. From such reasoning, it is deduced that Canada needs new tanks in Europe to help reduce the number of tanks in Europe. Ramsay Withers, a former chief of defence staff and now president of Government Consultants International, a defence lobby, responded to the cuts in the rearmament program, saying, 'You get to a point where you're not in any rational sense a viable nation.' In the same forum, Alex Morrison of the Canadian Institute for Strategic Studies concluded: 'There is in this country a malaise which has contributed to the passive attitude toward

national security and defence through lack of national leadership, the failure of the educational system and citizenship programs to inculcate the concept of service to the nation and patriotic responsibility in our youth.' Cited in Tim Harper, 'Cabinet D-Day looms on fate of armed forces,' *Toronto Star*, 7 October 1989

28 Martin Shadwick, 'Comment: Taking Stock,' *The Wednesday Report: Canada's Aerospace and Defence Weekly* 3, no. 31 (2 August 1989)

29 Mike O'Brien, 'Comment; Bracing for the 1990s,' *The Wednesday Report: Canada's Aerospace and Defence Weekly* 3, no. 35 (30 August 1989)

30 Mike Urlocker, 'On the defensive,' *Ottawa Citizen*, 22 August 1989. See also Keith Davies, 'Formation of Defence Industries Association,' *Canadian Defence Quarterly*, October 1989, 63, and Holly Porteous, 'Creating a Constituency for Defence in Canada,' *Canadian Defence Quarterly*, December 1989, 63

31 Tim Harper and Ron Lowman, 'Allies will help us protect Arctic McKnight says,' *Toronto Star*, 28 April 1989

32 John Thompson, 'Moving to Fortress North America,' *Strategic Datalink* 14 (May 1989)

33 Juliet O'Neill and Julian Beltrame, '87 defence policy outdated Mulroney says in Moscow,' *The Gazette*, 22 November 1989

34 See Tim Harper, 'Defence ducks another big chop,' *Toronto Star*, 21 February 1990.

35 John Lamb, 'Stalking the elusive peace dividend,' *Financial Times*, 12 March 1990

36 'Soviet attack called biggest threat,' *Toronto Star*, 7 March 1990

37 Cited by Dan G. Loomis, 'The meltdown of a dream,' *Ottawa Sun*, 31 August 1989

38 Ernie Regehr, *Arms Canada* (Toronto: Lorimer 1987), 185

39 Dalton Camp, Introduction to Lewis Hertzman, John W. Warnock, and Thomas Hockin, *Alliances and Illusions: Canada and the NATO-NORAD Question* (Edmonton: M.G. Hurtig Ltd. 1969), xxi

40 For an elaboration of the underlying assumptions of Canada's defence debate see Trudy Govier, 'Two Nuclear Logics,' Project Ploughshares Working Paper, 1988. Also see *Towards a World without War: The Defence Debate in Canada* (Halifax: Defence Research and Education Centre 1987).

41 Axel Dorscht, Tom Keating, Gregg Legare, and Jean-François Rioux, 'Canada's International Role and "Realism,"' *International Perspectives*, September/October 1986

42 Supported by multilateral, bilateral, and domestic pressure, Canada's

defence trap appears to be a component of a larger hegemonic system, structuring and reproducing relations within alliances, governments, the mass media, and even universities.

43 For an election-year polemic spelling out Canada's desperate need for NATO, see Larry Pratt and Tom Keating, *Canada, NATO and the Bomb: The Western Alliance in Crisis* (Edmonton: Hurting Publishers Ltd. 1988).

44 Douglas Roche, *Building Global Security: Agenda for the 1990s* (Toronto: NC Press 1989), 96

45 Ibid., 97

46 From an excellent review of these international changes see Dan Smith, 'The Changing Strategic Context,' in Smith, ed., *European Security in the 1990s*, 1–25

47 Cited in 'Big guns face Pentagon freeze,' *The Independent*, 4 December 1989

48 See a report of the Defence Research and Education Centre, *Towards a World without War: Next Steps in Canadian Defence Policy* (Halifax: Prepared for Veterans against Nuclear Arms, January 1987); *Canada and Common Security: The Assertion of Sanity*, a collection by members of the Group of 78 and others (Ottawa, 1987); and 'Alternative Defence Policy for Canada' by a working group of the Group of 78 (unpublished paper, Ottawa 1989).

49 Report of the International Affairs Committee of the New Democratic Party of Canada, *Canada's Stake in Common Security* (Ottawa: April 1988)

50 This idea was proposed by John Honderich, *The Arctic Imperative: Is Canada Losing the North?* (Toronto: University of Toronto Press 1987), 124

51 See John Best, 'Canada's military chiefs try to pick up pieces after budget cuts,' *Winnipeg Free Press*, 20 November 1989.

52 Report of the Special Committee of the Senate on National Defence, *Canada's Land Forces* (Ottawa: October 1989), 87.

53 SCEAND, *Independence and Internationalism* (Ottawa: 1986), 53

54 Gwynne Dyer, *War* (Toronto: Stoddart 1985), 263

55 Palme Commission on Disarmament and Security Issues, *A World at Peace*, 66

CHAPTER 6 Changing the Guard: From Defence Trap to Common Security?

1 Andrew Brewin, *Stand on Guard: The Search for a Canadian Defence Policy* (Toronto: McClelland and Stewart 1965), 6

2 Even in an atmosphere of improving East-West relations, the 1987 defence white paper warned: 'It is a fact, not a matter of interpretation that the West is faced with an ideological, political and economic adversary whose

explicit long-term aim is to mould the world in its own image.' Accordingly, it was stated that 'the principal direct threat to Canada continues to be a nuclear attack on North America by the Soviet Union.' Government of Canada, Department of National Defence, *Challenge and Commitment: A Defence Policy for Canada* (Ottawa, June 1987), 5, 10

3 Canada, Department of National Defence, Report of Study on Professionalism in the Canadian Forces, 1972. Cited in R.B. Byers, 'Peacekeeping and Canadian Defense Policy: Ambivalence and Uncertainty,' in Henry Wiseman, ed., *Peacekeeping: Appraisals and Proposals* (New York: Pergamon 1983), 145

4 See Rear-Admiral Elmar Schmaling, 'An Admiral Dissents on Germany, NATO and Modernization,' *Sanity*, May 1989, 16.

5 For an excellent and wide-ranging overview of this dilemma see Carl G. Jacobsen ed., *The Uncertain Course: New Weapons, Strategies and Mind Sets* (Oxford: Oxford University Press 1987).

6 The Palme Commission on Disarmament and Security Issues, *A World at Peace: Common Security in the Twenty-first Century* (Stockholm, April 1989), 67

7 The nuclear-winter theory has been most authoritatively explored by some 300 scientists from the United States, the USSR, and more than 30 other countries – working on a collaborative basis. See the World Commission on Environment and Development, *Our Common Future* (Oxford: Oxford University Press 1987), 295. Also see: Carl Sagan, 'Nuclear War and Climatic Catastrophe: Some Policy Implications,' *Foreign Affairs* 62, no. 3 (Winter 1983–4); SCOPE, *Environmental Consequences of Nuclear War* (Chichester: John Wiley and Sons 1985).

8 Schmaling, 'An Admiral Dissents,' 16

9 Peter Worthington, 'Our defence program prepares for the past,' *Financial Post*, 5 October 1987

10 Marek Thee, 'Prevailing security doctrines and armament dynamics,' PRIO Paper 9/84 (Oslo: International Peace Research Institute 1984), 2

11 As Stephenson says, 'A series of changed conditions, ranging from changes in technology to the reduction in the utility of military force and nuclear deterrence, to the breakdown of hegemonic leadership and of many of the regimes begun under that leadership, and to the growth of international dependence, have led to changes in the way international relations are conducted and in the ways in which scholars describe and explain international relations.' Carolyn M. Stephenson, 'The Need for Alternative Forms of Security: Crises and Opportunities,' *Alternatives* 13, no. 1 (January 1988), 65

12 Thomas Kuhn introduced the concept of the paradigm shift twenty-eight years ago in *The Structure of Scientific Revolutions* (Chicago: University of Chicago Press 1962). His paradigm shift described the process of radical reorientation by which basic science discards one world-view and adopts another. Mark Sommers has done an excellent job of summarizing Kuhn's thought. As he says: 'Observing the history of science, Kuhn noted that most research activity occurs in the realm of "normal science," a kind of "puzzle solving" within a set of assumptions so deeply imbued in the culture of the age that no other perspective seems possible let alone valid. It is only with the emergence of the "anomoly," in the form of recurring evidence which contradicts those assumptions, that extraordinary science is born ... Kuhn himself pointed out that no scientific world view is discarded by the culture and community it serves unless an alternative explanation is found which better conforms to present evidence. Once it has achieved the status of a paradigm, a scientific theory is declared invalid only if an alternative candidate is available to take its place.' Mark Sommers, *Beyond the Bomb: Living without Nuclear Weapons: A Field Guide to Alternative Strategies for Building a Stable Peace* (Boston: Expro Press 1985), 130–4

13 In the words of Canadian Secretary of State for External Affairs Joe Clark: 'In the past, it was the adherents of unilateralism who were known as realists and the advocates of cooperation who were labelled idealists. I submit that the reverse is now the case. Cooperation is now the new realism and pragmatism is the path to progress.' Speech delivered to the 44th Session of the United Nations General Assembly, 26 September 1989; cited in *The Disarmament Bulletin* 11 (Fall 1989), 10

14 See, for example, Don Munton, 'Uncommon Threats and Common Security,' *Peace and Security* 4, no. 4 (Winter 1989/90), 2.

15 Ibid.

16 These assumptions are at the core of the common-security alternative as outlined by the Independent Commission on Disarmament and Security (Palme Commission). See their initial report, *Common Security: A Blueprint for Survival* (New York: Simon & Schuster 1983).

17 Common security was the umbrella concept embraced by the Independent Commission on Disarmament and Security Issues in a 1982 report prepared for the United Nations Second Special Session on Disarmament. For a more thorough analysis of common security see: Independent Commission, *Common Security*; Palme Commission, *A World at Peace*; Stockholm International Peace Research Institute, *Policies for Common Security*, ed. Raimo Vayrynen (London: Taylor & Francis 1985); Report of the World

Commission on Environment, *Our Common Future* (Oxford: Oxford University Press 1987); United Nations Group of Governmental Experts, *Concepts of Security: Summary of a United Nations Study*, Disarmament Fact Sheet no. 48 (New York 1985).

For analysis situating the requirements of common security in a Canadian context see: Report of the International Affairs Committee of the New Democratic Party of Canada, *Canada's Stake in Common Security* (Ottawa, April 1988); Peter and David Langille, 'Freedom from Fear: Common Security and the Arms Race,' *Canadian Dimension* 22, no. 7 (October 1988); *Canada and Common Security: The Assertion of Sanity*, a collection by members of the Group of 78 and others (Ottawa 1987).

18 One of the central messages of the 1987 Bruntland Report was that 'Interdependence has become a compelling fact forcing nations to reconcile their approach to security.' *Our Common Future*, 295

19 Peter and David Langille, 'Freedom from Fear,' 4

20 Ibid., 5

21 Palme Commission, *A World at Peace*, 7

22 Ibid.

23 As stated in the Report of the Special Joint Committee on Canada's International Relations, 'All of Canada's major foreign policy goals, particularly the search for security and economic prosperity, as well as the preservation of justice and democracy are tied to the common interests of the international community.' *Independence and Internationalism* (Ottawa, June 1986), 137

24 Independent Commission, *Common Security*, 139

25 Government of Canada, Department of National Defence, *Defence in the 70s*, White Paper on Defence (Ottawa, August 1971), 7

26 Government of Canada, Department of National Defence, *Challenge and Commitment: A Defence Policy for Canada* (Ottawa, June 1987), 17

27 For a critical review of contemporary strategy see Leonard V. Johnson, 'A Mad, Mad World: The Evolution of Nuclear War-fighting Strategies,' in Simon Rosenblum and Ernie Regehr, eds, *The Road to Peace* (Toronto: James Lorimer 1988), 17–52. Also see Malcolm Dando and Paul Rogers, *The Death of Deterrence* (London: CND Publications 1984).

28 See Michael Tucker, 'Canadian Security Policy,' in Brian W. Tomlin and Maureen A. Molot, eds, *Canada among Nations / 1988: The Tory Record* (Toronto: James Lorimer & Co. 1989), 77

29 Jeff Sallot, 'P.M. warns U.S. on offensive use of Star Wars,' *Globe and Mail*, 25 May 1987

30 See Patrick Tyler and Jeffrey Smith, 'Study finds NATO war plans outdated;

Report concludes alliance overestimates Soviet attack capability,' *Washington Post*, 29 November 1989.

31 For a review of recent changes made to Soviet military posture see *NOD*, The Newsletter of Non-Offensive Defence (University of Copenhagen, Department of Peace and Conflict Studies), no. 13, September 1989.

32 International Institute for Strategic Studies, *The Military Balance 1989–1990* (London: Brassey's 1989), 231

33 Sir Michael Howard, '1989: A Farewell to Arms?' *International Affairs* 65, no. 3 (Summer 1989), 408

34 Senator Sam Nunn, 'Challenges to NATO in the 1990s: A Time for Resolve and Vision,' Speech to the International Institute for Strategic Studies, 4 September 1989, 7

35 Cited in Gwyn Prins, 'Naval Forces and "Defensive Defence,"' Paper presented to the International Studies Association Conference (London), 1 April 1989, 6

36 McKnight, 'Outlook for Canadian Defence,' Speech at ARMX dinner, 24 May 1989

37 See Franklin C. Spinney, *Defence Facts of Life: The Plans/Reality Mismatch* (Boulder: Westview Press 1985).

38 Personal conversation with former chief of defence staff, February 1989

39 Cited in John Best, 'Vital role remains for a strong NATO,' *Winnipeg Free Press*, 13 September 1989

40 See the proposal by Joseph T. Jockel and Joel J. Sokolsky, 'Defence White Paper Lives Again,' *International Perspectives*, July/August 1989.

41 Cited by Escott Reid, 'Canada and the North Atlantic Treaty: More than Just a Military Obligation,' *Canada and the World: National Interest and Global Responsibility* (Ottawa: Group of 78, 1985), 6

42 Stephen Clarkson writes that 'the more divisions there are within NATO between Europe and the U.S., the more Canada accepts its dominant partners' approach to strategic questions. It is as if the multilateral defence circuit is an optional extra; Canada's bilateral defence relationship is the standard vehicle.' See *Canada and the Reagan Challenge: Crisis and Adjustment 1981–85* (Toronto: James Lorimer & Co. 1985).

43 Colin Gray, *Canadian Defence Priorities: A Question of Relevance* (Toronto: Clarke, Irwin & Co. 1972), 207

44 For example, despite the revolutionary changes in the East, NATO's top military leaders have suggested that there is no reason to restructure alliance policy, that the strategy of forward defence and flexible response will remain valid for the 1990s. See 'Hardliners defend NATO plans,' *Toronto Star*, 16 February 1990.

45 Cited in Ish Theilheimer and Robert Cottingham, 'Time to consider quitting alliance,' *Winnipeg Free Press*, 2 July 1989

46 Tina Viljoen and Gwynne Dyer, 'Neutrality: A Choice Canada Can Make,' *Compass* 5, no. 5 (January 1988), 8

47 Nils Orvik, ed., *Semialignment and Western Security* (London: Croom Helm 1986), 6

48 Although Orvik suggested that semialignment might weaken Western solidarity and undermine alliance resolve, a number of others wrote that 'semialignment may thus provide hidden strength to an alliance for it guarantees, or at least augments, its capacity for sober reflection and ongoing consideration of the questions of peace and war from a variety of viewpoints. The semialigned members' continuing call for a return to *détente* illustrates the perspectives made available to the alliance by those countries. They succeed thereby in enhancing NATO's political and diplomatic efforts in its dealings with the Eastern bloc.' See Carsten Holbraad, Ruud Koole, Paul Lucardie, Constantine Melakopides, Christopher Rose, and Hugh Thorburn, 'The Reality of Semialignment,' *Semialignment and Western Security*, 271.

49 See Viljoen and Dyer, 'Neutrality.' For a wider range of discussion, also see: Major-General Leonard Johnson (ret.), 'A Military Perspective on Canadian Neutrality,' Address to the Conference 'Canada and Military Neutrality,' St Jean, PQ, 12 April 1987; Bjorn Moller, 'Disengagement and Non-offensive Defence in Europe: The Role of and Prospects of Cooperation between Neutrals and Semi-aligned Countries,' Paper presented to the Conference on Disarmament and Development: 'The Political and Moral Implications of Neutrality in Europe,' Irish School of Ecumenics, Dublin, 9–11 April 1987.

50 Rear-Admiral Fred Crickard (ret.), 'An Anti-Submarine Warfare Capability in the Arctic: A National Requirement,' *Canadian Defence Quarterly* 16, no. 4 (Spring 1987), 24

51 See the testimony of General Thériault to the Standing Committee on National Defence and Veterans Affairs, *Hansard*, no. 12, 25 January 1990, 12:6

52 See William Winegard, MP, 'Chairman's forword,' *NORAD 1986*, Report of the Standing Committee on External Affairs and National Defence, February 1986.

53 John Hamre, 'United States–Canada Defence Relations: A U.S. Perspective,' Paper prepared for the Annual Meeting of the Western Social Sciences Association, 22–24 April 1982, 13; cited in Clarkson, *Canada and the Reagan Challenge*, 254

54 *NORAD 1986*, 50

55 See the testimony of the Canadian Council of Churches and Project Ploughshares to the Standing Committee on External Affairs and National Defence, *NORAD 1986*, 55–7

56 Dalton Camp, Introduction to Lewis Hertzman, John Warnock, and Thomas Hockin, *Alliances and Illusions: Canada and the NATO-NORAD Question* (Edmonton: M.G. Hurtig Ltd. 1969), xvii

57 Cited in New Democratic Party of Canada, *Canada's Stake in Common Security*, 22

58 Richard Rohmer, 'Rethinking the unthinkable,' *Toronto Sun*, 18 July 1989

59 Palme Commission, *A World at Peace*, 21

60 Aside from outlining our defence objectives and commitments, it is important to establish the means by which such objectives are to be fulfilled. When declaratory policy can be flexibly interpreted, there is more room for the manipulation of operative policy. This can lead to internal contradictions that frustrate the pursuit of legitimate defence commitments.

61 Department of National Defence, *Defence in the 70s*, 7

62 Gray, *Canadian Defence Priorities*, 19

63 In addition to the six nations with nuclear-weapons capability, these countries are Afghanistan, Algeria, Cuba, Egypt, Greece, Indonesia, Iran, Iraq, North Korea, South Korea, Kuwait, Libya, Saudi Arabia, Syria, Taiwan, Turkey, North Yemen, and South Yemen. Cited in Douglas Roche, *Building Global Security: Agenda for the 1990's* (Toronto: NC Press 1989), 31

64 Ibid.

65 Brodie also noted: 'Nations that formerly thought it quite impossible to live together in a condition of expanding nuclear capabilities have now got considerably used to it ... We can predict over the longer term a much lesser inclination than in times past to take for granted the periodic recurrence of war ... We can predict also much greater earnestness about searching for alternatives to war ... That violence should continue indefinitely to take the specific institutional form known as war ... is now decidedly questionable. This could be wishful thinking, but we are not obliged to deny important visible changes simply because they happen to be done in a direction we like.' Bernard Brodie, *War and Politics* (London: Casell 1973); cited in Ken Booth, 'Alternative Defence,' in Ken Booth and John Baylis, *Britain, NATO and Nuclear Weapons: Alternative Defence versus Alliance Reform* (London: Macmillan 1989), 166

66 Over the past forty years public opinion has played a significant part in dissuading unwarranted aggression. Reliable information, made public through respected intermediaries, has generally constrained and often in-

hibited nations from using excessive force. In this respect the camera, especially the television camera, has had a profoundly defensive effect in uncovering military secrecy and limiting the offensive use of armed force. Accordingly, information can be a tremendous asset in the early resolution of international conflict.

67 As Major-General Leonard Johnson (ret.) writes, 'The ultimate test of Canadian security policy is whether it lessens the risk of nuclear war or makes it more likely.' 'A Military Perspective,' 2

68 This important distinction was made by David Cox in 'Canada's Military Options in the North,' Paper presented to Canada's Consultative Group on Arms Control and Disarmament, Cornwall, Ontario, 1–3 October 1987.

69 John Lamb, 'Stalking the elusive peace dividend,' *Financial Times*, 12 March 1990

70 Department of National Defence, *Challenge and Commitment*, 6

71 *Independence and Internationalism*, 48

72 George Kennan, 'Russia, the Atom and the West,' BBC Reith Lectures (London 1957); cited in Moller, 'Disengagement and Non-offensive Defence in Europe'

73 Ernie Regehr, *Arms Canada: The Deadly Business of Military Exports* (Toronto: James Lorimer & Co. 1987), 201

74 In a survey of public opinion conducted in 1988, 57 per cent of respondents were in support of Canada declaring NWFZ status. See Don Munton, 'Peace and Security in the 1980s: The View of Canadians,' Canadian Institute for International Peace and Security working paper, January 1988.

As of June 1987, there were already 169 nuclear-weapon-free zones in Canada, including numerous Canadian cities such as Montreal, Toronto, and Vancouver and several provinces. In fact, a majority (59.3 per cent) of Canadians already live in a NWFZ. Moreover, both of Canada's opposition parties have endorsed the initiative to make Canada a NWFZ. See 'Nuclear Weapon Free Zones in Canada,' Information provided by the Canadian Nuclear Weapon Free Zone Clearinghouse, Peace Research Institute (Dundas, Ont.), 15 June 1987.

75 Ernie Regehr, Bill Robinson, and Simon Rosenblum, *Making Canada a Nuclear Weapon Free Zone*, Ploughshares Working Paper no. 1 (April 1987), 1

76 Ibid., 2

77 Department of National Defence, *Defence in the 70s*, 7. There have been several recommendations for limiting Canadian military activity to de-

fensive operations. As stated in a 1985 Senate report: 'The committee recommends that the Canadian government define its objectives in North American aerospace defence as clearly as possible and concentrate on those aspects that are essentially defensive in nature.' Report of the Special Committee of the Senate on National Defence, *Canada's Territorial Air Defence* (Ottawa, January 1985), ix. In 1986, David Cox recommended several guidelines to establish a vigilant but pre-war doctrine for continental defence. He proposed to limit Canadian involvement to activities that would provide peace-time surveillance and crisis stability, and to desist from programs that, in the last resort, assume the possibility of nuclear war-fighting. David Cox, *Trends in Continental Defence: A Canadian Perspective* (Ottawa: Canadian Institute for International Peace and Security, Occasional paper no. 2, 1986)

78 For a general overview of non-offensive defence see: Anders Boserup, 'The Strategy of Non-Offensive Defence,' Peace Research Centre working paper, Australian National University, April 1986; the newsletter *Non-Offensive Defence*, nos 1–13, Centre of Peace and Conflict Research, University of Copenhagen; Peter Langille, 'Non-offensive Defence: A Canadian Option?' *Peace Magazine*, June/July 1988; Dietrich Fischer, 'Some Reflections on an Alternative Defence Policy for Canada,' unpublished paper, June 1987, and *Preventing War in the Nuclear Age* (New York: Rowman & Allanheld 1984); Bjorn Moller, *A Bibliography of Non-offensive Defence*, Centre of Peace and Conflict Research, University of Copenhagen, 1988; Johan Galtung, *There Are Alternatives: Four Roads to Peace and Security* (Nottingham: Spokesman 1984).

79 Randall Forsberg, 'Toward a Nonaggressive World,' *Bulletin of Atomic Scientists*, September 1988, 49

80 Anders Boserup, 'A Way to Undermine Hostility,' *Bulletin of Atomic Scientists*, September 1988, 18, 19

81 See Bjorn Moller, 'Disengagement and Non-offensive Defence in Europe: The Role and Prospects of Co-operation between Neutrals and Semi-aligned Countries,' Paper presented to Conference on Disarmament and Development, Dublin, 9–11 April 1987, 20.

82 Bjorn Moller notes: 'The guide-line when establishing a non-offensive defence should hardly be a search for specific "defensive weapons" as an alternative to offensive ones – like it has often been attempted in the past, and like it is still occasionally proposed. Applying the label "offensive" or "defensive" to individual weapons is a "pars pro toto" fallacy, identifying the whole with the sum of its parts. It ignores the fact that an offensive posture could often only be employed offensively, if it is supplemented with "defensive" elements – and that "defensive weapons" may therefore

perform the function of force multipliers when combined with offensive capabilities. The most radical example of this fact is probably the SDI program of the Reagan Administration, which only makes sense as a component of a war-fighting (and winning) strategy and posture.' 'A Non-offensive Maritime Strategy for the Nordic Area: Some Preliminary Ideas,' Paper presented to the Alternative Defence Working Group, Boston, Mass., February 1987, 6

83 See report of the Alternative Defence Commission, *Defence without the Bomb* (London: Taylor & Francis 1983), 121. Also see the follow-up study of the Commission, *The Politics of Alternative Defence: A Policy for a Non-nuclear Britain* (London: Paladin 1987).

84 Schmaling, 'An Admiral Dissents'

85 Although sharing several similar objectives, dissuasion was then primarily targeted at the allies of a potential opponent. In 1974, Karber and Wasaff wrote that the word 'dissuasion' was chosen for a new strategy 'because it met three conceptual needs: (1) to coin a descriptive word for a particular political situation where none existed; (2) to differentiate the requirements between deterring a primary opponent and inhibiting the offensive participation of his allies; and (3) the need for a concept to explain the type of international influence that falls between deterrence and friendly persuasion ... Conceptually, dissuasion differs from the more frequently employed term "deterrence" in that the latter is defined as forcing an opponent to desist from something he would otherwise do, that is, attack; an aggressive motivation is not presumed to be inherent in the dissuasion target.' See Phillip A. Karber and Charles R. Wasaff, 'A Dissuasion Strategy for NATO: Selective Threat Withdrawal as an Inhibition to Coalition Aggression,' in Morton A. Kaplan, ed., *NATO & Dissuasion* (Chicago: University of Chicago 1974).

86 See Frank Barnaby and Egbert Boeker, 'Non-nuclear Defence for Europe,' unpublished paper, 1985.

87 See Anders Boserup, 'The Strategy of Non-offensive Defence,' Working paper no. 2, Peace Research Centre, Research School of Pacific Studies, Canberra, 1986, 1.

88 See Anders Boserup, 'Non-offensive Defence in Europe,' in Derek Paul, ed., *Defending Europe: Options for Security* (London: Taylor & Francis 1985), 206.

89 R.B. Byers, 'Peacekeeping in the 80's,' in Byers and M. Slack, eds, *Canada and Peacekeeping: Prospects for the Future* (Centre for International and Strategic Studies, York University, 1983), 7–9

90 Andrew Cohen, 'Canada's role in keeping world peace is now likely to change,' *Financial Post*, 31 July 1989

91 John Hay, 'New role: Making DND budget-proof,' *Ottawa Citizen*, 14 May 1989

92 Cited in *Independence and Internationalism*, 60

93 Ibid.

94 See Hugh Thorburn, 'The New Democratic Party and National Defence,' in Orvik, ed., *Semialignment and Western Security*, 171.

95 Jonathan Power, 'UN must seize the initiative,' *Winnipeg Free Press*, 20 December 1989

96 See 'U.N. Peacekeeping: Canada should push for more,' *Ottawa Citizen*, 15 September 1989.

97 Interception for purposes of identification is one of the primary roles of Canada's air force. This point was made by a previous chief of the defence staff, General Paul Manson, in reference to the size of the Canadian fighter/interceptor fleet: 'In the sense that the airplane does not have the task of shooting down every bomber of a mass raid that might invade Canada, then the numbers we have are not that bad. Their purpose – and this is a very important point – is not primarily to shoot down bombers (but to) identify a raid ... The primary role, and I emphasize this, is detecting a classifying a potential raid.' See Ernie Regehr, 'A Framework for Canadian Disarmament and Arms Control in the Arctic,' Paper presented to the Consultative Group on Arms Control and Disarmament, Cornwall, Ont., 1–3 October 1987, 6.

98 Cited by David Todd, 'Open skies: Canada proposes unrestricted surveillance,' *Ottawa Citizen*, 30 September 1989

99 As Joe Clark noted in an op-ed piece in the *New York Times* (5 June), an open-skies agreement 'could be a clear, unequivocal gesture that a nation's intentions are not aggressive.' Cited in John Hay, 'Open skies: Middle power meddling wins,' *Ottawa Citizen*, 1 October 1989

100 The United States has paid considerably to develop the North Warning System. There are now fifty-two radar stations along the seventieth parallel, forty-seven of which are located in Canada and the rest in Greenland and Alaska. The present system is backed up with American-based over-the-horizon-backscatter radars with an approximate range of 1800 nautical miles, and U.S. Air Force AWACS (airborne warning and control systems) surveillance flights as well as CF-18s, both utilizing forward operating locations in the Canadian Arctic.

101 See Cox, *Trends in Continental Defence*, 31.

102 Report of the Defence Research and Education Centre, *Towards a World without War: Next Steps in Canadian Defence Policy* (Halifax: Prepared for Veterans Against Nuclear Arms, January 1987), 9

103 Ibid.

104 Cited in 'Defence Spending and the Federal Election,' Canadian Institute for International Peace and Security, *Communiqué*, 9 November 1988, 15

105 Two retired senior officers argued that the North Warning System should be deployed closer to the periphery of (northern) Canada, thereby providing a territorial surveillance capability that is currently lacking. In their view this would constitute a significant assertion of Canadian sovereignty, and obviate the need for U.S. patrols of northern Canadian territory from Alaskan bases. See Brig.-Gen. (ret.) C.E. Beattie and Brig.-Gen. (ret.) K.R. Greenaway, 'Offering up Canada's North,' *Northern Perspectives* 14, no. 4 (September 1986), 5–8; cited in Cox, 'Canada's Military Options in the North,' 8–9.

106 'Defence Spending and the Federal Election,' 15

107 The Senate report also noted: 'The number of satellites required for a viable system might consist of four to six air surveillance satellites, one or two maritime surveillance satellites, and three to four communication satellites, stationed most of the time over Canadian territory or areas relevant to Canadian military and diplomatic communications.' See *Canada's Territorial Air Defence*, 40.

108 Cox, *Trends in Continental Defence*, 39. Also see Brig.-Gen. John Collins (ret.), 'Military Use of Space by Canada in the Year 2000,' *Canadian Aeronautics and Space Journal* 32, no. 3 (September 1986), 193–201.

109 John C. Polyani, 'An International Satellite Monitoring Agency,' in Ernie Regehr and Simon Rosenblum, eds, *Canada and the Nuclear Arms Race* (Toronto: James Lorimer & Co. 1983), 236

110 Bhupendra Jasani and Frank Barnaby, *Verification Technologies: The Case for Surveillance by Consent* (Warwickshire: Berg Publishers 1984), 46. Also see *Towards a World without War*, 11.

111 Over nine years ago, it was estimated that the maximum yearly cost for an operational ISMA would be in the region of $3 billion. However, in the intervening period, many nations have developed the required technology and launching systems. It is conceivable that such a system might now be less expensive. It is unlikely that any participating nation would have to spend more than 1 per cent of its annual defence budget to bring this scheme to fruition. See Jasani and Barnaby, *Verification Technologies*, 46.

112 See Polyani, 'An International Satellite Monitoring Agency,' *236*.

113 The idea of a regional agency might also be worth pursuing. Research is now under way on developing a proposal for an international monitor-

ing agency for the Arctic. See Walter A. Doern, 'An International Monitoring Agency for the Arctic,' *Information North*, newsletter of the Arctic Institute of North America, January 1989.

114 For further elaboration and a range of similar proposals see Moller, 'A Non-offensive Maritime Strategy,' 18.

115 According to Danson, 'The real threat in the Arctic was to Canada's sovereignty and that was primarily from Canada's closest ally, the United States.' 'As for the Soviet Union's overall intentions in the North, the possibility of a threat from that direction except by air, still seems so remote that any diversion of Canada's limited military resources is unjustified. Landing Soviet troops, for example, would be ridiculous. For half of the year, the Arctic is mostly dark, and its climate is brutal. During the other half, the troops would be exposed in daylight virtually around the clock and vulnerable to an air attack that Canada is quite capable of mounting. In both cases, they would still be hundreds, even thousands of miles from any significant military objective.' B.J. Danson, 'Arctic military threat a red herring,' *Globe and Mail*, 22 May 1987, A7

116 One system that has an intrinsic appeal for all-terrain operations in the north is the air-inflated hovercraft. The hovercraft would appear as a cost-effective platform for working in search-and-rescue operations, cargo transport and resupply, regular patrol, coast-guard activities, and even anti-submarine operations. Its high speed, manoeuvrability, and capacity to work on land, sea, and over the ice speak strongly in its favour as a system suited to Canada's military requirements in the North.

117 Speaking to the Standing Committee on National Defence, Rear-Admiral Charles Thomas, chief of maritime doctrine and operations, stated: 'Given resources, we could put into the Arctic passages, at the choke points, a bottom-based trip wire, in real time, that would tell you something had gone by. If you are sufficiently discreet in your knowledges, you can identify what it is.' Minutes of Proceedings and Evidence of the Standing Committee on National Defence, House of Commons, issue no. 3, 27 January 1987, 3:27

118 See the testimony of Vice-Admiral Brodeur in Minutes of Proceedings and Evidence of the Standing Committee on National Defence, House of Commons, issue no. 3, January 27, 1987, 3:26. As Dr Derek Schofield, chief of research and development, Department of National Defence, noted, 'With regard to the areas in the Canadian Archipelago, I think we now have sufficient information so that we can specify the kinds of systems one would need, whether they are mobile systems or whether they are fixed systems in choke points. So from that point of view I do not

think we need any more information about the environment in order for us to specify a system. We would use a good deal of the technology we already have.' See Minutes of Proceedings and Evidence of the Standing Committee on National Defence, House of Commons, issue no. 7, 24 March 1987, 7:13.

119 According to a Swedish diplomat, two non-lethal systems were developed to counter submarine intrusions into Swedish territorial waters. They were referred to as the 'whoopee bomb' and the 'neutral bomb.' While both were affixed magnetically, one was designed to bang furiously and create an intolerable noise; the other actually bored a small hole into the top of the submarine allowing the crew plenty of time to discuss their problem before surfacing.

120 As Dan Smith writes, 'Part of the problem, of course, has been the tendency of military, bureaucratic and industrial institutions for various reasons, to increase their own size, standing and power.' *Non-Nuclear Defence Options for Britain*, Bradford University School of Peace Studies, Peace Studies Papers 6 (1982), 9

121 Department of National Defence, *Challenge and Commitment*, 26

122 Two studies by the Canadian Institute for International Peace and Security (CIIPS) and the Canadian Centre for Arms Control and Disarmament (CCACD) have begun to clarify the costs of an independent defence posture. The CCACD study estimated the annual cost of maintaining Canadian air and ground forces in Europe to be $1.225 billion for 1989. In addition, Canada's financial contribution to NATO infrastructure will amount to $2.19 billion for 1988/9. In turn, Canada will receive approximately $777 million in 1988/9 for NATO's use of military bases in Canada and for the maintenance of Canadian bases in Europe (cited in 'Defence Spending and the Federal Election,' 15). These figures are rather conservative estimates of the money that might be saved if these commitments were cancelled. See, for example, the assessment by Major-General Leonard Johnson (ret.), 'Canada and NATO: What Price Symbolism?' in Derek Paul, ed., *Defending Europe: Options for Security* (London: Taylor & Francis 1985), 50–62.

123 Peggy Hope-Simpson, 'Assuming Our Role: Canada as the Major Power in the International North,' unpublished paper, Wolfville, NS, 14 September 1989, 10

124 See the report of the Special Committee of the Senate on National Defence, *Canada's Land Forces* (Ottawa, October 1989), 17–18.

125 *Independence and Internationalism*, 135

126 See report of the Panel on Arctic Arms Control, prepared by David Cox

and Tariq Rauf, *Security Co-operation in the Arctic: A Canadian Response to Murmansk,* presented at the Canada-USSR Conference on Canadian-Soviet Arctic Co-operation, Ottawa, 24 October 1989. Also see: Ronald G. Purver, 'Arctic Arms Control: Constraints and Opportunities,' Canadian Institute for International Peace and Security, Occasional Papers, February 1988; Purver, 'Arms control Proposals for the Arctic: A Survey and Critique,' in Kari Mottola, ed., *The Arctic Challenge: Nordic and Canadian Approaches to Security and Cooperation in an Emerging International Region* (Boulder: Westview Press 1988); James Macintosh and Michael Slack, 'A Circumpolar Confidence Building Regime,' *Canadian Defence Quarterly,* Autumn 1988.

127 Numerous studies have demonstrated that high military spending and investment in defence industries contributes less to an economy than to similar investment in other sectors. A U.S. congressional research study showed that for each $1 billion spent on guided-missile production, some 14,000 direct jobs are created; for each $1 billion spent on local transit, 21,500; and for educational services, 63,000. Cited in Douglas Roche, 'Potential alternative strategies for Canada,' *Financial Post,* 7 November 1989. For a more thorough critique of a defence industrial strategy see Peter Langille, 'The Political Economy of Cruise Missile Testing in Canada: Cause and Consequences,' honours research essay, Carleton University, April 1985.

128 Clarkson, *Canada and the Reagan Challenge,* 265–6

129 An outstanding example of successful conversion is described in a 1981 study by the U.S. Defense Department's Office of Economic Adjustment of 94 communities affected by closures over the previous 20 years. It found that after a short initial period of hardship, the converted facilities had provided 50 per cent more jobs for civilians (in total, 45,000 more jobs) than the military installations had done. Cited in New Democratic Party, 'Canada's Stake in Common Security,' 28

130 Roche, 'Potential alternative strategies for Canada'

131 'Canadian industry holds its breath on defense budget decisions,' *Defense News,* 21 August 1989

132 Camp, Introduction to Hertzman, Warnock, and Hockin, *Alliances and Illusions,* xix–xx

133 Ibid., xx

Index